Security Disarmed

Security Disarmed

Critical Perspectives on Gender, Race, and Militarization

EDITED BY BARBARA SUTTON,
SANDRA MORGEN, AND JULIE NOVKOV

RUTGERS UNIVERSITY PRESS

NEW BRUNSWICK, NEW JERSEY, AND LONDON

LIBRARY OF CONGRESS CATALOGING-IN-PUBLICATION DATA

Barbara Sutton, Sandra Morgen, and Julie Novkov
    Security disarmed : critical perspectives on gender, race, and militarization / edited by
    Barbara Sutton, Sandra Morgen, and Julie Novkov.
        p. cm.
    Includes bibliographical references and index.
    ISBN 978–0-8135–4359–8 (hardcover : alk. paper)
    ISBN 978–0-8135–4360–4 (pbk. : alk. paper)
    I. Sociology, Military.   2.   Militarism.   3.   Women and the military.   I. Sutton,
Barbara, 1970–   II. Morgen, Sandra.   III. Novkov, Julie, 1966–
    U21.5.S42 2008
    306.2′7—dc22   2007048327

A British Cataloging-in-Publication record for this book is available from the British
Library.

CONTENTS

PART III
Localizing Militarization in the United States

PART IV
Demilitarization, Pedagogy, and Culture

ACKNOWLEDGMENTS

This book is the result of our engagement with the theme Gender, Race, and Militarization through a vital program organized by the Center for the Study of Women in Society (CSWS) and the Women's and Gender Studies Program at the University of Oregon. We are grateful to the Carlton Raymond and Wilberta Ripley Savage Endowment in International Relations and Peace for funding the program's activities, which contributed to generating many of the ideas and critical conversations expressed in the book. We thank the presenters and participants at the October 2005 conference on Gender, Race, and Militarization and at related colloquia and public talks held at the University of Oregon. Some of these events were cosponsored by the Ethnic Studies Program, the Wayne Morse Center for Law and Politics, the departments of Anthropology and Sociology, the Multicultural Center, and the Women's Center, as well as by the community group Progressive Response. Presenters included a number of authors in this book and other scholars, activists, and public intellectuals such as Lakshmi Chaudhry, Hilary Charlesworth, M. Jacqui Alexander, Monique Balbuena, Lamia Karim, Carol Van Houten, and Shaul Cohen. Their insights and participation helped shape the vision for this book. We also thank several people who provided assistance and support at different stages of the project, including CSWS staff members Shirley Marc, Peggy McConnell, Judith Musick, and Stephanie Wood, and the Women's and Gender Studies Program office manager Sabena Stark, as well as core faculty Judith Raiskin, Lynn Fujiwara, and Elizabeth Reis. They participated in various ways with the planning and implementation of program activities, such as colloquia, keynote presentations, courses, a visiting professorship, film series, and a conference on the mentioned theme. Katherine Kowalski and Elizabeth Doggett, graduate assistants at the University at Albany, SUNY, helped with book-related logistics, and Deborah LaFond, women's studies librarian at the same institution, traced some sources. We are also grateful to production editor Marilyn Campbell and particularly to copyeditor Kathryn Gohl for their excellent editorial work on this book. Finally, we thank Adi Hovav, social sciences editor at Rutgers University Press, for her vision, encouragement, and guidance throughout this journey.

PART I

=========================

Beyond Militarization

Alternative Visions of Security

1

Rethinking Security, Confronting Inequality

An Introduction

BARBARA SUTTON AND JULIE NOVKOV

Living in a time of war demands that we ask hard questions. Thinking critically, expressing dissent, and holding governments accountable are especially important when their policies lead to the killing of innocent people, massive human suffering, destruction of vital community infrastructure, and the degradation of the natural environment, with grave consequences for present and future generations. Justifications for war and militarization are diverse, but one reason we often hear in today's United States is the need to attain and maintain security, particularly national security. A yearning for security resonates with many people in the aftermath of the terrorist attacks of September 11, 2001. A sense of fear and insecurity enabled the political mobilization needed to support the post-9/11 U.S.-led invasions of Afghanistan and Iraq. Yet many people in the United States and around the world, particularly peace and social justice activists, have been asking the following questions: Is militarization an effective antidote to fear? What is the meaning of security? Whose security? What are the gaps between dominant conceptions of security and the interests of ordinary citizens, especially those in marginalized positions? What are the costs of embracing war and militarized violence as a solution to conflict? Might increasing militarization result in greater insecurity? What practical alternatives to militarism can we envision and implement?

In the period since 9/11 and encompassing the war in Iraq, the concept of homeland security in the United States has increasingly animated policies associating safety with aggressive military actions, growing military spending, patrolled borders, the erosion of civil liberties, and the recycling and creation of new racialized categories of potentially dangerous "suspects." U.S. foreign policy has long been heavily militarized, but some observers in the United States had hoped to reap a "peace dividend" as the cold war ended in the late 1980s and early 1990s. Instead, the United States has continued its long-standing pattern of military engagement, intervening in countries as diverse as Panama, Sudan, Somalia,

Colombia, Afghanistan, Iraq, and the former Yugoslavia. U.S. conventional military power, which is now unrivaled by that of any other country, grounds policies that promote empire—the political, cultural, economic, and military hegemony of the United States—on a global scale. In the wake of 9/11, rhetorical devices and doctrines such as "shock and awe," "preemptive strike," and the "war on terror" have come to embody this military drive, engaging other countries as allies, targets, or clients of the U.S. military machine. Militarization also undergirds the insidious dilution of the concept of torture, the erosion of international commitments to limit violence and aggression, and the weakening of civic life, politics, and truth as the U.S. president and his administration attempt to justify unrestrained war in the name of security.

The term *militarization* refers to how societies become dependent on and imbued by the logic of military institutions, in ways that permeate language, popular culture, economic priorities, education systems, government policies, and national values and identities (Enloe 2000a). Militarization is most visible in moments of armed violence and war. This book considers the scope and implications of militarization in multiple sites within the United States and in cross-national context in the present moment of global economic and political restructuring. At the same time, this book illuminates the fractures and continuities with past legacies of militarism. Individual chapters highlight political developments in various regions: Africa, Europe, North America, Latin America, the Middle East, and the South Pacific Islands. In exploring militarization and resistance to militarism in different corners of the world, the authors show the powerful influence of transnational social forces, including colonialism and globalization.

This project explores how social inequalities relate to war and militarism. As the culmination of a broader academic program on the theme of gender, race, and militarization, this volume emphasizes links among racial and gender relations and ideologies in a critique of various aspects of militarization.[1] Several chapters also investigate interconnections with other significant axes of power and difference: sexuality, ethnicity, nation, class, and global inequalities. We also attend to individual, community, and transnational responses to militarization that strive to reverse these processes. As feminist scholar Cynthia Cockburn suggests, we urgently "need to know more about *how peace is done*" (1998, 1, emphasis in original), how to envision and become proficient at crafting cultures of peace. This volume interrogates the meanings and consequences of competing ideas about security, proposing paradigms that underscore peacemaking, human rights, and social justice.

Although mostly grounded in academia, this book encompasses voices that bridge the distances among teaching, research, and politics. Book contributors include academics, activists, scholar-activists, public intellectuals, and a member of the U.S. House of Representatives. The book presents the perspectives of well-established academics as well as newer voices in the growing field of research and scholarship on war, militarization, state violence, and human rights. The volume also draws on the strengths of different disciplines such as history, sociology, anthropology, journalism, philosophy, international studies, political science, cultural studies, social work, women's and gender studies, and conflict analysis and resolution. The chapters' breadth of approach and location range from raising concerns about the rhetorical and ideological premises behind the U.S. "war on terror," to analyzing the global impact of militarization, to revealing the effect of the culture of militarized security on communities within the United States. Although topically diverse, the chapters grapple with relationships among militarization, human security, identity, and inequality. The authors take seriously the need to recognize the magnitude of the consequences and ripple effects of militarization for our cultures, our families, our nations, and our world.

The Problem of Militarization in U.S. History

Too often, residents of the United States perceive militarization as a recent phenomenon and view war as a temporary state of emergency. For the United States, however, war is neither unusual nor exceptional. Since 1776, the armed forces of the United States have been engaged in military conflict for 185 of its 231 years, waging six declared wars, ten undeclared wars, and a myriad of additional military campaigns across the world and within the territorial boundaries of the current nation (Brandon 2005, II, 31–35). Over time, we have seen an increase in the United States' military actions: troops were in the field during all but six years of the twentieth century and at war in every year of the twenty-first century. Most of these engagements have not been responses to national existential threats and have taken place under circumstances in which many of the ordinary trappings of domestic life have been maintained without visible disruption. We can thus justly categorize the United States as a "warrior state" and should think of national engagement in military conflict not as exceptional but as the ordinary and usual state of affairs (II–12).

U.S. budgeting priorities reflect this orientation. In 1940, before the nation's large-scale preparation for entry into World War II, national defense outlays had already reached $1.66 billion and totaled 1.7 percent of the gross domestic product. As the cold war began, military budgets increased steadily and continued to keep pace with the rapid economic expansion and accompanying increases in the gross domestic product of the United States. Although the pace of growth has varied, with only a few exceptions the overall pattern has been for military budgets to rise in times of active conflict and then to drop, but never to fall to the low levels that prevailed before and after World War II. In adjusted dollars, military budgets to fund the current belligerence are topping $400 billion for the only time in the post–World War II period except for the height of the Korean and Vietnam wars (U.S. Office of Management and Budget 2007, 119–125; see fig. 1.1). In unadjusted dollars, the projected military budget for 2008 is more than fourteen

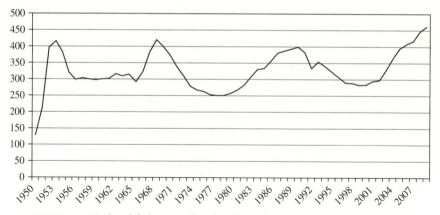

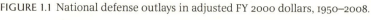

FIGURE I.I National defense outlays in adjusted FY 2000 dollars, 1950–2008.

Source: U.S. Office of Management and Budget 2007, 119–125 (amounts for 2007 and 2008 are estimates provided by the OMB).

times the sum total of all federal outlays in 1950 (46–54), and in adjusted dollars it is at the highest level since 1945 (119, 125).

During the Reagan era, those arguing for the escalation of military spending invoked the language of security and threat in persuading Congress and the American people to support the rapid ballooning of defense spending between 1980 and 1988. When the Berlin wall fell in 1989 and the cold war ended, many predicted a peace dividend in the United States specifically, but internationally as well, as the struggle between the Soviet Union and the United States ceased to structure international relations. Scholars and policy experts anticipated that the end of the cold war would bring peace as a public good, resulting in lower levels of international tension, fewer threats of war, and reduced actual conflicts. They argued further that nations would broadly reallocate resources from the military-industrial-political complex to the civilian economy, investing more generously in domestic social services and support as well as in international humanitarian aid. Finally, they predicted that scientific expertise that had been directed toward military research and development would be rapidly redirected toward other pressing technological and social problems (Hartley 1997, 32). Indeed, right after the end of the cold war, military spending across the globe declined rapidly in the early 1990s. Although the rate of decrease then slowed, global military expenditures continued to decline in the mid-late 1990s (Sköns 2005, 3).

In the United States, the end of the cold war affected discretionary spending for defense, leading to a flattening and then a decrease in spending during the 1990s. The lowest level, reached in 1996, was approximately $266 billion (or $289.2 billion in adjusted terms, that is, fiscal year 2000 dollars), with the next lowest in 1998 at $268 billion (or $282.4 billion in adjusted terms). The 1998 budget fell only to the level first surpassed in adjusted terms in 1981 and real terms in 1986 during the massive growth of military budgets under Ronald

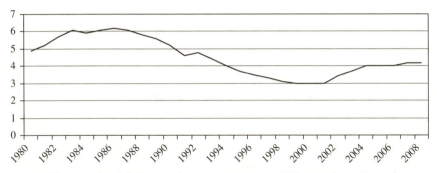

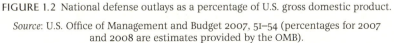

FIGURE 1.2 National defense outlays as a percentage of U.S. gross domestic product.

Source: U.S. Office of Management and Budget 2007, 51–54 (percentages for 2007 and 2008 are estimates provided by the OMB).

Reagan's leadership. In 1999, the steady upward trajectory resumed, sloping sharply upward with the initiation of hostilities in response to the terrorist attacks of 9/11 (U.S. Office of Management and Budget 2007, 124–125). Worldwide, military spending also began to increase again in 1999: "available estimates by the Stockholm International Peace Research Institute . . . of world military spending show an increase by an annual average rate of 6% in real terms in the period 2002–2004, and that the level is approaching that reached at the peak of the Cold War" (Sköns 2005, 3).

Even before 2001, the peace dividend had failed to materialize in the dramatic form that had been predicted. By 1997, analysts were calling for "recognition of the complexities of resource allocation and of disarmament as an investment process," noting the strength and persistence of structurally, economically, and politically embedded commitments to military spending not only in the United States but worldwide (Hartley 1997). Nonetheless, some economic analysts had hoped that, independent of the difficulties of retooling the defense industry, the end of the cold war would usher in a new era of prosperity in Western nations that would result in global economic growth and improvement. In fact, the gross domestic product of the United States did increase rapidly in the post–cold war years, rising at a faster rate than that of the defense budget (see fig. 1.2). But the rapid economic growth, as Ruth Colker and others have noted, rested on the emergence of a retooled vision of laissez-faire economics in the domestic sphere. This vision grounded the imposition of neoliberal economic policies abroad through international regulatory agencies influenced by the economic might of the U.S. government and large multinational corporations. The result, which Colker (1998) labels hypercapitalism, has prevented the realization of a meaningful peace dividend by the overwhelming majority of the world's population.

In fact, the economic growth of the United States has fueled calls for higher military budgets. With ongoing wars in Afghanistan and Iraq, the United States' military expenditures in 2004 accounted for 47 percent of the entire world's military spending (Sköns 2005, 4–5). Nonetheless, Harvard economist and president of the National Bureau of Economic Research Martin Feldstein recently argued that "national security expenditures today remain low relative to national income," that the current level of spending is inadequate to protect the United States, and that "handling the new threats facing the United States will require a significant rise in defense spending" (2007, 134–142). Although the current Democratic Congress seems willing to challenge troop deployments in at least a limited sense, disinvestment in militarization seems unlikely in a political climate in which security and military might are intimately linked.

Scholars are beginning to consider how the United States' identity as a warrior state has interacted with subordinated groups' efforts to advance change. In the late 1940s and 1950s, cold war politics had complex effects on U.S. labor's efforts to obtain social support from industry and on the struggles of the emerging civil rights movement. The years immediately following World War II were difficult for organized labor: 1947 saw passage of the Taft-Hartley Act, which drastically restricted unions' ability to strike; and 1949 saw the beginning of a recession, which sparked fears of a new depression. Trade unions' virulent anticommunist commitments resonated with the belligerent stance of the U.S. government against the Soviet Union, and mainstream organized labor supported "military Keynesianism" (Wehrle 2003, 527). Organized labor participated in defense planning with President Harry Truman and supported increasing military spending in exchange for Truman's engagement with labor's issues, as trade unionists "sought to commandeer the growing defense establishment—to make it as responsive to the goals of promoting employment and addressing social needs as to fighting the Cold War" (528). Although labor had ambiguous successes under Truman and significantly less national policy influence with Eisenhower, organized labor leader George Meany still sought to use cold war anxieties to promote labor-friendly policies, invoking the high unemployment rate during the recession of the late 1950s as a threat to U.S. security that "could give the Soviet Union a victory over us without firing a shot" (535). The AFL-CIO executive committee followed up with political attacks on Eisenhower's attempts to cut the military budget, explicitly linking prosperity and strong national defense (535).

Although wars have often resulted in dangerous curtailments of civil liberties, some subordinated groups have been able to use the experience of warfare to achieve advances toward equality. American feminism emerged from World War I revitalized and mobilized, and suffragists capitalized on the postwar ethos to achieve the vote (Ritter 2006). Mary Dudziak (2002) has shown how black civil rights leaders used American cold war rhetoric about liberty and democracy to push for the dismantling of the white supremacist state. American religious minorities achieved greater constitutional protection during and after World War II by "linking religious bigotry with the Nazi state" (Graber 2005, 106). And the U.S. Supreme Court, in its ruling in *Grutter v. Michigan* in which it upheld race-based affirmative action, acknowledged the influence of a brief filed by retired military officers that argued for the continued use of these policies in the inter-est of national security (Graber 2005, 115; *Grutter v. Michigan* 539 U.S. 206 [2003]).

Such opportunistic alliances have influenced how civil rights and economic advances have emerged for workers, women, and people of color. In some histor-ical periods, the most effective means for subordinated groups to achieve more inclusion and access to civic membership has been through their invocation of themselves as crucial and committed members of the warrior state. Klinkner and Smith argue that African Americans have been able to achieve advances in equal-ity when their participation has been crucial in achieving victory on the battle-field, enabling them to leverage arguments for inclusion based on military sacrifice in exchange for the benefits of manly citizenship (1999, 326–328). Graber argues more generally that the fate of civil rights during wartime depends on the nation's "mobilization needs, the ideological justification for the war, the identity of potential rights holders, and the predispositions of crucial political actors" (2005, 114). This has meant that the advances in rights that are linked to milita-rization have been conditioned upon the capacity of subordinated individuals to present themselves as crucial cogs in the American war machine and to frame their claims through the lens of American ideals that are simultaneously expan-sionist and classically liberal.

U.S. military and economic hegemony connect through the dominance of U.S. national and multinational corporate interests in the global economy. As the fore-going analysis suggests, the contemporary dynamics of militarization and its link-age to the American economy and American identity are not products of the Bush administration alone but rather have deeper roots as a bipartisan and historically continuous phenomenon (see, e.g., Bacevich 2005). Viewing the Bush administra-tion's actions, both domestically and abroad, as aberrations requires acceptance of what Bacevich (2002) labels the "myth of the reluctant superpower" or the idea that the United States has only grudgingly been persuaded to intervene in inter-national relations. Allowing this history to remain obscure is dangerous, as we may then fail to attend to and criticize the underlying dynamics of U.S.-led hege-monic neoliberalism and militarism that are likely to persist in some form regard-less of what happens in upcoming U.S. elections and even in Iraq itself.

We should note that efforts to achieve economic power and influence need not be related to the expansion of military power.[2] Although many historic and contemporary empires have been highly militarized and have depended on troops and warfare to expand their scope of economic influence, unmilitarized states and states with relatively low levels of militarization have achieved signifi-cant economic dominance. One need only consider the comparative military investments of Japan and the United States during the post–World War II era to illustrate this point. The relationship between the United States' efforts to achieve global military and economic dominance is a legacy of its experience with empire building and its ideological commitment to proselytizing on behalf of liberal idealism in international relations.

At the turn of the nineteenth century, the United States fought the Spanish American War and the longer and bloodier campaign to subjugate the Philippines. Having completed the task of extending the nation to the Pacific Ocean with the closure of the frontier in the late nineteenth century, American policymakers took the next step to extend the empire in territorial and colonial terms. This effort ultimately proved unsatisfactory because of the high costs of maintaining far-flung territorial possessions and the dissonance with a still vibrant revolutionary ethos that had in part helped whip up the war frenzy in the first place. The nation then shifted to commercial imperialism as the new form of empire—a policy inaugurated through Secretary of State John Hay's Open Door Notes, which advocated for and structured economic engagement with China and Japan (Bacevich 2002, 25–26). The modern American empire—one of capital market interpenetration—came of age during Woodrow Wilson's presidency as imperial ambition merged with liberal democratic idealism. Ultimately, "the essential aim of liberal internationalism was to open the world to American enterprise," and this kind of openness could only be achieved and sustained through the accumulation and exercise of military might (31).

The commitment to openness and free trade backed by U.S. military might came to fruition with the end of the cold war. President George H. W. Bush heralded the initiation of a new world order and provided substance to this rhetoric by using U.S. military power to overthrow General Manuel Noriega in Panama in 1989. He followed by organizing and implementing the multinational military response to Saddam Hussein's invasion of Kuwait in 1990 (Brandon 2005, 34). These actions were harbingers of a newly engaged interest on the part of the American state in exercising military force. Although the cold war featured massive spending on armaments and the accumulation of military might, from 1945 through 1988 U.S. troops were deployed in large-scale military actions only six times. Such deployments in the post–cold war era, however, have become commonplace (Bacevich 2005, 19). The first Bush administration used U.S. military power liberally to directly protect U.S. strategic and economic interests. President Bill Clinton's secretary of state, Madeleine Albright, however, criticized the previous administration's reticence to use military power in situations in which U.S. national interests were not directly at stake. Albright framed the new interventions as the use of military force rather than war making and argued for—as an extension of diplomacy—the deployment of remote, technological combat devices and methods that entailed low risk to U.S. service members (Bacevich 2002, 48–49). The vision of a protective and defensive, economically rational, and security-conscious American state was augmented by an expansive "moralism in American foreign policy," which grounded arguments for interventions framed as humanitarian. Thus, under Clinton, U.S. forces fought or conducted bombing campaigns in Iraq, Somalia, the Balkans, Haiti, and Kosovo (Brandon 2005, 14, 34). This stance of active engagement continued and expanded under George W. Bush, as military operations in Afghanistan commenced in 2001.

The significance of this continuity in the post–cold war era cannot be under-estimated. The scope of militarization and the range of justifications for the use of military force by the United States have grown consistently under two Republican presidents and a Democratic one. Resolutions authorizing these actions and funds to support them have been passed by Democratic and Republican Congresses. As Bacevich notes, a deep consensus has formed around four key imperatives:

> The imperative of America's mission as the vanguard of history, transforming the global order and, in doing so, perpetuating its own dominance . . . the imperative of openness and integration, given impetus by globalization but guided by the United States . . . the imperative of American "global leadership" expressed by maintaining U.S. preeminence in each of the world's strategically significant regions . . . the imperative of military supremacy, maintained in perpetuity and projected globally. (2002, 215–220)

These imperatives generate an intimate linkage among military prowess and U.S. military dominance, U.S. liberal democratic idealism, and U.S. economic hegemony, ultimately weaving these threads together around the theme of U.S. and international security. The human cost of these imperatives, either within or outside of the United States, is not part of the calculus.

Militarization and Social Inequalities

Militarization has painfully shaped the lives of millions of people around the world in recent history. From the scars of widespread state terrorism in Latin America, to the Hutu genocide against Tutsis in Rwanda, or the spiraling conflicts between Israelis and Palestinians—to name a few cases—we need to understand how these types of violence connect to broader systems of privilege and oppression. We need a better grasp of how ideologies and structures of inequality interact to permeate and fuel the militarization of communities and societies. Analytical approaches that move beyond focus on a single place and attend to transnational processes are particularly useful in looking at militarization because they can reveal similarities and variations across regions. They can also expose "linkages" among different places (Kim-Puri 2005, 148), underscoring how social processes and ideologies in one area of the world relate to crises, power struggles, or political designs in other areas. For instance, to understand state terror methods practiced during Latin America's latest round of military regimes, we must look beyond the "innovations" of local armed forces. A transnational perspective reveals joint counterinsurgency plans among different countries, the role of the U.S.-sponsored School of the Americas, hemispheric constructions of "national security," and in cases such as Argentina, the lessons from French officers expert in terror techniques applied in Algeria (Gill 2004; Menjívar and Rodríguez 2005; Randall 2003).

One often-mentioned factor in militarization processes has been the world-wide rise of religious fundamentalism as a political phenomenon. The ideological oppositions behind the cold war directly shaped and encouraged massive militarization worldwide. As the cold war wound down, some American scholars such as Samuel P. Huntington (1996) warned that a new ideological threat loomed on the horizon: the danger of religious fundamentalism, particularly Islam. In *The Clash of Civilizations,* Huntington warned that cultural and religious struggles would produce armed conflict worldwide and splinter formerly solid cold war alliances. Other scholars detailed the increased political salience of religion in multiple national contexts, tracing and comparing the rising significance of major religious movements in different nations and world regions (Marty and Appleby 1995). Religious fundamentalism is now perceived by many as a potent and dangerous force in politics, one that hardens agendas, closes down efforts at compromise, and encourages violence to achieve political ends.

Feminists have likewise criticized religious fundamentalisms of various stripes for contributing to gendered forms of oppression and violence worldwide as well as for increasing militarization (see, e.g., Engle 2005). Although feminist criticisms of fundamentalist religious agendas have been welcome, we urge caution in properly situating fundamentalisms and their effects. In the wake of the United States' struggles with al Qaeda and the war in Iraq, many observers have gone beyond even Huntington's broad cultural caricatures by conflating the multiple visions of Islam with a single-minded dedication to fundamentalist jihad against the West. This conception of the dangers of fundamentalism ignores the history and cultural and economic circumstances that have shaped violent expressions of Islam and other fundamentalist variants of major world religions. It also incorrectly perceives Islam as the only or primary militarized fundamentalist religion.

As Roksana Bahramitash's chapter in this volume attests, a straightforward Western feminist rejection of Islam as misogynistic plays into aggressive Western foreign policy agendas driven by the rhetorical device of saving women, as well as by racism and illegitimate stereotypes of Islam itself. As Mazoud Kazemzadeh notes, the rise of fundamentalism has provoked a complex response among Islamic women: "The misogynist programs of Islamic fundamentalists have provoked a backlash among many women who have organized resistance to fundamentalist groups. . . . At the same time, some women have embraced the veil and have become supporters of Islamist groups—both fundamentalist and anti-fundamentalist" (1998, 52). These cross-cutting internal alliances and challenges reflect the role that fundamentalist Islam has come to play in many nations as the purveyor of conservative values and gender roles as well as an important source of social support in the face of governmental failures relating to ruling regimes' neoliberal commitments and postcolonial legacies.

Fundamentalist Islamic groups have sought authority in the political sphere, but in many nations they have succeeded politically by taking on an increasingly prominent role in civil society (Berman 2003, 257). In the wake of failures by corrupt or ineffective regimes to provide basic social services, Islamic fundamentalists have stepped in to fill the gap, thereby strengthening their goodwill and influence (see Berman 2003). Fundamentalist Islam is thus not simply the product of a cultural backlash against the West and a rejection of the liberal values of democracy and peace. Its emergence as a political force should cause scholars to question their naive models of development and transition that predict a seamless path "from authoritarian crisis, to political liberalization, and finally to competitive democracy" (Brumberg 2001, 408). Rather, we must look to how modern postcolonial states have been produced and what bargains elites have made with traditional religious and ethnic leadership. Further, we must consider globalization's role in producing the economic deprivation and political dissonance that render states vulnerable to fundamentalist religious ideologies (385).

Consider the phenomenon of civil war, sometimes attributed to the rise of intolerant and dangerous fundamentalist insurgent movements and directly responsible for 16.2 million deaths worldwide between 1945 and 1999. Although Islamic fundamentalism has been present in many of these conflicts, careful statistical analysis shows that the conflicts themselves are more strongly related to poverty and strategic opportunities for insurgency campaigns than to the presence of fundamentalist Islamic or other religious fundamentalist groups (Fearon and Laitin 2003, 75, 85–86). Likewise, the perception that suicide terrorism is based solely in Islamic fundamentalist ideology is contradicted by scholars who note that "the world's leader in suicide terrorism is actually the Liberation Tigers of Tamil Eelam . . ., a group who recruits from the predominantly Hindu Tamil population in northern and eastern Sri Lanka and whose ideology has Marxist/Leninist elements. . . . Even among Islamic suicide attacks, groups with secular orientations account for about a third of these attacks" (Pape 2003, 343).

In considering the impact of fundamentalism, we must look beyond Islam (Howland 1999; Kazemzadeh 1998, 54). Across the globe, domestic politics and international affairs have been affected by "the rise of Christian fundamentalism in the United States, Jewish fundamentalism in Israel and the United States, the rise of Hindu fundamentalism in India, and the rise of militant, right-wing groups in countries like France, Germany, Canada, and the United States" (Kazemzadeh 1998, 54). Some comparative political analysts argue that, despite their doctrinal differences, these fundamentalist approaches all threaten "democracy, civil liberties, women's rights, secular life, and scientific progress" (54). And the impact of fundamentalisms on women is particularly worrisome. As the organizers of an international feminist conference on the international rise of religious fundamentalisms noted in 2004,

> although many women take part in fundamentalist movements, and some find them empowering, overall, fundamentalist politics tend to constitute a threat to women's freedom and autonomy and often their

lives. . . . [Women] are often used to symbolise the collectivity, its "culture and tradition," its boundaries and its future reproduction. For this reason, women tend to bear the brunt of identity politics in terms of control of their life choices; they are made to follow "authentic" notions of identity and behaviour. (Imam and Yuval-Davis 2004, ix)

Although fundamentalisms differ in their particulars, Imam and Yuval-Davis see most variants as constructing collective identities that are deeply interwoven with gender and emphasize "controlling women's sexuality and other aspects of their lives" (ix).

Christian fundamentalism's rise has profoundly affected politics in the United States as the Christian right's increased influence within the Republican Party helped to move the party to the extreme right of the political spectrum. Although religious fundamentalists' priorities and views have not coincided completely with the economic and ideological conservatives with whom they have built political coalitions, Republican Party platforms and policies have reflected the cultural influence and power of the religious right. The religious right has pressed upon the Republican Party its vision of gender roles and of America's divine mission in the world as foundational principles. The religious right's investment in cultural struggles over abortion and same-sex marriage are best understood not as idiosyncratic commitments to issues or as driven primarily by church doctrines but more as a reflection of a deep investment in women's remaining tied to traditional roles (see, e.g., Luker 1985).

Although religious fundamentalists generally believe strongly in the divine superiority of their own beliefs, the United States has recently experienced a "deepening political and economic alliance between Jewish and Christian fundamentalists, mainly from the US, which is encouraged by the Israeli lobby in the US" and linked to right-wing policies in the Middle East (Yuval-Davis 2004, 30). Fundamentalism among Jewish people has grown vigorously both in the United States and in Israel, where fundamentalism and militarism have intertwined destructively. In the occupied territories, fundamentalist Jewish women cleave to traditional roles. Although they are not permitted to serve as public leaders, they imbue an ideology of religious and racial supremacy. Yuval-Davis notes that "many of them spoke to the media and made bringing up as many children as possible in the frontline conditions of settlements in the Occupied Territories a fulfilling lifestyle" (32).

The rise of Hindu fundamentalism has profoundly shaped politics in Southeast Asia, particularly in India, where right-wing fundamentalist parties and movements have made startling gains within a democratic framework. Hindu fundamentalism, however, is not a new phenomenon, having been built incrementally and progressively since the foundation of the first fundamentalist organization, the Rashtriya Swayamsevak Sangh, in the mid-1920s (Shah 2004, 62). Fundamentalist Hindu organizations have sought to appropriate a long

Indian tradition of progressive movements rooted in shared oppression among the poor, the lower caste, and women by seeking believers and building an identity based on perceptions of religious persecution and inflamed memories of past wrongs. Women have been crucial in this agenda in that they are "considered important contributors to the creation of a Hindu nationalist culture, as nurturers, soldiers and propagators of the Hindu nationalist project. As mothers, daughters, sisters and wives, their role as defenders of the culture, values and ethos of Hinduism is projected as their main purpose in life" (64–65). This variant of religious fundamentalism drove mass retaliations against Muslims in 2002 after the intentional burning of a train killed 72 Hindus: enraged mobs of Hindus killed more than 2,000 Muslims over a three-day period and engaged in an orgy of property destruction that left more than 100,000 Muslims living in refugee camps. Rumors of rapes of Hindu women by Muslim men were used to whip up the frenzy, and fanatical Hindu men retaliated against Muslim women and girls with rape and murder (67).

The dangers of fundamentalisms should not, however, render us blind to strong historical and contemporary relationships among feminism, peace movements, and liberal theologies. In Israel and Palestine, Muslim and Jewish women have found common ground in their religious traditions' commitments to peace by working through groups such as Women in Black. Catholic liberation theology engaged in deep dialogue with feminist and antiracist thought, and nuns and female lay practitioners were crucial in extending its influence. Women within the American Indian Movement such as Wilma Mankiller have mobilized their indigenous religious traditions to resist assimilation and exercise leadership. And in the United States and internationally, people of multiple religious traditions have begun to come together to resist militarization and war and to heighten awareness about climate change from specifically religious standpoints. Nor should the existence of religious fundamentalism divert our attention from other forms of fundamentalism: at the 2003 World Social Forum, Latin American feminists launched a campaign—called Against Fundamentalisms, People Are Fundamental—in which they underscore nonreligious types of fundamentalisms, namely, market fundamentalism, that undermine women's lives.

In general, analyses of militarization, armed conflict, and violence need to pay attention to a range of social and economic disparities that inflect such problems. Intersectional analyses of inequality are apt to examine those relationships by emphasizing the mutually constitutive and reinforcing nature of different axes of subordination and advantage.[3] An intersectional lens renders visible how racist, nationalist, sexist, heterosexist, and class-related ideologies and practices interact, providing the impetus and becoming handy justifications for militarized violence (see, e.g., Alexander 2005; Eisenstein 2004). In exploring the impacts of militarization, we must unearth how militarization affects different groups of people, particularly those in subordinated positions, including women and racial-ethnic groups whose members have endured legacies of colonization, discrimination, and persecution. For instance, in many countries, militarization has reinforced social injustice against indigenous peoples, as when military forces occupy lands that are closely tied to indigenous identity, spirituality, and economic sustenance (Menchú 1984; Norrel 2006; Smith 2005), and when they violently squash resistance to transnational development projects—for example, gas and oil extraction, and mining—that threaten indigenous communities and the natural environment (Asian Indigenous Women's Network et al. 2003). Indigenous women from across the Americas have denounced the militarization of their territories by military, paramilitary, and guerrilla groups. They speak about how armed forces harass and even "disappear" indigenous leaders, foster the displacement of entire communities, perpetrate sexual attacks against indigenous women, and coerce them to provide food and shelter for armed units (Rights and Democracy, Enlace, and Quebec Native Women 2004; see also Amnesty International 2004).

A distinguished tradition of feminist scholarship and activism has drawn attention to aspects of armed conflict, political violence, and war—for example, women's experiences of militarization—that dominant narratives often gloss over.[4] Cynthia Enloe's groundbreaking work connecting cultural constructions of masculinity to militarized violence has, along with other feminists' analysis, advanced more nuanced understandings of militarization.[5] This work has successfully located women in what is generally perceived as a masculine arena—international relations, state conflicts, military institutions. It also reveals the interconnections between war and "peace," combat zones and home fronts. This book builds on such insights. In chapter 13, Catherine Lutz discusses how the violence inherent in military operations "comes back home" in the form of high rates of domestic violence against women who are partnered with military men in the United States (see also Lutz 2001).

Feminists have shown that gender matters in armed conflict. Although men are more likely to engage and die in combat, women and children, especially in developing countries, comprise significant numbers of civilian war casualties and are the majority of those displaced from their homes (Human Security Centre 2005; Turpin 1998). Yet, as international affairs scholar R. Charli Carpenter (2006) demonstrates, we need to be aware of how gender ideologies generate and project perceptions of vulnerability and innocence onto "women-and-children" while assuming that adult males and older boys are either combatants or potential combatants. Such assumptions, Carpenter argues, are crystallized in the implementation of humanitarian policies that leave civilian men without needed protection and at serious risk of death. Feminists have also shown that rape and other sexual attacks on women by men are pervasive in refugee camps, are used as weapons of war, and should be treated as war crimes (Bunch and Reilly 1994; McDougall 1998). In addition, feminists are analyzing how gender ideologies, racism, imperialism, and homophobia generate sexual violence against men during armed conflict (e.g., Eisenstein 2007; Petchesky 2005). In chapter 10 of this volume, Bonnie Mann develops such critiques, arguing that a sexualized project of "manning up" has been central to the "war on terror," including abuse against detainees in Iraq at the hands of U.S. male and female military personnel.

Feminists have examined how militarism jeopardizes the environment and the health of individuals, posing a particular burden on women as caregivers. Militarized violence and war have decimated agricultural and forest lands, water and fuel supplies, and basic infrastructure in war-torn countries, especially in developing areas, which negatively affects rural women engaged in subsistence production to ensure their families' survival. Feminists also note that harm to women's reproductive systems as a result of military-spread pollution has physical, emotional, and social dimensions, and particularly undermines women in cultures in which their status depends on their ability to bear children (Seager 1999). Joni Seager concludes that massive environmental degradation is closely associated with military presence in an area—"whether a base, a war zone, a storage facility, or a testing facility" (1999, 164). Not only do military projects and operations drain resources from international and national budgets, but militaries remain unaccountable for the environmental degradation and health problems they create even during so-called peacetime (Seager 1999). Native American scholar and activist Andrea Smith highlights environmental racism's connection to militarization, noting that "it is not an accident that virtually all uranium production takes place on or near Indian land" and that "military and nuclear testing also takes place almost exclusively on Native lands" (2005, 58). Feminists also note that despite powerful linkages among militarization, colonialism, and racism, efforts to break down and resist these forces continue. In chapter 9 of this volume, Katherine McCaffrey shows how women of Vieques Island, Puerto Rico, interrupted military environmental racism by confronting the threat to their homes, health, and environment posed by U.S. Navy maneuvers in the area.

Antiracist feminist analyses are particularly well equipped to illuminate the workings of militarization as it intersects with racism, colonialism/ neocolonialism, and globalization. In the United States, activist organizations such as the Women of Color Resource Center (Oakland, Calif.), Incite! Women of Color against Violence (national organization), and Women for Genuine Security, the U.S. partner in the International Women's Network against Militarism, have advanced these connections. They help to unravel the subtle and overt ways in which ingrained racist ideologies and practices become resources for increased violence and militarization (see, e.g., Incite! 2006). Congresswoman Barbara Lee— the only member of the U.S. Congress to vote against the Authorization for Use of Military Force, passed in the panic following the 9/11 attacks and signed by President Bush on September 18, 2001—urges us in chapter 3 to consider how the logic of militarization relates to the dehumanization of people perceived as "others," a process that also contributes to racism and violence against women. Under such ideological constructions, skin color, religion, language, and national origin often become markers of enemy status and are associated with threats to security.

Feminist scholar M. Jacqui Alexander, a foremost theorist of transnational, antiracist politics, highlights the growing salience of the figure of the "citizen patriot" as the United States has asserted its military power globally. The nation-state calls on the "citizen patriot" to support war as a patriotic duty and to join in the work of empire building. Yet, says Alexander, "not just (any) body can be a patriot" (2005, 233).[6] The citizen patriot is constructed in opposition to the large numbers of immigrants, poor people, and people of color who are criminalized and placed under the increased surveillance of the militarized state.[7] Paradoxically, as Leonard Feldman points out in chapter 11, empire building also relies on the labor and sacrifices of subordinated individuals who are summoned to embody the ideal of the citizen soldier, while elites are exempt from risking their lives in armed conflict and war. Feldman shows that the U.S. armed forces' reliance on the National Guard and the reserves as substitutes for the professional military rests on and obscures inequalities based on class, race-ethnicity, and citizenship status. The use of immigrants as soldiers who need to prove their loyalty to their adopted country, and who may be denied advancement opportunities otherwise, is a case in point. Feldman further suggests that we need to understand the U.S. armed forces' reliance on substitute soldiers, against the backdrop of a neoliberal logic of privatization and efficiency, as a cost-cutting strategy in line with other cost-effective practices such as the use of private security firms and subcontractors.

Neoliberalism plays a role in the militarization of civilians in yet another sense: by bolstering inequalities that push people into the military as a means of economic survival and social mobility. Neoliberal policies in the United States, including the 1996 welfare "reforms," cuts in social expenditures, and labor shifts driven by global capitalist imperatives, have undermined public education, reduced the quality of available jobs, and encouraged the severe underfunding of social programs. At the same time, more government spending is diverted to military priorities.[8] The resulting erosion of what should be basic entitlements in a democratic society (access to health care, education, food, and shelter) has disproportionably hurt marginalized individuals and communities. Thus among the military recruiters' selling points is the fulfillment of such needs. In chapter 12, Karen Houppert illustrates how the military aggressively recruits those it identifies as working class and youth of color, who are then drawn into the military by promises of access to social mobility and education not available to them in other realms. This recruitment style raises questions about the real meaning of "choosing" to participate in the "all-volunteer" military force and the perhaps too-high cumulative cost of this participation, especially for those sent to war. It also shows the disjuncture between those who command military operations from the political top (mostly elite white men who may not have experienced military service or war firsthand) and those who carry out such projects on the battlefield (mostly men, and increasingly women, from subordinated class and racial-ethnic groups).

Economic policies, social inequality, and militarization are dynamically related. In *The War at Home: The Domestic Costs of Bush's Militarism*, Frances Fox Piven (2004) suggests that U.S. military aggression post-9/11 is not only an empire-building strategy designed to secure U.S. capitalist interests abroad but also reflects the Bush administration's need to garner popular support around the war in order to comfortably implement its domestic agenda—one based on tax cuts for the rich, privatization, and welfare retrenchment. These policies can be expected to exacerbate existing inequalities and tensions at home. Conversely, U.S. military interventions abroad, in tandem with neoliberal economic policies advocated from the global North, have helped to create unbearable conditions of social tension, violence, and crisis in many developing countries. One of the outcomes of such a state of affairs has been northbound migration from those areas. In chapter 5, Lynn Stephen notes the United States' lengthy history of covert and overt military influence in Latin American countries in the name of "national security," a practice that has present-day ramifications in those countries and in racist anti-immigrant policies and sentiment in the United States, including the militarization of the U.S.-Mexican border. She also shows the dangerous paths and precarious existence of those Latin Americans who reach border zones—for example, migrants and women in export-processing towns—and who must endure in the face of economic violence, drug cartels, militarized borders, and the business of human smuggling.

Historically, colonial and imperialist enterprises have both rested upon and extended a racist and ethnocentric bias. Current versions of empire continue this tendency. The supposed right of imperial powers to use military force to "defend their interests," either political or economic, abroad—or to produce, sell, and use weapons of mass destruction (while expecting other countries not to take similar actions)[9]—is too often taken for granted or even required by government officials and ordinary citizens in powerful countries. The expansion of U.S. military and economic influence around the world builds on specific assumptions about good and evil, and civilization and barbarism, that not only legitimize U.S. military interventions but also place racial-ethnic "others" as cheap labor, likely enemies, or disposable casualties of war. In the context of the current "war on terror," we need to ask how racialized stereotypes (particularly as applied to Muslims) in North America and some European countries have facilitated wrongful detention, harassment, and other forms of discrimination against people who "look like" terrorists (see Grewal 2005). In chapter 6, Roksana Bahramitash discusses the gendered dimensions of such racialized stereotyping, which constructs Muslim men as terrorist suspects and Muslim women as oppressed beings in need of rescue. Focusing on the case of Iran, Bahramitash outlines the continuities between contemporary Orientalist ideologies and older Western colonialism. The far-reaching consequences of colonialism also figure prominently in other chapters of this volume. In chapter 8, Patricia McFadden analyses the damaging connections among neocolonial economic agendas, state-building processes, plunder, and militarization in Africa. In chapter 7, Teresia Teaiwa examines the legacies of British colonialism, shifts in global politics, and practices of inclusion and exclusion according to race and gender in the military in Fiji.

This volume contributes to and enhances the feminist critique of militarization's occupation of spaces that were not meant to be militarized. Militarization currently permeates mundane activities, shapes cultural values, and filters into paramount institutions such as the media and the education system. The pervasive presence of military symbols and viewpoints in such spaces greatly influences our everyday lives and worldviews. From the telling of history as a series of military campaigns and feats by military heroes, to the glorification of militarized violence in popular films, to the privileging of the opinions of military personnel by the news media over the perspectives of other concerned groups—such as peace activists or the victims of warfare (Goodman and HM IMC n.d.)—we are encouraged to internalize military values. Perhaps even without realizing it we may come to accept violence as normal or inevitable, we may stop questioning authority and uncritically accept the logic of war, or we may embrace ideals that equate love for one's country with allegiance to military priorities and objectives. Some of the chapters in this book challenge the role that militarization plays in cultural process and artifacts. Simona Sharoni's focus on demilitarizing education (chap. 16), Janell Hobson's arguments for decolonized feminist analyses of films on war and terror (chap. 14), and Cindy Sousa and Ron Smith's (chap. 15) reflection on the making and use of the counter-recruitment film *Army of None* show how sites of cultural production and dissemination can serve to contest militarization and social injustice.

Rethinking Security

Scholars, policy planners, and activists confronting militarization have articulated alternative visions of security, emphasizing demilitarization and state obligations to ensure the satisfaction of basic human needs in the age of globalization. The dominant concept of national security rests on the assumption that security, through the enforcement of militarized policies, surveillance, and state secrecy, will eventually trickle down to the majority of the population. (Perhaps this theory follows a logic similar to that of neoliberal market economics.) In contrast, a "human security" paradigm centers the everyday security of persons in the analysis. The Human Security Report Project explains that "for some proponents of human security, the key threat is violence; for others the threat agenda is much broader, embracing hunger, disease and natural disasters" (n.d., n.p.). The project, which focuses on the threat of violence, indicates that more often than not this threat emerges from state actors and is directed toward their own populations, rather than from external forces. The project emphasizes methods ranging from "preventive diplomacy, conflict management and post-conflict peacebuilding, to addressing the root causes of conflict by building state capacity and promoting equitable economic development" (Human Security Report Project n.d, n.p.).

The United Nations Development Programme adopts the more expansive approach and, in its *Human Development Report*, includes in the definition of human security the following dimensions (1994, 24–25):

- Economic security
- Food security
- Health security
- Environmental security
- Personal security
- Community security
- Political security

The report also explains the interdependency between these different facets of human security, highlighting how threats to everyday security sometimes result in greater intolerance, animosity, and ultimately violence within and across nations.

Although feminists have welcomed human security approaches, they also insist that even this more benign perspective must consistently take into account gender-based inequalities (McKay 2004). For example, with respect to food security, we must notice cultural norms that privilege boys' nutrition over girls' (McKay 2004); we must also recognize that capitalist patterns of production create scarcity of food, water, and other essentials, further disrupting women's access to resources in peripheral countries (Shiva 2005). In terms of health security, women in many communities disproportionately tend to the sick, while their own health is neglected (Chant and Craske 2003), a fact usually ignored by the gurus who promote neoliberal globalization. Feminists have also advocated for international laws and national policies that address how militarization and other forms of violence affect men and women differently (Charlesworth 1999). Feminists have argued that social arrangements and ideologies that encourage and condone everyday insecurity in the form of violence against women blur the boundaries between political and private violence, war and peace, domestic violence and torture. In that sense, personal security may be illusory for many women, even in peace times. The need for states to guarantee women's security, no matter whether the perpetrators of violence are state actors, organized criminals, or private individuals, is captured by activist women's rallying cry that "women's rights are human rights." The United Nations secretary-general endorsed this notion in a recent report (United Nations Division for the Advancement of Women 2006).

In considering community security, we must account for the role of cultural norms, group identities, structural violence, and their connections to gender. Feminists from different parts of the world have noticed how cultural values that supposedly assert the interests of the whole community may in fact undermine women's freedom, bodily integrity, and self-determination.[10] As noted earlier, many religious fundamentalisms endorse women's subordination as a cornerstone of traditional religious and cultural identities. Furthermore, versions of community grounded on intolerant ethnic-nationalist ideologies may not only fuel violent conflicts but also bolster gendered subordination as women are confined to the role of reproducers of the nation, repositories of tradition, or rapeable bodies upon which disputes among men of different groups are enacted (see Cockburn 1998; Giles and Hyndman 2004). Women of color in the United States and in other countries have also connected gender to the structural violence endured by racial-ethnic communities that historically experienced genocide, colonization, and slavery. In the United States, these communities are still targets of state violence in neighborhoods and prisons; they know all too well the violence of hunger and poverty, and live virtually under siege, even if these conditions are not technically defined as war (Incite! 2006). People of color bear the brunt of U.S. militarization, experiencing community insecurity in the flesh, in countries that the United States attacks and where the United States maintains bases and operations, and within the United States as populations (especially men) disproportionately incarcerated and targeted by police brutality, or by military recruiters.

With respect to political security, as linked to democratic political structures and citizenship rights, eco-feminist scholar and activist Vandana Shiva (2005) advocates for expanding our identities beyond narrow constructs of nationalism or religion, to visualize ourselves as citizens of the Earth. She decouples the notion of democracy from free trade, free market policies, and formal liberal democracy. Instead, Shiva advances a deeper conception of "earth democracy" as intimately tied to grassroots participation, more evenhanded economic arrangements, and positive notions of security: "Earth Democracy offers new freedoms to act, but it also offers new freedoms to think—to think of homeland security in terms of our real home—the earth, and in terms of our real security—the ecological security that the earth provides, and the social security that we create through community, through public systems, through shared wealth" (2005, 184). Shiva's specific vision is but one example of feminists' efforts to build positive and normative conceptions of security that go beyond both security as the absence of direct military threat and security as access to liberal rights of individual autonomy.

Community organizers and activists have historically and contemporaneously articulated critical paradigms of security and demands for peace. In 1915, the Women's International Congress assembled at The Hague and issued a critique of "the madness and the horror of war," calling for disarmament, abolition of the "right" of conquest, democratic accountability on issues of foreign policy, and participation of women in peace processes, among others. This statement is particularly poignant in the continued validity of many of its points (this vol., chap. 4, statement 1). In 1999, the Gender and Human Security Network, comprised of women from different countries, issued their manifesto, also for a large international gathering at The Hague. This statement articulates a positive vision of security as the eradication of inequalities and the creation of a "culture of peace" (chap. 4, statement 2). In the context of the "war on terror," a statement by the Esperanza Peace and Justice Center, an organization based in San Antonio, Texas, denounces the war in Iraq and other forms of violence from the perspective of peoples who have been multiply marginalized by oppressive ideologies and structures within the United States (chap. 4, statement 3). This manifesto is one of many important statements by organizations and individuals around the world opposing the U.S.-led military aggression of post-9/11, while also condemning other forms of violence and terror (see, e.g., Benjamin and Evans 2005; Hawthorne and Winter 2003; Joseph and Sharma 2003).

In July 2000, parallel to a G-8 meeting in Okinawa, participants at the International Women's Summit to Redefine Security argued that national security policies have done little for women and children but instead have promoted increased global militarization and bred insecurity as economic and environmental vulnerability of local communities worsened. As in the case of the Gender and Human Security Network, these women presented a statement offering a vision of security that included a healthy environment, state budgets that support basic needs, laws that respect human dignity and diversity, and policies that protect people and the natural world from avoidable harm (International Women's Summit to Redefine Security 2000). In chapter 2 of this volume, scholar and activist Gwyn Kirk, a signatory of both statements, elaborates and applies these views to her overarching analysis of militarization and description of actions that contest militarism at the personal, community, and social movement levels—nationally and internationally. She also draws attention to neoliberal globalization as a force undermining genuine notions of security. These contributions can be placed within a long and worldwide tradition of antiwar activism, which has gained strength in the past few decades and has become more focused on opposition to militarization and the crafting of positive alternatives. Women have led many of these struggles (see, e.g., National Women's Studies Association 2006).

In the midst of the war in Iraq, dissenting voices in the United States are embodied by independent media news programs such as *Democracy Now!* but are also emerging from within military institutions.[11] For example, in the film *Army of None* (see chap. 15), war veterans raise their voices against the military's misleading recruitment promises. Military families organized to resist the war denounce the lack of sound reasons behind the aggression and the risk it poses to the lives of their loved ones.[12] Women have critically situated themselves in these families' resistance, as military wives (Houppert 2005) and as mothers of U.S. soldiers killed or wounded in the war. Others have experienced firsthand the horrors of war and the ways it encourages individuals to dehumanize both the self and those constructed as enemy others. Here is how Camilo Mejía, a soldier who served in

Iraq and refused to return, exposes the tragic costs of war and his efforts to "regain [his] humanity":

> By putting my weapon down, I chose to reassert myself as a human being. . . . When I turned myself in, with all my fears and doubts, I did it not only for myself. I did it for the people of Iraq, even for those who fired upon me—they were just on the other side of a battleground where war itself was the only enemy. I did it for the Iraqi children, who are the victims of mines and depleted uranium. I did it for the thousands of unknown civilians killed in war. My time in prison is a small price compared with the price paid by Iraqis and Americans who have given their lives. Mine is a small price compared with the price humanity has paid for war. (Mejía 2005, 8–9)

The chapters of this book are animated by these generative critiques, which advance more expansive and deeper definitions of security, democracy, and freedom than those implicit in current militarized policies and actions.

This volume is organized into four main parts. Part I argues for alternative paradigms of security based on demilitarization, peace, and social justice. Part II addresses the implications of militarization in diverse regional contexts, most of which lie outside the United States but are often influenced by U.S. global hegemony and economic and military interests: Puerto Rico, Mexico, El Salvador, Iran, Fiji, and different regions of Africa. Part III focuses on processes of militarization in the United States and their relationship to the "war on terror," national identity, and social inequality. The section illuminates some of the sites where effects of militarization are felt: homes, high schools, National Guard quarters, and immigrant communities. Part IV analyzes gender, race, and militarization in the realms of popular culture, education, and antiwar activism, showing these sites as complex but potentially productive arenas of resistance. A brief conclusion situates the positive agenda for change and transformation supported by the volume. Through this book, we seek to engage readers in critical dialogues about some of the most pressing global problems. We hope this collection will contribute to contemporary political and scholarly debates on militarization and at the same time inspire actions toward a "just peace."

ACKNOWLEDGMENTS

We thank Jane Cramer (University of Oregon) and Nancy Wadsworth (University of Denver) for their insights and comments on this chapter.

NOTES

I. This two-year initiative at the University of Oregon consisted of a conference, colloquia, a visiting professorship, courses, and film screenings on the topics of gender, race, militarization, war, political violence, armed conflict, and genocide. The program was organized by the University of Oregon's Women's and Gender Studies Program and the Center for the Study of Women in Society and funded by the Carlton Raymond and Wilberta Ripley Savage Endowment in International Relations and Peace.

2. Thanks to Jane Cramer at the University of Oregon for clarifying the relationship between militarization and U.S. efforts to achieve economic hegemony.

3. See Collins (2000), Crenshaw (1989), Glenn (1985), hooks (1984), McCall (2005), and Moraga and Anzaldúa (1984).

4. See, e.g., Cockburn (1998), Cohn and Ruddick (2004), Enloe (1989, 1993, 2000a, 2000b), Hawthorne and Winter (2003), Lorentzen and Turpin (1998), and Moser and Clark (2001).

5. For example, Enloe's work (1989, 1993, 2000a, 2000b) points to how notions of masculinity that enshrine violence percolate through all levels of society, from children's toys and television shows to military training, foreign policy, and war.

6. As co-editors of this book, we have benefited from Alexander's insights, not only through her written work, but also through dialogue during her visit to the University of Oregon as one of the Gender, Race, and Militarization program's guest speakers.

7. This surveillance is evident in ever more sophisticated tools of bio-control employed by U.S. authorities, from extensive use of fingerprinting, to the implementation of programs for reading passengers' facial expressions as a way of detecting suspects in major airports (e.g., SPOT—Screening Passengers by Observation Techniques), to an increase in bodily searches and investment in body scanning technologies.

8. Over 50 percent of the 2006 discretionary federal budget has gone to the Pentagon, whereas funds for housing and income security, health, education, training, employment, and social services pale in comparison (see Women's Action for New Directions 2006).

9. For a feminist analysis of ethical issues concerning weapons of mass destruction, see Cohn and Ruddick (2004).

10. For example, feminists in India have rallied against the practice of suttee (widow immolation) and violence against women in connection with dowry (Kumar 1995). In England, the Southall Black Sisters, an organization that works with immigrant, refugee, and minority women, has launched a campaign against the forced marriages experienced by some women in those communities and challenged the idea that, out of cultural sensitivity, it would be racist to intervene in cases of domestic violence in the context of such marriages (Southall Black Sisters n.d.). Although these kinds of violence demand redress, Chandra Mohanty (2003) also warns us against dominant views that portray Third World women as mainly bound by backward, traditional communal norms and Western women as homogeneously free from such constraints. Her analysis points in the direction of paying attention to how cultural practices in the West also condone and encourage violence against women.

11. See http://www.democracynow.org.

12. See, for example, the organization Military Families Speak Out (http://www.mfso.org/).

REFERENCES

Alexander, M. Jacqui. 2005. "Transnationalism, Sexuality, and the State: Modernity's Traditions at the Height of Empire." In *Pedagogies of Crossing: Meditations on Feminism, Sexual Politics, Memory, and the Sacred,* 181–254. Durham, NC: Duke University Press.

Amnesty International. 2004. *Colombia: Scarred Bodies, Hidden Crimes.* London: International Secretariat.

Asian Indigenous Women's Network, Cordillera Peoples Alliance Philippines, Indigenous Environmental Network, Indigenous Initiative for Peace, Indigenous Women's Network, International Indian Treaty Council, Na Koa Ikaika Kalahui Hawai'i, and Tebtebba Foundation. 2003. "The International Cancún Declaration of Indigenous Peoples." Fifth WTO Ministerial Conference, Cancún, Quintana Roo, Mexico. September 12. http://www.ifg.org/programs/indig/CancunDec.html (accessed April 5, 2007).

Bacevich, Andrew. 2002. *American Empire: The Realities and Consequences of U.S. Diplomacy.* Cambridge: Harvard University Press.

———. 2005. *The New American Militarism: How Americans Are Seduced by War.* Oxford: Oxford University Press.

Benjamin, Medea, and Jodie Evans, eds. 2005. *Stop the Next War Now: Effective Responses to Violence and Terrorism.* Maui: Inner Ocean Publishing.

Berman, Sheri. 2003. "Islamism, Revolution, and Civil Society." *Perspectives on Politics* 1(2): 257–272.

Brandon, Mark. 2005. "War and the American Constitutional Order." In *The Constitution in Wartime: Beyond Alarmism and Complacency,* ed. Mark Tushnet, 11–39. Durham, NC: Duke University Press.

Brumberg, Daniel. 2001. "Dissonant Politics in Iran and Indonesia." *Political Science Quarterly* 116(3): 381–411.

Bunch, Charlotte, and Niamh Reilly. 1994. *Demanding Accountability: The Global Campaign and Vienna Tribunal for Women's Human Rights.* New Brunswick, NJ: Center for Women's Global Leadership, Douglass College, Rutgers University; New York: United Nations Development Fund for Women.

Carpenter, R. Charli. 2006. *Innocent Women and Children: Gender, Norms and the Protection of Civilians.* London: Ashgate Press.

Chant, Sylvia, with Nikki Craske. 2003. *Gender in Latin America.* New Brunswick, NJ: Rutgers University Press.

Charlesworth, Hilary. 1999. "Feminist Methods in International Law." *American Journal of International Law* 93(2): 379–394.

Collins, Patricia Hill. 2000. "It's All in the Family: Intersections of Gender, Race, and Nation." In *Decentering the Center: Philosophy for a Multicultural, Postcolonial, and Feminist World,* ed. Uma Narayan and Sandra Harding, 156–176. Bloomington: Indiana University Press.

Cockburn, Cynthia. 1998. *The Space between Us: Negotiating Gender and National Identities in Conflict.* New York: Zed Books.

Cohn, Carol, and Sara Ruddick. 2004. "A Feminist Ethical Perspective on Weapons of Mass Destruction." In *Ethics and Weapons of Mass Destruction: Religious and Secular Perspectives,* ed. Sohail H. Hashmi and Steven P. Lee, 405–435. New York: Cambridge University Press.

Colker, Ruth. 1998. *American Law in the Age of Hypercapitalism: The Worker, the Family and the State.* New York: New York University Press.

Crenshaw, Kimberlé. 1989. "Demarginalizing the Intersection of Race and Sex: A Black Feminist Critique of Antidiscrimination Doctrine, Feminist Theory, and Antiracist Politics." *University of Chicago Legal Forum,* 139–167.

Dudziak, Mary. 2002. *Cold War Civil Rights: Race and the Image of American Democracy.* Princeton: Princeton University Press.

Eisenstein, Zillah. 2004. *Against Empire: Feminisms, Racism and the West.* London: Zed Books.

———. 2007. *Sexual Decoys: Gender, Race and War in Imperial Democracy.* London: Zed Books.

Engle, Karen. 2005. "Feminism and Its (Dis)contents: Criminalizing Wartime Rape in Bosnia and Herzegovina." *American Journal of International Law* 99(4): 778–816.

Enloe, Cynthia. 1989. *Bananas, Beaches and Bases: Making Feminist Sense of International Politics.* London: Pandora.

——. 1993. *The Morning After: Sexual Politics at the End of the Cold War.* Berkeley: University of California Press.

——. 2000a. *Maneuvers: The International Politics of Militarizing Women's Lives.* Berkeley: University of California Press.

——. 2000b. "Masculinity as Foreign Policy." *Foreign Policy in Focus* 5(36). http://www.fpif. org/briefs/vo15/v5n36masculinity.html (accessed August 26, 2007).

Fearon, James, and David Laitin. 2003. "Ethnicity, Insurgency, and Civil War." *American Political Science Review* 97(1): 75–90.

Feldstein, Martin. 2007. "The Underfunded Pentagon." *Foreign Affairs* 86(2): 134–142.

Giles, Wenona, and Jennifer Hyndman. 2004. *Sites of Violence: Gender and Conflict Zones.* Berkeley: University of California Press.

Gill, Lesley. 2004. *The School of the Americas: Military Training and Political Violence in the Americas.* Durham, NC: Duke University Press.

Glenn, Evelyn Nakano. 1985. "Racial Ethnic Women's Labor: The Intersection of Race, Gender and Class Oppression." *Review of Radical Political Economics* 17(3): 86–108.

Goodman, Amy, and HM IMC (Hudson Mohawk Independent Media Center). N.d. "Independent Media in a Time of War." *IndyMedia War and Peace Trilogy* [DVD]. Hudson Mohawk Independent Media Center and Democracy Now!

Graber, Mark. 2005. "Counter-Stories: Maintaining and Expanding Civil Liberties in Wartime." In *The Constitution in Wartime: Beyond Alarmism and Complacency,* ed. Mark Tushnet, 95–123. Durham, NC: Duke University Press.

Grewal, Inderpal. 2005. *Transnational America: Feminisms, Diasporas, Neoliberalisms.* Durham, NC: Duke University Press.

Hartley, Keith. 1997. "The Economics of the Peace Dividend." *International Journal of Social Economics* 24(123): 28–45.

Hawthorne, Susan, and Bronwyn Winter, eds. 2003. *After Shock: September 11, 2001. Global Feminist Perspectives.* Vancouver: Raincoast Books.

hooks, bell. 1984. *Feminist Theory: From Margin to Center.* Cambridge, MA: South End Press.

Houppert, Karen. 2005. *Home Fires Burning: Married to the Military—For Better or Worse.* New York: Ballantine Books.

Howland, Courtney W., ed. 1999. *Religious Fundamentalisms and the Human Rights of Women.* New York: St. Martin's Press.

Human Security Centre. 2005. *Human Security Report 2005: War and Peace in the 21st Century.* New York: Oxford University Press.

Human Security Report Project. N.d. "Human Security Explained." http://www.hsrgroup.org/ (accessed September 15, 2007).

Huntington, Samuel P. 1996. *The Clash of Civilizations and the Remaking of World Order.* New York: Simon and Schuster.

Imam, Ayesha, and Nira Yuval-Davis. 2004. Introduction to *Warning Signs of Fundamentalisms,* ed. Ayesha Imam, Jenny Morgan, and Nira Yuval-Davis, xi–xviii. London: Women Living under Muslim Laws.

Incite! Women of Color against Violence. 2006. *Color of Violence: The INCITE! Anthology.* Cambridge, MA: South End Press.

International Women's Summit to Redefine Security. 2000. "Final Statement of the International Women's Summit to Redefine Security." Naha, Okinawa, Japan. June 22–25. http://devnet.anu.edu.au/GenderPacific/pdfs/20_gen_peace_summit.pdf (accessed April 6, 2007).

Joseph, Ammu, and Kalpana Sharma. 2003. *Terror, Counter-Terror: Women Speak Out.* New York: Zed Books.

Kazemzadeh, Masoud. 1998. "Teaching the Politics of Islamic Fundamentalism." *PS: Political Science and Politics* 31(1): 52–59.

Kim-Puri, H. J. 2005. "Conceptualizing Gender-Sexuality-State-Nation: An Introduction." *Gender and Society* 19(2): 137–159.

Klinkner, Philip, and Rogers Smith. 1999. *The Unsteady March: The Rise and Decline of Racial Equality in America.* Chicago: University of Chicago Press.

Kumar, Radha. 1995. "From Chipko to Sati: The Contemporary Indian Women's Movement." In *The Challenge of Local Feminisms: Women's Movements in Global Perspective,* ed. Amrita Basu, 58–86. Boulder, CO: Westview Press.

Lorentzen, Lois, and Jennifer Turpin. 1998. *The Women and War Reader.* New York: New York University Press.

Luker, Kristen. 1985. *Abortion and the Politics of Motherhood.* Berkeley and Los Angeles: University of California Press.

Lutz, Catherine. 2001. *Homefront: A Military City and the American Twentieth Century.* Boston: Beacon Press.

Marty, Martin, and R. Scott Appleby, eds. 1995. *Fundamentalism Comprehended.* Vol. 5 of *The Fundamentalism Project.* Chicago: University of Chicago Press.

McCall, Leslie. 2005. "The Complexity of Intersectionality." *Signs: Journal of Women in Culture and Society* 30(3): 1771–1800.

McDougall, Gay J. 1998. *Contemporary Forms of Slavery: Systematic Rape, Sexual Slavery and Slavery-Like Practices during Armed Conflict.* Special Rapporteur Final Report. United Nations Doc. E/CN.4/Sub.2/1998/13. June 22.

McKay, Susan. 2004. "Women, Human Security, and Peace-Building: A Feminist Analysis." In *Conflict and Human Security: A Search for New Approaches of Peace-Building,* ed. Hideaki Shinoda, and How-Won Jeong, 152–175. English Research Report Series, vol. 19. Hiroshima, Japan: Institute for Peace Science, Hiroshima University. IPSHU.

Mejía, Camilo. 2005. "Regaining My Humanity." In *Stop the Next War Now: Effective Responses to Violence and Terrorism,* ed. Medea Benjamin and Jodie Evans, 8–9. Maui: Inner Ocean Publishing.

Menchú, Rigoberta. 1984. *I, Rigoberta Menchú: An Indian Woman in Guatemala.* Ed. Elisabeth Burgos-Debray. Trans. Ann Wright. London: Verso.

Menjívar, Cecilia, and Néstor Rodríguez, eds. 2005. *When States Kill: Latin America, the U.S., and Technologies of Terror.* Austin: University of Texas Press.

Mohanty, Chandra Talpade. 2003. *Feminism without Borders: Decolonizing Theory, Practicing Solidarity.* Durham, NC: Duke University Press.

Moraga, Cherríe, and Gloria Anzaldúa, eds. 1984. *This Bridge Called My Back: Writings by Radical Women of Color.* 2nd ed. New York: Kitchen Table Press.

Moser, Caroline O. N., and Fiona C. Clark. 2001. *Victims, Perpetrators or Actors? Gender, Armed Conflict and Political Violence.* London: Zed Books.

National Women's Studies Association. 2006. "Feminist Perspectives on Peace and War: Before and After 9/11." Special issue. *NWSA Journal* 18(3).

Norrel, Brenda. 2006. "Indigenous Border Summit Opposes Border Wall and Militarization." *Citizen Action in the Americas,* October 31. http://americas.irc-online.org/amcit/3648 (accessed April 5, 2007).

Pape, Robert. 2003. "The Strategic Logic of Suicide Terrorism." *American Political Science Review* 97(3): 343–361.

Petchesky, Rosalind P. 2005. "Rights of the Body and Perversions of War: Sexual Rights and Wrongs Ten Years Past Beijing." *International Social Science Journal* 57(2): 301–318.

Piven, Frances Fox. 2004. *The War at Home: The Domestic Cost of Bush's Militarism.* New York: New Press.

Randall, Margaret. 2003. *When I Look into the Mirror and See You: Women, Terror, and Resistance.* New Brunswick, NJ: Rutgers University Press.

Rights and Democracy, Enlace—The Continental Network of Indigenous Women, and Quebec Native Women, Inc. 2004. "Indigenous Women and Militarization of Their Territories." Indigenous Women of the Americas. http://www.dd-rd.ca/english/commdoc/publications/indigenous/sheetsWomen/5en.pdf (accessed August 27, 2007).

Ritter, Gretchen. 2006. *The Constitution as Social Design: Gender and Civic Membership in the American Constitutional Order.* Stanford, CA: Stanford University Press.

Seager, Joni. 1999. "Patriarchal Vandalism: Militaries and the Environment." In *Dangerous Intersections: Feminist Perspectives on Population, Environment, and Development,* ed. Jael Silliman and Ynestra King, 163–188. Cambridge, MA: South End Press.

Shah, Chayankia. 2004. "Hindu Fundamentalism in India: Ideology, Strategies, and the Experience of Gujarat." In *Warning Signs of Fundamentalisms,* ed. Ayesha Imam, Jenny Morgan, and Nira Yuval-Davis, 61–70. London: Women Living under Muslim Laws.

Shiva, Vandana. 2005. *Earth Democracy: Justice, Sustainability, and Peace.* Cambridge, MA: South End Press.

Sköns, Elisabeth. 2005. "Military Expenditure." *Disarmament Forum* 3: 3–10.

Smith, Andrea. 2005. *Conquest: Sexual Violence and American Indian Genocide.* Cambridge, MA: South End Press.

Southall Black Sisters. N.d. "The Forced Marriage Campaign." http://www.southallblacksisters.org.uk/campaign_forcedmarriage.html (accessed April 6, 2007).

Turpin, Jennifer. 1998. "Many Faces: Women Confronting War." In *The Women and War Reader,* ed. Lois Lorentzen and Jennifer Turpin, 3–18. New York: New York University Press.

United Nations Development Programme. 1994. *Human Development Report.* New York: Oxford University Press.

United Nations Division for the Advancement of Women. 2006. *In-Depth Study on All Forms of Violence against Women: Report of the Secretary-General.* United Nations. http://daccessdds.un.org/doc/UNDOC/GEN/N06/419/74/PDF/N0641974.pdf?OpenElement (accessed February 25, 2007).

U.S. Office of Management and Budget. 2007. *Historical Tables: Budget of the United States Government, Fiscal Year* 2008. Washington, DC: Office of Management and Budget. http://www.whitehouse.gov/omb/budget/fy2008/pdf/hist.pdf (accessed April 27, 2007).

Women's Action for New Directions. 2006. *WAND News Bulletin,* February. http://www.wand.org/issuesact/060214/index.html#2 (accessed March 13, 2007).

Wehrle, Edmund. 2003. "Welfare and Warfare: American Organized Labor Approaches the Military-Industrial Complex, 1949–1964." *Armed Forces and Society* 29(4): 525–546.

Yuval-Davis, Nira. 2004. "Jewish Fundamentalisms and Women." In *Warning Signs of Fundamentalisms,* ed. Ayesha Imam, Jenny Morgan, and Nira Yuval-Davis, 7–32. London: Women Living under Muslim Laws.

2

Contesting Militarization

Global Perspectives

GWYN KIRK

Currently, 80 percent of women working in bars and clubs near U.S. bases in South Korea are from the Philippines; Korean women have found other opportunities for making a living. In the Philippines, however, low wages, high unemployment, and no sustainable economic policy force roughly 10 percent of the country's workers to seek employment abroad. In 2005, these workers sent home $10.7 billion (or 12 percent of GNP) in official remittances. President Gloria Mapacalang Arroyo has proudly called these overseas workers "the backbone of the new global workforce" and "our greatest export" (Paddock 2006, A1).

Following the division of the Korean peninsula after World War II, the United States maintained approximately a hundred military bases and facilities in South Korea. Although the U.S. military is restructuring and reducing the number of its bases there, South Korea is still considered a war zone and a "hardship" posting, as no formal peace treaty has been signed between North and South Korea to conclude the Korean War (1950–1953). Typically, most U.S. service members based there are young, their tours of duty are short, and the military prefers them to be unencumbered by family members. They are usually posted to Korea after basic training, often en route to Iraq or Afghanistan.

Korean and U.S. officials' shared beliefs about the soldiers' sexuality have led to policies that ensure the availability of women in bars and clubs near U.S. bases. Racist and sexist assumptions about Asian women—as exotic, accommodating, and sexually compliant—are an integral part of these arrangements. Moreover, Filipinas have a reputation for friendliness, and many speak some English. They come to Korea on six-month entertainer visas to work as singers or dancers. They have varying expectations, but a major goal is to send money home. They arrive already indebted to club owners for their plane fare, passport costs, and agent's fees. In addition, their pay is often much lower than they were promised by recruiters, and they may be fined by owners for infractions of club rules. To pay

30

off their debts they need to earn more, so they "go out" with U.S. soldiers. Thus, prostitution continues despite the U.S. military's declared "zero tolerance" policy.[1] Servicemen have privilege, as men and as buyers, in these encounters, whether the liaisons are one-night stands or longer-term live-in relationships. The servicemen's U.S. citizenship also privileges them and protects them from prosecution for many infringements of Korean law and customs. In class terms, many U.S. servicemen may be, like these women, part of a "poverty draft." But this analogous situation does not necessarily translate into sympathy or respect. Often the opposite is true, with some U.S. soldiers, notably white men, committing serious crimes of violence against bar women.

Nowadays soldiers prefer live-in relationships, and women often choose to live with them rather than be exploited in the clubs. If they leave the clubs, however, they lose both their work permits and residence permits, which are tied to the job. If caught by immigration officials, the women are fined and deported. They may get jobs in small Korean factories that employ undocumented workers. They may engage in street prostitution, usually for low fees, or rely on their military boyfriends for support. U.S. soldiers with live-in girlfriends are not, strictly speaking, engaging in prostitution or trafficking. Thus U.S. military authorities can talk about "zero tolerance" while, at the same time, their troops have sexual servicing (Kim 2006; Kirk 2006).

Approximately 2.5 million Salvadorans—out of a population of 6.5 million—live abroad, primarily in the United States, where they work in construction, gardening, child care, domestic work, restaurant service, and other areas of the service sector. They send remittances to relatives back home, estimated at $2.8 billion a year (Aizenman 2006). Some have temporary protected status, a category negotiated between the two governments after a devastating earthquake wiped out homes, farms, and jobs in El Salvador in 2001. El Salvador took the dollar as its currency in 2001 and joined the Central America Free Trade Agreement (CAFTA) two years later. In August 2003, El Salvador reinforced its close ties to the United States by committing 360 soldiers to the war in Iraq (Garamone 2004).

As a colony of Spain for almost three hundred years, El Salvador developed an economy based on cash crops for export, especially sugar and coffee. A few families continue to control much of the nation's wealth, and most people are very poor. A third of the rural population survives thanks to remittances from abroad. For decades, peasants and workers organized to change the gross inequalities that have characterized the country since colonization. These efforts met with severe governmental repression. From 1980 to 1992, U.S.-backed government troops fought insurgents of the Frente Farabundo Martí para la Liberación Nacional (FMLN), who were struggling for land redistribution, genuine democracy, and an end to inequality and oppression. An estimated 80,000 people were killed and 7,000 more "disappeared" in this war (Ready, Stephen, and Cosgrove 2001, 184–185). Over a million were displaced. In many areas it was too dangerous to plant or tend crops, and people fled for their lives, some to Honduras or the United States.

Women were profoundly affected by the war in that they were usually the ones responsible for generating household income, caring for children, and finding medical help, food, and shelter for their families. During the war up to 51 percent of households were headed by women (Ready, Stephen, and Cosgrove 2001, 184–185). Some had to leave their children in the care of others or send them abroad for safety because government forces made a practice of abducting infants and young children. Thousands of women were killed. Thousands more lost family members and suffered from war trauma, including rape, abuse, and torture by the military, government security forces, and death squads.

A military stalemate brought the two sides to negotiate a peace settlement, finalized in 1992, which included political changes, downsizing of the military, demobilization of left-wing forces, and the legalization of the FMLN as a political party. There has been little improvement in the nation's persistent inequality, however. Economic policy has favored the financial sector and the *maquiladoras* surrounding San Salvador, rather than promoting land redistribution. The government is committed to "free market" principles, and hopes to stimulate the sluggish economy by opening new export markets and encouraging foreign investment. Remittances now make up 67 percent of El Salvador's foreign exchange, compared to the *maquila* sector (16 percent) and agro-exports (6 percent) (Rosa 2004). Before the civil war, coffee exports were the backbone of the economy, but from 1999 to 2001 world coffee prices slumped dramatically to an all-time low. A key factor was oversupply, mainly the result of a massive increase in production in Vietnam, as part of economic rebuilding in the aftermath of the Vietnam War (Greenfield 2002).

A United Nations truth commission that investigated human rights abuses perpetrated during the war in El Salvador found that the government and government-sponsored death squads had committed 90 percent of the atrocities; at the same time, it also condemned FMLN violence. The commission admonished the right-wing Nationalist Republican Alliance (ARENA) government to set up a legal process to deal with war crimes. Instead, the government pushed an amnesty law through parliament (Rubin 2004).

Reconstruction has been slow and uneven. Many elderly people, especially women whose husbands and children were killed, have no family support. During the war, adults and children witnessed—and committed—terrible atrocities. An "estimated 80 percent of government troops and 20 percent of FMLN recruits were under 18 years of age" (Hertvik 2006, n.p.). Unknown numbers suffer from injuries and war-related trauma. In many communities people report increasing gang-related violence—a manifestation of ongoing poverty, lack of opportunities, the disruptive effects of war, and culture of violence.

The former Federal People's Republic of Yugoslavia in the mountainous Balkan region of eastern Europe was created after World War II as a socialist state, with

Bosnia-Herzegovina, Croatia, Macedonia, Montenegro, Serbia, and Slovenia as member republics. Vojvodina and Kosovo were autonomous provinces within Serbia. From 1991 to 2001, the member republics all experienced the devastation of war. Western media reports invariably emphasized aggressive nationalisms and age-old enmities among the many ethnic groups, suggesting that the Yugoslav federation was imploding from the inside. In addition to ethnic divisions and the political ambitions of Serbian president Slobodan Milosevic to create a Greater Serbia, economic factors and the role of Western governments and the International Monetary Fund (IMF) were also a major cause of bloodshed.

Yugoslavia declared autonomy from the Soviet Union in 1948. It developed a distinctive form of workers' self-management, with economic ties to western Europe and the United States. By the 1980s, however, the economy was in trouble, with high levels of inflation and mounting national debt. The IMF, dominated by Western powers, agreed to make loans on condition that a series of harsh austerity measures were enacted. Taken together, these led to a wage freeze, widespread unemployment, shortage of basic commodities, increased external debt, and the gradual dismantling of the welfare state (Chossudovsky 1996). People protested. Leaders of the republics argued among themselves and with federal officials. Federal funding that should have gone to the republics was diverted to debt repayment, which fueled "secessionist tendencies that fed on economic factors as well as ethnic divisions" (Chossudovsky 1996, 33).

In multiparty elections in 1990, separatist coalitions won in Croatia, Bosnia, and Slovenia. Croatia and Slovenia announced their secession from the federation in 1991 and were quickly recognized as independent states by the European Union. Serbian forces and the Yugoslav Army supported violent opposition to this move by the Serbian minority in Croatia. Bosnia, significant for its ethnic diversity and with considerable intermarriage among groups, held a referendum that called for independence in March 1992, and the Republic of Bosnia and Herzegovina was also recognized by European states. However, Bosnian Serb nationalists resisted secession. Bosnian Croats and Muslims fought together against Bosnian Serbs, but increasing polarization along ethnic lines, exacerbated by local media reporting, spiraled into a fury of violence and atrocity by armies and armed militias. Nationalist groups pursued "ethnic cleansing" by intimidation, forced expulsion or killing, and the destruction of cultural and historical buildings such as places of worship and cemeteries. Their practices included the systematic rape and forced impregnation of women by men from "other" groups.

War in Bosnia formally ended in 1995 with the Dayton Peace Accords, brokered by the United States. The new state of Bosnia and Herzegovina comprises two ethnic entities: the Federation of Bosnia and Herzegovina with a Bosnian Muslim and Croat majority, and the Republic Srpska with a Bosnian Serb majority. During the 1990s, Serbia took steps to reduce the autonomy of Kosovo, and Serb forces fought a secessionist movement in Kosovo. In March 1999, the United States and NATO (North Atlantic Treaty Organization) intervened with seventy-nine days of devastating air strikes against Serbia. This step was justified as necessary to stop Serbian brutality against ethnic Albanians and Muslims, who made up 85 percent of the population of Kosovo. Press reports, however, noted that these air strikes actually "precipitated a sharp escalation of ethnic cleansing and other atrocities" (Chomsky 1999, 37).

These wars redrew the map of the Balkans along ethnic lines. They resulted in shattered communities, people's acute distrust of "others," high unemployment, and poverty. Governments of the new states pledged themselves to "free market" principles, including extensive privatization of formerly state-owned enterprises and outside investment from Western companies. Economic recovery has been slow, and the multilayered process of healing and rebuilding will take many years.

These examples illustrate intersections between militarization and the globalization of the economy. They show how war and militarism uproot people and make them available, indeed force them, to look for livelihood elsewhere. They detail interlocking systems of inequality based on gender, race/ethnicity, class, and nation. I separate economic, political, and ideological dimensions of militarism briefly in what follows, but they must be understood as intersecting, as shown in these examples.

Virtually all nations make huge economic, political, and ideological investments in militaries and militarism—a broad system of institutions, practices, values, and cultures that take their meaning and value from war. By contrast, for everyday security, people need clean air and water, meaningful sources of livelihood, respectful systems of health care, community ties, and nourishment for body, mind, and spirit. To contest militarization and develop alternative views of security teachers, researchers, and activists need nuanced understandings. Although much is being done in this regard there is scope—and need—for very much more.

This chapter deals in generalizations and broad strokes, with a focus on intersections among gender, race, and militarization. Given the power of the dollar, the dominance of U.S.-based corporations, the United States' influence on World Bank and IMF policies, the worldwide reach of CNN and U.S. popular culture, and with more than seven hundred U.S. military bases spanning the globe, this account inevitably emphasizes U.S. militarism.

The Permanent War Economy

World military spending rose to a massive $1,118 billion in 2005 (Stockholm International Peace Research Institute 2006). Characterized as having a "permanent war economy" since World War II (Melman 1974, 2003), the United States spent 48 percent of this staggering total, almost as much as the rest of the word combined. In general, war is big business. A U.S. Department of Defense Web site describes the Pentagon as the "oldest," "largest," "busiest," and "most successful" U.S. company, boasting a budget bigger than ExxonMobil, Ford, or General Motors, and with wider geographical scope (U.S. Department of Defense 2002). Indeed, U.S. military policies and budget priorities are driving militarization worldwide. On leaving office in 1960, U.S. President Dwight Eisenhower warned against the power of the "military-industrial complex," now more accurately described as the "military-industrial-congressional-academic-media complex," to refer to institutional interconnections based on the overlapping goals, financial investments, and revolving-door job opportunities among top levels of government, the military, corporations, and academia.

Steven Staples, chair of the International Network on Disarmament and Globalization, argues that the large U.S. military budget "is for all practical purposes a corporate subsidy" siphoning public money into private hands and protected under article 21 of the General Agreement on Tariffs and Trade (GATT), which allows "governments free rein for actions taken in the interest of national security" (Staples 2000, 19). He notes that

> globalization and militarism are two sides of the same coin. On the one side, globalization promotes the conditions that lead to unrest, inequality, conflict, and, ultimately war. On the other side, globalization fuels the means to wage war by protecting and promoting the military industries needed to produce sophisticated weaponry. This weaponry, in turn, is used or is threatened to be used to protect the investments of transnational corporations and their shareholders. (18)

The U.S. military is both a state agency and a highly profitable sector that contracts with corporations like Lockheed Martin, Raytheon, Northrop Grumman, General Electric, and Boeing to produce weapons. Public funds underwrite the lengthy research and development process, and the government is the main customer for these weapons.

Nation-states, militaries, and corporations are intertwined through international trade in weapons, with the United States and Russia as the top weapons-exporting countries. The United States earned nearly $21 billion in overseas arms sales in fiscal year 2006 (Wayne 2006). Europe's main arms-manufacturing nations—Britain, France, and Germany—maintain a significant market share, whereas Israel and China seek to increase arms sales. Major bombing and missile strikes like the 1999 bombardment of Kosovo and more recent attacks on Afghanistan and Iraq serve as advertising campaigns for arms manufacturers. War-tested planes and weapons systems command a price double or triple that of those without such testing (Merle 2003; Pae 2003). Moreover, weapons must be used to justify continued production.

Worldwide, most people are killed by small arms that are cheap and easily available rather than by sophisticated weapons systems. The international trade in small arms is a central part of the global economy as an earner of hard currency

and as a way for indebted nations to repay foreign loans. More than 1,135 companies in a hundred countries manufacture small arms, and nearly 60 percent of
them are in civilian hands (Soto 2004). A good deal of the cross-border trade in
small arms is illegal, but it is highly profitable for manufacturers, dealers,
brokers, shippers, and financiers (Lumpe 2000). This trade sustains many of the
conflicts currently going on, for example, in Burundi, Congo, Sudan, Myanmar,
Nepal, the Philippines, Sri Lanka, Colombia, Peru, and Russia (Chechnya).

The outsourcing and privatization of U.S. military functions is a growing
trend (Avant 2005; Ferguson and Turnbull 2004). Singer (2004) identifies
provider firms (for example, Executive Outcomes) that offer direct, tactical military assistance; consulting firms (for example, Military Professional Resources
Inc.) that provide strategic and administrative expertise; and support firms such
as Halliburton's Kellogg Brown and Root that provide logistic and maintenance
services to armed forces. Private military companies are active in the war in Iraq,
with their own weapons supplies (Leigh 2004). Blackwater Security Consulting
has engaged in full-scale battle, using its own helicopters, to resupply its commandos (Mokhiber and Weissman 2004). In 2004, an estimated 20,000 private-
enterprise soldiers worked for dozens of companies, mainly hired by the Iraqi
Coalition Provisional Authority. Some were former Special Forces military personnel; others, for example, hired by Global Risk of London, were formerly unem-
ployed men from the Pacific island of Fiji (Leigh 2004). Privatized soldiering is a
cost-cutting measure using employees on short-term contracts, in contrast with
regular troops who rely on the government to provide pensions and benefits,
including medical insurance for their families. It shields military operations from
congressional oversight and poaches troops who can earn much more from private companies. The practice also places employees in a legal grey area in which
the military has no jurisdiction over them, as, for example, the private interroga-
tors accused of abusing Iraqi prisoners, or the Dyncorp employees who were
implicated in the trafficking of young women and other sex crimes in Bosnia
(Singer 2004). If killed in war, such individuals do not appear on lists of official
military deaths.

For centuries, colonial expansion and the quest for control of strategic locations and scarce resources have been motivating factors in military intervention.
The economic reasons for contemporary wars are not always made clear in news
reports, which often emphasize a conflict's ethnic, cultural, or religious aspects
said to be based on old enmities and histories of aggression. Recent wars in the
Balkans, the oppression of the Palestinians by Israel, and the sixty-year conflict
between India and Pakistan over Kashmir all have strong cultural and religious
elements. But in addition, Bosnia, Serbia, and Kosovo have valuable mineral and
oil deposits; Israel wants control of land and water supplies; and the watershed
region of Kashmir provides control of rivers flowing to the Indus. In Sierra Leone,
the lucrative diamond trade has fueled and financed decades of civil war. In
Colombia, coca and processed cocaine play a similar role.

The economic imperative to get business running again in the aftermath of war means that peace agreements rarely address the root causes of conflict or make provisions for meaningful reconciliation or reparations but instead focus on reconstruction and economic normalization (Lipschutz 1998). The rebuilding of destroyed factories, oil pipelines, dams, and bridges is highly lucrative. In the case of the bombing of Kosovo, Western corporations were maneuvering for rebuilding contracts as soon as the bombing stopped; in the war against Iraq, this positioning began before the bombing started. Economic and military policies are not always a smooth fit, however. For example, John Feffer (2000) notes significant contradictions underlying U.S. policy in East Asia, where the United States seeks to open up new markets, especially in China with its more than one billion potential customers, but still pursues cold war foreign policy objectives in the region.

Some commentators argue that the nation-state is becoming weaker as a corollary of increased corporate power. Fifty-one of the world's top hundred economies are corporations. WalMart is bigger than Indonesia, and General Motors is roughly the size of Ireland, New Zealand, and Hungary combined (CorpWatch 2001). Under a market economy, a major role for the nation-state is to create and maintain conditions for business profitability. States also finance their militaries, buy from military contractors, and generate ideological support for militarization by invoking patriotism, ethnocentrism, nationalism, and national security.

National Security

A "realist" paradigm in international relations has dominated political, military, and academic thinking about state security for decades. It assumes "a hostile international environment" in which "sovereign, self-interested states" seek their own security through a balance of political and military power among them (Tickner 2001, 38). National security is thus equated with military security, which places militarism at the center of public policy, justifies vast military expenditures, and naturalizes military activities.

Many nations were founded as a result of military conquest or postwar territorial changes. In general, state violence is considered legitimate violence. War veterans are often highly respected and their sacrifices honored in national commemorations and ceremonies. Military cemeteries are important national symbols (Ferguson and Turnbull 1999). Military service and connections facilitate running for political office or gaining appointment to high-ranking government positions. Departments of Defense are key government ministries. Militaries can also be a source of organized political opposition. They may limit the political potential of fragile democratic regimes and, on occasion, may take power through coups d'état. Armed struggle by popular forces, often characterized as rebels or insurgents, has been a key strategy in overthrowing colonial powers or achieving greater social and economic equality, and more democratic political institutions. Currently, more wars are being fought within nation-states than between states.

Serving in the military is considered a responsibility of citizenship. In the 1860s, African Americans wanted to fight in the American Civil War as part of their claim to equal citizenship. In the 1990s, gay men and lesbians in the United States also claimed this right. Nations where military service is compulsory for men include Austria, Chile, Egypt, Mexico, and South Korea, although with varying exemptions that include health and educational status. Peru, Libya, and Israel require military service from both men and women. In Britain, Germany, Greece, and the United States, women may volunteer for the military. Britain and the United States do not have conscription, but structural inequalities within these societies—based on race/ethnicity and class—constitute a "poverty draft." In many nations, job opportunities depend on military service and contacts. Much is made of military service as a rite of passage into manhood. Feminist scholars point to the construction of militarized masculinity in recruits, as well as the role of masculinity in national foreign policy, and argue that the nation-state, which the military is said to protect, is a patriarchal, heterosexist institution (Allen 2000; Enloe 2000b; Peterson 2000; Plumwood 1993).

Since the attacks on the World Trade Center and the Pentagon, the United States has pressed its allies especially throughout Europe and the Asia-Pacific region—by flattery, bribery, bullying, or coercion—to support its open-ended "war on terrorism." In their adherence to U.S. foreign policy, allied governments trade national sovereignty for U.S. support and protection, real or imagined. They also jeopardize their own internal political processes in that their alignment with U.S. dominance is often at great cost to their citizens. Allied governments support this war despite their own people's opposition to their nation's involvement. In addition, taxpayers' resources and some citizens themselves are expropriated for it.

Within the United States the commonplace distinction between foreign and domestic policy masks the continuities between them. The U.S. government is pursuing an integrated imperial policy that affects communities at home and abroad. Since the collapse of the Soviet Union in the late 1980s, the United States has been the sole superpower. On May 30, 2000, over a year before the attacks of September 11, 2001, the United States announced a policy of "full spectrum dominance" or "the ability of U.S. forces, operating alone or with allies, to defeat any adversary and control any situation across the range of military operations" on land, at sea, in the air, and in space (Garamone 2000). The United States has bases on every continent and has begun the militarization of space. In December 2006, NASA announced its intention to establish a permanent base on the moon by 2024.

Embedded with the Military: Information, Ideologies, and Culture

The term *embedded journalist,* referring to a reporter attached to a military unit involved in armed conflict, first came into use during the 2003 U.S. invasion of Iraq, when the U.S. military offered journalists the opportunity to undergo a period of boot camp-style training before allowing them into the combat zone. The much-repeated comment, "In war, truth is the first casualty," is attributed to the Greek dramatist Aeschylus (525–456 B.C.). Contemporary forms of this include press censorship, restricted access to war zones, one-sided reporting, highly conjectural "reports," and deliberate misinformation.

The mainstream U.S. media are owned and controlled by megacorporations like Disney/ABC and Time Warner/Turner, which Robert McChesney (2004) describes in terms of "hypercommercialism." When militarization plays a central role in the global economy and in government policies, one of the mainstream media's jobs is to enlist people's support for such a role and to convince us that military priorities are legitimate (Chomsky 1997; Herman and Chomsky 2002). Mainstream news media typically endorse militarism as the only feasible approach to security. After the attacks of September 11, 2001, "experts" brought in by U.S. television networks to discuss military and foreign policies were invariably high-ranking, middle-aged military men who supported military action. Since then, however, the picture has become more complicated. Only 35 percent of those members of the U.S. military polled in 2006 said they approved of the way the president was handling the war in Iraq, and 41 percent said the United States should not have gone to war (Hodierne 2006). Senior military officers have also criticized the Bush administration's political agenda as preventing them from making properly reasoned choices regarding U.S. withdrawal. Nevertheless, television viewers rarely learn of alternative approaches to resolving conflicts. Presidents can simply declare that diplomacy has "failed." The development of nonmilitary forms of strength is assumed to be "unrealistic," and such notions are scorned as soft, wimpy, even laughable.

Feminist philosopher Val Plumwood (1993) highlights dualistic thinking as the methodology that underpins hierarchal systems such as militarism, colonialism, racism, sexism, and environmental destruction in that various attributes are thought of in terms of oppositions—culture/nature, mind/body, male/female, self/other, and so on. These systems all rely on the creation of "otherness," of enemies and inferiority, to justify superiority and domination. These dualisms are mutually reinforcing and should be viewed as an interlocking set. For members of dominant groups and nations, the construction of identity continually reinforces a belief in the group's superiority. This belief, in turn, involves the dehumanization of "others" and encourages ignorance of how policies of the dominant group or nation affect people outside its borders, and how citizens and residents benefit from such policies, including those who are otherwise marginalized by racism or class inequality.

Media reports use language and images, subtly or crudely, in service of these ends. In Israel, this practice includes gross dehumanization of Palestinian people as well as governments and citizens of Arab nations. In the Balkans, local media sowed distrust and hatred among people who had lived alongside each other for generations. The independent Rwandan radio station, Radio Télévision Libre des

Milles Collines, broadcast hate propaganda against Tutsis, moderate Hutus, Belgians, and the UN mission (UNAMIR), greatly contributing to the racial hostilities that led to genocide. Since the attacks of September II, 2001, U.S. government policies and news reporting have relied on explicit ideologies of racism in the demonization of very diverse peoples, conveniently lumped together as Arabs, Muslims, Arab Americans, and "people who look like Muslims." In an analysis of *New York Times* articles from 2000 to 2004, Suad Joseph and Benjamin D'Harlingue revealed "a predominantly negative representation of Islam. In article after article, Islam is presented as reactionary, violent, oppressive, anti-American, and incomprehensible to the 'Western mind.' Muslim leaders are represented as dangerous fanatics rather than as respected spiritual leaders, and Muslim places of worship as sites of insurgencies rather than sites of the sacred" (2007, 464).

Drawing on such beliefs, U.S. president George W. Bush and British prime minister Tony Blair argued that the bombing of Afghanistan and Iraq would liberate Afghan and Iraqi women from domination by Muslim men. Their wives, Laura Bush and Cherie Blair, made public statements to this effect that were widely published by mainstream media: that is, the first ladies deployed gender arguments while their own gender was also being deployed. Anthropologists Lila Abu-Lughod (2002) and Charles Hirschkind and Saba Mahmood (2002) have critiqued the assumptions underlying this savior discourse as reminiscent of colonial and missionary rhetoric. Gayatri Spivak (1988, 297) notes that colonial ideology often seeks to justify domination as being in the interests of women and that arguments for intervention often are cast in terms of "white men saving brown women from brown men." By contrast, Afghan and Iraqi women argue that they desperately need military operations to stop. They need physical safety, resources to rebuild their homes and communities, genuine solidarity and support from feminists of other countries, and full involvement in peacemaking processes (Heyzer 2005; Kolhatkar 2004, 2005).

U.S. women were among the troops deployed ostensibly to "liberate" Muslim women. The differing experiences of three women who served in the U.S. Army 507th Maintenance Company unit ambushed after taking a "wrong turn in the desert" (Bragg 2003) are instructive in showing how news is created. Lori Piestewa, a single mother aged twenty-three, became the first Native American woman to die in combat as a U.S. soldier and the first female soldier killed in Iraq. Shoshanna Johnson, the first black female prisoner of war in the history of the United States, was shot in the legs and held prisoner for twenty-two days. Neither woman was given much attention, whereas Jessica Lynch, described as petite, pretty, blonde, and a plucky little fighter, made the front cover of *Time* magazine. Her story, which reverberated throughout the U.S. media, was cast in terms of a fairy-tale rescue narrative involving U.S. Marines flying Black Hawk helicopters. Lynch was alleged to have suffered multiple gunshot wounds. She was said to have fought to near death rather than be taken prisoner. These details turned out to be fiction—she survived partly due to the generosity and skills of Iraqi doctors—but they made a much better national story at a time when the war was going badly, and as a young white woman from Appalachia, Jessica Lynch made a better national hero than her colleagues of color.[2]

Whether or not women take part in combat, militaries need women's support and participation in many ways: as mothers who believe in heroism and patriotic duty and who support sons and daughters who enlist; as nurses who heal the wounded and the traumatized; as wives and girlfriends who anxiously wait to welcome soldiers home and help them adjust to civilian life; and as workers who produce food supplies, uniforms, and weapons (Enloe 2000a). Their experiences provide material for a steady stream of human-interest stories that affirm women's contribution to the war effort and the importance of the "home front."

The militarization of the English language includes commonplace usage in which ads "target" consumers and leaders "spearhead" reforms. The power of language is further co-opted to distract us from the reality of war: rocket-launched intercontinental ballistic missiles are code-named "Peacekeepers"; smaller surface-to-air missiles are "Patriots." A bloodless phrase such as "collateral damage" refers to the destruction of homes and hospitals, and to civilian casualties, an unfortunate side effect of bombing so-called military targets. The seemingly neutral term "national security" masks the fact that torture is an explicit part of U.S. national policy, even if its practice is defined as interrogation, for example.

The global "war on terrorism" is described as a "mission"—replete with religious overtones—by the Bush administration, part of its conflation of church and state. Forms of religious extremism and fundamentalism are one response to poverty and insecurity generated by the global economic system. U.S. responsibility for having promoted, supported, and armed Islamic fundamentalist groups to create a wedge against communism must be noted here. Religious fundamentalism—Christian, Hindu, Jewish, and Muslim—has increased intolerance and violence in many regions and reinforced "misogyny, homophobia, xenophobia and aggression, while narrowing secular space" (Global Fund for Women and Women of Color Resource Center n.d., 11). These developments have limited or closed down cultural and political spaces for critique and resistance, with significant impacts on antimilitary organizing.

Consequences of Militarized Security

Militarized national security undermines everyday human security and imposes vast personal, economic, political, cultural, and environmental costs. Indeed, the current international system of militarism, together with overconsumption in countries of the global North, is the main impediment to genuine security worldwide.

Killing, Trauma, Crisis, Destruction

Direct effects of wars include the killing of soldiers, mainly men, and of non-combatants—mainly women, children, and elders; the trauma of experiencing or witnessing destruction, torture, or rape; the chaos of everyday life, with hunger and loss of home, family, and livelihood; and the trauma of being forced to flee from home and live as refugees. Other effects are physical injuries and disabilities, post-traumatic stress disorders, loss of community, economic crisis, broken sewers, contaminated water, environmental devastation, and the prevalence of guns. War trauma greatly affects those in combat, particularly those who kill (Lifton 2005; MacNair 2002). Combatants experience brutalization as they learn to dehumanize others so as to be able to torture, rape, or kill. The proportion of civilians killed in war has leapt from 5 percent of casualties (after World War I) to over 90 percent by the end of the twentieth century. Over 80 percent of casualties of small arms are women and children. There are approximately 50 million uprooted people around the world—refugees who have sought safety in another country and people displaced within their own nation. About 75–80 percent of these are women and children, many of them war orphans (Fritz 2000; International Rescue Committee n.d.). Economic collapse resulting from war causes lack of food, water, and basic supplies; exorbitant prices; destruction of farms and gardens, factories, and other workplaces; and endless queuing for necessities. This situation impacts women severely as they try to care for children and sustain their families and communities.

Cultures of Violence

Cynthia Enloe argues that "things start to become militarized when their legitimacy depends on their associations with military goals. When something becomes militarized, it appears to rise in value. Militarization is seductive. But it is really a process of loss" (2002, 15). The militarization of everyday culture, often unnoticed, is a critical tool of militarism. War toys, video games, movies, and television shows all teach children what it means to be a "real man." War movies are a Hollywood staple and screened worldwide, with heroes and adventure shown in military terms. As part of the "war on terrorism," the Bush administration called on the U.S. film industry to make more pro-war movies (Saunders 2001; Schneider and McDermott 2001). G.I. Jane Boot Camp exercise programs co-opt ideas of military strength and fitness. Toy manufacturer Ever Sparkle Inc. produced a bombed-out dollhouse in which grenades replaced salt and pepper shakers, ammunition boxes littered the kitchen, and G.I. Joe, armed with a bazooka, was on the balcony ready for action. Fashion designers promote the "military look" and camouflage chic. Backpacks, cell-phone covers, baby clothes, and condoms all come in "camo" (Ahn and Kirk 2005).

Dynamics of dehumanization link violence against women by male family members, acquaintances, or strangers to state violence perpetrated by police officers, prison guards, immigration officers, and military personnel. The stress of war leads to increased violence against women, whether they are wives or girlfriends, or women who sexually service soldiers, in that they absorb the aggression and fear of men returning from training or from battle. Crisis and disruption invariably generate additional responsibilities for women to support their families as cultivators, breadwinners, or decision makers. Possibilities for greater authority and independence may emerge during such times, but in the aftermath, patriarchal relations are usually reinstated and many women say they are even less secure after the fighting stops, especially when men are armed and weapons remain in circulation (Rehn and Sirleaf 2002, 118).

In the United States, "rates of domestic violence are 3 to 5 times higher in military couples than in comparable civilian ones" (Lutz 2004, 17; and this vol., chap. 13). Women in the U.S. military have reported sexual assault by their colleagues in the service academies, in basic training, and in Iraq. Peacekeeping forces also subject women to forced prostitution, sexual abuse, and rape (Rehn and Sirleaf 2002, 64). As a weapon of war, rape involves a complex intertwining of gender and race/ethnicity, and is a strategic and systematic way of dishonoring and attacking enemy men. Examples include Korean and Chinese "comfort women" forced to provide sexual services for the Japanese Imperial Army in World War II (Hicks 1994; Kim-Gibson 1999; Sajor 1998). In the 1990s, armies conducted systematic rapes in the Balkans (Cockburn 1998; Kesic 2000; Walsh 2001) and in Rwanda (Newbury and Baldwin 2001; Rehn and Sirleaf 2002). More recently, pro-government militias have raped women and girls in the Darfur region of Sudan (Kristof 2005; Lacey 2004). Sexual abuse and torture committed by U.S. military personnel and contractors against Iraqi prisoners in Abu Ghraib prison illustrate a grim new twist on militarized violence, where race and nation "trumped" gender. White U.S. women were among the perpetrators (appropriating the masculinist role); Iraqi men were violated (forced into the feminized role).

Diverting Resources Needed for Everyday Security

Resources committed to war and militarization could provide for everyday security. In 2002, the Stockholm Peace Research Institute estimated that approximately $200 billion would allow nations to provide decent housing, health care, and education for everyone worldwide; this amount was one-quarter of the sum then invested in militaries (as quoted in Rehn and Sirleaf 2002, 123). A change in budget priorities could also provide resources for developing renewable energy and cleaning up environmental contamination as well as stopping global warming, easing the debt burden, disarming nuclear weapons, and ridding the world of landmines.

People's time, creativity, opportunities, and talents are valuable resources. In many countries it is much easier for young men to obtain and use guns than to hold a paying job or make a constructive contribution to their society. Militaries take capable young men and women from their home communities, in the process often depriving those communities of young people's energy and potential leadership. In industrial nations, especially the United States, a significant number of scientists, technologists, and researchers spend their professional lives creating ever more sophisticated ways of killing, with an increasing reliance on robotics. Scientists in fields like meteorology, cosmology, astrophysics, and complex chemistry must compete with military researchers for time on government-funded supercomputers.

Environmental Destruction and Effects on Human Health

Militarism and wars have serious long-term effects on the environment and human health (Kirk 2008). Take, for example, catastrophic wartime events such as the atomic bombing of Hiroshima and Nagasaki in 1945, use of the defoliant Agent Orange in the Vietnam War, the burning of oil fields and use of depleted uranium in the 1991 Persian Gulf War, and the bombing of Kosovo, Afghanistan, and Iraq. Environmental destruction for military ends occurs throughout the entire nuclear weapons cycle: from uranium mining, processing, development, and testing to disposal of weapons-grade plutonium and recirculation of depleted uranium in "conventional" weapons. Land mines in Bosnia-Herzegovina, Cambodia, Colombia, and Kosovo, for example, make the use of large areas a long-term danger. Mine removal is slow, expensive, and painstaking work. Routine military training also damages crops and agricultural land. Fuels, oils, solvents, and heavy metals used in the maintenance and repair of armored vehicles, ships, and planes contaminate land, water, and the ocean. Land used for bombing training is pulverized to dust and rubble. Unexploded ammunition and debris litter bombing ranges and live-fire artillery ranges as well as parts of the seabed.

Undermining Participatory Governance Structures and Processes

Increasing militarization happens through the accumulation of thousands of daily decisions taken by elected officials, political advisers and aides, voters, administrators, news editors, scientists, investors, corporate employees and executives, as well as members of the military. As nations move toward becoming more militarized, their decision-making processes become more centralized or autocratic. This change may involve the increasing use of presidential edicts, surveillance, secrecy, arbitrary arrests, military courts, extra-judicial killings, the "disappearance" of "suspects," or the shutdown of decision-making bodies. It may include outlawing opposition groups, closing down community newspapers, radio stations, and presses, banning books, or firing teachers. It invariably includes the demonization of enemy groups, as mentioned earlier. Governments may jettison citizens' rights to organize, to assemble lawfully, or to speak freely, for example, which they justify as necessary for national security. Ferguson and Turnbull (1999) argue that compared with "war talk," national security discourse is seen as rational and bureaucratic, and hence more difficult to challenge. However, Seager maintains that national security "is a vague and constantly shifting concept—it has no real or absolute meaning; it is whatever the military defines it to be (with the agreement of other men in the national security loop)" (1993, 38).

Socially and culturally, militarization requires and serves to enforce conformity, leading human rights law professor Zorica Mrsevic to comment: "The opposite of war is not peace—it is creativity" (2000, 41). Militarism operates through hierarchy and the sacrosanct nature of the "chain of command." In civil wars, people with visions of an alternative society may be killed or forced to flee for their lives. The bloated budgets and distorted spending priorities required to sustain militarism take resources from many potential creative and generative projects.

Contesting Militarization

Contesting militarization means understanding and opposing this web of interconnected economic, political, and ideological factors and working for demilitarization along all these dimensions. It involves developing nonmilitary forms of strength to counteract military threats; expanding and disseminating knowledge and experiences of peaceful resolution to conflicts; and articulating visions of true security based on sustainable environmental and economic principles, participatory political systems, and sturdy connections among people that both acknowledge and go beyond narrow identities and territories.

The increasing integration of the world economy requires and has given rise to new political movements across national and regional boundaries. It is clear to many people that neither capitalism nor militarism can guarantee genuine security for the majority of the world's population or for the planet itself. Activists draw on various overlapping and diverging theoretical and political frameworks: feminisms, nationalisms, anti-imperialism, internationalism, critiques of neoliberal globalization, indigenous peoples' demands for sovereignty and reparations, and environmental justice. Given the centrality of militarization in the world economy, conventional thinking about international relations, and the imaginative hold of militarism in popular culture, creating genuine security is a huge undertaking involving four interconnected levels of analysis and action: the individual (micro), community (meso), institutional (macro), and transnational/global levels. It is both oppositional and reconstructive, and includes work to

- alleviate poverty;
- maintain a healthy environment;
- struggle against structural violence and discrimination based on gender, race, ethnicity, class, sexuality, ability, or culture;
- establish a just economic and social order;
- change priorities in government spending away from military budgets and toward social needs;
- ensure universal access to resources;
- promote peace education and conflict mediation;
- enhance health and education policies and practices;

- analyze mechanisms that endanger peace at community, national, or international levels;
- promote gun control;
- protect women's rights and human rights;
- document war crimes and violations of human rights; and
- care for survivors of armed conflicts, promote reconciliation and healing, and contribute to peaceful reconstruction and demilitarization of the society.

These criteria were generated by a feminist project originating in Switzerland and organized by an international coordinating group to recognize, honor, and make visible women's ongoing efforts to create peace and genuine security. This project had two components: nominating a group of a thousand outstanding women from over 150 countries for the 2005 Nobel Peace Prize and creating a permanent record of their work. Choosing a thousand was symbolic—a way of saying that one cannot make peace alone (PeaceWomen n.d.). These remarkable women did not win the Nobel Peace Prize, but the documentation of their work through video, photography, and writing continues to spread knowledge of their contributions to peacemaking. I refer to some of the organizations they participate in and the methods they use in the following examples.

At the Personal/Micro Level

Resistance to militarization at the microlevel includes thinking about how we are each affected by militarization and how we contribute to it, which varies greatly according to location and context. It may include individual decisions to turn in or destroy weapons, not to enlist in the military, to support or become a conscientious objector, or to undertake the personal work of healing from trauma after military service or experiencing military violence. Personal resistance to militarization may include joining antimilitary demonstrations, vigils, and organizations, supporting antimilitary candidates for political office, and urging them to promote sustainable development polices and projects. It may mean limiting our financial support for militarism through, for example, tax resistance; demilitarizing our knowledge by being more critical of what the mainstream media feed us; and seeking alternative sources of information.

On the positive side, it means using our personal resources—skills, talents, time, money, and imagination—to create ways of living that support everyday security and sustainability. Examples include teaching conflict resolution skills to children, cultivating gardens, supporting farmers' markets, making art, sharing in community events that affirm and celebrate nonviolence, and opening ourselves to connections and friendships across lines of race, class, religion, and culture.

At the Community/Meso Level

Women's peace work is most visible at the community level, where women draw on their skills and creativity to analyze their situation, define needs, and provide services. This work may include organizing workshops or rallies where women can speak about violence related to war, as has happened in Guatemala, Colombia, and Sierra Leone. It includes establishing women's centers to heal military violence (for example, Medica Women's Therapy Center in Bosnia-Herzegovina), helping women deal with the daily impact of Israeli occupation as well as the sexism of their society (Women's Center for Legal Aid and Counseling in Palestine), supporting Philippine women who work in bars and clubs around U.S. bases (My Sister's Place in South Korea), and providing health care and income-generating projects for women affected by war (Association of Widows of the Genocide of April 1994 in Rwanda). Organizations that support young men and women who oppose military service include the Central Committee for Conscientious Objectors (United States), Peace and Human Rights Solidarity (South Korea), and New Profile and Yesh Gvul (Israel).

Resisting militarization at the community level may include creating cultural spaces to explore the meaning of demilitarization and peace, such as the Center for Education for a Culture of Peace and Folk Art Museum (El Salvador), the Chicago Peace Museum (United States), Space Peace (South Korea), or the antimilitary fashion shows initiated by the Women of Color Resource Center (United States) to contest the militarization of everyday culture through camouflage "chic." It involves demonstrations and vigils. Women in Black stood in silent witness outside government offices in Belgrade and denounced Milosevic, their president. Dialogue projects—among Israeli and Palestinian people, across ethnic lines in the Balkans, or between Catholic and Protestant communities in Northern Ireland—have created spaces for listening and the deepening of understanding (Cockburn 1998). Community media projects that use street theater, comic books, storytelling, video, radio shows, alternative newspapers, or the Internet all distribute information and perspectives missing from mainstream media. Community resistance also includes music, poetry, writing, painting, theater, dance, and other cultural events that are healing and inspirational.

At the Institutional/Macro Level

Resistance at the institutional level involves lobbying governments, pushing them to uphold treaties, and holding them accountable to commitments made in ratifying international agreements such as the UN Charter, the 1993 Vienna Declaration on Human Rights, and the Platform for Action adopted by the 1995 UN Conference on women in Beijing. South Africa's postapartheid constitution is the first in the world to ban "speech that incites hatred of a person because of race, religions, gender, or sexual preference"—an example of demilitarizing the notion of free speech (Rehn and Sirleaf 2002, 107–108).

The demilitarization of education includes curriculum changes, as with the contentious debate over history textbooks used in Japanese classrooms and what students are taught about atrocities perpetrated by the Japanese Imperial Army before and during World War II, especially against China, Korea, and Okinawa.

It also includes peace education in schools and community discussions in which people can assert their peacemaking traditions. In communities in Albania, Cambodia, and Niger, such discussions generated agreements to destroy knives and guns (Hague Appeal for Peace n.d.). In the United States, it means learning deeply about people from diverse communities and many nations, as well as about this nation's profound historic investment in colonialism, genocide, militarization, and imperialism. It includes creating an alternative curriculum to replace the JROTC presence in schools and fostering resistance to military recruiters in schools. The military is the only employer that systematically targets inner-city African American and Latino youth with promises of a disciplined lifestyle, enhanced pride and self-esteem, professional training, and money for college. For every college counselor at Roosevelt High School in East Los Angeles, for example, there are five military recruiters (Joiner 2003). Demilitarizing education includes refusing to undertake military-related research. It includes the actions of faculty, staff, students, and community members who opposed a proposed U.S. Navy University-Affiliated Research Center at the University of Hawai'i–Manoa. It means that feminist research and teaching must confront the centrality of militarism, a defining dimension of the nation-state and the articulation of state power.

In many nations, people are organizing to push for a larger share of public funds to be devoted to education rather than military operations. Closely related is the demilitarization of national budget priorities, which requires that people understand the relationship between military spending and socially useful government spending. Organizations in Britain, South Korea, and Sweden have started to do this. In the United States, the National Priorities Project, the War Resisters' League, and Women's Action for New Directions publish accessible materials on military spending.

Resistance to militarization at the institutional level means including women's meaningful participation in peace processes and efforts to demilitarize societies in the aftermath of war. In October 2000, the UN Security Council adopted Resolution 1325 on women, peace, and security. This is the first time the Security Council has addressed the disproportionate impact of armed conflict on women; recognized the undervalued contributions that women make to conflict prevention, conflict resolution, and peace building; and stressed the importance of women's equal and full participation as active agents in peace and security. Although not binding on governments, Resolution 1325 sets a new standard of inclusiveness and gender sensitivity in peace negotiations and provides leverage for women's efforts to influence policy in postconflict reconstruction (Lynes and Torry 2005).

In June 2006, for example, women's organizations in Southern Sudan relied on this resolution in calling for UN support for women in conflict areas ("Message from the Women from Southern Sudan" 2006). They argued that women's rights violations, women's low social status, and continued gender-based discrimination are a result of high levels of poverty, twenty-one years of war, and a confluence of culture, religions, and traditions. They requested that the UN Security Council press the government of Southern Sudan for urgent reforms in the areas of family law, legal aid, psycho-social counseling, and health services for women; for increased participation of women in decision-making at all levels of conflict resolution, peace building, and development; for increased recruitment of female police who better understand the plight of women; and for support for women's organizations to undertake civic education, skills training, and consciousness raising on HIV/AIDS and gender issues. They also requested that the UN Security Council continue to support the parties to the Comprehensive Peace Agreement (CPA) in Southern Sudan; report on the protection of women and children from violence; and continue to provide necessary resources to UN agencies such as UNIFEM and UNFPA to ensure women's full participation in the implementation of the CPA.

At the Transnational/Global Level

Working across national borders builds on activities at other levels. This work needs guides and interpreters, opportunities to listen and learn, time, resources, organizational capacity, patience, perseverance, and the willingness to be uncomfortable at times. It includes networking at meetings and conferences, sharing information through journals and the Internet, and organizing coordinated activities.

The Pan-African Women's Conference on a Culture of Peace (Zanzibar, Tanzania, 1999), the International Women's Summit to Redefine Security (Okinawa, Japan, 2000), and international gatherings of Women in Black groups from North America, Europe, and the Middle East (Jerusalem, 2006) serve as examples of women organizing across borders. Such gatherings build on the work of networks like the Federation of African Women's Peace Networks, the Mano River Union Women's Network for Peace, and the International Women's Network against Militarism. Women's groups in Croatia, Serbia, Bosnia, and Kosovo have done remarkable work across ethnic lines in supporting Serb, Croat, and Muslim women during war and in the aftermath to build bridges within their communities and between states. Long-standing organizations such as the Women's International League for Peace and Freedom (founded in 1915 and currently active in thirty-seven countries) can play an important role at this level, as can UN-sponsored gatherings, and other opportunities for dialogue and exchange such as the World Social Forum.

Transnational organizations that seek to prevent conflicts include Global Action to Prevent War and Armed Conflict, and Search for Common Ground, both of which work with partner organizations in various nations to find culturally appropriate ways for nations to strengthen their capacity to deal constructively with conflicts. These organizations use media production—radio, television, film, and print—mediation and facilitation, training, community organizing, sports, theater, and music to promote individual and institutional changes. The Nonviolent Peaceforce, with over ninety member organizations from around the world, works to build a trained, international civilian peace force able to intervene in conflicts. In December 2002, 130 delegates from forty-seven nations chose Sri Lanka as the site of the first pilot project. The goal is for field team members to contribute to protecting human rights, deterring violence, and creating space for local peacemakers to carry out their work. Peace Brigades International (PBI) has a similar mission, currently with volunteers in Colombia, Guatemala, Indonesia, and Mexico. Any kind of solidarity work needs clear understandings about whose needs, perspectives, and decisions are central to the task in order to avoid allowing individuals and groups with class or national privilege to define the direction in which projects should go, thereby reinforcing unequal relationships, even if this is not the intent. Many people working in transnational networks and solidarity organizations draw on what Chandra Talpade Mohanty (2003, 50) calls "a common context of struggle," with a shared framework opposing militarization.

Transnational work includes support for UN initiatives such as UNESCO's Culture of Peace, as well as the International Criminal Court (ICC), independent of the UN, which can try individuals accused of the most serious crimes of international concern: genocide, crimes against humanity, and war crimes. The ICC, based on a treaty that entered into force in 2002, has been joined by 105 countries so far.

Militarism's reach and power are vast. Increased intolerance and violence in many regions have reduced cultural and political spaces for critique and resistance, as mentioned earlier. Nevertheless, millions of people worldwide oppose and reject war, as shown on February 15, 2003, a day of unprecedented coordinated protest against the not-yet-begun U.S.- and British-led war on Iraq. Journalist Patrick Tyler (2003) wrote that "the huge anti-war demonstrations around the world this weekend are reminders that there may still be two superpowers on the planet: the United States and world public opinion." The "second superpower" has not yet stopped the war against Iraq, but it contests militarization in a myriad ways, including the examples mentioned in this chapter.

Betty Burkes, former president of Women's International League for Peace and Freedom (U.S. section) and among the thousand women nominated for the 2005 Nobel Peace Prize, comments: "We will succeed in building a strong base for transforming . . . power when together we weave a vision that in practice offers a way of life so *vital* it is impossible to resist." [3]

ACKNOWLEDGMENTS

An earlier version of this essay was given at the Gender, Race, and Militarization Conference, October 28, 2005, at the University of Oregon. I thank the editors of this volume for their insights and support, and also Margo Okazawa-Rey, longtime friend and colleague, with whom I shared and developed many of these ideas. This chapter's section "The Permanent War Economy" partly draws on ideas developed in *Social Justice* 27(4), a special issue on neoliberalism, militarism, and armed conflict, edited by Gwyn Kirk and Margo Okazawa-Rey (2000). Reprinted by permission; see www.socialjusticejournal.org.

NOTES

1. In January 2004, the U.S. Department of Defense issued a memorandum restating its opposition to "prostitution and any related activities that may contribute to the phenomenon of trafficking in persons as inherently harmful and dehumanizing" (as quoted in Equality Now 2006, n.p.). On October 14, 2005, President Bush signed Executive Order 13387, which makes "patronizing a prostitute" a violation of article 134 of the Uniform Code of Military Justice.

2. Margo Okazawa-Rey alerted me to the unequal treatment and visibility these women received.

3. Betty Burkes, pers. comm.; this is a version of her statement in *1000 Peace Women across the Globe* (1000 Women for the Nobel Peace Prize 2005, 718).

REFERENCES

Abu-Lughod, Lila. 2002. "Do Muslim Women Really Need Saving? Anthropological Reflections on Cultural Relativism and Its Others." *American Anthropologist* 104(3): 738–790.

Ahn, Christine, and Gwyn Kirk. 2005. "Why War Is All the Rage." *San Francisco Chronicle,* May 29, D5.

Aizenman, N. C. 2006. "Money Earned in U.S. Pushes up Prices in El Salvador." *Washington Post,* May 14, A17. http://www.washingtonpost.com/wp-dyn/content/article/2006/05/13/AR2006051300879.html?nav=rss_world/centralamerica (accessed December 12, 2006).

Allen, Holly. 2000. "Gender, Sexuality and the Military Model of U.S. National Community." In *Gender Ironies of Nationalism: Sexing the Nation,* ed. Tamar Mayer, 306–327. New York: Routledge.

Avant, Deborah. 2005. *The Market for Force: The Consequences of Privatizing Security.* New York: Cambridge University Press.

Bragg, Rick. 2003. "Wrong Turn in the Desert." *Time Magazine,* November 17. http://www.time.com/time/magazine/article/0,9171,1213025-1,00.html (accessed December 26, 2006).

Chomsky, Noam. 1997. *Media Control: The Spectacular Achievements of Propaganda.* New York: Seven Stories Press.

——. 1999. "Kosovo Peace Accord." *Z Magazine* (July): 36–42.

Chossudovsky, Michel. 1996. "Dismantling Yugoslavia, Colonizing Bosnia." *Covert Action Quarterly* 56: 31–37.

Cockburn, Cynthia. 1998. *The Space between Us: Negotiating Gender and National Identities in Conflict.* London: Zed Books.

CorpWatch. 2001. "Corporate Globalization Fact Sheet." http://www.corpwatch.org/article.php?id=378 (accessed December 12, 2006).

Enloe, Cynthia. 2000a. *Maneuvers: The International Politics of Militarizing Women's Lives.* Berkeley: University of California Press.

——. 2000b. "Masculinity as a Foreign Policy Issue." *Foreign Policy in Focus* 5(36). http://www.fpif.org/fpiftxt/1502 (accessed February 13, 2007).

——. 2002. "Sneak Attack: The Militarization of U.S. Culture." *Ms.* (December/January): 15–16.

Equality Now. 2006. "United States: The Role of Military Forces in the Growth of the Commercial Sex Industry." Women's Action 23.2, March. http://www.equalitynow. org/english/actions/action_2302_en.html (accessed October 20, 2006).

Feffer, John. 2000. "Gunboat Diplomacy: The Intersection of Economics and Security in East Asia." *Social Justice* 27(4): 45–62.

Ferguson, Kathy, and Phyllis Turnbull. 1999. *Oh, Say, Can You See? The Semiotics of the Military in Hawai'i.* Minneapolis: University of Minnesota Press.

——. 2004. "Globalizing Militaries." In *Rethinking Globalism,* ed. Manfred B. Steger, 79–91. Lanham, MD: Rowman and Littlefield.

Fritz, Mark. 2000. *Lost on Earth: Nomads of the New World.* New York: Routledge.

Garamone, Jim. 2000. "Joint Vision 2020 Emphasizes Full-Spectrum Dominance." http:// www.defenselink.mil/news/Jun2000/n06022000_20006025.html (accessed December 24, 2006).

——. 2004. "El Salvador to Continue Iraq Deployment." American Forces Press Service. http:// www.defenselink.mil/news/Jul2004/n07222004_2004072207.html (accessed December 20, 2006).

Global Fund for Women and Women of Color Resource Center. N.d. *Building a 21st Century Transnational Women's Movement.* San Francisco: Global Fund for Women and Women of Color Resource Center.

Greenfield, Gerard. 2002. "Vietnam and the World Coffee Crisis: Local Coffee Riots in a Global Context." http://www.cb3rob.net/~merijn89/ARCH2/msg00037.html (accessed December 20, 2006).

Hague Appeal for Peace. N.d. *Peace and Disarmament Education: Changing Mindsets to Reduce Violence and Sustain the Removal of Small Arms.* New York: HAP.

Herman, Edward S., and Noam Chomsky. 2002. *Manufacturing Consent: The Political Economy of the Mass Media.* New York: Pantheon.

Hertvik, Nicole. 2006. "El Salvador: Effecting Change from Within." *UN Chronicle.* http://www. un.org/Pubs/chronicle/2002/issue3/0302p75_el_salvador.html (accessed December 12, 2006).

Heyzer, Noeleen. 2005. "Seating Women at the Peace Table." In *Stop the Next War Now,* ed. Medea Benjamin and Jodie Evans, 167–168. San Francisco: Inner Ocean Publishing.

Hicks, George. 1994. *The Comfort Women.* New York: Norton.

Hirschkind, Charles, and Saba Mahmood. 2002. "Feminism, the Taliban, and the Politics of Counterinsurgency." *Anthropological Quarterly* 75(2): 339–354.

Hodierne, Robert. 2006. "Down on the War. Poll: More Troops Unhappy with Bush's Course in Iraq." http://www.militarycity.com/polls/2006_main.php (accessed January 9, 2007).

International Rescue Committee. N.d. "Frequently Asked Questions about Refugees and Resettlement." http://www.theirc.org/what/frequently_asked_questions_about_refugees_ and_resettlement.html (accessed February 13, 2007).

Joiner, Whitney. 2003. "The Army Be Thuggin' It—The New Black and Latino Recruitment Hustle." *Salon,* October 17. http://dir.salon.com/story/mwt/feature/2003/10/17/army/ index.html (accessed December 13, 2006).

Joseph, Suad, and Benjamin D'Harlingue. 2007. "Media Representations and the Criminalization of Arab Americans and Muslim Americans." In *Women's Lives: Multicultural Perspectives,* 4th ed., ed. Gwyn Kirk and Margo Okazawa-Rey, 464–468. New York: McGraw-Hill.

Kesic, Vesna. 2000. "From Reverence to Rape: An Anthropology of Ethnic and Gendered Violence." In *Frontline Feminisms: Women, War, and Resistance,* ed. Marguerite R. Waller and Jennifer Rycenga, 23–36. New York: Garland.

Kim, D. S. 2006. "Human Rights Situation of Foreign Women in the Korean Sex Industry." In *Out of the Trap, Hope One Step: Case Studies of Prostitution and Sex Trafficking in Korea*, ed. Dasi Hamkke Center, 39–48. Seoul: Dasi Hamkke Center.

Kim-Gibson, Dai Sil. 1999. *Silence Broken: Korean Comfort Women*. Parkersburg, IA: Mid-Prairie Books.

Kirk, Gwyn. 2006. "Genuine Security for Women." Paper marking the twentieth anniversary of My Sister's Place, South Korea, including information from interviews with Yu Young Nim and Dong Shim Kim, July–September 2006.

——. 2008. "Environmental Effects of U.S. Military 'Security': Gendered Experiences from the Philippines, South Korea, and Japan." In *Gender and Globalization in Asia and the Pacific: Method, Practice, Theory*, ed. Kathy E. Ferguson and Monique Mironesco. Honolulu: University of Hawai'i Press.

Kirk, Gwyn, and Margo Okazawa-Rey, eds. 2000. "Neoliberalism, Militarism, and Armed Conflict." Special issue. *Social Justice* 27(4).

Kolhatkar, Sonali. 2004. "Afghan Women Continue to Fend for Themselves." *Foreign Policy in Focus*, March. http://www.fpif.org/papers/2004afghanwom.html (accessed February 13, 2007).

——. 2005. "Freedom through Solidarity—The Lie of 'Liberation.'" In *Stop the Next War Now*, ed. Medea Benjamin and Jodi Evans, 87–89. San Francisco: Inner Ocean Publishing.

Kristof, Nicholas. 2005. "A Policy of Rape." *New York Times*, June 5, D14.

Lacey, Marc. 2004. "Amnesty Says Sudan Militias Use Rape as Weapon." *New York Times*, July 19, A.

Leigh, David. 2004. "Who Commands the Private Soldiers?" *Guardian UK*, May 17. http://www.truthout.org/cgi-bin/artman/exec/view.cgi/9/4500/printer (accessed January 11, 2007).

Lifton, Robert J. 2005. *Home from the War: Learning from Vietnam Vets*. New York: Other Press.

Lipschutz, Ronnie D. 1998. "Beyond the Neoliberal Peace: From Conflict Resolution to Social Reconciliation." *Social Justice* 25(4): 5–19.

Lumpe, Lora. 2000. *Running Guns: The Global Black Market in Small Arms*. New York: Palgrave/St. Martins.

Lutz, Catherine. 2004. "Living Room Terrorists." *Women's Review of Books* 21(5): 17–18.

Lynes, Krista, and Gina Torry, eds. 2005. *From Local to Global: Making Peace Work for Women*. New York: NGO Working Group on Women, Peace and Security.

MacNair, Rachel. 2002. *Perpetration-Induced Traumatic Stress: The Psychological Consequences of Killing*. Westport, CT: Praeger.

McChesney, R. W. 2004. *The Problem of the Media: U.S. Communications Politics in the 21st Century*. New York: Monthly Review Press.

Melman, Seymour. 1974. *Permanent War Economy: American Capitalism in Decline*. New York: Simon and Schuster.

——. 2003. "In the Grip of a Permanent War Economy." *Counterpunch*, March 15. http://www.counterpunch.org/melman03152003.html (accessed December 13, 2006).

Merle, Renae. 2003. "Battlefield Is a Showcase for Defense Firms." *Washington Post*, April 1, E1.

"Message from the Women from Southern Sudan to the UN Security Council in Relation to UN Security Council Resolution No. 1325." 2006. June 8. http:// www.peacewomen.org/ campaigns/Sudan/Sudan.html (accessed January 5, 2007).

Mohanty, Chandra Talpade. 2003. *Feminism without Borders: Decolonizing Theory, Practicing Solidarity*. Durham, NC: Duke University Press.

Mokhiber, Russell, and Robert Weissman. 2004. "The Rising Corporate Military Monster." CommonDreams.org News Center, April 23. http://www.commondreams.org/views04/0423–12.htm (accessed February 13, 2007).

Mrsevic, Zorica. 2000. "The Opposite of War Is Not Peace—It Is Creativity." In *Frontline Feminisms: Women, War, and Resistance,* ed. Marguerite R. Waller and Jennifer Rycenga, 41–55. New York: Garland.

Newbury, Catharine, and Hannah Baldwin. 2001. "Profile: Rwanda." In *Women and Civil War: Impact, Organizations, and Action,* ed. Krishna Kumar, 29–38. Boulder, CO: Lynne Rienner.

1000 Women for the Nobel Peace Prize. 2005. *1000 Peacewomen across the Globe.* Zurich: Scalo.

Paddock, Richard G. 2006. "The Overseas Class." *Los Angeles Times,* April 20, A1, A20–22.

Pae, Peter. 2003. "Iraq a Proving Ground for Defense Firms." *Los Angeles Times,* April 1, C1.

PeaceWomen. N.d. http://www.1000peacewomen.org/ (accessed March 19, 2007).

Peterson, V. Spike. 2000. "Sexing Political Identities/Nationalism as Heterosexism." In *Women, States, and Nationalism: At Home in the Nation?* ed. Sita Ranchod-Nilsson and Mary Ann Tétreault, 54–80. New York: Routledge.

Plumwood, Val. 1993. *Feminism and the Mastery of Nature.* New York: Routledge.

Ready, Kelley, Stephen, Lynn, and Cosgrove, Serena. 2001. "Women's Organizations in El Salvador: History, Accomplishments, and International Support." In *Women and Civil War: Impact, Organizations, and Action,* ed. Krishna Kumar, 183–204. Boulder, CO: Lynne Rienner.

Rehn, Elisabeth, and Ellen Johnson Sirleaf. 2002. *Women, War, Peace: The Independent Experts Assessment on the Impact of Armed Conflict on Women and Women's Role in Peace- Building.* New York: UNIFEM.

Rosa, Herman. 2004. *Economic Integration and the Environment in El Salvador.* San Salvador: PRISMA.

Rubin, Joe. 2004. "El Salvador: Payback." *Frontline World,* October 12. http://www.pbs. org/frontlineworld/elections/elsalvador/ (accessed January 11, 2007).

Sajor, Indai Lourdes, ed. 1998. *Common Grounds: Violence against Women in War and Armed Conflict Situations.* Quezon City, Philippines: Asian Center for Women's Human Rights.

Saunders, Doug. 2001. "Hollywood, D.C." *Toronto Globe and Mail,* November 17. http://www.theglobeandmail.com/series/hollywood/ (accessed February 19, 2007).

Schneider, Bill, and Anne McDermott. 2001. "Uncle Sam Wants Hollywood." CNN.com. http://archives.cnn.com/2001/SHOWBIZ/Movies/11/09/hollywood.war/ (accessed February 19, 2007).

Seager, Joni. 1993. *Earth Follies: Coming to Feminist Terms with the Global Environmental Crisis.* New York: Routledge.

Singer, P. W. 2004. *Corporate Warriors: The Rise of the Privatized Military Industry.* Ithaca, NY: Cornell University Press.

Soto, Jessica U. 2004. *Human Rights: A Cross-Cutting Issue in Peace and Conflict Situations and Violence against Women.* Report prepared for the International Meeting on Human Security and Development, November 21–28, Manila, Philippines.

Spivak, Gayatri Chakravorty. 1988. "Can the Subaltern Speak?" In *Marxism and the Interpretation of Culture,* ed. Cary Nelson and Lawrence Grossberg, 271–313. Urbana: University of Illinois Press.

Staples, Steven. 2000. "Globalization and Militarism." *Social Justice* 27(4): 18–22.

Stockholm International Peace Research Institute. 2006. *SIPRI Yearbook 2006.* Stockholm: SIPRI. http://yearbook2006.sipri.org/chap8 (accessed January 12, 2008).

Tickner, J. Ann. 2001. *Gendering World Politics: Issues and Approaches in the Post–Cold War Era.* New York: Columbia University Press.

Tyler, Patrick. 2003. "A New Power in the Streets: A Message to Bush Not to Rush to War." *New York Times,* February 17, A1.

U.S. Department of Defense. 2002. "DOD 101: An Introductory Overview of the Department of Defense." http://www.defenselink.mil/pubs/dod101/dod101_for_2002.html (accessed March 19, 2007).

Walsh, Martha. 2001. "Profile: Bosnia and Herzegovina." In *Women and Civil War: Impact, Organizations, and Action,* ed. Krishna Kumar, 57–67. Boulder, CO: Lynne Rienner.

Wayne, Leslie. 2006. "Foreign Sales by U.S. Arms Makers Doubled in a Year." *New York Times,* November 11, Business sec. http://www.nytimes.com/2006/11/11/business/11military.html?_r=1&scp=88&sq=Wayne%2C+Leslie&oref=slogin (accessed January 12, 2008).

3

Gender, Race, and Militarism

Toward a More Just Alternative

BARBARA LEE

The twentieth century was a period of profound destructiveness. In terms of human violence, it was the bloodiest and most destructive century that humankind has ever known. It was marked not only by the development of the capacity to annihilate people by the millions, but, as the Holocaust showed us, by the capacity to convince entire nations that such destruction was necessary or even desirable.

Yet despite today's so-called war on terror, the period since the end of the cold war has seen a steep decline not only in the number of wars but also in the number of deaths resulting from war. Given our enormous technological and ideological capacity for destruction, we must ask *why* there is quantitatively less conflict and fewer deaths as a result of conflict than there were fifty or even fifteen years ago.

In looking at this question, the *Human Security Report* (Human Security Centre 2005) has pointed to several reasons: the end of the cold war and the proxy wars supported by the United States and the USSR, and the end of colonialism and wars of liberation. The report concluded, however, that the most significant factor in the decline of war was the growth of international activism on behalf of peace, conflict resolution, human rights, and international law. In their words "the main driver of change has been the extraordinary upsurge in activism by the international community that has been directed towards conflict prevention, peacemaking, and peacebuilding" (155).

In 1963, Dr. Martin Luther King Jr. suggested that peace is not the "absence of tension" but "the presence of justice" (King 1963, n.p.). I believe that in looking at this information, which describes a decrease in tension and the growth of the network of organizations, individuals, and principles that made it possible, we can see a glimmer of justice. What does this notion of justice consist of? It is rooted in the idea of equality and the institutions that protect it. It gives meaning to the idea of human dignity by offering every human being protection against its abuse. In its most basic form, justice is the right to security in one's person, and the freedom from violence and persecution.

Amid the violence of the twentieth century we saw the establishment of the United Nations and the Universal Declaration of Human Rights. We have seen dictators who operated with impunity called to stand trial and persons who presided over genocide sent to jail. This realization of justice was the result of diverse people coming together around principles whose value they agreed transcended the boundaries of the nation-state. These people outlined a trajectory of hope, based on a broad consensus of the sacredness of human life and a commitment to ending violence as a means of resolving conflict.

As a result of this work, the families of victims of the Pinochet regime or the Rwandan genocide will likely see their persecutors punished, but the greater promise is that through this action, such violence to human dignity may be prevented in the future. In the United States, this notion of justice is something that is deeply ingrained in our sense of ourselves as a nation, one that at times in our history we have been profoundly at odds with yet one that we continue to strive to achieve.

Sister Rosa Parks died this week,[1] and with her we lost a courageous American. Yet the courage she showed in insisting, in the face of hatred and the threat of violence, on the essential nature of equality and human dignity is a powerful lesson about justice that has strengthened all of us, and will live on and continue to inspire us by its example.

In our own history, from the women's suffrage movement to the civil rights movement, we can see the intimate connection between the fight against racial and sexual discrimination, the struggle for human dignity, and the movement internationally toward establishing basic, inalienable human rights.

I think it is important to recognize that there is a reason why Dr. King came out so forcefully against the Vietnam War, and why Jeannette Rankin, the first woman elected to Congress, would risk her career to vote against going to war in Europe. It is not simply that war is a brutal enterprise, or, as Rankin once said, "You can no more win a war than you can win an earthquake" (as quoted in Josephson 1974, 135). It is that, as persons steeped in the struggle for justice, they understood that militarism is, on a basic level, opposed to the very rights and principles that they were fighting for.

In the context of this concept of justice, I would like to discuss some of the elements of militarism as they relate to race and gender and the failures of predominantly military efforts to promote justice. I would also like to highlight the threat the Bush administration's foreign policy poses to the movement toward justice internationally and outline elements of an alternative.

Militarism is, in many ways, the opposite of this concept of justice. Where justice proceeds from equality and a faith in shared principles, militarism proceeds from suspicion, division, and the insistence on the need for violence to dominate or protect against those who are perceived as different. Militarism is inherently dehumanizing. It can only function if one group of people is seen by another as somehow less than human. Militarism relies on making other peoples appear different or threatening, making their lives seem expendable, and making their deaths seem inevitable or even desirable.

One of the primary ways that militarism achieves this dehumanization is through racism. The dehumanizing nature of racism is evident in our own nation's history. The belief that allowed whites to accept the enslavement of black Africans was actually documented in our country's founding. Blacks' status as less than human was officially enshrined in our constitution with a numerical value: three-fifths. According to the document that established our nation, blacks were barely more than half human.

The value of being able to produce this sort of racial animosity was not lost on colonial governments. In fact, it was often central in their divide-and-conquer efforts to pit native populations against one another in order to consolidate their rule. Before the colonial rule of Rwanda by Germany and later Belgium, Hutus and Tutsis coexisted peacefully. Animosity began to grow only after the Belgian colonial government pitted them against one another by installing Tutsis as the bureaucratic elite, tasked with implementing the authoritarian rule of the colonial regime. Yet the supposed racial differences, a fiction created by the ignorance of the colonial government, were at the center of the 1994 genocide, in which Hutu extremists slaughtered more than 800,000 Tutsis and moderate Hutus over the course of a hundred days. Hutus came to accept and participate in the slaughter of Tutsis who were once their friends and neighbors only through massive propaganda that incessantly repeated the message that Hutus were less than human. The radio station RTLMC played a role in organizing militias, it broadcast lists of people to be killed, and above all, it incited hatred, continuously repeating the call to "exterminate the Tutsi cockroaches."

The similarities with the process that allowed Germans to accept and participate in the slaughter of more than six million Jews are striking. This same dehumanizing process has been consistently used to mobilize support for war. During World War II, the U.S. government routinely distributed posters, designed to support the war effort, that featured grotesque racial caricatures of the Japanese and often simply referred to them as "japs." One poster portrayed Emperor Hirohito against a background of flames with a gun in one hand and a naked white woman over his shoulder. The caption on the poster said "This Is the Enemy," underscoring the government's direct appeal to racial fears to generate support for the war.

The racism of militarism also functions more subtly. There is no question but that Americans are sympathetic to the Iraqi people. The degree to which that sympathy is at odds with the Bush administration's policies in Iraq is obscured by a more subtle form of racism—one that portrays Iraqis, like Africans, as a more primitive, violent people. This racism serves to justify the detentions at

Guantánamo and the atrocities of Abu Ghraib and reinforces the notion that some lives are more expendable and that some deaths are just inevitable. It is reinforced each day as the precise counts of U.S. casualties come in, whereas no effort is made to give an official count of the Iraqi dead. Only through this process can a war, that by some estimates has killed more than 100,000 Iraqi civilians, be cast as a war of liberation.

If we understand that militarism undermines our concept of justice by enforcing racial divisions and playing on racial fears to dehumanize the perceived enemy, we must also understand the threat to justice that is posed by militarism's perpetuation of gendered violence. The *Human Security Report* highlights the history of sexual violence in wars. Here are just a few examples:

- During Japan's infamous assault on the Chinese city of Nanking in December 1937, more than 20,000 and possibly as many as 80,000 women were raped and killed. In 1934–1945 the Japanese forced between 100,000 and 200,000 mostly Asian women, most of them Korean, into prostitution as "comfort women." . . .
- In the 1994 Rwandan genocide, as many as 500,000 women and girls may have been victims of sexual violence. According to Gerald Chamina, Rwanda's prosecutor general, "Rape was the worst experience of victims of the genocide. Some people paid to die, to be shot rather than tortured. Their prayers were for a quick and decent death. Victims of rape did not have that privilege."
- In the war in Bosnia, an estimated 20,000 to 50,000 women were sexually assaulted. . . .
- In Sudan in early 2005, government forces and militias were responsible for rape and other acts of sexual violence throughout the region of Darfur. These and other acts were conducted on a "widespread and systematic basis, and therefore may amount to crimes against humanity." (Human Security Centre 2005, 107).

The changing nature of war has meant a shift from battles fought by heavily armed conventional forces with the resultant high military casualties to an increase in "low-intensity" conflicts. Although the total number of casualties has decreased, the overwhelming number are now civilians, many of them women and children. The deliberate targeting of civilian populations has meant an enormous increase in the number of displaced persons; this displacement puts women at much higher risk of rape and sexual violence. In one instance, displaced women were found to be almost twice as likely to face sexual assault. Consider that information when looking at the fact that between 1964 and 2003, the number of displaced persons worldwide increased from less than 5 million to approximately 33 million.

The *Human Security Report* also points out, however, that during the past decade, the international community seems to have begun to take the issue of war and sexual violence more seriously:

- In 1993 and 1994 the statutes of the International Criminal Tribunals for the former Yugoslavia and for Rwanda defined rape as a crime against humanity.
- In September 1998 the International Criminal Tribunal for Rwanda convicted Rwandan mayor, Jean-Paul Akayesu, of committing rape as genocide and a crime against humanity. This was the first such finding by an international tribunal.
- In February 2001 the International Criminal Tribunal for the former Yugoslavia convicted three Bosnian Serbs of rape, which it designated a crime against humanity.
- The statutes of the new International Criminal Court (ICC) stipulate that when rape is committed as part of a widespread attack against a civilian population it is both a war crime and a crime against humanity. (Human Security Centre 2005, 112).

Unfortunately, the issue of sexual violence illustrates the limitations of a predominately military approach to promoting human rights, particularly women's rights. In 2005, the United Nations issued a report that confirmed allegations of sexual abuse on the part of UN peacekeepers in the Democratic Republic of Congo. The report and subsequent revelations highlighted the degree to which the forces that dehumanize women in military institutions are present even outside an environment of direct hostilities.

The forces that perpetuate this gendered violence are not limited to UN troops. Sadly, we find evidence of the dehumanization of women in our own military institutions. From the Air Force Academy to the battlefield in Iraq, there is ample evidence that women in the military are victims of rape and sexual assault at rates much higher than those of their civilian counterparts. According to "A Considerable Sacrifice: The Costs of Sexual Violence in the U.S. Armed Forces"—a report given by Christine Hansen, executive director of the Miles Foundation, at the Military Culture and Gender conference at the University of Buffalo in September 2005—a "survey conducted within the Veterans' Administration system has assessed sexual assault at 30 percent of female veterans. Further, the researchers found that 14 percent of the victims were gang raped and 20 percent of the victims were raped more than once" (Hansen 2005, 2).

These figures raise grave questions about the culture of our military institutions, but they also raise the larger issue of the nature of our commitment to justice. It is time to question the logic of placing the primary burden of advancing human rights on institutions that train people to kill people. It is important here to draw a distinction between military institutions and militarism, and the distinction lies precisely in the values the two models uphold. Militarism is precisely the point where the recourse to force, the reliance on military means to achieve some end, supersedes the commitment to justice. The case of women illustrates the challenge we must meet of developing and supporting nonmilitarist means of promoting justice. Unfortunately, the Bush administration not only is uninterested in this challenge, but it is aggressively pursuing militarist policies that threaten the fragile but growing framework upon which the hope for justice on the international level rests.

It is critical to understand that the war in Iraq is not an isolated mistake but rather a central part of a larger foreign policy vision. It is a vision of the United States as an unrivaled superpower whose supremacy is consolidated through an aggressive military foreign policy, and as a nation ultimately unconstrained in the pursuit of its interests by concerns about the international community's opinion or concepts like international law. Central to this vision is the idea of preemptive war, the right claimed by the Bush administration to invade another nation solely on the premise that that nation may one day threaten us. In addition to the fact that this policy is a stark violation of international law, it is inherently destabilizing. Imagine the results if India or Pakistan, to name one example, embraced this precedent. That is why I have introduced House Resolution 82, legislation that would renounce the doctrine of preemption.

In place of multilateral arms control agreements, the Bush administration envisions stopping the spread of weapons of mass destruction in part through the development of a new "more useable" generation of nuclear weapons and has actively undermined the framework for international arms control. Then-undersecretary of state for arms control and disarmament John Bolton effectively ended international efforts to create an enforcement mechanism, the Biological Weapons convention. The administration's attitude was summed up by one of the far-right architects of the Bush foreign policy, who said, "Treaties are popular among weak nations."

Although it has been quick to invoke human rights and humanitarian concerns to justify the military action in Iraq, the administration's concern is more propagandistic than substantive. The White House insisted that the ban, recently passed by the Senate, on the use of "cruel, inhuman or degrading treatment" of any detainee held by the United States government not be applied to the actions of the CIA. They advocate torture in the name of "freedom."

The administration has been openly hostile to efforts to strengthen international law and the growing international framework for protecting human rights. Under the Bush administration, the United States was one of only seven countries, including Iraq, that voted against the creation of the International Criminal Court, a jurisdiction of last resort to investigate and prosecute cases of genocide, crimes against humanity, and war crimes.

In short, we have seen the rejection of the principles of diplomacy and cooperation, and a rejection of the commitment to justice, in favor of a strategy of military dominance. The problem with these policies is not only that they are morally bankrupt but that they will fail, and in failing undermine the very security they are designed to create.

We stand at a historic crossroads. The shape of the twenty-first century will be determined in large part by whether the United States' relationship with the rest of the world is defined by our hopes, the values we share with the world, and our commitment to justice, or whether the Bush administration ultimately succeeds in establishing a unilateral, military approach that is based on our fears. As people who are committed to justice, we must act not only to challenge militarism in our foreign policy but to redefine the way our nation talks about security and to advocate for alternatives that support multilateralism, human rights, and international law.

First off, challenging militarism means ending this unnecessary war in Iraq and bringing our troops home. I have opposed this war from the beginning, and I offered an alternative to the authorization to use force in Iraq that would have allowed the weapons inspectors to complete their job and avoided this terrible war altogether. The American people are increasingly rejecting the Bush administration's policy in Iraq and increasingly calling for our troops to be brought home. I am a cosponsor of the bipartisan Abercrombie-Jones Homeward Bound legislation, which sets a timeline both for the president to submit a withdrawal plan to Congress and to begin bringing our troops home.

As the 2006 congressional elections approach, members of Congress from both parties will be under increasing pressure to do something about the war. We must make sure that the Bush administration doesn't announce cosmetic reductions in troops to dispel public dissatisfaction yet maintain the military occupation of Iraq. That is why I introduced legislation that would make it U.S. policy that we will not establish permanent military bases in Iraq. Members of Congress should be asked whether they support being in Iraq permanently. If they do not, they should support my bill.

And as critical as it is that we force a debate on withdrawing our troops, the debate on Iraq cannot be allowed to substitute for a debate on the larger issue of the aggressive militarism of our current foreign policy. We must formally renounce the doctrine of preemptive war and the development of new nuclear weapons and reaffirm our commitment to international law if we are to begin shaping a foreign policy that fosters justice.

Challenging militarism also means redefining how we talk about security. It is past time to reject the outdated idea that pouring money into wasteful military spending makes you strong on defense. My colleague Congresswoman Lynn Woolsey from California has introduced legislation calling for a SMART security policy (see U.S. Congress 2007). SMART stands for Sensible, Multilateral American Response to Terrorism, and the platform calls for a policy that

1. prevents future acts of terrorism by strengthening international institutions and respect for the rule of law;
2. reduces the threat and stops the spread of weapons of mass destruction and reduces the proliferation of conventional weapons;

3. addresses the root causes of terrorism and violent conflict;
4. shifts U.S. budget priorities to more effectively meet the security needs of the United States; and
5. pursues, to the fullest extent, alternatives to war.

Finally, we must support international institutions and develop our nation's capacity to foster justice internationally. My colleague Congressman Dennis Kucinich from Ohio has introduced legislation to create a cabinet-level Department of Peace (U.S. Congress 2005). The department would have both an international and domestic influence, directing policy concerned with peaceful conflict resolution, democracy, and human rights globally and coordinating policy on domestic violence, abuse, and other civil injustices domestically. The legislation would also establish a peace academy, modeled after the military service academies, to provide a four-year concentration in peace education. Graduates would be required to perform five years of public service in programs dedicated to domestic or international nonviolent conflict resolution.

The United States is the richest nation in the world, yet we spend less on international aid per capita than virtually any other country. Our entire budget for foreign humanitarian aid and development is equivalent to what we spend for military operations in Iraq in two months. We would get a lot more security out of increasing foreign aid and addressing the root causes of terrorism than by fanning the flames of anti-Americanism in Iraq.

We face a significant challenge in building the political support needed to pass this legislation and to begin constructing a foreign policy that reflects our commitment to justice. I encourage you to rise to the challenge. Political action is key to any strategy toward a more just alternative. Dr. King once said, "The arc of the moral universe is long, but it bends toward justice" (1967, n.p.). It is important to understand that the movement toward justice that Dr. King described is not accidental—nor is it inevitable. It is not the result of the hand of Providence but of the work of men and women like you.

Looking back on our own history, it is easy to assume that it was inevitable that women and African Americans would gain the right to vote. But it was not inevitable. It was the result of decades of work by committed members of the women's suffrage movement and the civil rights movement, who were challenging the prevailing wisdom without any assurance that they would prevail. In other words, our belief in justice should give us cause for hope, but it should also give us cause for action.

In closing, I am reminded of my friend and mentor, a great African American woman, Shirley Chisholm. Shirley was another courageous champion in the struggle not only for civil rights but for women's rights and the rights of the oppressed and vulnerable everywhere. She passed away in January 1, 2005, but her legacy and what she taught our nation about justice live on. I learned a great many things from Shirley Chisholm, but I will never forget when she said, "You don't make progress by standing on the sidelines, whimpering and complaining. You make progress by implementing ideas." We have a clear idea and vision of what we must do, and I look forward to working with you to implement it.

ACKNOWLEDGMENTS

This chapter is based on a speech prepared by Congresswoman Barbara Lee for the Gender, Race, and Militarization conference at the University of Oregon, October 28, 2005.

NOTE

1. Rosa Parks died on October 24, 2005.

REFERENCES

Hansen, Christine. 2005. "A Considerable Sacrifice: The Costs of Sexual Violence in the U.S. Armed Forces." http://www.law.buffalo.edu/baldycenter/pdfs/MilCult05Hansen.pdf (accessed March 16, 2007).

Human Security Centre. 2005. *Human Security Report 2005: War and Peace in the 21st Century.* New York: Oxford University Press.

Josephson, Hannah. 1974. *Jeanette Rankin: First Lady in Congress: A Biography.* Indianapolis: Bobbs-Merrill.

King, Martin Luther Jr. 1963. "Letter from the Birmingham Jail," April 16. http://www.stanford.edu/group/King/frequentdocs/birmingham.pdf (accessed April 22, 2007).

———. 1967. "Where Do We Go from Here." Tenth Anniversary Convention of the Southern Christian Leadership Conference, Atlanta. August 16. http://www.indiana.edu/~ ivieweb/mlkwhere.html (accessed April 22, 2007).

U.S. Congress. House of Representatives. 2005. "To Establish a Department of Peace and Nonviolence." 109th Cong., 1st sess., H.R. 3760. September 14.

———. 2007. "Calling for the Adoption of a Sensible, Multilateral American Response Terrorism (SMART) Security Platform for the 21st Century." 110th Cong., 1st sess., H.R. 227. March 7.

4

==

Activist Statements

Visions and Strategies for a Just Peace

STATEMENT I. INTERNATIONAL CONGRESS
OF WOMEN AT THE HAGUE

This statement originally appeared in 1915 in the volume *Women at The Hague: The International Congress of Women and Its Results,* by Jane Addams, Emily Green Balch, and Alice Hamilton. The document is one of the products of a meeting of more than a thousand women from Europe and North America at The Hague, from April 28 to May 1, 1915. The goal of the gathering was to devise an international agenda to end World War I and to promote strategies and principles for a peaceful coexistence between nations and peoples from around the world. This statement is a vital testimony to the historic role of women in crafting a peace movement during the early twentieth century and to the crucial connections between demands for peace and the advancement of women's rights worldwide.

Resolutions Adopted by the International Congress of Women at The Hague, May 1, 1915

I. Women and War

1. Protest

We women, in International Congress assembled, protest against the madness and the horror of war, involving as it does a reckless sacrifice of human life and the destruction of so much that humanity has laboured through centuries to build up.

2. Women's Sufferings in War

This International Congress of Women opposes the assumption that women can be protected under the conditions of modern warfare. It protests vehemently against the odious wrongs of which women are the victims in times of war, and especially against the horrible violation of women which attends all war.

II. Actions Towards Peace

3. The Peace Settlement

This International Congress of Women of different nations, classes, creeds and parties is united in expressing sympathy with the suffering of all, whatever their nationality, who are fighting for their country or labouring under the burden of war.

Since the mass of the people in each of the countries now at war believe themselves to be fighting, not as aggressors but in self-defence and for their national existence, there can be no irreconcilable differences between them, and their common ideals afford a basis upon which a magnanimous and honourable peace might be established. The Congress therefore urges the Governments of the world to put an end to this bloodshed, and to begin peace negotiations. It demands that the peace which follows shall be permanent and therefore based on principles of justice, including those laid down in the resolutions[1] adopted by this Congress, namely:

- That no territory should be transferred without the consent of the men and women in it, and that the right of conquest should not be recognized.
- That autonomy and a democratic parliament should not be refused to any people.
- That the Governments of all nations should come to an agreement to refer future international disputes to arbitration or conciliation and to bring social, moral and economic pressure to bear upon any country which resorts to arms.
- That foreign politics should be subject to democratic control.
- That women should be granted equal political rights with men.

4. Continuous Mediation

This International Congress of Women resolves to ask the neutral countries to take immediate steps to create a conference of neutral nations which shall without delay offer continuous mediation. The Conference shall invite suggestions for settlement from each of the belligerent nations and in any case shall submit to all of them simultaneously, reasonable proposals as a basis of peace.

III. Principles of a Permanent Peace

5. Respect for Nationality

This International Congress of Women, recognizing the right of the people to self-government, affirms that there should be no[2] transference of territory without the consent of the men and women residing therein, and urges that autonomy and a democratic parliament should not be refused to any people.

6. Arbitration and Conciliation

This International Congress of Women, believing that war is the negation of progress and civilisation, urges the governments of all nations to come to an agreement to refer future international disputes to arbitration and conciliation.

7. International Pressure

This International Congress of Women urges the governments of all nations to come to an agreement to unite in bringing social, moral and economic pressure to bear upon any country, which resorts to arms instead of referring its case to arbitration and conciliation.

8. Democratic Control of Foreign Policy

Since war is commonly brought about not by the mass of the people, who do not desire it, but by groups representing particular interests, this International Congress of Women urges that Foreign Politics shall be subject to Democratic Control; and declares that it can only recognise as democratic a system which includes the equal representation of men and women.

9. The Enfranchisement of Women

Since the combined influence of the women of all countries is one of the strongest forces for the prevention of war, and since women can only have full responsibility and effective influence when they have equal political rights with men, this International Congress of Women demands their political enfranchisement.

IV. *International Coöperation*

10. Third Hague Conference

This International Congress of Women urges that a third Hague Conference be convened immediately after the war.

11. International Organization

This International Congress of Women urges that the organization of the Society of Nations should be further developed on the basis of a constructive peace, and that it should include:

a. As a development of the Hague Court of Arbitration, a permanent International Court of Justice to settle questions or differences of a justiciable character, such as arise on the interpretation of treaty rights or of the law of nations.

b. As a development of the constructive work of the Hague Conference, a permanent International Conference holding regular meetings in which women should take part, to deal not with the rules of warfare but with practical proposals for further International Coöperation among the States. This Conference should be so constituted that it could formulate and enforce those principles of justice, equity and good will in accordance with which the struggles of subject communities could be more fully recognized and the interests and rights not only of the great Powers and small nations but also those of weaker countries and primitive peoples gradually adjusted under enlightened international public opinion.

This International Conference shall appoint:

A permanent Council of Conciliation and Investigation for the settlement of international difference arising from economic competition, expanding commerce, increasing population and changes in social and political standards.

12. General Disarmament

The International Congress of Women, advocating universal disarmament and realizing that it can only be secured by international agreement, urges, as a step to this end, that all countries should, by such an international agreement, take over the manufacture of arms and munitions of war and should control all international traffic in the same. It sees in the private profits accruing from the great armament factories a powerful hindrance to the abolition of war.

13. Commerce and Investments

a. The International Congress of Women urges that in all countries there shall be liberty of commerce, that the seas shall be free and the trade routes open on equal terms to the shipping of all nations.

b. Inasmuch as the investment by capitalists of one country in the resources of another and the claims arising therefrom are a fertile source of international complications, this International Congress of Women urges the widest possible acceptance of the principles that such investments shall be made at the risk of the investor, without claim to the official protection of his government.

14. National Foreign Policy

a. This International Congress of Women demands that all secret treaties shall be void and that for the ratification of future treaties, the participation of at least the legislature of every government shall be necessary.

b. This International Congress of Women recommends that National Commissions be created, and International Conferences convened for the scientific study and elaboration of the principles and conditions of permanent peace, which might contribute to the development of an International Federation.

These Commissions and Conferences should be recognized by the Governments and should include women in their deliberations.

15. Women in National and International Politics

This International Congress of Women declares it to be essential, both nationally and internationally to put into practice the principle that women should share all civil and political rights and responsibilities on the same terms as men.

V. *The Education of Children*

16. This International Congress of Women urges the necessity of so directing the education of children that their thoughts and desires may be directed towards the ideal of constructive peace.

VI. *Women and the Peace Settlement Conference*

17. This International Congress of Women urges, that in the interests of lasting peace and civilisation the Conference which shall frame the Peace settlement after the war should pass a resolution affirming the need in all countries of extending the parliamentary franchise to women.

18. This International Congress of Women urges that representatives of the people should take part in the conference that shall frame the peace settlement after the war, and claims that amongst them women should be included.

VII. *Action to Be Taken*

19. Women's Voice in the Peace Settlement

This International Congress of Women resolves that an international meeting of women shall be held in the same place and at the same time as the Conference of the Powers which shall frame the terms of the peace settlement after the war for the purpose of presenting practical proposals to that Conference.

20. Envoys to the Governments

In order to urge the Governments of the world to put an end to this bloodshed and to establish a just and lasting peace, this International Congress of Women delegates envoys to carry the message expressed in the Congress Resolutions to the rulers of the belligerent and neutral nations of Europe and to the President of the United States.

These Envoys shall be women of both neutral and belligerent nations, appointed by the International Committee of this Congress. They shall report the result of their missions to the International Committee of Women for permanent Peace as a basis for further action.

NOTES

The discussion of these Resolutions and others which were not carried is to be found in the official report of the International Congress of Women at The Hague. [Footnote in original.]

1. The Resolutions in full are Nos. 5, 6, 7, 8, 9. [Footnote in original.]
2. The Congress declared by vote that it interpreted no transference of territory without the consent of the men and women in it to imply that the right of conquest was not to be recognized. [Footnote in original.]

REFERENCE

Addams, Jane, Emily Green Balch, and Alice Hamilton. 1915. Appendix III to *Women at The Hague: The International Congress of Women and Its Results*. New York: Macmillan.

At the end of the twentieth century, a group of women from diverse national and cultural backgrounds formed the Gender and Human Security Network. The goal of the group was to attend and bring a "gender perspective" to The Hague Appeal for Peace, an international civil society conference that took place in May 1999 at The Hague, Netherlands, with about 10,000 attendees from over a hundred countries. Its timing coincided with the centenary of an earlier international gathering in the same location: the First Hague Peace Conference in 1899, called by Nicholas II, czar of Russia. The 1999 Hague Appeal for Peace Conference was meant to convey

> *a clear message to the world's policy makers on issues with which they failed to address in the first two peace conferences of 1899 and 1907: How to eliminate the causes of war; including racism, colonialism, poverty and other human rights violations, the limitation of arsenals to a reasonable level for territorial defense, the elimination of all weapons of mass destruction including nuclear ones, the establishment and utilization of conflict resolution mechanisms as an interim measure on the way to abolish war, improvements in humanitarian law, and most importantly, the creation of a culture of peace for the world's war-oppressed people. (Hague Appeal for Peace n.d.)*

The members of the Gender and Human Security Network spoke on several conference panels on the topic of gender and human security from the perspective of their own countries and their organizing work. Their collective statement follows.

Gender and Human Security Network Manifesto

We are women from the Earth's five continents. We are moved by profound anger, fear, hope, determination, patience, impatience, stubborn conviction, common sense, the real possibility of change, a belief in the miracle of life and human community, and a commitment to justice. To realise justice, we must renounce the war system and adopt alternatives to it.

We believe that human security begins in the home and in our communities. A nation is secure only when its most vulnerable are secure. We want to create and share a new reality of a culture of peace where women have full participation in the decisions that affect our lives, our communities, and our relations with the world.

A culture of peace grows from full democratic participation of all members of society, replacing the top-down system of the present globalizing economic/military structure. These power relationships pervade all levels of our lives, from personal to global, bringing multiple forms of violence into all human relationships.

Women bear the most oppressive weight of the violence from the home to the war zone. Human security calls us to recognise the interconnectedness among all forms of violence and address them in a holistic and systematic way. For these forms of violence are the means by which both women and the natural environment are treated as resources to be controlled and exploited by these same male-dominated structures.

Our security is based on deep respect for life and the right to resist oppression. Our security involves an ongoing commitment to staying connected to each other, to nurturing bonds of trust and caring, and to constructive forms of contention and conflict.

Our security is to live, to think, to love, to choose, to express, to decide, to move, to work, to relax, and to organise.

Human security is our ability to speak about the effects of violence on our bodies, minds, and hearts and those of our children. We cannot tolerate violence in the home, on the streets, in schools and communities.

Human security includes diversity, self-determination and freedom—freedom from deprivation, all forms of discrimination, and from injustice and oppression; freedom of expression and in establishing personal and social relationships. Security is about accountability and responsibility—of parents to children; teachers to students; of leaders, governments, and corporations to all people; and people to the chain of life that sustains us.

Our security requires the sharing of resources. It is daily violated by the unequal distribution of wealth, over-consumption and waste by countries of the North and elites in countries of the South, and by inequalities within and between families, communities, and countries.

Human security can be achieved through the wise and just use of the Earth's resources. We can craft ways to share these resources, drawing on people's caring attitudes, skills, knowledge, experience, and creativity, transcending the greed, consumerism, and pursuit of profit that characterise the present global system.

A culture of peace means we are respected and heard; we have education, health care, and a dependable source of livelihood. We have nourishing food, clean and accessible water, clean air, adequate shelter with a good place to sleep, clothing, and physical and psychological safety. We have love and a sense of belonging, and participate in all decisions that affect us. We have time, exercise, rest, peace of mind and spirit. We have music, dance, laughter, joy. To live in a culture of peace, we have a code of ethics that denounces all forms of violence. We have spiritual growth and fulfillment and bodily integrity.

Human security is based upon respect for human life as a foundational principle of politics and economics; just and effective international laws; people-to-people communication; a commitment to peaceful conflict-resolution; equitable distribution of resources (material and information); democratic control of economic institutions; and the health of the biosphere.

Human security in a culture of peace depends on all people from all countries and all walks of life being convinced that it is possible. It depends on us all working to bring this vision closer to reality, and to making choices that honour the sacredness of life.

We pledge to do all in our collective power and call upon our respective societies to foreswear militarised security, and to develop alternatives to violence as we struggle toward the realising [of] a culture of peace.

We are:

Kozue Akibayashi	Margo Okazawa-Rey
Krishanti Dhamaraj	Ursula Oswald Spring
Janet Gerson	Alicia Pieterse
Mila de Guzman	Hillka Pietila
Elli Nur Hayati	Betty Reardon
Vesna Kesic	Sandra Nineth Moran Reyes
Gwyn Kirk	Igball Rugova
Wenny Kusuma	Izelia Rucateluane Vilanculo Simbine
Elizabeth Lu	Slavica Stojanovic
Leni Marin	Suzuyo Takazato
Armene Modi	Alison Timme
Bernedette Muthien	Maria Elena Valenzuela Ponce de Leon
Norma Neneh	Xheraldina Vula

REFERENCE

Hague Appeal for Peace. N.d. "Why Was the Conference Called?" http://www.haguepeace.org/index.php?action=history&subAction=conf&selection=why (accessed April 27, 2007).

STATEMENT 3. ESPERANZA PEACE AND JUSTICE CENTER

The Esperanza Peace and Justice Center–based in San Antonio, Texas–issued the following statement in an effort to organize against the U.S.-led invasion of Iraq in 2003. This antiwar statement was produced in a particularly adverse context, as San Antonio is a highly militarized city, home of military bases and other related facilities, and populated by many people who have supported the war. The Esperanza Center joined the voices of grassroots activists from marginalized communities whose perspectives on the causes and effects of violence sharply differ from the hegemonic analysis advanced by groups in power. The Esperanza Center "advocates for those wounded by domination and inequality–women, people of color, lesbians and gay men, the working class and poor" and "works to preserve and promote artistic and cultural expression of and among diverse communities." This organization fosters networking, cross-cultural communication, and community building that "helps individuals and grassroots organizations acquire knowledge and skills so that we can control decisions that affect our day-to-day lives in a way that respects and honors shared goals for a just society" (Esperanza Peace and Justice Center n.d.).

Esperanza Peace Statement: *Unidos por la Paz*

As
people of color, as poor and working class people,
as immigrant and native people, as women, men, old and young,
queer and straight,
as people moved by a vision of social justice,
we denounce
ACTS OF WAR,
we denounce
acts of violence.

We,
the survivors of institutional and systematic violations
on our bodies, our communities, our cultures, our histories
are committed to creating a world
where many worlds exist,
cooperatively, creatively,
in
peace.

We the survivors
of:
colonization, of exploitation,
of racism, of homophobia, of sexism,
of economic and social inequality
are committed
to working for a world
of
justice.

We firmly believe in a world where cultures, languages, histories, and
    traditions
will not be
distorted, disrespected, erased.

We firmly believe in a community's right to self-determination.

We,
the Esperanza Peace and Justice Center
publicly denounce
ACTS OF WAR

We denounce and resist war
where the only goal is that of empire building.
We denounce and resist war
that singles out communities based on their race and nationality.
We denounce and resist war
that privileges profit over people.
We denounce and resist war
that targets communities for their political and religious beliefs.
We denounce and resist war
that tears communities apart and destroys the environment.
We denounce war
that disguises itself in progress and globalization.
We denounce and resist war
that keeps people homeless and hungry.
We denounce and resist war
that eradicates human rights and civil rights.
We denounce and resist war
that covers itself with the shroud named free trade.

We denounce sexism, homophobia, racism, economic inequality, and
environmental degradation as all
ACTS OF WAR.

We mourn the tragic loss of life and the pain of all who suffered
from the assaults on the
World Trade Center and the Pentagon.
In our grief,
we
demand
that no more lives are destroyed
in a war
waged in our name.

We view the assaults on the World Trade Center and the Pentagon as
a tragic response
to the violence the United States government
inflicts, coordinates and sponsors
throughout
the
world.

U.S. foreign and domestic policies have
waged official and unofficial wars
on women, people of color, poor people, the elderly, differently-abled
people, queer people, young people, indigenous peoples
for centuries.

Families and communities have been devastated and decimated
here and throughout the Third World
in the name of U.S. interests.

The call to war
by the Bush Administration
will not stop
the violence at home and abroad.
The violence
will only
escalate.

Our grief
is not
a cry
for war!

REFERENCE

Esperanza Peace and Justice Center. N.d. "Vision and Mission of Esperanza."
http://www.esperanzacenter.org/somosmissionstatement.htm (accessed April 27, 2007).
Reprinted by permission from the Esperanza Peace and Justice Center.

PART II

============================

Cross-National Militarization

5

==

Los Nuevos Desaparecidos y Muertos

Immigration, Militarization, Death, and Disappearance on Mexico's Borders

LYNN STEPHEN

During the 1980s and 1990s, groups that identified themselves as families and kin of the disappeared in Latin America came to exert significant political presence in their countries. Identified primarily as "mothers" of the disappeared, groups such as the Madres de la Plaza de Mayo from Argentina and CO-MADRES of El Salvador drew worldwide attention to the brutal practices of military dictatorships in the Southern Cone and the pseudo-democracies of Central American that were in fact run by the military. Analyses in the 1990s have provided ample evidence of U.S. involvement and knowledge of the kinds of practices that resulted in widespread assassination, disappearances, and rape as weapons of political intimidation. Since the end of the cold war, marked by most with the fall of the Berlin wall and, in the Americas, with the peace processes in El Salvador and Guatemala, public oversight of the continued role of the U.S. military and foreign policy in the region has decreased, with the exception of Colombia.

In this chapter I draw our attention to what I call *los nuevos desaparecidos, asesinados, y muertos* or the new disappeared, assassinated, and dead of the late twentieth and early twenty-first century who have met their fates on the U.S.-Mexican border. The toll includes hundreds of women who have been raped, sexually brutalized, and murdered in a range of border cities and now on the Mexican-Guatemalan border and within Guatemala, as well as the thousands of men, women, and children who die crossing the U.S. border or are simply never found. The militarization of both borders, high rates of immigration from Mexico (of people from a variety of nations), and the integration of various kinds of smuggling operations in the 1980s and 1990s at key points on both of Mexico's borders are at the heart of the patterns of the dead and disappeared that we are seeing now. I focus on the murders of women in Ciudad Juárez and Chihuahua as well as the stories of migrants who have disappeared while crossing the

U.S.-Mexican border to illustrate how this new intersection of militarization, human and drug smuggling, and undocumented immigration produces the dead and disappeared of the twenty-first century. Although the context of militarization and the pattern of abuses perpetrated against women and men who were labeled "subversives" during the civil war in El Salvador are distinct from those we encounter on the border regions of Mexico in the 1990s and beyond, related elements should draw our attention.

There are several distinct patterns of the disappeared and dead on the U.S.-Mexican border. In Ciudad Juárez, most of the victims of rape and murder are young, brown, working-class women who have come to work in the area from their homes in the interior of Mexico, where employment opportunities are poor. Women who cross the border to enter the United States are from a wider range of class backgrounds, from working poor to middle class, but all can become victims of rape and violence as they enter the war zone of the border. The disappeared highlighted in this chapter are indigenous people—men and women—who increasingly form a major part of the migrant stream. The patterns of racialized, gendered, and class-based violence that people living and working near the border as well as those who attempt to cross the border experience are linked to U.S. immigration policy, which since 1994 has pushed would-be migrants into the most inhospitable terrain for crossing, which is controlled by integrated drug- and people-smuggling businesses. The brutality these migrants encounter in the border zone is also directly linked to U.S. security priorities, which label as criminals all those attempting to get into the United States without documentation. Although the U.S. border patrol tries to keep out those without documentation, the true enforcers of the border—drug cartels staffed by ex–counterinsurgency troops from Central America and Mexico—produce the brutal context in which the new disappeared and dead are found.

Guns, Military and Paramilitary Violence, and the Gendered Dynamics of the National Security Discourse: El Salvador

Throughout the period of the Salvadoran civil war that lasted from 1979 until 1992, the United States spent $6 billion to shore up various branches of the Salvadoran Armed Forces in an effort to prevent a victory by the Farabundo Martí National Liberation Front (FMLN) (Lauria-Santiago and Binford 2004, 3–4). In this civil war, more than 80,000 people died, at least 8,000 were disappeared, and massive human rights violations occurred. Human rights organizations such as Amnesty International have linked the Salvadoran military, different police forces, and death squads to thousands of cases of assassination, torture, rape, and imprisonment of peasants, union leaders, students, and others who were politically unaffiliated. The final report of the UN Truth Commission (Naciones Unidas 1993) blamed the military and far-right death squads with ties to the army for 85 percent of the 25,000 civilian deaths the commission investigated.

The United States justified its support for the Salvadoran military on the grounds of national security. From the Carter presidency to the George H. Bush administration, El Salvador was an obsession of U.S. policy. As a brutal civil war raged on the ground, Washington's cold war concerns ensured massive and continued U.S. support for the Salvadoran government and military against the guerrilla forces of the FMLN (Digital National Security Archive 2004). President Ronald Reagan declared his intention to "roll back communism" in Central America. As post–civil war analyses and documents make clear, subsequent U.S. governments continued to work with and support the Salvadoran government and armed forces at all costs, and despite massive evidence of the involvement of key figures in death squads and widespread repression (see Digital National Security Archive 2004). U.S. national security doctrine—now called homeland security—centered on the discourses of the cold war and fighting communism. In El Salvador, Guatemala, and other Central American states dependent on U.S. aid and political influence, the doctrine of national security assigned to the armed forces and their allies was the role of "safeguarding internal security and waging war against 'subversive elements' within their borders" (Fisher 1993, 10). In El Salvador, the pattern of those persons targeted for assassination, torture, rape, and other forms of violence reveals how the word "subversive" was translated to mean any type of idea, project, event, individual, or organization that threatened the status quo politically, economically, or even culturally.

As many have documented, the labeling of subversives is gendered as well as racialized in the contexts of war and militarization. The feminization of the enemy and the imposition of dichotomizing labels on "the female and the feminine" that justify dehumanizing treatment of men, women, and children can be found in any context of war and militarization—but with important contextual differences. In Afghanistan, U.S. soldiers were purportedly videotaped shouting to enemy soldiers whom they presumed to be Taliban, "You allowed your fighters to be laid down facing west and burned. You are too scared to retrieve the bodies. This just proves you are the lady boys we always believed you to be" (Serrano 2005, n.p.).[1] In Mexico, Central America, and border regions, links between Catholic images of femininity and their use by men in positions of power to control women, children, and other men are a part of the context of the gendering of militarization. Although dichotomous models of femininity ignore women's own understanding and construction of their gendered and sexual beings, larger cultural stereotypes of femininity that divide women into virgins and whores operate to subject particular women in particular circumstances to treatment that categorizes them as deserving of inhuman treatment. A basic ingredient in any human rights violation is a system of categorization that places particular individuals or groups outside the standards for dignified and respectful treatment. The image of the Virgin Mary, and by extension that of a woman who exhibits appropriate female behavior, reveals an obedient, self-sacrificing mother, one who subordinates her needs to those of her children. She is asexual, obedient to authority, and remains close to home. The counterpart to this image is that of the Whore: aggressive, impure, disconnected from motherhood, and an object of male sexual interest. Her own sexuality is constructed to service men and promote masculinity, and her personhood is embodied in this role. She is a symbolic whore.

In earlier work I have discussed how the Salvadoran Armed Forces and the death squads inscribed ordinary Salvadoran women as well as participants in CO-MADRES in El Salvador as subversives through a reading of women who took part in grassroots movements, occupied public spaces, and confronted authority as whores; this dynamic led all women in public places to be viewed with suspicion and treated as subversive (Stephen 1995, 1997). As Jennifer Schirmer has pointed out, once a woman is perceived as a subversive or as having become political, regardless of whether she in fact is, another standard of gendered behavior is applied to her. If a male in a position of power reclassifies her from "wife, mother, daughter" to "subversive," her femaleness is read as "tainted, soiled, and by definition sexually aggressive and active—she becomes a whore" and thus a suitable target for sexual assault and sexual violence (Schirmer 1993, 55). This logic has also been extended to men. In the 1990s, I wrote about the Mexican Federal Judicial Police's sexual torture of Zapotec indigenous men from the Loxicha region of Oaxaca (Stephen 1999). They were racialized as "Indian others," and their brownness was a further dimension of suitability for torture and detention.

Prisoners or captives who are reclassified as feminine and whores—regardless of gender—are punished with rape, sexual brutality, and often death. In El Salvador, the Salvadoran Army, National Guard, National Police, and Treasury police have all been implicated in the use of rape as a systematic method of torture. Many of the women who were active participants in CO-MADRES and survived were detained, raped, and tortured. Rape as a routine part of torture was a common experience not only for women in CO-MADRES but for other Salvadoran women during the course of the civil war—as it continues to be for women in wars around the world. The rape of women in the border city of Ciudad Juárez, Mexico, before their brutal murders continues this trend.

Migration to the United States from El Salvador and Mexico

One of the consequences of the civil war in El Salvador was large-scale migration both within El Salvador and to Guatemala, Mexico, Honduras, and the United States. By 1981, some 60,000 refugees, who had fled from some of the most conflict-ridden zones of the country, were housed in camps in Honduras. Some 20,000 Salvadoran refugees also sought sanctuary in Nicaragua, and an estimated 80,000 to 110,000 more relocated to Guatemala and then to Mexico, many ultimately hoping to reach the United States (Helms 1990). Between 1979 and 1988 as many as 500,000 Salvadorans may have reached the United States, the majority via Mexico (Helms 1990). The number of Salvadoran refugees and displaced persons in general was estimated at 1 million, or 20 percent of the population, roughly half of whom had left the country. Approximately 20 percent of the Salvadoran population still resides outside the country. The 2000 U.S. census found that 655,165 Salvadoran immigrants live in the United States (U.S. Census 2000). A majority migrated during the 1980s, with the numbers slowing by the 1990s when the civil war ended. The presence of Salvadoran workers in the United States, however, has been crucial to the Salvadoran economy. In 2002, Salvadorans in the United States sent home $1.9 billion in remittances (Orozco 2003), or three to four times the foreign exchange generated by the coffee industry.

Dramatically increased migration from Mexico in the 1980s and 1990s is tied to economic downturns in Mexico and earlier U.S. immigration policy. In 1982, Mexico experienced a deep economic crisis linked to the slashing of oil prices, expanded international borrowing at high interest rates, runaway inflation, and problems of corruption and accountability in the government (Cockcroft 1998, 271). In August 1982, Mexico announced that it could not meet its IMF debt payments and devalued the peso by 100 percent. A U.S.-led financial bailout of Mexico totaled $10 billion, but in exchange Mexico was required to radically change its economic model by ending import substitution and protectionism and entering full tilt into a program of neoliberalism.

The North American Free Trade Agreement (NAFTA) solidified changes made in Mexico during the 1980s in order to facilitate debt repayment. Agriculture in Mexico changed drastically: subsidies and loans for small farmers disappeared, and approximately three million corn farmers and their families moved into other sectors. These alterations had serious consequences for many. Self-employed farmers experienced dramatic wage losses during the 1990s. In 1991, they had earned an average of 1,959 pesos per month, but by 2003 they were earning 228 pesos for the same amount of work (as measured in constant 1994 pesos) (White, Salas, and Gammage 2003 19). NAFTA thus caused a devastating loss of income for subsistence farmers in that by 2003, farmers were earning only 11.6 percent of what they had in 1991. These harsh economic realities in Oaxaca and elsewhere in Mexico compelled Mexicans to immigrate to the United States, and during the 1990s their numbers in the United States doubled. The Mexican foreign-born population grew by 104 percent during the 1990s, from 4.3 million to 8.8 million persons overall (American Immigration Law Foundation 2002).

Since the 1920s, U.S. immigration policy in relation to Mexico has served primarily as a labor policy: inviting workers in when they are needed and then showing them the door when it becomes politically expedient to "defend" the border. U.S. immigration policy has consistently maintained the theater of "defending" the border from what are called "illegal aliens." Yet deeper historical analysis of particular policies—the Bracero Program from 1942 to 1964, and the Immigration Reform and Control Act (IRCA) and Special Agricultural Workers Program (SAW) of 1986—and a close examination of the accelerated integration of the U.S. and Mexican economies under economic neoliberalism and NAFTA suggest that

U.S. immigration policy toward Mexico has in fact encouraged and facilitated increased immigration (see Massey 1997; Martin 2003). In many ways, past U.S. immigration policy is directly responsible for the increased levels of undocumented immigrants of the 1980s and 1990s.

The fact that so many Mexicans (2.3 million) took advantage of IRCA's legalization provisions reflects economic circumstances in Mexico as well as opportunities in the United States (Durand, Massey, and Parrado 1999). By March 2006, the undocumented population of the United States was estimated at between 11.5 and 12 million, of which approximately 56 percent hailed from Mexico (Passel 2006). "About 80 to 85 percent of the migration from Mexico in recent years has been undocumented" (Passel 2005, 1). The length of stay of such a migrant has notably increased in the 1990s as a result of stronger mid-1990s border enforcement and the increasing cost and dangers of the crossing (see Cornelius 2005; Massey, Durand, and Malone 2002, 128–133; Reyes 2004, 299–320). In 1992 about 20 percent of Mexico-to-United States migrants returned home after six months; in 1997, however, about 15 percent did, and by 2000 only 7 percent did (Cornelius 2005; Reyes, Johnson, and Van Swearingen 2002, 32–33).

These undocumented U.S. residents, in combination with those who are here legally, make a major economic contribution to Mexico. During 2005, Mexicans living outside the country sent home US $23.05 billion in remittances (Remittances EU 2007). In 2003, a total of 18 percent of the adult population reported receiving such remittances (Suro 2003). This contribution to the Mexican economy is second only to that of international oil sales.

The Business of Smuggling

The high numbers of Salvadorans along with other Central Americans and Mexicans who sought to make it into the United States during the 1980s, the 1990s, and beyond offered a unique business opportunity. Moving people across countries and over borders where their status is that of an illegal, or at best is questionable, has become extremely lucrative—particularly when the borders become harder to cross. "Around the world, the U.N. Population Division found in a 2002 survey that 175 million people were living in countries where they were not born. More than 11 million people moved into industrialized nations between 1995 and 2000, and more than five million of them landed in North America" (Crossette 2004, n.p.).

One consequence of Salvadorans' migration to the United States was their concentration in cities such as Los Angeles and Washington, D.C. Many who fled El Salvador grew up in the violence described earlier and were socialized to protect themselves from violence. In Los Angeles, however, Salvadoran youth were victimized by other gangs. I do not discuss the complexity of how and why young people join gangs and the different dimensions to their existence, but the kind of violence that came to characterize some sectors of the Mara Salvatrucha gangs formed in Los Angeles and then re-imported into El Salvador, and subsequently exported to Guatemala, Honduras, Mexico, and various parts of the United States, has direct links to the kind of violent climate that existed in El Salvador during and after the war.[2] Over time, the growth of the Mara Salvatrucha and other groups in Los Angeles came to include some former paramilitaries and others who were trained in weapons and had carried out the kind of atrocities that characterized the civil war. In the 1990s, as gang members were deported from the United States to El Salvador, they began to move into other areas of business, collaborating with those who controlled border smuggling routes, particularly on the southern border of Mexico.

Beginning with President Bill Clinton in 1994, U.S. border defense policy moved away from focusing on internal detentions to fortifying the border in highly trafficked crossing points through the construction of large walls and other barriers, the use of high-tech equipment to track migrants, an increase in the number of border patrol agents, and implementation of a new system of identification linked to fingerprinting all who are detained. By early 1998, Operation Gatekeeper, launched in the San Diego/Tijuana area, had been in place for more than three years; arrest rates fell significantly. The second phase of the border "defense plan" focused on classic crossing routes in central Arizona and south Texas. The enforcement offensive south of Tucson, dubbed Operation Safeguard, was launched just a few weeks after Gatekeeper in San Diego. By 1999, defense walls and agents were being planted along the full length of the border. Operation Rio Grande targeted the zone of south Texas that included McAllen, Brownville, and Laredo. Arrests were dropping in these sectors. Thus by late 1999 all of the traditional border-crossing areas had been blocked by walls and the increased presence of agents. These efforts led greater numbers of migrants to attempt to cross in the rugged mountains to the west of San Diego in Imperial County. Here people began dying in the cold of winter. Others were pushed into the desert in western Arizona. Significantly increased migration during the 1990s, coupled with a border defense policy that squeezed people into extremely rugged terrain in California and increasingly in Arizona, produced a killing field.

As migrants were pushed into more marginal areas, they could no longer cross with the help of village-based guides or coyotes who knew routes into San Diego or other well-traveled areas. Hopping the border zone fence near San Diego had allowed migrants to walk into the United States and then quickly board some form of transportation, but crossing in isolated desert areas with no populations, roads, and few access points required more infrastructure. Smugglers needed staging strategies for moving persons from remote areas of Mexico into the Arizona desert and then getting them across the border, for which they charged much more money. According to Ken Ellingwood, as smuggling got more lucrative, organized smuggling groups increasingly came to resemble crime syndicates: "A coyote's trade that once relied on gumption and quick feet now stacked its arsenal with cellular telephones, global-positioning navigational aids and computer technology" (2004, 85). Some of the new routes being used to move people over the border in remote areas had previously been used to move drugs and guns. As human smuggling and drug smuggling came to occupy overlapping turf, the two businesses became integrated—a predictable result of globalization. The kinds of equipment that had been used for drug smuggling now served to smuggle people as well. "You'll see a lot of alien smugglers who used to be drug smugglers, or they'll be doing both," stated a top INS antismuggling official (Ellingwood 2004, 87). Ellingwood described the far reach of one immigrant-smuggling syndicate: it was estimated to have brought thousands of immigrants into the United States, including many whose journey originated outside of Mexico, from places such as Egypt and Central America. One human rights activist and researcher reported that this group took in $250,000 per week to bring in a thousand immigrants (87). The group used top-end cellular phones to communicate, owned a fleet of vans and safe houses, and rented apartments and hotel rooms on both sides of the border. A seven-year investigation revealed that they paid police officers in Mexico to ignore their operations and bribed a U.S. customs inspector, who waved through vans full of immigrants in his lane at the San Ysidro border crossing (89). Ellingwood's account demonstrates the ways in which people now enter the United States, the profits to be made, and the integration of the human-smuggling business with the drug business. Estimates of the number of major smuggling organizations operating in Mexico and the United States range from fifteen to twenty-four (86–87).

The southwestern border is the most popular gateway for drugs into the United States (U.S. Drug Enforcement Administration 2003). Desert areas have offered smugglers tremendous opportunities. The estimated street value of illegal drugs sold in the United States in the year 2000 was $62 billion (National Drug Intelligence Center 2000). Although we might like to think that drug cartels exist only in Mexico, clear evidence shows drug-related police corruption in major cities in the United States. According to the U.S. General Accounting Office, "half of all police officers convicted as a result of FBI-led corruption cases between 1993 and 1997 were convicted for drug-related offenses" (1998, 35).

Mexico has been a country of drug transshipment for quite some time. Drugs produced in Colombia, Peru, and elsewhere have been shipped through Mexico to the U.S. market. And Mexico's own drug production has increased. The National Drug Intelligence Center's 2007 "National Drug Threat Assessment" stated that the "Mexican DTOs [drug transshipment organizations] and criminal groups are the most influential and pervasive threats with respect to drug transportation and wholesale distribution in nearly every region of the country and continue to increase their involvement in the production, transportation, and distribution of most major illicit drugs" (27). It has also pointed out that "with Mexican and Colombian DTOs responsible for most wholesale-level drug money laundering in the United States, a significant amount of illicit drug proceeds are moved across the Southwest Border into Mexico annually. Therefore, the

Southwest Border remains a serious area of concern for U.S. drug money laundering" (24).

These findings underline the corrupting influence of narcotics money that
reaches the highest levels in the Mexican military, police forces, and justice system and leaves traffickers immune from prosecution for most crimes. The complete lack of accountability of police, military commanders, and many judges in
Mexico produces a nonfunctional justice system that lacks the trust of Mexican
citizens. One estimate states that the Mexican cartels spend about 10 percent of
their gross income on bribes on both sides of the border, which in 2000 would
have amounted to about $6.2 billion (Builta 1997). In 2001, the Special Rapporteur
on the Independence of Judges and Lawyers, an officer of the United Nations, visited Ciudad Juárez, Chihuahua City, and Mexico City. His report stated, "in general, there is a perception of a high-level of impunity (95 percent) for all types of
crimes. Many crimes are never reported, many arrest warrants are never exe-
cuted" (Mexico Solidarity Network 2004, n.p.).

In Ciudad Juárez and other border towns, drug dealers buy off new officers as
soon as they are hired, either with huge bribes or threats. In 2005, in Nuevo
Laredo alone, 136 people were killed, including 21 current and former police officers and a city council member (Corchado and Eaton 2005). The center of power
of the Latin American drug trade has shifted to Mexico, where it is quickly infil-
trating every corner of the country. What is most disturbing is evidence that
some members of Mexico's elite counterinsurgency unit called the Zetas and
Guatemala's fierce Kaibiles, famous for atrocities carried out during the
Guatemalan civil war, are now working for Mexico's drug cartels and involved in
cross-border activities. The Department of Homeland Security issued a warning
to Sheriff Rick Flores of Webb County, Texas, and other law enforcement officers
who work in Nuevo Laredo about a possible alliance between the Zetas and rogue
members of the Kaibiles, whose members are known for their jungle-fighting
skills. Seven Guatemalans, including four thought to be former Kaibiles, were
arrested on the southern Mexico border in September 2005 (Corchado and Eaton
2005). The Zetas have also been tracked operating within the United States. FBI
and Texas law officials have reported Zeta activity in the Dallas area since 2003.
In June 2005, a U.S. Justice Department report stated that the Zetas have been
setting up trafficking routes in Texas, California, Oklahoma, Tennessee, Georgia,
and Florida (*WorldNetDaily* 2005).

According to FBI officials, the Zetas are attempting to consolidate their grip
on the smuggling route along I-35. "Anyone caught not paying the 10% commission they charge on all cargo—drugs or humans—is killed, according to U.S. and
Mexican law enforcement sources" (Corchado 2005, n.p.). Between October 1,
2004, and August 1, 2005, border patrol agents in the Tucson sector, which
includes 260 miles of U.S.-Mexican border in Arizona, were assaulted 196 times.
According to *Washington Times* reporter Jerry Seper, "the sector is the busiest
alien- and drug-trafficking corridor in the country" (2005b, n.p.). The Zetas are

expanding their routes and seek to protect them at any cost. Several Zetas operating in Texas, according to the Mexican government, were trained at the School of the Americas in Fort Benning, Georgia. The school, now known as the Western Hemisphere Institute for Security Cooperation, is the U.S. Army's principal Spanish-language training facility for Latin American military personnel (Seper 2005a).

The following exchange occurred between Rick Flores, the sheriff of Webb County, Texas, and Brad Sherman, a U.S. Representative from California, during a hearing on border vulnerabilities and international terrorism, held in the U.S. House of Representatives in July 2006. Flores's statements confirm the presence of U.S.-trained former Mexican Zetas who now protect smuggling routes on the Texas border.

MR. FLORES: First of all, and I welcome any of you to come to our neck of the woods, you will see first hand that we are having gunfights lasting 2 hours right across our border and [neither] the police, nor the military, appears to be able to stop that siege, what is that telling you? That the Mexican Government is in on the narcotrafficking and human smuggling. They're getting paid. They're getting paid off. Is this something new? This has been going on for decades. This has been going on since Mexico's been Mexico.

MR. SHERMAN: So the military units of the Army of Mexico located near your border are not helpful in controlling the drug-control problem?

MR. FLORES: Mr. Sherman, when you've got 37 defectors of the Mexican military who are trained in Fort Benning, Georgia by us [references to the Zetas] to go and fight narco-terrorism in Mexico and they defected from the Mexican Government or the Mexican military and are now working for the drug cartel, and now they've got the biggest, sophisticated equipment, and training. (U.S. Congress, House of Representatives, Subcommittee on International Terrorism 2006, 136–137).

During the same set of hearings, Flores and other witnesses testified to the integration of the drug- and human-smuggling routes under the protection of the Zetas along the Texas-Mexico border. Flores stated that "the cartels are in control of not only the narcotrafficking, but also the human smuggling" (357).

On Mexico's southern border, the Mara Salvatrucha has come to dominate trafficking routes for humans from the Chiapas border to the state of Veracruz, operating along the railroad line used by undocumented travelers to move from the south to the north of Mexico. Ciudad Hidalgo and Tapachula, like the northern border cities of Juárez and Nuevo Laredo, are major smuggling points controlled by the Mexican Gulf cartel, the Juárez cartel, and reputedly also by the San Marcos cartel, a Guatemalan drug cartel (Balboa 2004). Reports suggest that Mexican municipal police, immigration officials, and army elements are also involved, as well as Guatemala's National Civil Police (Balboa 2004; Grayson

2002). An atmosphere of impunity has congealed along the southern border, where, like the region around the northern border, drug traffic, human traffic, and prostitution are the most lucrative sources of income.

The integration of counterinsurgency military and paramilitary forces that were once supported by the United States into lucrative linked businesses such as drug and human smuggling should not come as a surprise. Drug cartel control of Mexico's borders and, increasingly, parts of its interior, combined with further militarization of the northern border by the United States since 1995, has produced a climate of war. Those living in border cities and those who must pass through the border zone on their way to the United States face risks similar to those of being caught in the middle of a war they neither chose nor created. U.S. border defense policy has forced migrants into the most violent sector of the border in western Arizona and into some of the most inhospitable territory in the continent. I now focus on two examples of what I call *los nuevos desaparecidos y muertos*, who have come out of this unofficial war.

The Women of Ciudad Juárez, U.S-Mexican Border Area

From 1993 to 2004, at least 370 young women and girls were murdered in the cities of Ciudad Juárez and Chihuahua (Amnesty International 2005). Other estimates run to more than 400 (Mexico Solidarity Network 2004).[3] Almost a third of them suffered sexual violence. Many people believe that these crimes are serial because of the victims' similar traits. They were young and slender, and had brown complexions and long hair. All came from poor families, and many were lured to Ciudad Juárez by job prospects at maquiladoras.[4] Many were raped and their mutilated bodies dumped in ditches or vacant lots.

In February 2004 the Mexican government issued a report describing the murders and disappearances as follows:

> Between 1993 and 2003, Ciudad Juárez experienced the homicide of 328 women. In some of these, the victim disappeared for a length of time before being murdered. 92 of the homicides were perpetrated by violent sexual aggressors and the rest were motivated by varied causes, among them domestic and interfamily violence, theft, fights and crimes of vengeance. 16% of the victims had less than 15 years of age, 43% were between 16 and 30, and 31% were older than 30. In addition, from the disappearances reported during the same period of time, forty four women remain missing. (Secretaría de Relaciones Exteriores 2004, n.p.)

The slayings of these women have occurred against a backdrop of violence in Juárez that also took the lives of 1,600 men.

After significant public pressure, campaigns by a wide range of groups within Mexico, and visits from a special rapporteur from the UN as well as representatives from Amnesty International, the Mexico Solidarity Association, and others, the Mexican government began to respond. A special federal prosecutor's office worked with local prosecutors and conducted federal investigations into some of the cases. This office was led by María López Urbina, whose mandate was to "carefully review each of the existing investigations regarding both missing women and homicides, as well as identify negligent or inefficient handling of these, as well as tolerant attitudes by public officials toward those who should have been brought to justice or when these officers did not carry out their duties" (Secretaría de Relaciones Exteriores 2004, n.p.). After reviewing the 150 case files handled by Chihuahua's state prosecutor's office, López Urbina concluded that there was probable cause for "criminal and administrative investigations into more than 100 Chihuahua state public officials for negligence, omission, and other related offences" (Amnesty International 2005, n.p.). Human rights activist Guadalupe Morfin was appointed to head a special commission to oversee federal intervention and to foster contact with families of victims and human rights organizations. However, because federal authorities insist that they lack jurisdiction to officially investigate the cases, the cases have been remanded to the local prosecutor's office and the courts in Chihuahua. Although the Mexican government claims that of the 328 murder cases, 103 have been solved and the perpetrators convicted, human rights organizations such as Amnesty International have documented that several of those convicted were tortured before confessing (see Amnesty International 2005; Mexico Solidarity Network 2004).

The most controversial theory about the source of the murders and disappearances is that advocated by Diana Washington Valdez, a reporter for the *El Paso Times*. "Mexican federal authorities have conducted investigations, which reveal who the killers are," she claims. "Five men from Juárez and one from Tijuana who get together and kill women in what can only be described as blood sport. Some of those involved are prominent men with important political connections—untouchables." Others supply new victims: "They capture the girls and bring them to their masters" (Jordan 2003). Washington Valdez alleges that at least a hundred women have been killed by men with ties to the Juárez cartel, who have used their money to move into legitimate business (Jordan 2003).

Although many officials deny Washington Valdez's accusations, even the Mexican government's own special federal prosecutor has turned up evidence to confirm what human rights organizations and women's organizations have been saying for almost a decade: a climate of impunity exists, and it is highly unlikely that most of the murders and disappearances will be solved because many in the police and judicial system have been bought off by drug money.

The documented patterns of violence against those young women who were the victims of violence and murder in Ciudad Juárez and Chihuahua (and elsewhere) suggest parallels to the gendered rationales of violence perpetuated against women such as the CO-MADRES in the 1980s by the Salvadoran Armed Forces. In a report issued in 2003 on the Juárez murders, the Inter-American

Commission on Human Rights, an autonomous organ of the Organization of American States, determined the following:

> A significant number of the victims were young, between 15 and 25, and many were beaten and/or subjected to sexual violence before being strangled or stabbed to death. A number of the killings that fit this pattern have been characterized as multiple or "serial" killings ... the response of the authorities to these crimes has been markedly deficient. There are two aspects of this response that are especially relevant. On the one hand, the vast majority of the killings remain in impunity; approximately 20% have been the subject of prosecution and conviction. On the other hand, almost as soon as the rate of killings began to rise, some of the officials responsible for investigation and prosecution began employing a discourse that in effect blamed the victim for the crime. According to public statements of certain highly placed officials, the victims wore short skirts, went out dancing, were "easy" or were prostitutes. Reports document that the response of the relevant officials to the victims' family members ranged from indifference to hostility. (Inter-American Commission on Human Rights 2003, n.p.)

This description suggests that some officials categorized the Ciudad Juárez victims as "whores" who were somehow responsible for, if not deserving of, their own murder and sexual assault. The climate of militarization that surrounds these murders suggests that we don't have far to look for the origins of a gendered ideology that inscribes masculinity in the hands of powerful men through the feminization and sexualization of their victims. In Ciudad Juárez, Chihuahua, and elsewhere, groups of mothers and relatives of the victims lead the grassroots organizations demanding an end to the femicides and justice for the perpetrators. Casa Amiga, a shelter for battered women in Ciudad Juárez, has worked to compile data on women's disappearances and murders. Nuestras Hijas de Regreso a Casa was formed in 2002 in Ciudad Juárez, and in 2003, Justicia para Nuestras Hijas was formed in Chihuahua. Other organizations and NGOs have formed in support of the mothers of Juárez and Chihuahua. Their demands are strikingly similar to those of the CO-MADRES in the 1980s.

The Disappeared, the Dead, and the Future Dead on the Northern Border

The cases of the women murdered and sexually assaulted in Ciudad Juárez and Chihuahua city are part of a larger landscape of border violence that extends to those who are coming to the United States as undocumented workers. Each year up to one million undocumented immigrants cross the U.S.-Mexican border, primarily on foot, on their way to seeking work in the United States. The U.S. Bureau of Customs and Border Protection has reported that, during the fiscal year ending September 30, 2005, at least 464 immigrants died crossing the 2,000-mile border—a rise of 43 percent from the previous year and the highest number on record (Marosi 2005). Well over half of the deaths occurred in Arizona, often in the Tucson sector referred to earlier. For the fiscal year ending September 30, 2006, the slightly lower number of 426 deaths was reported (U.S. Immigration Support 2006).

As many as 3,500 people are believed to have died crossing the U.S.-Mexican border from 1995 to 2005 (Berenstein 2005). Beginning with the Clinton administration in 1995, U.S. border protection policy has pushed migrants out of classic crossing areas such as San Diego/Tijuana and Ciudad Juárez/El Paso and into more desolate areas such as the inhospitable western Arizona desert. In 2006 approximately 11,000 border patrol agents worked along the 2,000-mile U.S.-Mexican border. In contrast, approximately 980 agents work along the 4,000-mile U.S.-Canadian border (Migration Policy Institute 2006). Customs and Border Protection, and Immigration and Customs Enforcement deploy four operations to apprehend unauthorized border crossers in the Southwest: Operation Hold-the-Line in El Paso, Operation Gatekeeper in San Diego, Operation Rio Grande in El Paso, and Operation Safeguard in Tucson. The agents use a combination of electronic sensors, night vision scopes, ground vehicles, and aircraft (Migration Policy Institute 2006).

The results of this aggressive enforcement have been increasing fatalities due to exposure to extreme heat or cold, unprecedented inflation in the cost of crossing (averaging from $2,000 to $3,000 in 2005), and the replacement of locally run border-crossing operations with those that integrate human smuggling with gun- and drug-running operations on routes often controlled by drug cartels. Because today most migrants coming over the border now need a guide to cross, business is booming. But as human smuggling has gotten more profitable, it has become more dangerous. In addition to the physical risks of walking long distances in the desert are the risks of robbery, rape, and kidnappings of groups of border-crossers by competing coyotes or by Mexican police or others. So although the U.S. border patrol has focused on border defense during the past ten years, officers increasingly are spending their time rescuing people along the border. In FY 2005 they rescued a total of 2,570 migrants (Migration Policy Institute 2006). Those they encounter are men, women, and children, even babies, attempting to enter the United States to work and to be united with their families.

The U.S. border patrol records the deaths of people found near the U.S.-Mexican border every year, but it is possible that even greater numbers of people disappear in the process of crossing. A part of the community history of every single migrant and every immigrant-sending town in Oaxaca where I have worked in the past several years includes chapters about *los desaparecidos* who set out to cross the border into the United States and never returned. Although there are the inevitable stories and some real cases of men or women who left, probably started new families, and never returned, there are far more well-documented cases of people who set out and were never heard from again, and who didn't arrive where they were supposed to in the United States.

In the town of San Agustín Atenango in the Mixteca Baja region of Oaxaca, where I conducted fieldwork during the summers of 2004, 2005, and 2006, two different cases of the disappeared have scarred the community. San Agustín Atenango is a transborder community with a long history of migration within Mexico and emigration to the United States. Beginning with participation in the U.S. bracero program, people from San Agustín have been coming to the United States. By 2006, clusters of families from San Agustín lived in more than twelve locations in the United States and an equal number in other parts of Mexico. The greatest numbers of immigrants in the United States have settled in Santa Maria, Ventura, and Madera (California), Portland and Salem (Oregon), Flagstaff and Grand Canyon (Arizona), and Chicago (see Stephen 2007). San Agustín has ten desaparecidos from the past five years.

The first case began and ended in tragedy. In 2003, Mariano González, a man in his late twenties who was living and working in Santa Maria, California, returned to his hometown to bury his brother after the brother died in the United States in an accident. The man went back to Mexico with his wife, leaving their two children with relatives in Santa María. After the funeral, he and his wife set off to return to the United States with a locally known coyote. During the trip through the Arizona desert, according to the coyote, he went off to look for water for the couple, but when he returned they were gone. They were never found. Their children—who are U.S. and Mexican citizens—were brought back to San Agustín to live with their grandparents, but they didn't adjust. They missed both the United States and their parents. Now they are back in the United States living with other relatives. The couple never turned up. Community members went to look for them to no avail.

A neighbor of Mariano's commented, "It was so sad for the children. They were told that their parents went home and then they never saw them again. The kids don't really know what happened to them, why can't they see them and they are not happy living in San Agustín. They went back to Santa María but they miss their parents. They want to know where they are."[5]

The second case comes from the summer of 2005. On July 16, 2005, seven people left San Agustín Atenango on a bus to go to the border town of Sonoyta, Sonora, where they expected to cross over to the United States. Sonoyta is located across the border from Lukeville, Arizona, and crossings take migrants into the most desolate areas of the western Arizona desert, which incorporate the Tohono O'odham Indian Reservation and Organ Pipe Cactus National Monument. In July, the daily temperature often goes well above 110 degrees Fahrenheit. The group of seven that left San Agustín Atenango included five men between the ages of 26 and 49 and two boys aged 15 and 16. By August 16, 2005, a month after they had left, there was no word from any of them. With local officials, their families created flyers with their photographs to circulate, called and faxed family members in California, Oregon, Arizona, and elsewhere, and began to phone and fax Mexican consulates in Arizona and elsewhere. The offices of the Indigenous Front of Binational Organizations (FIOB) were alerted in Juxtlahuaca, Tijuana, Los Angeles, and Fresno, and other NGOs and government organizations such as the Oaxacan Institute for Attention to the Migrant (Instituto Oaxaqueño de Atención al Migrante) were notified of details of the seven desaparecidos. The mothers of Pablo and Ubaldo, the two boys, were unable to eat or sleep and circulated endlessly around San Agustín, Juxtlahuaca, and elsewhere seeking help in locating their children.

Pablo's mother pleaded for any information long after his disappearance: "We want to hear from someone, anyone. Please give us some information. Let me know what happened because we are so worried about our son. If anyone knows where he is, what town he is in, please let us know. We just want to know anything. If you find him in the road, if you find him, please communicate. We just want to know. We just want to know." The wife of one of the missing men emphasized wanting to know as well, not only for herself but for her other children: "Please let me know anything about him. My son is asking for his father. 'How is my Dad?' he asks. 'Did something bad happen to him? Is he ok or what happened?' We are always thinking about him and the others."[6]

The term used by people from San Agustín Atenango to describe those who set out to cross the border and are never heard from again is *desaparecidos* or "disappeared." The consequences for the relatives of the disappeared are that they have no knowledge of what became of their loved ones—where they are, whether they are dead or alive, and how they may have suffered. They can only imagine, hope, and pray that the *desaparecidos* are alive; at the same time, they must grapple with the horror of how their loved ones may have suffered and died. The lack of information, of not knowing, leaves families in suspended animation as they continue to hope but also fear the worst. A permanent hole is created in family and community histories by the disappeared, who continue to exist as a bracketed pause, a suspended silence, a permanent question mark in social relations. And although the disappeared are counted in their families and in their communities, they are not counted by either the U.S. or Mexican governments. If, as a rough estimate, we assume that each community has five to ten disappeared people, then we are talking about thousands of people in that each of Oaxaca's 570 municipalities has from two to more than a dozen communities within it.

The people from San Agustín who have disappeared were attempting to pass through the most deadly sector of the Arizona border. The seven who disappeared in 2005 were to be led by a town-based guide who may not have known about the 10 percent tax charged to people passing through or about the extreme heat. They had to cross a border that is militarized two or three times over—by

Mexican police and border guards, by the U.S. border patrol, and by the smug-gling cartels and their enforcers who control the routes and charge people passage. Undertaking this crossing is to look death in the face in different forms and often multiple times.

In the eyes of some, crossing the U.S.-Mexican border and migrating to the United States is similar to going off to war. One is ready to make the ultimate sacrifice for a worthy cause. In this case, nationalism is not the motivator but instead a strong desire to support and nourish beloved family members. Migration not only entails the emotional isolation and loss of connection with family members left behind (Zavella 2006) but also requires that someone literally risk her or his life in order to arrive, work, and help to support those at home. Going is not a choice but a necessity. Attached to that necessity is the risk of death.

Ninety-seven year-old Valentina Lorenzo from San Agustín herself migrated to Veracruz and Sinaloa. She has watched her children, grandchildren, and great grandchildren also migrate throughout Mexico and to the United States. To her the risk of death associated with migration is linked to the poverty in Mixtec communities like San Agustín Atenango, which drives peoples to leave. Her analysis says it all. She stated,

> There are no rich people here. We don't have anyone whose dishes we can wash, whose clothes we can wash, whose gardens we can tend or whose houses we can clean. No, now we have to go to the north, El Norte, to be able to make a living. Here there are only poor people. For years and years everyone has left to go to the north. Mostly the men leave to work and the women stay here alone, especially old women like me. It is a sad town because so many are gone and there is no work. When they go to the north they can die. Many die on the way there and once they arrive. They can't stay here.[7]

Lorenzo's sentiments about the sadness of living in an empty town and sorrow for those who risk their lives and those who die are part of the emotional political-economy of migration linking transborder communities together in multiple sites. Her vision of past deaths and future deaths on the border merges with the unstable status of the disappeared. All who have migrated, including the dead, the disappeared, and the potentially dead who risk their lives every time they go, are a part of the consequences of current U.S. immigration policy and the militarization of the border. The integration of the U.S.-Mexican economies, the increasing stratification and poverty in rural Mexico that make migration a sixth- or eighth-grade graduation rite, and the ease with which undocumented laborers are absorbed into the U.S. economy come together in the bodies of migrants and immigrants. They carry trade and immigration policies deep within their hearts, minds, and arms and legs as they walk, work, and wonder about those who are not with them.

Conclusions

U.S. border defense policy since the mid-1990s has converged with the relocation of the Mexican drug trade on the northern and southern border regions of Mexico to produce what can aptly be termed war zones. The victims in these war zones are *los nuevos desaparecidos, asesinados, y muertos*—the new disappeared, assassinated, and dead. The intense violence and danger that have become ordinary in these border zones relate directly to the presence of drug cartels, high levels of impunity for crimes such as rape, murder, and mutilation, and high levels of corruption on both sides of the border, funded with narco dollars. Yearly profits totaling in the billions of dollars make human smuggling extremely lucrative.

Although U.S. officials are quick to condemn drug and human traffickers, they seldom pause to consider the role that U.S. border defense policy has had in pushing migrants into such dangerous circumstances. Military and paramilitary cultures of masculine violence based on the feminization of victims and their sexualization are certainly factors in the nature of the violence perpetuated against girls and women from Ciudad Juárez and Chihuahua. In addition, such cultures of violence seem to permeate smugglers and their accomplices who are in the business of moving Mexican men, women, and children across the U.S.-Mexican border. Current U.S. immigration and border defense policy, which focuses on securing four major ports of entry, does nothing to alleviate the dangerous situation for migrant border-crossers. Missing from the analysis is a consideration of how forcing migrants into isolated sectors of the desert has contributed to the situation and how not providing a channel to legalization continues to push people to come in undocumented, and feeds into established patterns of militarized violence against women on the border.

We need to recognize and adjust the status of large numbers of people who are already north of the border and contributing economically, socially, culturally, and politically to both the United States and Mexico. In addition, we need to radically rethink the current strategies for militarizing and patrolling the border. Much higher levels of cooperation and teamwork are necessary between the justice system and various police and armed forces of Mexico. The primary routes for crossing from Mexico into the United States are not controlled by the U.S. border patrol but by interlinked groups of drug and human smugglers based on both sides of the border who clearly pay protection money to armed forces and the police. Until the high levels of corruption within the armed and police forces of the Mexican and U.S. justice systems are addressed on a binational basis, the high levels of danger currently associated with crossing will not decrease. Finally, the United States should reverse its policy of forcing undocumented migrants through dangerous and isolated regions such as the Arizona desert. Until this happens, gendered patterns of militarization and violence linked to human and drug smuggling will continue as part of an undeclared war in the border zones of Mexico.

NOTES

1. The empowerment and accompanying masculinization of military, paramilitary, and what are now called drug cartel and gang men through feminization and sexualization of their victims, is a common colonial and contemporary theme (see Aretxaga 1997).

2. When the Salvadoran civil war ended, thousands of weapons that had been in the hands of the FMLN and the government's armed forces made their way into the hands of the larger population. Many of these weapons, such as the M16 rifle and the M67 fragmentation hand grenade, as well as the AK-47 often associated with the FMLN, are commonly reported as the instruments of organized criminal activity (Godnick, Haven, and Martinez-Henriquez 2000, 1). Between 1980 and 1993, U.S. foreign military sales of light weapons to El Salvador included 32,374 M16 rifles and 266,420 fragmentation hand grenades (Godnick, Haven and Martinez-Henriquez 2000, 2). Although there have been efforts to encourage voluntary repatriation of weapons such as these, the numbers have been small.

3. According to a 2006 report, "an average of 1,000 women a year were murdered in Mexico, a country of 103 million, between 1995 and 2005, according to official figures" (Cevallos 2006). The largest number of killings occurred in Toluca and Guadalajara—not in Ciudad Juárez. In Guatemala, which has a population of 13 million, 566 women were killed in the first ten months of 2006, whereas in El Salvador, a country of 6.9 million, 286 were killed between January and August 2006.

4. A maquiladora is an in-bond assembly plant in which duty-free goods, materials, and equipment are imported, assembled, and then exported.

5. Author interview, San Agustín Atenango, Oaxaca, Mexico, August 18, 2005.

6. Author interview, San Agustín Atenango, August 18, 2005.

7. Author interview, San Agustín Atenango, August 15, 2005.

REFERENCES

American Immigration Law Foundation. 2002. "Mexican Immigrant Workers and the U.S. Economy: An Increasingly Vital Role." *Immigration Policy Focus* 1, no. 2. http://www.ailf.org/ipc/ipf0902.asp (accessed January 11, 2008).

Amnesty International. 2005. "Mexico: Justice Fails in Ciudad Juárez and the City of Chihuahua." *Amnesty International USA*, February 29. http://www.amnestyusa.org/countries/mexico/document.do?id=5AB197BCEE37D92D80256FB600689A74 (accessed April 19, 2007).

Aretxaga, Begoña. 1997. *Shattering Silence: Women, Nationalism, and Political Subjectivity in Northern Ireland.* Princeton: Princeton University Press.

Balboa, Juan. 2004. "La frontera sur, territorio sin ley bajo dominio de la Mara Salvatrucha." *La Jornada,* December 6. http://www.jornada.unam.mx/2004/12/06/006n1pol.php (accessed April 19, 2007).

Berenstein, Leslie. 2005. "This Year Likely to Be Worst in Migrant Deaths." *San Diego Union Tribune,* August 10. http://www.signonsandiego.com/uniontrib/20050810/news_1n10deaths.html (accessed September 12, 2005).

Builta, Jeff. 1997. "Mexico Faces Corruption, Crime, Drug Trafficking and Political Intrigue." *Crime and Justice International,* 13 (February). http://www.cjcenter.org/cjcenter/publications/cji/archives/cji.php?id=407 (accessed April 19, 2007).

Cevallos, Diego. 2006. "Juárez Femicides, Just a Drop in the Ocean of Blood." *Inter Press News Services Agency,* November 24. http://www.ipsnews.net/news.asp?idnews=35603 (accessed April 19, 2007).

Cockcroft, James. 1998. *Mexico's Hope: An Encounter with Politics and History.* New York: Monthly Review Press.

Corchado, Alfredo. 2005. "Cartel Enforcers Operate in Dallas." *Dallas Morning News,* June 18. http://narcosphere.narconews.com/comments/2005/6/15/204155/304/2?mode=alone;showrate=1 (accessed April 19, 2007).

Corchado, Alfredo, and Tracey Eaton. 2005. "Surging Mexican Violence Draws Comparisons to Colombia." *Dallas Morning News,* October 20. http://www.highbeam.com/doc/1G1-137749567.html (accessed April 23, 2007).

Cornelius, Wayne. 2005. "Controlling 'Unwanted' Immigration: Lessons from the United States, 1993–2004." *Journal of Ethnic and Migration Studies* 31(4): 775–794.

Crossette, Barbara. 2004. "Millions of People Worldwide on the Move." *Atlantic Online,* May 17. http://www.theatlantic.com/foreign/unwire/crossette2004-05-17.html (accessed April 23, 2007).

Digital National Security Archive. 2004. "El Salvador: War, Peace, and Human Rights, 1980–1994." http://nsarchive.chadwyck.com/el_essay.htm (accessed October 20, 2005).

Durand, Jorge, Douglas S. Massey, and Emilio A. Parrado. 1999. "The New Era of Mexican Migration to the United States." *Journal of American History,* September. http://www.historycooperative.org/journals/jah/86.2/durand.html (accessed December 18, 2006).

Ellingwood, Ken. 2004. *Hard Line: Life and Death on the U.S.-Mexico Border.* New York: Vintage Books.

Fisher, Jo. 1993. *Out of the Shadows: Women, Resistance, and Politics in South America.* London: Latin American Bureau.

Godnick, William, Erick Haven, and Ivonne Martinez-Henriquez. 2000. "SAND Brief: El Salvador, Periodic Brief Prepared for the Small Army Survey." Monterrey Institute of International Studies, Security and Development Program. http://sand.miis.edu/research/2000/mar2000/elsbrief.pdf (accessed December 19, 2006).

Grayson, George. 2002. "Mexico's Forgotten Southern Border: Does Mexico Practice at Home What It Preaches Abroad?" Center for Immigration Studies. http://www.cis.org/articles/2002/back702.html (accessed August 31, 2007).

Helms, Mary W. 1990. "Chapter 2: The Society and Its Environment. Migration" In *El Salvador: A Country Report,* ed. James Haggerty. Washington, DC: U.S. Library of Congress. Electronic Book. http://lcweb2.loc.gov/cgi-bin/query/r?frd/cstdy:@field(DOCID+sv0042 (accessed December 19, 2006).

Inter-American Commission on Human Rights. 2003. "The Situation of the Rights of Women in Ciudad Juárez, Mexico: The Right to Be Free from Violence and Discrimination." Trans. from Spanish. March 7. Washington, DC. http://www.cidh.org/annualrep/2002eng/chap.vi.Juárez.htm (accessed April 23, 2007).

Jordan, Sandra. 2003. "Rich Killers Stalk City of Lost Girls." *Guardian,* November 2. http://observer.guardian.co.uk/international/story/0,6903,1075952,00.html (accessed December 19, 2006).

Lauria-Santiago, Aldo, and Leigh Binford. 2004. "Local History, Politics, and the State in El Salvador." In *Landscapes of Struggle: Politics, Society, and Community in El Salvador,* ed. Aldo Lauria-Santiago and Leigh Binford, 1–12. Pittsburgh: University of Pittsburgh Press.

Marosi, Richard. 2005. "Border Crossing Deaths Set 12 Month Record." *Los Angeles Times,* October 1. http://www.ccis-ucsd.org/news/latimes10-1-05.pdf (accessed April 26, 2007).

Martin, Philip. 2003. *Promise Unfulfilled: Unions, Immigration, and the Farm Workers.* Ithaca, NY: Cornell University Press.

Massey, Douglas. 1997. "March of Folly: U.S. Immigration Policy after NAFTA." *American Prospect* 37: 1–16.

Massey, Douglas, Jorge Durand, and Nolan J. Malone. 2002. *Beyond Smoke and Mirrors: Mexican Immigration in an Era of Economic Integration.* New York: Russell Sage Foundation.

Mexico Solidarity Network. 2004. "Femicides in Ciudad Juárez." http://www.mexicosolidarity. org/site/specialreports/2004femicides (accessed December 19, 2006).

Migration Policy Institute. 2006. "The U.S.-Mexico Border." *Migration Information Source,* June. Washington, DC: Migration Policy Institute. http://www.migrationinformation. org/Feature/display.cfm?ID=32 (accessed December 19, 2006).

Naciones Unidas. 1993. *De la locura a la esperanza: La guerra de 12 años en el Salvador: Informe de la Comisión de la Verdad para el Salvador.* San Salvador and New York: United Nations. http://www.uca.edu.sv/publica/idhuca/cv.pdf (accessed January 11, 2008).

National Drug Intelligence Center. 2000. "National Drug Threat Assessment 2001—The Domestic Perspective." http://www.indianadea.com/public_docs/pubs/647/index.htm (accessed April 23, 2007).

——. 2007. "National Drug Threat Assessment 2007." http://www.justice.gov/dea/concern/18862/2007.pdf (accessed April 26, 2007).

Orozco, Manuel. 2003. "The Impact of Migration in the Central American and Caribbean Region." Canadian Foundation for the Americas. http://meme.phpwebhosting.com/ ~migracion/modules/documentos/manuel_orozco1.pdf (accessed October 20, 2005).

Passel, Jeffrey. 2005. *Report: Estimates of the Size and Characteristics of the Undocumented Population.* Washington, DC: Pew Hispanic Center. http://pewhispanic.org/files/reports/ 44.pdf (accessed April 27, 2007).

——. 2006. "The Size and Characteristics of the Unauthorized Migrant Population in the U.S." March 7. Washington, DC: Pew Hispanic Center. http://pewhispanic.org/files/ reports/61.pdf (accessed January 11. 2008).

Remittances EU. 2007. "Mexico in Fact and Figure." January 17. http://www.remittances.eu/ content/view/19/53/ (accessed January 11, 2008).

Reyes, Belinda. 2004. "U.S. Immigration Policy and the Duration of Undocumented Trips." In *Crossing the Border: Research from the Mexican Migration Project,* ed. Jorge Durand and Douglas S. Massey, 299–320. New York: Russell Sage Foundation.

Reyes, Belinda, Hans P. Johnson, and Richard Van Swearingen. 2002. "Holding the Line? The Effects of the Recent Border Build-up on Unauthorized Immigration." Public Policy Institute of California. http://www.ppic.org/content/pubs/R_702BRR.pdf (accessed March 29, 2005).

Schirmer, Jennifer. 1993. "Those Who Die for Life Cannot Be Called Dead: Women and Human Rights Protest in Latin America." In *Surviving beyond Fear: Women, Children and Human Rights in Latin America,* ed. Marjorie Agosin, 31–57. Fredonia, CA: White Pine Press.

Secretaría de Relaciones Exteriores. 2004. "Updated Document Regarding the Situation of Women in Ciudad Juárez." http://www.sre.gob.mx/substg/derechoshumanos/docs/ infoJuárezen.doc (accessed April 23, 2007).

Seper, Jerry. 2005a. "Ex-Troops Aiding Drug Traffickers." *Washington Times,* February 24. http://www.washtimes.com/national/20050224-123713-6092r.htm (accessed April 23, 2007).

——. 2005b. "Mercenaries Expand Base into U.S." *Washington Times,* August 1. http://washingtontimes.com/functions/print.php?StoryID=20050801-122047-2623r (accessed April 23, 2007).

Serrano, Richard. 2005. "U.S. Looks into Videotaped Desecration of Taliban Corpses by Army Unit." *Los Angeles Times,* October 20. http://pqasb.pqarchiver.com/latimes/access/ 913776121.html?dids=913776121:913776121&FMT=ABS&FMTS=ABS:FT&type=current&date =Oct+20%2C+2005&author=Richard+A.+Serrano&pub=Los+Angeles+Times&edition=&startpage=A.3&desc=THE+WORLD (accessed April 23, 2007).

Stephen, Lynn. 1995. "Women's Rights Are Human Rights: The Mothers of the Disappeared (CO-MADRES)." *American Ethnologist* 22(4): 807–827.

——. 1997. *Women and Social Movements in Latin America: Power from Below*. Austin: University of Texas Press.

——. 1999. "The Construction of Indigenous Suspects: Militarization and the Gendered and Ethnic Dimensions of Human Rights Abuses in Southern Mexico." *American Ethnologist* 26(4): 1–22.

——. 2007. *Transborder Lives: Indigenous Oaxacans in Mexico, California, and Oregon*. Durham, NC: Duke University Press.

Suro, Roberto. 2003. "Remittances Senders and Receivers: Tracking the Transnational Channels." Washington, DC: Pew Hispanic Center. http://pewhispanic.org/reports/report.php?ReportID=23 (accessed March 29, 2005).

U.S. Census. 2000. "Profile of Selected Demographic and Social Characteristics 2000. Population Universe: People Born in El Salvador." http://www.census.gov/population/cen2000/stp-159/stp159-el_salvador.pdf (accessed April 23, 2007).

U.S. Congress. House of Representatives. Subcommittee on International Terrorism and Nonproliferation of the Committee on International Relations. 2006. "Border Vulnerabilities and International Terrorism." 109th Cong., 2nd sess., July 5 and 7. Serial no. 109–203. Washington, DC. http://commdocs.house.gov/committees/intlrel/hfa28499.000/hfa28499_of.htm (accessed on April 23, 2007).

U.S. Drug Enforcement Administration. 2003. "Statement of Sandalio Gonzalez, Special Agent in Charge of El Paso Division Drug Enforcement Administration before the U.S. House of Representatives Committee on Government Reform." Subcommittee on Criminal Justice, Drug Policy, and Human Resource. April 15. http://www.dea.gov/pubs/cngrtest/ct041503.html (accessed December 19, 2006).

U.S. General Accounting Office. 1998. "Report to the Honorable Charles B. Rangel, House of Representatives, Law Enforcement: Information on Drug-Related Police Corruption." Washington, DC: GPO.

U.S. Immigration Support. 2006. "Stats Show Immigrant Deaths Decreased Along U.S.-Mexico Border." *U.S. Immigration Newsletter* (New York), October. http://www.usimmigrationsupport.org/newsletter/2006/oct_17.html (accessed on December 19, 2006).

White, Marceline, Carlos Salas, and Sarah Gammage. 2003. *Trade Impact Review: Mexico Case Study. NAFTA and the FTAA: A Gender Analysis of Employment and Poverty Impacts in Agriculture*. Washington, DC: Women's Edge Coalition.

WorldNetDaily. 2005. "Mexican Drug Commandos Expand Ops in 6 U.S. States." June 21. http://www.worldnetdaily.com/news/printer-friendly.asp?ARTICLE_ID=44899 (accessed December 19, 2006).

Zavella, Patricia. 2006. "Where You Go Is What You Want: Immigration and Mexican Family Formation." Paper presented to the Center for the Study of Women and Society, University of Oregon, Eugene, Oregon, October 26.

6

==

Saving Iranian Women

Orientalist Feminism and the Axis of Evil

ROKSANA BAHRAMITASH

In the aftermath of September 11, wars have been waged on two Muslim countries as part of a global war on terror. The image of the terrorist is undoubtedly that of a Muslim man, one who holds the Koran in one hand and carries a machine gun in the other. This image is particularly powerful in major airports of the United States, where I find myself from time to time. Every trip I take to the United States, often in order to attend a conference, is nightmarish. Each time I leave Canada for the United States I have to register at the border. Regardless of the fact I hold a dark blue Canadian passport, I still have to register because of my birthplace, Tehran. The fact that I was born in Tehran makes me a special Canadian. For me, every border crossing has to take place at a port where the U.S. Department of Homeland Security (USDHS) has a branch. The ritual is as follows: I present myself at the border to an immigration officer, and he gets up and asks me to follow him—reluctantly, because I have just created more work for him. People behind me in the queue stare at me and feel frustrated because I am a person with a problem who has delayed their departure.

On one particular occasion I needed to use the washroom, and the immigration officer told me I could not leave without a guard. A security officer was called to follow me to the ladies' room, stand outside until I was out, and accompany me back to the Department of Homeland Security. It was hard for me to understand how I had lost my status as a respectable citizen and become a potential terrorist. I kept asking myself at what point had I turned from a beauty into a beast, from a respectable citizen who could use a public washroom freely into a suspect who needed to be followed by a guard.

To continue the ritual, once I am in the Department of Homeland Security office, I am asked to sit and wait while the officer hands my passport to another officer. My luggage is put in a designated area, and I am not allowed to touch it until I have been cleared. The next step is a long wait, after which finally my name is called. I enter a room. Often my heart is pounding and my hands trembling, and I am not always able to control my emotional reactions to the proceedings. I am fingerprinted, every finger. Often the computer does not register my fingerprints because the lines on my skin are fine. As a result, the fingerprinting process takes a long time and often has to be repeated several times. After the fingerprinting, I am photographed, and then I wait again while the computer finds my profile. I have a long profile—I found this out once when I was asked several questions about a trip I had taken twelve years ago. I had forgotten about it and as a result I did not give the right answers; the officer had to remind me of certain details. At the time, the expression of fear in my face alarmed the officer, who had to comfort me and tell me that there was nothing wrong and that I should calm down.

Sometimes the computer takes a long time to find my profile. Finally, the officer hands me a form; I fill it in and the process comes to an end. He stamps my passport and I am set free. I leave the room to pick up my luggage and head toward the door, passing the large dogs that are waiting outside the office. The same process is repeated when I leave the country. I have to leave from a border where there is a USDHS, and go through one terminal after another in order to have my passport stamped. If I fail to do this, my next entry can be refused. On a couple of occasions I have failed to register when leaving, and this has caused major delays.

Undoubtedly, border crossing must be even worse for Iranian men or all men of Muslim background, because it is the Muslim man who is the terrorist suspect. Although Iranian men and women both have to register, the men are the main targets of current racial profiling, as they are the ones who have taken action against President Bush's foreign policy for remapping the region and his "Greater Middle East" plan. What is interesting is that none of the perpetrators of September 11 were Iranian. But that fact seems irrelevant; as far as U.S. foreign policy is concerned, Muslim men are the enemy. They are the enemy of "democracy" and human rights in general, and of women's rights in particular.

The justification for U.S. foreign policy has been the rhetoric of bringing democracy to the region and defending women's rights. This type of legitimization for an empire's domineering actions is not new. The ideas of implementing democracy and defending women's rights as human rights are the modern-day equivalent of the "civilizing" missions of the European empires during the colonial era. During that period, countries of the Muslim world had to be forcibly civilized because of the uncivilized way in which they treated their women. It was a male colonial mission to save Muslim women from barbaric Muslim men. This idea has persisted into the postcolonial world. The current administration has pursued "saving" Muslim women in the same fashion. The campaign for war against Afghanistan is a clear example. President George W. Bush argued for war to free women from the Taliban, forgetting that the United States had bred and fed the Taliban during the cold war.

The Taliban is the creation of empire. During the time of British colonial power, "Saudi Arabia" was severed from the Ottoman Empire. The British supported the eighteenth-century puritanical reformer Ibn Wahhab, who came to be the ruling force of Saudi Arabia. Followers of Ibn Wahhab went to the Indian subcontinent and established seminaries out of which, two centuries later, the Taliban movement that ruled most of Afghanistan from 1996 to 2001 emerged. These facts have critical links to twentieth-century international politics: the United States, for more than fifty years, supported the Saudi royal family—the self-proclaimed guardians of Wahhabi interpretations of Islam—and initially welcomed the Taliban's ascent to power. Those who follow the interpretations of Ibn Wahhab, called the Wahhabi, are the most conservative and reactionary voices in Islam regarding the role of women. In contrast to Bush's rhetoric, it would seem that for the United States, Wahhabi treatment of women is not a problem as long as this faction of Muslims supports the United States and its allies. This is clearly the case with Saudi Arabia, where Wahhabi are in power. The United States has made no proclamations about women's rights there, despite insisting on the necessity for a regime change to defend women's rights in Iran.

Saving Muslim Women from Their Men: A Colonial Agenda

In the context of colonial rule, a body of knowledge about the Orient formed. Critical literature on Orientalism, based on Edward Said's (1978) pioneering work, elaborates on the depiction of the Orient in the West. In his groundbreaking book, Said explained how Orientalists regard the Orient as a place of corrupt despotism, mystical religiosity, irrationality, and backwardness, whereas the Occident is seen as rational, democratic, and progressive. From a colonialist perspective, the position of women in the Orient is evidence of this backwardness and despotism, something that colonial rule aimed to address. In the case of Algeria, which the French invaded and conquered in 1830, "civilizing the Arabs," particularly because of their treatment of women, was the reason the French used to justify depriving Algerians of the right to vote. As Frantz Fanon (1967) has demonstrated, civilizing Algerian men meant de-veiling women by force to save them from the ravages of Algerian men. Ironically, the forced de-veiling and Gallicization that ideologically grounded French colonial power in Algeria were being carried out while many women in France were fighting for their rights against those very men who dreamed of liberating Muslim women. As Gayatri Spivak (1988, 297) has noted, "white men saving brown women from brown men" is a major underlying theme of the colonial project. Because Algerian men oppressed their women, they were "uncivilized," and their behavior, argued the French, was conditioned by their religion, Islam. In the case of British rule, imperial power's project to save Muslim women has a long history. During the late nineteenth century and early twentieth, when the British Empire ruled Egypt, the British embarked on a campaign to liberate Muslim women. In 1882, when the British took control, Lord Cromer "argued that veiling was the 'fatal obstacle' that prevented Egyptians from participating fully in Western civilization. Until it was abolished, Egypt would need the benevolent supervision of the colonialists. But Cromer had cynically exploited feminist ideas to advance the colonial project. Egyptian women lost many of their new educational and professional opportunities under the British, and Cromer was co-founder in London of the Anti-Women's Suffrage League" (Armstrong 2006, n.p.). Such attitudes, of course, reinforced colonialism, for the more "uncivilized" the natives, the more necessary it was for the French, the British, (or other "civilized" Europeans) to rule them. These altruistic "feminist" framings enabled the silencing of colonialism's exploitative agenda.

The Postcolonial World, Orientalist Feminism, and the Greater Middle East

In the postcolonial world, women's rights are similarly contextualized. There are some differences, namely, a history of a feminist movement that was established by the 1950s. There is now a huge body of literature on women's rights written by feminists. Some of the literature, however, particularly that concerned with women in the Orient, tends to fall into the same discourse that existed during colonial times. The United States' foreign policy can thus benefit from certain types of gender rights advocacy and feminism. The work of Antonio Gramsci, and his analysis of hegemonic knowledge, explains this seemingly contradictory observation. Gramsci (1971) argues that hegemonic knowledge is a system of thought that represents and serves the interests of those in the position of power. This body of knowledge is extremely authoritative and can become universalized to the extent that it can subvert forces that are a potential challenge to the hegemony. In the case of some types of feminist advocacy, a potentially liberating movement comes to serve the interests of the imperial power. According to Gramsci, hegemonic knowledge is not only successful in forming an ideological base to protect the interests of the powerful elite but also in engaging the opposition in such a way as to serve the hegemony. Here, a certain type of feminism not only poses no challenge to U.S. foreign policy but in fact supports it (Bahramitash 2005).

To give an example, Canada's new Conservative government endorses U.S. foreign policy in Afghanistan and has changed its own mandate from that of peacekeeping to military deployment. Penni Mitchell, a prominent Canadian feminist who is managing editor of the national feminist magazine *Herizons*, has implicitly endorsed Canada's military mission in Afghanistan and supports the Conservative government's foreign policy, even though at home the government's record on women's and minority rights is poor. According to Mitchell, "human rights of linguistic minorities and women are worth Canadians fighting for in Afghanistan, but advancing the rights of minorities and women in Canada's courts are a luxury Ottawa says it can little afford" (as quoted in Carastathis 2006).

The type of feminism that supports U.S. foreign policy under the pretext of defending women's rights can be called Orientalist feminism. Paidar (1995) describes certain characteristics of Orientalist feminism as expressed in the literature about women in the Muslim world. This type of feminism, based on Orientalist thinking, assumes a binary relationship between the West and the Orient. The West is progressive and is the best place for women, whereas the backward and uncivilized Muslim world of the Orient stands in direct contrast and provides the worst conditions for women. This binary perspective is problematic in that it assumes women in the West are homogenous and all of them liberated, whereas all women in the Muslim world, and in this case Iran in particular, are enslaved and victims. A homogenous picture of Muslim women as categorically oppressed implies that these women are unable to defend their rights. Once this image is established, it is only natural that the women need saviors.

Although there is no doubt that the position of women in Iran needs to be seriously criticized, just as in Afghanistan, the context in which such criticisms are raised is problematic. The uses, or rather misuses, of women's rights rhetoric to legitimate war—and, in the case of Iran, regime change—is at the heart of the issue. The United States has been pushing for international pressure, first, to impose economic sanctions on Iran, just as it did in Iraq, and then to follow these with a military air strike to prevent Iran from building nuclear power. Before the invasion of Iraq, the drums for war began after President Bush called Iran, Iraq, and North Korea members of an axis of evil. In the case of Iraq, weapons of mass destruction (WMD) became justification for invading the country and crushing Saddam Hussein.

Looking back to the 1980s, we see that it was the Americans who gave Saddam Hussein weapons of mass destruction, such as chemical bombs to be used against the Iranians, Iraqi Shias, and Kurds. However, Saddam Hussein fell out of favor during the Gulf War. Iraq was placed under international sanctions, followed by an invasion to find WMD, even though Saddam Hussein had been armed mainly by Europeans, in particular the British, and by the Americans. Currently we are witnessing the consequences for Iraq, and Iraqi women, of the search for WMD and the attempt to institute democracy.

The issue of women's rights in Iran continues to be a focal point, as evidenced by the popularity of the best-selling *Reading Lolita in Tehran,* a book about the lives of Iranian women written by Azar Nafisi (2003), an American woman of Iranian origin. For several months the book remained number one on the *New York Times Book Review* list. Although the book is about Iranian women's lives and their oppression, it was eventually endorsed by neoconservatives Bernard Lewis and Fouad Ajami. *Reading Lolita in Tehran* is about Azar Nafisi's experience teaching weekly English literature classes to eight young middle-class urban Iranian women and her attempts to shed light on their oppression through the teaching of nineteenth- and early twentieth-century Western literature. But Nafisi's account of her experience with a handful of middle class urban women has come to represent all oppressed Iranian women. This book is similar to another "feminist" book written by an American woman married to an Iranian man, titled *Not without My Daughter* (Mahmoody 1987), in which Betty Mahmoody flees Iran with her daughter to the United States, her home country. The book stirred up considerable antagonism toward Iranians in North America and Europe, and when it was turned into a movie of the same name it led to racist attacks on Iranians in Western countries. The book has been criticized heavily by Iranian feminists. Nafisi's work, unlike that of Mahmoody, has been supported by Washington and highly recommended and promoted by the neoconservatives of the Bush administration. Nafisi names her neoconservative mentor Fouad Ajami, her superior at the School of Advanced International Studies in Washington, as one of her best supporters. At the back of the book is a quote from Bernard Lewis, guru of the neoconservatives, who describes the work as "a memoir about teaching Western literature in revolutionary Iran with profound and fascinating insights into both." Hamid Dabbashi, however, has argued in a different direction:

> So far as its unfailing hatred of everything Iranian—from its literary masterpieces to its ordinary people—is concerned, not since Betty Mahmoody's notorious book *Not without My Daughter* . . . has a text exuded so systematic a visceral hatred of everything Iranian. Meanwhile, by seeking to recycle a kaffeeklatsch version of English literature as the ideological foregrounding of American empire, *Reading Lolita in Tehran* is reminiscent of the most pestiferous colonial projects of the British in India, when, for example, in 1835 a colonial officer like Thomas Macaulay decreed: "We must do our best to form a class who may be interpreters between us and the millions whom we govern, a class of persons Indian in blood and colour, but English in taste, in opinions, words and intellect." Azar Nafisi is the personification of that native informer and colonial agent, polishing her services for an American version of the very same project. (Dabbashi 2006, n.p.)

Nafisi's book is a prime example of what Paidar defines as Orientalist feminism, a type of feminism that assumes binary opposition between the West and the Orient. Because Orientalist feminism regards Oriental women only as victims and not as agents of social transformation, it is blind to the ways women in the East resist and empower themselves. Western women therefore conclude that Muslim women need saviors, that is, as in the case of Afghan women, they are seen as unable to become agents of their own liberation. Even President Bush, not a man known for advocacy of feminist causes, has spoken about the need to save Afghan women. Another aspect of feminist Orientalism assumes that all societies in the Orient are the same and that all Muslim women there live under the same conditions (Bahramitash 2005, 224). This type of feminism not only provides support for militarized foreign policy but also exacerbates racism domestically, in this case anti-Muslim/anti-Iranian sentiment.

Nafisi's work not only celebrates U.S. foreign policy but equally makes a major contribution to the existent Islamophobia in North America. In the quote that follows, she portrays the backwardness of religious Iranian men within the context of her teaching of Jane Austen's *Pride and Prejudice*, a novel written at the height of the British Empire: "It is a truth universally acknowledged that a Muslim man, regardless of his fortune, must be in want of a nine-year-old virgin wife" (Nafisi 2003, 257). Nafisi repeats this portrayal again and again throughout her book. She also depicts secular Iranian men as not very different from their religious countrymen, and portrays them as fanatical, hypocritical, and generally oppressive behind their liberated appearance.

Orientalist feminism has been criticized heavily by postcolonial feminists (Abu-Lughod 2001; Yegenoglu 1998; Moallem 2005; Olmsted 2005). The portrayal of Iranian women as victims unable to transform their situation, and the resulting idea that these women are therefore in dire need of saviors, is at the core of the Orientalist feminist agenda. As I show in the next section, such assumptions are erroneous. In postrevolutionary Iran, Iranian women have resisted; they have fought and renegotiated their position; and they have indeed managed to bring about change.

Facts and Fictions about Iranian Women

There is no doubt that gender inequality exists in Iran, and there is a great need to enhance the role of women. However, Azar Nafisi's representation of Iranian women in *Reading Lolita in Tehran* as a group who are universally and categorically victims needs to be criticized as well. Iranian women, like other women from different parts of the world, divide along issues related to class and ethnic background. Postrevolutionary Iran shows clear indications of class divisions, which testifies to the different experiences of women from different social classes.

In the aftermath of the Iranian revolution, Islamist forces came to dominate the country's political scene. At the time, the ruling government made great efforts to exclude women from the public sphere. This policy primarily affected middle-class and elite women, who had taken on professional roles during the previous pro-American regime of the shah. Ironically, the Islamist followers of Ayatollah Khomeini have in fact contributed to mobilizing women from the low-income peasant class and the traditionalist class to engage in the revolution. The ayatollah had called for women to break the curfew, leave their homes, and go into the streets for demonstrations. This directive was given in the form of a *fatwa*, a religious decree, making it mandatory for Muslim men and women to participate in the revolution (Bahramitash 2007).

Once the revolution was won, the regime needed women to continue their support in order to provide the social services the ayatollah had promised. With Iraq's invasion of Iran, women became still more vital. During the 1980s, many women from low-income backgrounds and the traditional classes were drawn into the public sphere from the private space of their homes. These were the same women who, during the previous regime, had been excluded by the ruling elite because they wore the veil. To some extent they were veiled because they were from the lower-income groups—rural and urban peasants. But after the revolution, and ironically with the imposition of compulsory veiling, many of these women were able to engage in a variety of activities. Their access to public space came at the expense of excluding women from middle-class and elite backgrounds, many of whom became alienated and, like Azar Nafisi, either stayed at home or left the country by force or by choice.

Nonetheless, the fact that the majority of women were mobilized by the Islamist regime, often as volunteers, paved the way for future changes. The revolution was inspired by the idea of social justice. Social services, ranging from literacy campaigns to universal health care and education, had to be delivered. These services relied heavily on the work of millions of women. The nationwide literacy campaign in particular mobilized women in great numbers, bringing masses of illiterate women to mosques for education. As a result of such mass programs, women who had no access to education under the previous secular regime became literate. This initial mass literacy campaign led to increasing numbers of educated women, who currently constitute more than 60 percent of Iran's 1.6 million university students. Now, not only are more women than men enrolled in higher education, but they also have a higher propensity than men to finish their education. In her book, Nafisi is preoccupied with eight middle-class women who are studying English literature. They seem to be a major point of fascination to North American readers as well, erasing the millions of women who worked as volunteers to teach basic literacy to illiterate women. Nafisi is the heroine of Iran in the eyes of the neocons, whereas the work of millions to fight illiteracy is overlooked.

The literacy campaign in Iran has had enormous ramifications. With the rising number of women earning secondary and university educations, many young women are postponing marriage until graduation. The overall social trends have been toward an increase in the age of first marriage for women, a decrease in the age gap between spouses, a decline in the role played by the bride's family in the selection of the spouse (that is, a decline in arranged marriages), a decrease in the number of married women (as a percentage of all women) over the age of fifteen, an increase in divorce rates, and a decrease in the number of children per family. Rising literacy and educational attainment have resulted in declining infant mortality and fertility rates, both of which decrease family size. Low infant mortality means that women tend to have fewer children because they no longer have to bear extra children in an attempt to secure their family's size (Bahramitash and Kazemipour 2006).

Nafisi mentions that after the Iranian revolution, the age at which a female could marry was reduced to nine years, in accordance with Islamic jurisprudence—an act she believed reinforced the misogyny of Islam. However, in reality, as Moslem (2002, 16) points out, the legal age of marriage was indeed lowered after the regime change, but the average age of marriage has risen from 18.7 in 1956 to 21 in 1991, and any deviation from this pattern is statistically marginal. In other words, although there is no doubt that such a legal age is unacceptable, the law hardly reflects social reality.

The same applies to polygamy. Regardless of Nafisi's negative account of Iranian men and their desire to have many wives, in reality polygamy is an uncommon practice. Only 1 percent of all marriages are polygamous, according to recent research conducted at the University of Tehran (Shaditalab 2003). These are just two examples of how Nafisi intertwines facts and fiction to create a book that pretends to give a true story of Iran and of the oppression of Iranian women but in fact provides a skewed perspective.

The denunciation of Iran as a backward, barbaric place for women because of Islam is taking place in a context in which Muslim men throughout North America are being profiled as potential terrorists. Anti-Muslim/Iranian/Arab sentiment has risen significantly in North America, as documented by the Council on American-Islamic Relations (CAIR), North America's largest Muslim organization. The council has reported that hate crimes against Muslims have increased more than 50 percent since 2003, and its recent report (CAIR 2006) indicates that complaints involving anti-Muslim discrimination, harassment, and violence jumped about 30 percent in 2005 compared to 2004.

The situation of women in the Muslim world in general and in Iran in particular leaves much to be desired, and feminists in Iran and other parts of the Muslim world, as well as in many other countries, have a huge battle to fight. What is unclear is how neoconservatives and their current foreign policy are going to help the situation. It is likely that further destabilization of the region will make the situation worse for men as well as women.

REFERENCES

Abu-Lughod, Lila. 2001. "Orientalism and Middle East Feminist Studies." *Feminist Studies* 27 (1): 101–113.

Armstrong, Karen. 2006. "My Years in a Habit Taught Me the Paradox of Veiling." *Guardian,* October 26. http://www.guardian.co.uk/comment/story/0,1931544,00.html (accessed April 1, 2007).

Bahramitash, Roksana. 2005. "The War on Terror, Feminist Orientalism and Orientalist Feminism: Case Studies of Two North American Bestsellers." *Critique: Journal of Middle Eastern Studies* 14(2): 223–237.

———. 2007. "Female Employment and Globalization during Iran's Reform Era (1997–2005)." *Journal of Middle East Women Studies* 3(2): 56–86.

Bahramitash, Roksana, and Shahla Kazemipour. 2006. "Myth and Realities of the Impact of Islam on Women: Women's Changing Marital Status in Iran." *Critique: Journal of Middle Eastern Studies* 15(2): 111–128.

CAIR (Council on American-Islamic Relations). 2006. "The Status of Muslim Civil Rights in the United States, 2006: The Struggle for Equality." http://www.cair.com/pdf/2006-CAIR-Civil-Rights-Report.pdf (accessed February 19, 2007).

Carastathis, Anna. 2006. "Dust in the Eyes of the World." *Dominion: News from the Grassroots,* October 19. http://www.dominionpaper.ca/foreign_policy/2006/10/19/dust_in_th.html (accessed April 2, 2007).

Dabbashi, Hamid. 2006. "Native Informers and the Making of the American Empire." *Al-Ahram Weekly,* June 1–7. http://weekly.ahram.org.eg/2006/797/special.htm (accessed March 16, 2007).

Fanon, Frantz. 1967. *Black Skin White Masks.* New York: Grove Press.

Gramsci, Antonio. 1971. *Selections from the Prison Notebook,* ed. Quinton Hoare and Geoffrey Nowell-Smith. New York: International Publishers.

Mahmoody, Betty, with William Hoffer. 1987. *Not without My Daughter.* New York: St. Martin's Press.

Moallem, Minoo. 2005. *Between Warrior Brother and Veiled Sister.* Los Angeles: University of California Press.

Moslem, Mehdi. 2002. "The State and Fractional Politics in the Islamic Republic of Iran." In *Twenty Years of Islamic Revolution: Political and Social Transition in Iran since 1979,* ed. Eric Hooglund, 19–35. New York: Syracuse University Press.

Nafisi, Azar. 2003. *Reading Lolita in Tehran: A Memoir in Books.* New York: Random House.

Olmsted, Jennifer. 2005. "Is Paid Work the (Only) Answer? Neoliberalism, Arab Women's Well-Being and the Social Contract." *Journal of Middle East Women's Studies* 1(2): 112–139.

Paidar, Parvin. 1995. *Women and the Political Process in Twentieth-Century Iran.* Cambridge: Cambridge University Press.

Said, Edward. 1978. *Orientalism.* New York: Vintage Books.

Shaditalab, Zhaleh. 2003. "Women in the Twentieth Century Iran." Paper presented at the Symposium on Women's Struggle for Peace in the Middle East, Concordia University, Montreal, Canada. November 23.

Spivak, Gayatri Chakravorty. 1988. "Can the Subaltern Speak?" In *Marxism and the Interpretation of Culture,* ed. Cary Nelson and Larry Grossberg, 271–313. Chicago: University of Illinois Press.

Yegenoglu, Meda. 1998. *Colonial Fantasies: Towards a Feminist Reading of Orientalism.* Cambridge: Cambridge University Press.

7

===

On Women and "Indians"

The Politics of Inclusion and Exclusion in Militarized Fiji

TERESIA K. TEAIWA

W hy should the primary audience for this book, likely North Americans, be interested in or concerned with militarization in the South Pacific republic of Fiji? The United States' foreign policy reaches into the farthest corners of the globe, but surely North Americans cannot be expected to be responsible for knowing, let alone understanding, the impact of their governments' and corporations' actions in every tiny developing nation. Besides, the United States has territories and former colonies in the Pacific (see Camacho 2005; Hattori 2004; Kent 1993; Trask 1999; Underwood 1985) that would seem to demand attention before Fiji. So why should Fiji receive serious consideration from Americans as anything other than an exotic tourist destination?

One immediate answer to this question lies in the current U.S.-led global war on terror and the initially U.S.-led occupation of Iraq that is now being assisted by UN peacekeeping forces. As the reconstruction of Iraq has proven more and more challenging, it has become mortally dangerous for those U.S. and allied forces occupying Iraq, and consequently it has become increasingly difficult to recruit soldiers domestically (United Kingdom 2003; Brooke 2005). In tandem, we have seen growth in the United States' and, especially, in Great Britain's interest in recruiting new members of the armed forces from their former colonial territories (BBC News 2004; Brooke 2005; Haglelgam 2005; Teaiwa 2008) and growth in private, corporate militias—two key by-products of the occupation of Iraq and the global war on terror (Kelsey 2006; Maclellan 2006; *Fiji Times* 2007a).

Fiji becomes significant at three levels in this context. First, it is a preferred supplier of peacekeeping personnel for the UN Assisted Mission for Iraq (UNAMI) Guard Unit, even when its domestic politics (e.g., governments brought to power as the result of coups d'état in 2000 and 2006) may otherwise demand sanction and exclusion from participation in UN activities. Second, it has become a reliable source of military recruits for its former colonial ruler, Great Britain, with over a thousand Fiji citizens serving in Iraq and Kuwait under the British flag in 2006 (Kelsey 2006; Maclellan 2006). Third, it is a dependable provider of personnel for multinational private security firms engaged for the most part in Iraq and the Middle East, with no less than three thousand Fiji men on their books (Maclellan 2006).

Thus, a relatively small South Pacific nation, with a relatively small population, and a relatively small standing army, experiences intensified processes of militarization as a result of decisions made by the president of the United States and the prime minister of Great Britain in consultation with one another—decisions that profoundly affect international movements of capital, investment, and labor. So indeed it behooves readers of this book to become aware of and understand what militarization in Fiji means. In addition, the texture of militarization in Fiji offers alternative perspectives on, and invites further consideration of, the possible range of gender and race dynamics in nations built on plural foundations. It bears repeating that the majority of Fiji's citizens enlisted in the Fiji Military Forces (FMF) and serving in UN peacekeeping forces, the British Armed Forces, and multinational private security firms are indigenous Fijian males.

Given the demographic makeup of the country, women and "Indians" become obvious "others" against which both the Fiji military as an institution and militarism as a hegemonic ideology can be defined. The term *Indians*, as used colloquially and on many official documents, refers to Fiji citizens of East Indian descent. However, since the coup of 1987, many Fiji citizens and academics have preferred the term *Indo-Fijian* instead of *Indian* to more accurately represent the history of Indo-Fijian settlement in Fiji since the nineteenth century. Advocates of the term *Indo-Fijian* argue that continuing use of *Indian* serves to further entrench ideologies that would exclude this group from acceptance as full citizens in the nation-state that is Fiji. Throughout, I place the term *Indians* in quotation marks to signify the politics around the use of the term.

In this chapter, I analyze the extent to which women and "Indians" are either included or excluded historically, practically, and discursively in militarized constructions of Fiji. My purpose is twofold: to bring into relief a range of the cultural and political stakes invested in the militarization of Fiji and to raise questions about how "race" and gender intersect in the context of militarization.

As Cynthia Enloe (2000) and others (Katzenstein and Reppy 1999) have noted, military service continues to function in modern nation-states, for better or worse, as a rarefied crucible of citizenship. According to Enloe, "the most optimistic calculation is to figure that when a country's military admits a once excluded or despised group, that institution is transformed and made more compatible with democratic culture. In this perhaps too-sanguine scenario, the outsider group campaigning to enter the military doesn't become militarized; rather, the newly diversified military becomes democratized" (2000, 16).

Of course, Enloe retains a healthy skepticism about how effectively the military is democratized by its selective inclusions of "once excluded or despised" groups. She calculates that the more likely scenario is that, in fact, those groups have become militarized. But contemporary U.S. military history records a steady stream of women and ethnic minorities queuing up for military service and clamoring for equitable treatment within the military (Katzenstein and Reppy 1999)—in effect, bolstering rather than challenging the military's position in society, and ensuring the indefinite march and progression of U.S. militarization. By contrast, Fiji's military history culminates in the current curious historical moment, in which the once excluded or despised groups—women and "Indians"—are both being differentially treated by and responding to the process of militarization.

Some Background

Fiji is made up of over three hundred islands situated north northeast of New Zealand, east of Australia, and south southwest of Hawai'i. After Papua New Guinea, Fiji is the next most populous Pacific Island nation and has the most developed social and economic infrastructure of all the independent Pacific Island nations. Fiji is a hub of the Pacific: a major crossroads for both shipping and air routes, and home to key regional institutions such as the twelve-member University of the South Pacific and the Pacific Islands Forum Secretariat.

A former British colony granted independence in 1970, Fiji has the most visibly "racially" diverse population in the South Pacific,[1] with 54 percent of its residents claiming indigenous Fijian heritage, over 38 percent claiming Indo-Fijian descent (these are largely the descendants of East Indian indentured laborers brought to Fiji by the British in the nineteenth century), and about 7.5 percent categorized as Others (Fiji Bureau of Statistics 2006), consisting of the indigenous ethnic minority Rotumans as well as communities of Europeans, Chinese, and Pacific Islanders of Melanesian, Micronesian, and Polynesian heritage.

Per capita, Fiji is the most militarized of the independent states in the Pacific Islands region. Papua New Guinea, with a total population of over six million, has a defense force of just over 4,000 (U.S. Navy 2005), yet Fiji, with a total population of just under 900,000, maintains military forces only a few hundred smaller than that of Papua New Guinea.[2] As might be expected, the Fiji military is predominantly male. With the nation's multiracial makeup, the fact that the rank and file of the armed forces are overwhelmingly indigenous Fijians raises serious questions about the neutrality of the institution within the highly politicized domestic arena.

Indeed, although Fiji has distinguished itself internationally through service during World War II, in the Malaya Campaign, and as United Nations peacekeeping forces in the Middle East and elsewhere, the roots of Fiji's modern military are in a colonial constabulary established to pacify rebellious groups within the country (Kaplan 2001; Nicole 2006; Teaiwa 2001b). Inevitably, it has been the Fiji military's domestic interventions and subversions of government that have attracted the most international attention and censure. May 14, 2007, marked the twentieth anniversary of the country's first military coup d'état, whereas December 5, 2006, became the occasion for its fourth. Modern militarization and militarism in Fiji have been dynamic processes, and in this chapter I describe some of their gendered and racialized dimensions.[3]

Before proceeding further, however, an explanation of who I am and what my interest in militarization in Fiji is may be in order. Although I am a U.S. citizen by birth, African American by maternal descent, and heir to a militarized genealogy in that three generations of my mother's family served in the U.S. armed forces, my formative years were spent in Fiji, the adopted homeland of my father. My father and his family had been resettled to Fiji after World War II, when he was a child. Despite his not being ethnically indigenous Fijian, my father considers Fiji his home and is fiercely patriotic. I have inherited some of his passion for Fiji and was indelibly marked by growing up in that country during its golden days of early independence from Great Britain (Teaiwa 2004).

I grew up singing the Fiji national anthem—"Blessings grant, oh God of nations, on the isles of Fiji." I grew up proud of the multiculturalism I lived, and I believed the political rhetoric I heard on the radio and read in the newspapers as an alert child. I knew I was a member of a racial and ethnic minority in Fiji, and I knew well the power of social exclusion on the school playground. But I believed I was growing up in an increasingly inclusive Fiji, a nation that would allow all of us who sang the national anthem, played and watched sports together, shared each other's food, celebrated each other's religious holidays, and did all those other "soft multiculturalism" things together, to belong.

This personal background evolved into political, professional, and civic engagements. As a young adult observing the two coups that occurred in Fiji in 1987 (the first in May and the second in September of that year) from a distance resulting from my pursuit of a university education in the United States, my relationship with and perspective on Fiji was inevitably politicized. Over time I found useful frames for analysis in Marxism, indigenous rights discourse, women-of-color feminism, and cultural studies. Although initially I was drawn to a Ph.D. topic on women's resistance to land alienation in my own ethnic community, Fiji became the central case study site for my eventual Ph.D. dissertation on militarism and tourism in the Pacific (Teaiwa 2001b).

While still working on my Ph.D., I elected to leave the United States to return to Fiji for extended fieldwork, during which time I had my first child, joined the academic staff of the University of the South Pacific (USP), and became actively involved in several civic organizations ranging in focus from feminist education to the antinuclear movement, and constitutionality and political consensus-building. But after five years at USP, an unforeseen opportunity arose to relocate with my son to New Zealand and take up a position coordinating the Pacific Studies program at Victoria University of Wellington. In the last seven years I have observed two further coups in Fiji from my location here in New Zealand (having had the strange fortune of never being in country for any of the coups). Significant populations of both indigenous and nonindigenous immigrants from Fiji reside in New Zealand, and with only four hours of air travel separating the two countries, the frequency of two-way visits is greatly facilitated.

The combination of my professional, academic, personal, political, and civic attachments to Fiji and my marginal identity location (as a patriotic noncitizen ethnic minority member) has infused my thinking with passion and anxiety, insight and confusion, outrage, and empathy. Like most people in Fiji, I have family members and close friends serving in the military with whom I have maintained social relations. In a way I have found it easier to disagree with and disassociate myself from fellow civilians with opposing political views than to detach myself from my relations in the military. Because soldiers in Fiji are not highly paid, do not have the best working conditions, and have few employment alternatives in any case (Teaiwa 2001b), it is easier for me to sympathize with them, even if I am opposed in principle to militarism.

Furthermore, it has become increasingly apparent to me that my position as an analyst of militarism is not uncompromised, and not just because I have friends and relatives in the military. More disturbingly, I have come to see how aspects of social and cultural life in Fiji, in which I had participated and even enjoyed—the educational system, sports, religion, even performances for tourists—are all implicated in reifying the same values that crystallized in the institution of the military (Teaiwa 2001b). Cynthia Enloe (2000) has described a similar process by which the ostensibly civilian roles of mother, wife, nurse, prostitute, and even an inanimate can of soup can be militarized. Under such conditions, authentic demilitarization requires a radical transformation of social and cultural values—a transformation predicated on understanding and not blind opposition, however principled it may be.

I have continued to research and write about militarization in Fiji and am presently preparing to undertake an oral history project with indigenous Fijian women in the Fiji and British armed forces. This chapter grows out of both my previous and ongoing research. I offer it here in hopes that Fiji may benefit from being brought into a robust dialogue on race, gender, and militarization.

At this writing, Fiji has been under military rule since December 2006, when Commander Frank Bainimarama dismissed elected Prime Minister Laisenia Qarase and his nationalist government and formed an interim government with significant civilian backing. As emergency rule continues there, media freedom and other basic human rights have not been allowed full expression, with international concerns raised by reports of torture and several confirmed deaths of civilians in military custody (*Fiji Times* 2007b; V. Lal 2007). At the same time, there are counterreports of citizens testifying their support of the military regime and claiming that Fiji has never been safer for women and Indo-Fijians especially (e.g., Nadan 2007). Needless to say, these contradictory circumstances make research into the military a delicate task at this time.

Key sources for this chapter have necessarily been literature-based: newspaper reports, a 1997 *Defence White Paper,* and secondary scholarship on Fiji have supplemented my own personal observations and insider knowledge of Fiji society and culture. It is understood here that news media cannot be taken as showing a simple or value-free reflection of contemporary events but also are likely to project the views of vested interests, and in this way media may shape social perceptions as much as reflect them. In spite of its limitations, the 1997 *Defence White Paper,* published by the Parliament of Fiji, is the result of the most comprehensive review of the Fiji Military Forces ever. It provides a valuable official account of both military history and policy.

There are few focused secondary studies of Fiji's modern military forces (Halapua 2003; Nawadra 1995; Ravuvu 1988). One publication documents the oral histories of Fijian soldiers exposed to Britain's Pacific nuclear testing campaign at Christmas Island (Pacific Concerns Resource Centre 1999). More scholarly and analytical attention has been given to the background and consequences of the military coups of 1987 than to any other aspect of the military in Fiji (Dean and Ritova 1988; B. Lal 1988; V. Lal 1990; Griffen 1989; Robertson and Tamanisau 1988; Scarr 1988; Sutherland 1992). Little of this 1987 coup literature, however, illuminates the dynamics of militarization in Fiji.

A literature has emerged on the coup of 2000 (Field, Baba, and Nabobo-Baba 2005; Lal and Pretes 2001; Ratuva 2000), and no doubt the coup of 2006 will generate a slew of new publications (Ratuva 2007). A recent master's thesis by Luisa Senibulu (2005) looks at professionalism within the FMF and provides summaries of interviews with senior military officers, all of whom profess a firm belief in the responsibility of the military to keep its distance from parliamentary politics—ironic in that they all gave their full support to the 2006 coup. In this context of professionalization, Senibulu's thesis offers occasional insights into the limits and possibilities for women in the Fiji military but says nothing about the implications for Indo-Fijians.

Much of the literature reinscribes cultural biases and political prejudices without questioning them. And as the preponderance of coup-focused literature suggests, analyses of militarism in Fiji have been skewed more toward dramatic events than deep structures. Halapua's work initiated the critical task of identifying and closely interrogating some of the collusions among the Methodist church, the indigenous chiefly system, and the military hierarchy in Fiji (Halapua 2003), but there is yet more work to be done to illuminate the likely trajectory of militarized developments in Fiji. This chapter contributes to the field of Fiji

military studies most significantly by attempting an unprecedented consideration of the histories of both women and "Indians" in the Fiji military.

Fiji as a Militarized Society

Statistics from Fiji indicate that in 2000, a total of 3,163 servicemen and women
were enlisted in the regular armed forces. Of that total, 3,131 or 98.98 percent
were male. Of the 32 women in the regular forces in 2000, all of them were
recorded as being of indigenous descent. Only 14 of the men or 0.44 percent were
not indigenous: 12 were Indo-Fijian, and 2 were categorized as "other" (Fiji Bureau
of Statistics 2006). Given this gendered and ethnic profile of the Fiji military, it is
safe to deduce that the institution's inferred alterities are either or both nonindigenous and female. However, the military's official policy of targeted and
timetabled recruitment of women since 1988, without a comparable target or
timetable for recruiting nonindigenous men, indicates a significant asymmetry
between "race" and gender, at least as far as the culture of the Fiji military forces
is concerned. Under conditions of militarization, "race" thus seems to subsume
gender for indigenous Fijians, whereas gender, or more specifically masculinity, is
not able to similarly subsume "race" for the nonindigenous.

These figures and disaggregations provided by the Bureau of Statistics may be
based on blurred categories of ethnicity, resulting in the inclusion of Rotumans
and part Europeans in the figures for Fijians.[4] In any case, the level of formal militarization in Fiji cannot be judged based on the size of the country's regular
forces alone. Unfortunately, figures for territorial and reserve forces are not easily accessible, although they probably contribute to between 1,000 and 3,000
additional personnel, with the predominant number of them again likely indigenous men.

The military is an institution with a high public profile in Fiji. On the basis of
my current research on media coverage during the immediate first postcoup
period of 1987–1988, I find that military-related images and reportage occurred
daily. In a survey of Fiji's daily newspapers conducted during the postcoup years
of 1995 and 1996, I found that publication of military-related images and
reportage occurred no less than once a week (Teaiwa 2001b). I have no doubt that
analyses of the immediate postcoup and intercoup periods of this century will
show similar patterns of Fijian media coverage of the military. The institution
had evidently become normalized in Fiji society. The military is expected to cast
a shadow or leave an impression, if not always appearing in full color or three
dimensions in every day life.

The shadow or impression that the media provide reflects the statistical
demographics: the Fiji military is dominated by indigenous Fijian men; when
enlisted women or female officers are portrayed, it seems done for its curiosity
value; and Indo-Fijian men are rarely featured in news coverage. It is entirely possible that simply by browsing the Fijian daily newspapers, one could come away

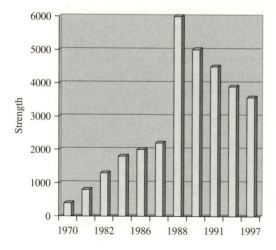

FIGURE 7.1 Fiji Military Forces
Development since 1970.

Source: Fiji Parliament 1997, 96.

with the idea that the militarization of Fiji is tautologically attributable to the presence, size, and activities of the Fiji military.

Fiji's military reached its largest size during World War II. Although an official history estimates that more than 11,000 males passed through the military during the war, the peak of enlistment saw a total of 8,513 in the Fijian armed forces. Of these, 1,070 were local Europeans, 6,371 were indigenous Fijians, 808 were New Zealanders, and 264 Indians (Howlett 1948, 149). With the return to peacetime, most soldiers returned to civilian life, and the military ceased its efforts at recruitment. By 1970, the year of Fiji's independence from Great Britain, the number in Fiji's regular forces stood at 400 (fig. 7.1).

The leaders of the newly independent and developing nation, however, sought economic opportunities for its citizens—especially the indigenous population, whose members had been "protected" under British colonial rule from commercial activity (Nicole 2006). In the 1970s, circumstances on the global scene seemed to provide a new opportunity for the employment of indigenous Fijians and a valuable source of foreign revenue for Fiji: the United Nations required international peacekeeping forces to support multilateral attempts to stabilize the Middle East. Because Fijians had distinguished themselves in service during World War II and had demonstrated their commitment to dominant British and American ideas of a "free world" in their contributions to the anti-communist Malaya campaign of the 1950s, they were approached by the UN as a reliable and capable force.

Fiji's engagements in peacekeeping in the Middle East thus led to a gradual increase in its armed forces again. When the first contingent of Fijian peacekeepers was deployed to Lebanon in 1978, the regular forces had grown to a total of 1,300. According to the *Defence White Paper* of 1997, 120 men were dispatched per month (for each of eleven months of the year) for service in the Middle East. Each tour of duty was a year long. In subsequent years, as the UN's peacekeeping requirements in the Middle East expanded, Fiji forces were also posted to the Sinai beginning in 1982 (Fiji Parliament 1997, 97). By 1986, and after a fairly steady pattern of growth, the Royal Fiji Military Forces had reached 2,200 in size.[5] Then in 1987 there was a dramatic spike, with the number of regular forces rising meteorically to 6,000. The year 1987 also saw Fiji's first two military coups, and understandably the military came to be perceived by many as a threat to democratic society. In the decade after the 1987 coups, the force was gradually reduced in size until it reached its present numbers.

The 1997 level represented in the last bar on the graph in figure 7.1 seems, by official reckonings, not to have changed significantly since then—even though there have been two more military coups. A constitutional review conducted during 1995–1996 offered the opportunity of reconsidering the role of the military in Fiji's democratic future, but the final report of the Constitutional Review Commission did not take up that challenge (Reeves, Vakatora, and Lal 1996). In May 2000, a civilian-led coup, during which members of the Labour coalition cabinet were held hostage for fifty-two days, received armed support from FMF personnel—specifically, breakaway members of the Counter Revolutionary Warfare (CRW) unit. The military eventually gained control of the situation and arrested the coup makers, but the split within military ranks illustrated by the CRW members' participation in the coup led to an attempted mutiny against the commander and the loss of eleven lives in November that year (Field, Baba, and Nabobo-Baba 2005; Lal and Pretes 2001).

The civilian government put into place by the military subsequently gained legitimacy and then a critical degree of independence from the military through an electoral victory in 2001. The government's unwillingness to prosecute or alienate key participants in the 2000 coup and mutiny led to a growing alienation between the prime minister and the commander of the FMF, with regular threats by the prime minister, Laisenia Qarase, to replace the commander and reduce the military budget (Field 2006; Field, Baba, Nabobo-Baba 2005). A further insult to the FMF came when the prime minister established a national security council in which the military was not invited to participate.

In 2006, with the government's introduction of controversial bills on "reconciliation and national unity" (a euphemism for immunity from prosecution for the 2000 coup makers) and indigenous fishing rights, government and military relations in Fiji had reached such a low that the government of New Zealand was compelled to step in to mediate the developing conflict. The prime minister and commander held talks in the capital of New Zealand, Wellington, facilitated by the governor general of New Zealand (Judge Anand Satyanand, the New Zealand–born son of Indo-Fijian migrants) and the New Zealand minister of foreign affairs (Winston Peters, a New Zealand Maori). However, within a few weeks of the talks, on December 6, 2006, the commander had made good on his threat to remove the prime minister and his government in what has been described as Fiji's first antinationalist coup (Ratuva 2007).

The impact of militarization on the modern history of Fiji is indisputable, but further studies of the military and the specific articulations of an FMF culture are necessary to appreciate the peculiar dynamics of militarization in Fiji. I do not have space here to examine the institutionalization of indigenous cultural norms and religion in the FMF (see Halapua 2003), nor the social and psychological impacts of international peacekeeping on returned soldiers. In writing elsewhere about the phenomenon of former military officers being appointed to key civilian public service roles in postcoup administrations, I have questioned, as Enloe suggests, whether this action can be reliably read as a civilianizing of the military or, in fact, as the militarization of civilian life (Enloe 1990; Teaiwa 2001b).

Suffice to say, militarization offers complex and troubling challenges for understanding contemporary Fiji. Absent opportunities to study the FMF from the inside, we must examine it at its borders. Indo-Fijians and women are the ostensible "others" for this profoundly male and indigenous institution. By surveying the extent to which the military is prepared and able to include and exclude key groups in society, we may find that what emerges is a mirror image of ways in which those same groups are prepared to include and exclude the military from their respective visions of a good society.

On "Indians": Military Inclusions and Exclusions

According to Vijay Naidu, "the predominance in the army of members of one ethnic category who are closely affiliated to the chiefly hierarchy that wields political power is a matter of concern. There is something immoral and sinister about the arming and training of one ethnic category in a multi-ethnic community" (1986, 13–14). A drastic underrepresentation of a major ethnic group in the nation-state's armed forces is also a matter of grave concern. In 2006, according to official estimates, 0.38 percent of the FMF were of Indo-Fijian descent, and all were males. Such an imbalance in ethnic representation is all the more disconcerting when one takes into account that approximately 40 percent of Fiji's unarmed police force is made up of Indo-Fijians (Fiji Parliament 1997, 73). Although a comparative analysis of racialized or ethnic politics of inclusion and exclusion in Fiji's police and military is beyond the scope of this chapter, I suggest that part of the reason for the disparity between the two institutions can be explained by the histories of Indians in Fiji and their relations with Fiji military forces.

Indo-Fijian identity emerges from a fusion of East Indian and Fijian histories and cultures. Between 1879 and 1916, the British colonial government in Fiji imported approximately 61,000 indentured laborers from the Indian subcontinent to work on white settler–owned plantations. The *girmitiyas* were a diverse group of northern and southern Indians, Muslims and Hindus, of different caste origins. *Girmitiyas* were offered the opportunity of repatriation at the end of their term of indenture, but the majority chose to stay on in Fiji, many of them taking up agricultural land leases to continue working in the sugar industry. The need for Indian workers had been determined by a colonial policy explicitly aimed at protecting the native population from the ravages of modernization and the corrupting influences of a waged system of labor (B. Lal 1983). *Girmitiyas*, as waged laborers, on the other hand, were by definition paid for their labor, and of course were by and large well aware of the need for thrift and financial prudence as they planned for lives after indenture. Sadly, these fine traits would eventually come to be held against them by both their European colonizers and the indigenous population.

The British fostered a climate of racialized suspicion between their two subject groups, which future unscrupulous leaders would readily exploit in an independent Fiji (Dean and Ritova 1988; B. Lal 1988). Although the majority of Indo-Fijians are descendants of indentured laborers, Gujarati and Punjabi free migrants came to Fiji in the postindenture period. Resentment by indigenous Fijians of "Indian wealth" is often based on their perceptions of Gujarati merchant activity (B. Lal 1988); they erroneously generalize, on the basis of "race," what in effect needs to be understood as the product of the economic histories of distinct migrant groups. The diversity contained tenuously by the label "Indo-Fijian" must be kept in mind when investigating that community's relationship with the FMF.

The origins of the modern Fiji military forces lie in a colonial armed constabulary that was initially established not to defend against external threats but to pacify and domesticate the indigenous hill tribes, which had not been party to the negotiated Deed of Cession by the coastal chiefs, a process that continued well into the twentieth century (Kaplan 2001; Nicole 2006). This history is worth remembering because it is too easy to see Indo-Fijians as primary "other" to an institution such as the military, so overwhelmingly indigenous in membership and character. Nevertheless, Indo-Fijians were eventually brought into the military's line of fire when it was mobilized to put down the industrial actions of Indo-Fijian workers in the 1920s and 1940s.

Indo-Fijians have not uniformly been positioned as the "other" in relation to the military, however. As most colonial histories demonstrate, specific individuals and communities may have a particular interest in cooperating or collaborating with colonial authorities. In an exchange on the on-line "Great War Forum," New Zealand genealogist Christine Liava'a refers to a soldier from Fiji, one W. Rajah Gopaul Naidu, who served in "Basra, Mesopotamia" in 1919 as an Indian translator for the British Indian Army's 1st King George's Own Sappers and Miners, and 2nd Queen Victoria's Own Madras Sappers and Miners (Liava'a 2006). Fijian scholar Asesela Ravuvu notes that an Indo-Fijian platoon had been formed in 1934 but provides no further details on it (Ravuvu 1988, 8–9). Inexplicably, Indo-Fijian scholars routinely fail to highlight the significance of this historical legacy in their analyses of postcoup politics (e.g., B. Lal 1988; V. Lal 1990). Eventually, as previously mentioned, 264 Indo-Fijians were recorded as having served during World War II (Howlett 1948, 159). The full nature of their

participation is not easily assessed from the secondary sources, but Howlett provided some insight when he described the Reserve Motor Transport unit as composed entirely of Indians except for the officers, who were of course European.

Among the "Honours and Awards" listed in Howlett's official history of the
FMF in World War II, there was only one Indo-Fijian, a staff sergeant Manzoor Beg
from the Fiji Medical Corps, who earned a Mention in Dispatches. This stands in
contrast to the numerous honors and awards for Fijians, who earned an impres-
sive 2 Foreign Awards (both from the United States), 24 Mentions in Dispatches,
3 Medals of the Order of British Empire (OBE), 16 Military Medals, 1 Victoria Cross,
1 Member of the OBE, 2 Military Crosses, and 4 Distinguished Conduct Medals
(Howlett 1948, 155). Given the numbers of enlisted Indo-Fijians relative to Fijians
(Howlett 1948, 159), the lack of medals presented to Indo-Fijians is understand-
able. However, military honors and awards are used to affirm not only military
skill and valor but a combined ideal of masculinity and citizenship. The lack of
medals earned by Indo-Fijians in World War II could be used to impugn the ethnic group as inherently disloyal to the crown (prior to independence in 1970) and,
by default, of questionable loyalty to the independent state. In such scenarios, it
becomes easy to justify excluding Indo-Fijians from full citizenship rights in Fiji.

In popular discourse, the terms of Indo-Fijians' inclusion or exclusion from
the Fiji military have historically revolved around two questions: appropriate
remuneration and necessary masculine attributes for military service. During
World War II, Indo-Fijian community leaders condemned the graduated pay rate
that saw Indo-Fijian and indigenous Fijian servicemen paid at a lower rate than
Europeans, which perhaps explains the low levels of Indo-Fijian enlistment during the war. Unfortunately, the matter has been popularly interpreted by members of other communities in Fiji as an excessive (and typically "Indian") interest
in money rather than as a worthy stand on the principles of racial equality
(Ravuvu 1988, 16; Fiji Parliament 1997, 10, 73).

Fijians' (and indeed, Europeans' and other Pacific Islanders') assumptions
about the "racial" character or cultural heritage of Indo-Fijians have tended to
take essentialist turns, as the dismissal in the postwar period of Indo-Fijian
males' physical suitability for soldiering demonstrates: "During the recruitment
for the Malayan Campaign in 1951 a number of Indians volunteered but were not
accepted because it was alleged they had inadequate 'soldierly qualities' for jungle warfare" (Ravuvu 1988, 10). In Fiji's colloquial terms, Indo-Fijians are often
disparaged as "kai Idia, skinny malila"—a comment formed by the perception that
Indo-Fijians' physical frames tend to be not as robust as those of indigenous
Fijians and other Pacific Islanders. Ravuvu's reference to Indo-Fijian volunteers as
not having adequate "soldierly qualities" for jungle welfare tells us more about
racialized perceptions in Fiji than it does about the actual attributes of those volunteers. The *Defence White Paper* also makes ambiguous reference to an official
attempt in 1968 to recruit Indo-Fijian men for officer training: "The product of
this policy was a number of Indian officers who served the RFMF well in various

capacities but whose service did not bring them to top rank or long service with the regular forces" (Fiji Parliament 1997, 72).

Indeed, whether the derision is overt or subtle, such complacency about Indo-Fijian representation in the FMF flies in the face of the rich military history of the Indian Subcontinent. Indians (as opposed to Indo-Fijians) served with distinction in both World War I and World War II (Indian Army n.d.). There is no explicit recognition of this distinction and no consideration in the literature of what India's proud military history means for understanding the Indo-Fijian position vis-à-vis the Fiji military, but the Fiji government has in fact had limited although significant exchanges with the Indian Army during the postcolonial period. In the late 1970s, the FMF engaged in training exercises and exchanges with the elite Gurkha forces of the British Army. As a schoolgirl growing up in the Fijian town of Lautoka during 1976–1979, I vividly recall Gurkha and FMF units marching and jogging through the suburban streets while on training exercises. Public awareness in Fiji of the strong military heritage of Indians also results from the fact that the key actor in the coups of 1987, Sitiveni Rabuka, is widely known to have received his master's degree in defence studies from the Indian Armed Forces Staff College in Tamil Nadu, India (Sharpham 2000, 65–66). Strangely, the *Defense White Paper* acknowledges neither Fiji's official defense exchanges with India nor the martial history of Indians (Fiji Parliament 1997, 37).

Space limitations prevent me from tracing in more detail the ways in which Indo-Fijians have been included in and excluded from the FMF. If further evidence is needed, I can only gesture with one hand toward the overarching postcoups trajectory that has seen Indo-Fijian academics and businessmen become targets of military surveillance and violence in 1987, to Commander Frank Bainimarama's appointment of Fiji's first Indo-Fijian prime minister Mahendra Chaudry (deposed by nationalists in the 2000 coup) to the current interim government cabinet in the pivotal role of minister of finance. With my other hand, I point to the remarkably unsensationalized media reporting around an Indo-Fijian soldier's murder of an indigenous Fijian fellow soldier in 2000 (Field, Baba, and Nabobo-Baba 2005, 243) and the fact that in 2005, the top military lawyer was Lieutenant Colonel Mohammed Aziz, an Indo-Fijian male who had received his law training in Australia with FMF sponsorship (Senibulu 2005, 74).

Mine has been a preliminary account of a previously unsynthesized history, but I hope I have demonstrated sufficiently that the historical relationship between Indo-Fijians and the Fiji military has been marked by both deliberate and unreflexive acts of inclusion and exclusion. Although "race" or racialized perceptions and assumptions have been a crucial factor in explaining or justifying the military's exclusions of Indo-Fijians, they are patently insufficient for explaining any successful inclusive engagements of "Indians" or Indo-Fijians by the FMF. Furthermore, in light of Indo-Fijian acknowledgments in the postcoups era that they need to more publicly prove their patriotism and worthiness,[6] the significance of the continued—even if apolitical—withholding of Indo-Fijian labor from military service cannot be underestimated.

On Women: Military Inclusions and Exclusions

Recall for a moment that Fiji's military strength was at an all-time high during World War II, and allow world history to remind us that women were assigned roles as both enlisted nurses and members of the auxiliary forces, especially in the Allied efforts (Nathan 2004). But in the official postwar history of the Fiji Military Forces, the only acknowledgment of women's role in Fiji's World War II efforts came in a cursory noting of the presence of the New Zealand Women's Army Auxiliary Corps and a glowing description of the large canteen set up at the "old Government Buildings to provide recreation and light refreshment for troops on leave. This canteen, most ably managed by Lady Adi Maria, wife of Lieutenant-Colonel Ratu Sir Lala Sukuna, and a party of Fijian girls, proved a great success and was an immense boon to troops on leave with no homes in Suva" (Howlett 1948, 40, 267). Fiji's women were clearly not expected to play much of a role in World War II other than keeping the home—and canteen—fires burning.[7]

Women were first admitted into Fiji's modern armed forces in 1988, when the Republic of Fiji Military Forces (RFMF) was eager to restore its credibility on the world scene after carrying out two unprecedented military coups in 1987. A classified advertisement in the January 14 edition of Fiji's premier daily newspaper, the *Fiji Times,* offered "Officer Training for Young Women in the Fiji Military Forces" (*Fiji Times* 1988a, 1988e). By February 1, the newspaper was able to publish a complete list of 227 successful applicants for military selection, and among the names were those of forty-one women (*Fiji Times* 1988d). After three months of training, on April 1, 1988, in what was clearly not an April Fool's prank, forty-one women marched in the Fiji Military Forces convocation parade (*Fiji Times* 1988c; Ravu 1988).[8]

In 1999, when I invited four women serving in the Fiji military to speak to the only women's studies course offered at the University of the South Pacific, they reported that of the original number of women recruited in 1988, only twenty-two chose to stay on in the military, and only six of them had actually been made officers (Kau et al. 1999). According to the women on the panel, there were two main reasons for the Fiji Military Forces' decision to admit women in 1988. Captain Kau suggested, and this was corroborated in the *Defence White Paper* (Fiji Parliament 1997), that women were intended to replace men in administrative duties at headquarters, thereby freeing up men for deployment in the postcoup recovery period. Lieutenant Ana Rokomokoti referred to the pressure of international trends in providing women equal employment opportunities: "If you don't have women in the army, there's something wrong with the army" (Kau et al. 1999). Additional intakes of women into Fiji's regular forces did not recur until

1998–1999, when only two women were recruited, and then again in 2006 and 2007. The latest official figure of a total of thirty-two women in the regular forces does not account for these recent recruitments. Informal inquiries have provided the estimate that in early 2007 there were between eighty and ninety women in the Fiji Military Forces. In 2003 and 2007, women were among Fiji troops deployed to serve with UNAMI.

To date, there has been no focused scholarship on or analysis of women's experiences in Fiji's military, but occasional insights are gained from more general studies of the Fiji military or journalistic features. In Luisa Senibulu's master's thesis on professionalism in the Fiji military, she cites a *Daily Post* article claiming that "service women share the belief that even though the army is a great job and provides great benefits, a woman in the army will not climb the ranks if she does not have a specialized skill" (Senibulu 2005, 60, citing the *Daily Post*, Jan. 1, 2003). To illustrate this point, Senibulu provided the examples of Captain Karalaini Serevi, an army dietician; Staff Sergeant Karolina Vunibaka, a physiotherapist; Sergeant Raisili, a dental therapist; Major Kau, a dentist; and Major Davina Chan and Captain Samanunu Vaniqi, both commissioned lawyers for the army (2005, 59–60).

Debates about women in combat that have pervaded public discourse in nations such as the United States and Great Britain have not come to the fore in Fiji's public life (see BBC News 2000; Katzenstein and Reppy 1999), in part because the Fiji Military Forces have not engaged in overt combat since the Malaya campaign. But the *Defence White Paper* clearly took its cue from international practice at the time, stating that "servicewomen should not be employed in combat type postings such as the infantry battalion and the anti-terrorist unit (this restriction is common to most armies)" (Fiji Parliament 1997, 75). However, with the core force and peacekeeping force balanced at about 41 percent and 39 percent, respectively (Senibulu 2005, 45), women's role in peacekeeping duties, which was officially sanctioned in 1995, remains unexamined in the literature.[9] I hope to begin to fill this gap with ongoing research, and return to consider Fiji's official position on women in peacekeeping shortly.

The military institutions of Fiji, dominated as they are by men, retain a distinctly conservative analysis of gender issues in the military. The *Defence White Paper* notes that initial reluctance to enlist servicewomen "was based not so much on prejudice as on the expense of providing special accommodation and clothing for females" (Fiji Parliament 1997, 74). Similar reasons were given for preventing women from serving on patrol vessels (75). Insisting that "no great allowances" were made for the first female recruits in terms of field and physical training, the report also refers to the

> high proportion of the servicewomen [who] have married, many of them
> to servicemen; therein lay several problems for which the RFMF had to
> make new policies, namely maternity leave . . . and husbands and their

wives serving within the same formal chain of command which introduced difficulties (though not insoluble ones) into the military legal and
command system. (75)

Finally, in regard to women participating in international peacekeeping missions, the *Defence White Paper* explains that

> Until 1995 servicewomen were not sent . . . overseas. This was not because
> they had no value there but because of the element of operational dan-
> ger involved. Further because servicewomen in such employment, being
> vastly outnumbered by men of many nationalities, tend to be subjected
> to continual sexual pressure. In addition because they often are called
> on to work on combined national staffs away from the support of their
> countrymen, such pressure can prove intolerable. (74)

Such concerns for preserving the sexual propriety and dignity of servicewomen,
protestations about the logistical inconvenience of separate facilities for women,
and distinct policies for married and pregnant women emerge from patriarchal
values and androcentric inertia. Clearly, the inclusion of women in Fiji's military
was never intended to be about achieving gender parity or full equality for
women in the military.

While gender becomes an obvious matter for consideration when it comes to
women in the military, "race" intersects with gender in significant ways. In that
first intake of forty-one women in 1988, three of them bore identifiably Indian last
names,[10] and one each had an identifiably European, Rotuman, or Chinese last
name (*Fiji Times* 1988b). The 2006 Bureau of Statistics report states that all thirty-
two servicewomen at the time were indigenous Fijian women,[11] but this information cannot be treated with complete confidence—as I showed earlier, the
ethnicity figures for males are arguable. Yet what the figure suggests is that for
whatever reason, the few women of racial or ethnic minority communities in Fiji
who initially had signed up for military service in 1988 found that the military no
longer fulfilled their career or personal aspirations. The majority of women in the
Fiji military, like the majority of men, are thus indigenous Fijians, and this incidence puts servicewomen in an interesting position in relation to the phenomenon of women's rights organizing and feminist consciousness-raising in Fiji,
which perhaps coincidentally has risen along a parallel timeline.

Conclusion: "Race," Gender, and Militarism in Fiji

What the record on inclusive and exclusive militarization in Fiji seems to show is
that "race" is read primarily as masculine (i.e., Indo-Fijians in the military will be
male), and gender is assumed to be "raced" (i.e., women in the military will be
indigenous Fijian). Put another way, in a situation in which practically all the soldiers are indigenous Fijian males, "race" thus seems to subsume gender for

indigenous Fijians, whereas gender, or more specifically, masculinity, is not able to similarly subsume "race" for Indo-Fijian males.

Inasmuch as the discussion in this chapter of "race" and gender in Fiji's military has demonstrated that the inclusion and exclusion of "once despised groups"—women and "Indians"—have not been uniform, it is useful to close with reflections on the context of feminism in Fiji. The postindependence feminist and women's rights movement in Fiji has by necessity been a "multiracial," "multiethnic," multicultural project.[12] This diversity makes a feminist lens useful for understanding the topic at hand, enhancing the sort of bifocal approach that would continue to separate perspectives on "race" from ones on gender. In particular, a feminist lens draws into clearer view a group that so far has been even more marginalized than the (indigenous Fijian) women and the (male) "Indians" who have preoccupied most of this chapter: nonindigenous women.

Women's activism and awareness of women's rights issues have grown in Fiji since the 1975 UN International Decade for Women.[13] Within little over a decade, both the Fiji Women's Crisis Centre and the Fiji Women's Rights Movement were formally established as nongovernmental organizations dedicated to critiquing gender inequalities and achieving positive social change for women. Although there was certainly critical engagement by indigenous Fijian women with emerging feminist ideas, nonindigenous women were most visible in this early consciousness-raising phase and have continued to play prominent roles as advocates for women's and human rights in more recent times.[14] Indo-Fijian women in particular, situated as they are at crucial intersections of "race" and gender in Fiji, have risen to prominence in the Fiji women's movement.[15]

The FMF's initial move to recruit women in 1988 and its ongoing efforts in this area are, quite simply, no mere coincidence. Rather, whether by conscious or intuitive design, the FMF has been able to co-opt the feminist agenda by providing proto-feminist career opportunities for indigenous Fijian women. Before the two 1987 coups, the government had made no significant policy statements or major budgetary commitments to women's development outside of traditionally female occupations. But in 1988, struggling to regain international respect, the postcoup interim government established for the first time a full-fledged Ministry of Women, with a cabinet portfolio, and opened the doors of the military to women.

Fiji feminists were aware in 1988 of this possible co-optation. When the longest-publishing daily, the *Fiji Times,* ran an editorial on International Women's Day crediting the first 1987 coup with ushering in a new, enlightened era for women in Fiji (*Fiji Times* 1988b), a group of Fiji's pioneering feminists responded:

> Far from improving the lot of women in Fiji, on the contrary the coup
> and its side effects have raised the level of tension within families often
> to the point of physical abuse and made poverty a frightening reality.
> Women have little to thank the coup for.

> The statement is ... an insult to all the women of Fiji who have
> worked for women's rights for many years. Only time will tell if the cre-
> ation of the Ministry of Women's Affairs will improve women's status in
> Fiji, as in many countries a Ministry of Women's Affairs has been created
> merely as a token gesture to appease the women of the country.
> (Tuidomo, Ali, and Moore 1988)

Rooted as they were in independent and community-based initiatives, Fiji feminists were rightfully suspicious of governmental moves to institutionalize and
bureaucratize a process for women's development. Yet my research has failed to
turn up any public statements by the women's rights activists of the time on
which they either lobbied for allowing women into the military or congratulated
the government on its foresight. The feminist silence in Fiji around women soldiers can be seen then as counterpoint to the historical fact that Indo-Fijians
have never publicly lobbied to have the number of women in military service
increased. This feature of militarization in Fiji needs to be understood better,
because I believe it may contain the seeds of visions of an unmilitarized or demilitarized nation-state.

Fiji women's rights organizations work with and against the military in complex ways. The Fiji Women's Rights Movement (FWRM) and the Fiji Women's
Crisis Centre (FWCC) have protested against each coup since 1987, and more
women and NGOs have emerged with similar pro-democracy standpoints. Let me
sketch most inadequately the role of Indo-Fijian women in this area: FWRM's
Imrana Jalal was among seventeen pro-democracy activists arrested in 1988 for
protesting on the anniversary of the first coup (Griffen 1997), femLink Fiji's Sharon
Bhagwan Rolls was a key leader of the women's blue ribbon campaign and peace
vigil during the coup and hostage crisis of 2000, and FWCC's Shamima Ali has
been an outspoken critic of all of the coups. The FWCC under Ali's leadership was
pivotal in the period between the 1987 and 2006 coups in brokering dialogue with
the FMF on issues of domestic violence and HIV/AIDS. The inroads made by the
FWCC are perhaps exemplified by the gender-sensitivity workshops it was commissioned to run for the military before the most recent coup disrupted relations
between government and NGOs. As outsiders to the military, women—and Indo-
Fijian women prominent among them—have come to the fore both as peace and
democracy advocates and as reformers or educators for the military. The complex
context for "race," gender, and militarization in Fiji demands further description
and analysis. What will my audience, so far away from Fiji, make of all of this?

In the United States, where discrimination in the military on the basis of
race, gender, religion, or sexuality has by no means been resolved (Enloe 2000;
Katzenstein and Reppy 1999), it may be difficult to appreciate the context in
which women and Indo-Fijians find themselves in relation to the FMF. In addition, given the persistent and dramatic marginalization of ethnic minorities in
the FMF, it may seem pointless to draw comparisons with the U.S. Armed Forces,

where ethnic minorities, unlike women, and religious or sexual minorities, are in fact overrepresented (Kane 2005). Furthermore, what may be even more opaque for the U.S.-based audience of this book is the lack of activism or community mobilization around issues of representation for women and Indo-Fijians in the Fiji military. Nevertheless, I hope this chapter has helped stimulate some critical reflection on the following questions: In what circumstances might ethnicity, "race," gender, and militarization intersect in universal ways, and under what conditions might we find their intersections so historically and culturally specific as to defy generalization?

As I argued at the beginning of this chapter, the contemporary militarization of Fiji is closely bound up with economic and political processes (what some would describe as globalization) determined by the governments of nations and of people who may be unaware of their effects on others. As Cynthia Enloe has reminded us, a persistent stream of thought promotes the idea that military institutions can be democratized if they would only more closely reflect the demography and diversity of wider society within their ranks (Enloe 2000, 16).[16] I hope that what I have shared of the story of women and Indo-Fijians in militarized Fiji will help strengthen in others the resolve to question such a proposition.

ACKNOWLEDGMENTS

My sincerest thanks go to Barbara Sutton for inviting me to contribute to this exciting volume and for patiently encouraging me to finish my chapter. Thanks also to Judith Raiskin and all her colleagues at the Center for the Study of Women in Society at the University of Oregon for so warmly hosting me and providing the initial opportunity to air the ideas contained in this chapter as part of their Carlton Raymond and Wilberta Ripley Savage International Studies and Peace seminar series in 2006. Rachel Yates, a promising undergraduate student at Victoria University of Wellington, has ably assisted me with archival newspaper research and provided me with valuable feedback on theoretical and conceptual approaches to my continuing research on militarism in Fiji. My mother, Joan Martin Teaiwa, is my unpaid research assistant extraordinaire, who vigilantly looks out for and shares with me all the contemporary reporting and images of the Fiji military and women soldiers that she finds. A scoping visit to Fiji in the early postcoup period of 2007 was made possible by a grant from the Victoria University of Wellington University Research Fund. My enduring gratitude goes out to my husband Sean for enthusiastically supporting my interest in militarism and feminism—it is always a joy to be able to celebrate the completion of a major piece of writing with Sean and our sons, Manoa and Vaitoa. Finally, I pay my respects to the pioneering feminists and women's rights activists of Fiji, and all the young women of Fiji who, from 1988 to the present, have taken up the challenge of a military career. My work here cannot do justice to the courageousness of theirs, but I hope this chapter will inspire others to want to learn more and perhaps publish their own accounts. I accept full responsibility for any errors of fact or other failings in this chapter.

NOTES

1. It is tempting to describe Fiji as an ethnically diverse society. However, in the context of other South Pacific nations such as Papua New Guinea, Solomon Islands, and Vanuatu,

which may seem to be racially homogenous but in fact are extremely diverse ethnically (e.g., Papua New Guinea has over 800 distinct language groups among its six million citizens), it is more appropriate to distinguish Fiji as having a "racially" diverse population. In this chapter, quotation marks are used around the words "race" and "racially" because the whole concept of race as a biological fact has been contested by scientists and scholars for some time, but these words are the only ones adequate at the moment to describe the particular diversity of Fiji's population.

2. In 1995 the size of the Papua New Guinea Defence Force (PNGDF) was 3,800, only slightly larger than Fiji's during the same period (New Internationalist 1998). With the 2005 estimate, it becomes clear that with a regular force more than six times smaller than Papua New Guinea's, Fiji has the highest per capita ratio of military to civilian population among independent nations of the Pacific Islands region.

3. In postindependence Fiji, colloquial discourse utilized the terms of race. Indigenous Fijians, "Indians," and "others" were described as "races" or "racial" groups, and Fiji was touted as an ideal of "multiracialism." After the 1987 coups, a discourse of ethnicity came to replace the one of race both within ordinary conversation and within the language of government. Postcoup Fiji saw the establishment of the Department of Multiethnic Affairs, which replaced the precoup Ministry of Indian Affairs and combined the concerns of the large minority population of Indo-Fijians with those of smaller minority groups such as the Chinese, Europeans, Melanesians, Micronesians, part Europeans, and others.

4. It was in fact surprising to see only two "others" accounted for in the statistics, as I could from personal acquaintance identify several more "other" males in the Fiji military at the time.

5. While Fiji was still a member of the British Commonwealth, the force was known as the Royal Fiji Military Forces or RFMF. After the first coup of 1987, when Fiji was expelled from the Commonwealth, the name was changed to the Republic of Fiji Military Forces, retaining the same acronym. After elections in 1992, when Fiji was once again able to return to the Commonwealth fold, the R was dropped altogether, and the institution called simply, the Fiji Military Forces or FMF. Fiji society has a penchant for acronyms, and many institutions, from schools (RKS, QVS, SJSS, MBHS) to churches (AG, SDA, LDS) and corporate entities (CML, NBF, MPI), are known by their abbreviations. The FMF shares its letters with Flour Mills of Fiji, which advertises itself by its acronym as well, although in lower case (i.e., fmf).

6. See Teaiwa (2001b) for a discussion of the militarized construction of rugby as the national game of Fiji, and its parallel domination by indigenous Fijian men. There have been no Indo-Fijian rugby players of note at the national level. After the Constitution Review of 1995–1996, as Fiji seemed to be moving toward a new era or "race" conciliation, an Indo-Fijian rugby league was formed with the stated purpose of breeding loyal Indo-Fijian rugby warriors for the nation. This initiative has yet to bear fruit, but in the meantime, Indo-Fijians have thrown their full support behind the national rugby team both at the level of the individual fan and as corporate sponsors. Some of Fiji's most well-known Indo-Fijian-owned businesses have begun to make sizable investments in indigenous Fijian and Pacific Islander rugby development. The best example is Punja's sponsorship of the (Fiji, Tonga, and Samoa) Pacific Islanders rugby team in 2004.

7. Growing up in Fiji, I was aware from an early age of a particularly close relationship between soldiers and (civilian) nurses. It was thought that the two professions were highly compatible on a social scale, and members of each profession considered the

other desirable life partners. This was manifested in the fraternizing that took place around regularly sponsored dance parties and socials and was evidenced in the significant number of married households made up of soldiers and nurses. In Enloe's terms (2000), the nurse's role becomes militarized as consensual sexual partner or wife for the soldier. A more specific and customarily informed role for women in relation to the military surrounds the practice of launching or blessing the vessels in Fiji's small naval fleet with a Fijian ritual known as *cere*. This ceremony involves older or married Fijian women charging boisterously around the vessel with reams of cloth billowing at their sides. The last reported performance of *cere* took place in 1995 (Teaiwa 2001b, 2005).

8. The newspaper reports that 45 women were accepted for officer training but only 41 completed the course (*Fiji Times* 1988c; Ravu 1988, 8). The figure of 45 does not match the list of 41 names published in the *Fiji Times* (1988d) and the 42 reported verbally by Fiji women in the military in 1997 (Kau et al. 1999). The discrepancies will have to be followed up with research into official military records.

9. The remaining 20 percent of the military constituted a so-called nation-building force (Senibulu 2005, 45). One female officer was posted on a six-month tour of peacekeeping duties to the Sinai in 1995. Another female officer replaced her, and a further one was scheduled to replace her in 1996 (Fiji 1997, 75).

10. Two of these, however, were personally known to me as women of mixed Tongan and Indo-Fijian heritage.

11. It is possible that Major Davina Chan, to whom Senibulu refers in her thesis, was awarded her officer's commission by the army after the Bureau of Statistics data were compiled (Senibulu 2005, 59).

12. From the 1970s onward, there has been a lingering discomfort around the term *feminist* in Fiji women's organizations (e.g., V. Griffen 1989).

13. There has been no feminist revision of Fiji's history to date, and no major survey of contemporary developments in the Fiji women's movement. Amratlal et al. (1975), Gokal (1978), and V. Griffen (1989) are exemplary of early attempts at raising awareness about women's issues and profiling women leaders at both the community and national levels. Knapman's history of white women in Fiji (1986) remains the only sustained examination of women in Fiji's history, and Robert Nicole's thesis (2006) on people's resistance in the colonial era includes an examination of women's resistive acts. A great deal of political writing by Fiji feminists and pro-democracy activists has emerged in the last thirty years (e.g., A. Griffen 1997; Emberson-Bain 1994), but those same feminists have not prioritized documenting their own stories. One focused analysis of women's NGOs in Fiji lays a heavy-handed theoretical critique over their organizational practices and intellectual rigor—in effect, charging them with mimicry of international aid donor-provided templates at the expense of developing more organic local models for social change (Riles 2000).

14. The late Amelia Rokotuivuna was an indigenous Fijian woman activist who is often acknowledged by early nonindigenous feminists as a catalytic influence on their praxis. See her brief biography in Gokal (1978). Nonindigenous women active in the early phrase were, for example, Vanessa Griffen, a key facilitator of national and regional conferences for women from the 1970s through the 1980s (e.g., Griffen 1989); Peni Moore and Shamima Ali, founding members of the Fiji Women's Crisis Centre and Fiji Women's Rights Movement (Tuidomo, Ali, and Moore 1988); and 'Atu Emberson-Bain and Claire Slatter, along with Vanessa Griffen, writers of pivotal texts using feminist analysis to critique development agendas that undermine women's well-being (Emberson-Bain 1994; Emberson-Bain and Slatter 1995).

15. Since the 1990s, lawyer Imrana Jalal has joined Shamima Ali as two of the most high-profile Indo-Fijian women and feminists in the country (see Jalal 1998; Teaiwa 2001a).

16. The same point is made by Katzenstein and Reppy (1999).

REFERENCES

Amratlal, Jyoti, Eta Baro, Vanessa Griffen, and Geet Bala Singh. 1975. *Women's Role in Fiji*. Suva: South Pacific Social Sciences Association in association with the Pacific Women's Conference.

BBC News. 2000. "Women Soldiers Could Serve on Front Line." October 2. http://news.bbc.co.uk/1/hi/uk/912738.stm (accessed May 6, 2007).

——. 2004. "Fiji Agrees to Protect UN in Iraq." October 20. http://news.bbc.co.uk/2/hi/middle_east/3761448.stm (accessed May 6, 2007).

Brooke, James. 2005. "On Farthest U.S. Shores, Iraq Is a Way to Dream." *New York Times*, July 31.

Camacho, Keith Lujan. 2005. "Cultures of Commemoration: The Politics of War, Memory and History in the Mariana Islands." Ph.D. diss., University of Hawai'i.

Dean, Eddie, and Stan Ritova. 1988. *Rabuka: No Other Way*. Suva: Marketing Team International.

Emberson-Bain, 'Atu, ed. 1994. *Sustainable Development or Malignant Growth? Perspectives of Pacific Island Women*. Suva: Marama Publications.

Emberson-Bain, 'Atu, and Claire Slatter. 1995. *Labouring under the Law*. Suva: Fiji Women's Rights Movement.

Enloe, Cynthia. 1990. *Bananas, Beaches and Bases: Making Feminist Sense of International Politics*. Berkeley: University of California Press.

——. 2000. *Maneuvers: The International Politics of Militarizing Women's Lives*. Berkeley: University of California Press.

Field, Michael. 2006. "Military a Threat to Peace, Says Fiji's PM." *Dominion Post*, March 15, A10.

Field, Michael, Tupeni Baba, and Unaisi Nabobo-Baba. 2005. *Speight of Violence: Inside Fiji's 2000 Coup*. Auckland: Reed Publishing.

Fiji Bureau of Statistics. 2006. "Paid Employment by Occupational Categories, Ethnic Group and Sex, 2000." Suva, Fiji.

Fiji Parliament. 1997. *Defending Fiji: Defence White Paper*. Parliamentary Paper no. 3. Suva, Fiji: Parliament of Fiji.

Fiji Times. 1988a. "Army Looks for Female Officers." January 14, 3.

——. 1988b. "Editorial Comment: Women's Rights." March 8.

——. 1988c. "Eyes Right!" April 2, 1.

——. 1988d. "List of Applicants Passing Selection Board 1/88." February 1, Classifieds.

——. 1988e. "Officer Training for Young Women in the Fiji Military Forces." January 14, classifieds.

——. 2007a. "Fiji Soldiers Earn $750,000 for 3 Month Tour in Iraq." April 18. http://pidp.eastwestcenter.org/pireport/2007/April/04-19-15.htm (accessed April 28, 2007).

——. 2007b. "Heffernan Takes Military to Court." March 16, 2.

Gokal, Sumitra. 1978. *Women of Fiji*. Suva: Lotu Pasifika Productions.

Griffen, Arlene, ed. 1997. *With Heart and Nerve and Sinew: Post-Coup Writing from Fiji*. Suva: Christmas Club.

Griffen, Vanessa, ed. 1989. *Women, Development and Empowerment: A Pacific Feminist Perspective*. Kuala Lumpur: Asian and Pacific Development Centre.

Haglelgam, John. 2005. "Duty, Honor and Country? Values Aren't the Same for FSM Soldiers." *Pacific Magazine*, December. http://www.pacificislands.cc/pm12005/pmdefault.php?urlarticleid=0004 (accessed May 6, 2007).

Halapua, Winston. 2003. *Tradition, Lotu and Militarism in Fiji*. Lautoka: Fiji Institute of Applied Studies.

Hattori, Anne. 2004. *Colonial Dis-Ease: U.S. Navy and Health Policies and the Chamorros of Guam, 1898–1941*. Honolulu: University of Hawai'i Press.

Howlett, R. A. 1948. *The History of the Fiji Military Forces, 1939–45, Compiled from Official Records and Diaries by Lieutenant R. A. Howlett*. Christchurch, New Zealand: Crown Agents for the Colonies on behalf of the Government of Fiji.

Indian Army. N.d. "History." http://indianarmy.nic.in/arhist1.htm (accessed May 5, 2007).

Jalal, Imrana. 1998. *Law for Pacific Women: A Legal Rights Handbook*. Suva: Fiji Women's Rights Movement.

Kane, Tim. 2005. "Who Bears the Burden? Demographic Characteristics of U.S. Military Recruits before and after 9/11." In *Center for Data Analysis Report #05–08*. November 7. Washington, DC: Heritage Foundation. http://www.heritage.org/Research/National Security/upload/95512_1.pdf (accessed January 27, 2008).

Kaplan, Martha. 2001. "Blood on the Grass and Dogs Will Speak: Ritual Politics and the Nation in Independent Fiji." In *Represented Communities: Fiji and World Decolonization,* by John D. Kelly and Martha Kaplan, 121–144. Chicago: University of Chicago Press.

Katzenstein, Mary Fainsod, and Judith Reppy, eds. 1999. *Beyond Zero Tolerance: Discrimination in Military Culture*. Lanham, MD: Rowman and Littlefield.

Kau, Naina, Ana Rokomoti, Sera Motokilagi, and Silipa Tagicaki. 1999. Panel discussion in SE201, Women in Society. University of the South Pacific.

Kelsey, Jane. 2006. "Taking Nurses and Soldiers to Market." Opening plenary paper, Fifteenth Annual Conference on Feminist Economics, Sydney. July 7–9.

Kent, Noel J. 1993. *Hawai'i: Islands under the Influence*. Honolulu: University of Hawai'i Press.

Knapman, Claudia. 1986. *White Women in Fiji, 1835–1930: The Ruin of Empire?* Sydney: Allen and Unwin.

Lal, Brij V. 1983. *Girmitiyas: The Origins of the Fiji Indians*. Canberra: Journal of Pacific History.

——. 1988. *Power and Prejudice: The Making of the Fiji Crisis*. Wellington: New Zealand Institute of International Affairs.

Lal, Brij V., and Michael Pretes. 2001. *Coup: Reflections on the Political Crisis in Fiji*. Canberra: Pandanus Books.

Lal, Victor. 1990. *Fiji, Coups in Paradise: Race, Politics and Military Intervention*. London: Zed Books.

——. 2007. "Military Beatings, Command and Responsibility." *Sunday*, March 11, 5.

Liava'a, Christine. 2006. "The Great War Forum." Comment posted on January 22. http://1914–1918.invisionzone.com/forums/lofiversion/index.php/t45561.htm (accessed May 6, 2007).

Maclellan, Nic. 2006. "Fiji, the War in Iraq, and the Privatisation of Pacific Island Security." http://www.nautilus.org/~rmit/forum-reports/0611a-maclellan.html (accessed May 6, 2007).

Nadan, Keshwan. 2007. "Crime Rate" (letter to the editor). *Fiji Times*, March 27, 10.

Naidu, Vijay. 1986. "Militarization and Nuclearization of the Pacific: A Call to Strengthen the Anti-Nuclear Movement." Paper presented at Pacific Week, October 4–10.

Nathan, Amy. 2004. *Count on Us: American Women in the Military*. Washington, DC: National Geographic.

Nawadra, Tevita. 1995. *"Ai Matai" Malaya: 1st Battalion, Fiji Infantry Regiment, Far-East Land Forces, 1952–1956*. Suva: Republic of Fiji Military Forces.

New Internationalist. 1998. *The World Guide, 1997/98: A View from the South*. Oxford: Instituto del Tercer Mundo.

Nicole, Robert. 2006. "Disturbing Histories: Aspects of Resistance in Early Colonial Fiji, 1874–1914." Ph.D. diss., University of Canterbury, New Zealand.

Pacific Concerns Resource Centre. 1999. *Kirisimasi: Na Sotia kei na Lewe ni Mataivalu e Wai ni Viti e na vakatovotovo iyaragi nei Peritania mai Kirisimasi/Fijian Troops at Britain's Christmas Island Nuclear Tests*, edited by Losena Tubanavau-Salabula, Josua M. Namoce, and Nic Maclellan. Suva: Pacific Concerns Resource Centre.

Ratuva, Steven. 2007. "Couped up Again: The Anatomy of the 2006 Military Takeover in Fiji." Paper presented in Va'aomanu Pasifika Seminar Series, Victoria University of Wellington, New Zealand. March 20.

Ratuva, Sitiveni. 2000. "Analysis: The Failed Rebel Coup: Episode 2." *Wansolwara*. http://www.usp.ac.fj/journ/docs/news/nius3090shoot.html (accessed May 6, 2007).

Ravu, Joseph. 1988. "Army's New Recruits." *Fiji Times*, April 2, 8.

Ravuvu, Asesela. 1988. *Fijians at War, 1939–1945*. Suva: Institute of Pacific Studies of the University of the South Pacific.

Reeves, Sir Paul, Tomasi Rayalu Vakatora, and Brij Vilash Lal. 1996. *The Fiji Islands towards a United Future: The Report of the Fiji Constitution Review Commission 1996*. Parliamentary Paper No. 34. Suva: Parliament of Fiji.

Riles, Annelise. 2000. *The Network Inside Out*. Ann Arbor: University of Michigan Press.

Robertson, Robbie, and Akosita Tamanisau. 1988. *Fiji: Shattered Coups*. Leichardt, New South Wales: Australian Council for Overseas Aid.

Scarr, Deryck. 1988. *Fiji: Politics of Illusion, the Military Coups in Fiji*. Kensington, New South Wales: New South Wales University Press.

Senibulu, Luisa Matanisiga. 2005. "Professionalism in the Military: A Case Study of the Fiji Military Forces." M.A. thesis, University of the South Pacific, Suva, Fiji.

Sharpham, John. 2000. *Rabuka of Fiji: The Authorized Biography of Major-General Sitiveni Rabuka*. Rockhampton, Queensland, Australia: Central Queensland University.

Sutherland, William. 1992. *Beyond the Politics of Race: An Alternative History of Fiji to 1992*. Canberra: Department of Political Science, Research School of Pacific and Asian Studies, Australian National University.

Teaiwa, Teresia K. 2001a. "Imrana Jalal and Shamima Ali." In *20th Century Fiji: People Who Shaped the Nation*, ed. Stewart Firth and Darryl Tarte, 207. Suva: USP Solutions, the University of the South Pacific.

——. 2001b. "Militarism, Tourism and the Native: Articulations in Oceania." Ph.D. diss., University of California, Santa Cruz.

——. 2004. "Lomani Viti: Reflections on Patriotic Literature from Post-Coup(s) Fiji." *SPAN: Journal of the South Pacific Association for Commonwealth Literature and Language Studies* 53: 82–104.

——. 2005. "Articulated Cultures: Militarism and Masculinities in Fiji during the Mid-1990s." *Fijian Studies* 3(2): 201–222.

——. 2008. "Globalizing and Gendered Forces: The Contemporary Militarization of Pacific/Oceania." In *Gender and Globalization in Asia and the Pacific: Method, Practice, Theory, Hawai'i*, edited by Kathy Ferguson and Monique Mironescu. Honolulu: University of Hawai'i Press.

Trask, Haunani-Kay. 1999. *From a Native Daughter: Colonialism and Sovereignty in Hawai'i*. Rev. ed. Honolulu: University of Hawai'i Press.

Tuidomo, Veniana, Shamima Ali, and Peni Moore. 1988. "Women Protest." *Fiji Times*, March 11.

Underwood, Robert. 1985. "Excursions into Inauthenticity: The Chamorros of Guam." In "Mobility and Identity in the Island Pacific," ed. Murray Chapman and Philip S. Morrison. Special issue. *Pacific Viewpoint* 26: 160–184.

United Kingdom. 2003. *Hansard Parliamentary Debates.* Commons, 5th ser. vol. 412, col. 515 (November 3). http://www.publications.parliament.uk/pa/cm200203/cmhansrd/vo031103/debtext/31103-01.htm (accessed May 6, 2007).

U.S. Navy. Naval Health Research Center. 2005. "Department of Defense HIV/AIDS Prevention Program, Papua New Guinea Yearly Country Report." http://www.nhrc.navy.mil/programs/dhapp/countryreports/yearly05/papuanewguinea05.pdf (accessed May 6, 2007).

8

===

Plunder as Statecraft

Militarism and Resistance in Neocolonial Africa

PATRICIA McFADDEN

In this chapter I situate, both theoretically and empirically, the notions of military rampancy and plunder as historically recognizable features of the state, with specific reference to their deployment within the current process of class consolidation on the African continent. This deliberate, inherently violent process—most dramatically reflected in the ubiquity of wars and through the seeming normalization of impunity—is juxtaposed with the struggles for an inclusive and secure idea and practice of citizenship across the societies of the African continent.

My arguments draw directly, in conceptual and activist terms, from a vibrant tradition of debate on various political and theoretical positions and experiences with regard to the state and militarization in Africa, ranging from colonial (and precolonial) times to the present. These debates provide an invaluable perspective from which to consider the state as it is defined and used within the specific context of the African continent. In this regard, my perspectives are informed predominantly by the thinking and visioning of African scholars and activists located within the purview of the state as well as outside its boundaries.

The Proverbial Elephant in the Africanist Academy

Western academic discourse and policy analysis about Africa derive largely from a liberal approach and are predicated on an often undeclared pro-capitalist stance, which tends to *peculiarize* the state in Africa by drawing curiously from anthropological representations and racist characterizations that are old-fashioned yet persistently popular. This Eurocentric approach manifests itself in a particular analysis (both conservative and liberal) that describes the state on the continent as the "African state" and tends to conflate moralistic notions of individual or group behavior with those of the state as an overarching, objective phenomenon at a national and continental level.

This developmentalist literature on African societies and their political systems in the Western academy tends to be based on certain generalizations regarding the African state that for the most part derive from an established discourse informed by conservative, colonial-inspired racist biases about Africans and their political behavior. Although increasing numbers of scholars from the "former colonies" have rebutted such patronizing, reactionary discourses with scathing and often brilliant critiques (Said 1994; Ahmad 2000), the persistence of conservative approaches and perspectives on the state in Africa indicates a much larger challenge than first meets the intellectual eye.

Such representations of Africa, which are drawn from the romanticized travelogues and journals of colonial adventurers, reflect the unacknowledged exotica that accompanies the often vilifying descriptions of the state and of those Africans who occupy it at the present time. This adoption of a conceptual consensus about the supposed characteristics of the state in Africa, which pervades the writing of Africanists in the West and has frequently drawn the ire of African male scholars,[1] lends itself to a deeply conservative and often facile approach to matters of state practice on the continent.

Conservative discourses pervade Western scholarship even in supposedly progressive analyses of African politics. An excellent example of this genre is a recent publication by Richard Sandbrook (2000), containing the beguiling inscription on the dedication page that encapsulates the exotic imagery often accompanying such liberal analyses of African politics.[2] Among the most disconcerting features of such scholarship is the inaccuracy of the paradigm through which the state on the continent is framed. The critique of liberal notions of the state and its rhetoric of inclusiveness and universal protections, especially in relation to particular classes and social groups within societies of the West, is well established, albeit still largely contentious. Increasingly, in North America and Europe such critiques have influenced and informed the emergence of lively debates concerning the relationship (or lack thereof) between citizens and the state with regard to issues of security, health care, reproductive rights, sexual choices, and the like.

The often-repeated assertion that the African state is a corrupted and mismanaged state derives its supposed credibility from the largely unarticulated (and unquestioned) assumption that those who control the state in Africa today inherited a functioning, Westernized (read democratic) state at the moment of independence, which they have tainted and destroyed. In other words, the allegedly civilizing project of colonialism has been undone by the reckless and unstatesmanly behavior of the likes of Moi in Kenya, Mugabe in Zimbabwe, and Kaunda in Zambia.

However, the very construction of the state on that continent as the African state is a generic expression that, in my opinion, creates the fundamental pretext of peculiarity, which in turn feeds a range of often-repeated generalizations, most of which are erroneous and anchored in colonial representations of politics of Africa. In addition to parochializing the phenomenon of the state and dislocating it from Africa's long historical trajectory prior to the colonial moment, such constructions of the state as peculiarly African imbue the analysis with sensibilities and features of Otherness, conceptually and rhetorically placing Africa and state politics outside the realm of more conventional discourses about states as phenomena that bear certain universally shared features. The use of the moment of colonial conquest and occupation to signal the emergence of state politics in Africa is itself a Westernized, Eurocentric notion and theoretical invention (Davidson 2001).[3] From a more radical, feminist perspective, this extensive developmentalist genre has not yielded any valuable insights, particularly in terms of clarifying the urgent issues emerging between discontented communities of African citizens and a rapidly consolidating neocolonial state across the continent.

The "natural" relationship between the state and the military in Africa can be traced back to feudal, precolonial times. During the colonial period, this relationship was further consolidated by the overt collaboration between these two arms of class rule in every instance of European occupation on the continent. Therefore, the construction of the state in Africa as somehow pathologically flawed and deficient in relation to the state elsewhere, particularly in comparison to the state in the West, smacks of a double standard. More specifically, such judgments are basically false and dangerously misleading. Repetitions of the same obfuscating, partial constructions of the state as dysfunctional, highly conflict-ridden, and violent (Engel, Gentili, and Chabal 2005; Basedu, Erdmann, and Mehler 2006) in the African context sidestep the debates and imagining that African scholarship desperately needs to provoke a transformational agenda and practice.

Africans inherited a colonial state that represented and performed all that colonialism meant for subjugated, exploited, and disposed people. It was a fundamentally undemocratic, racist, exclusionary institutional and ideological system, constituted of deeply racist, misogynistic relationships of power and suppression. Additionally, it was a socially, legally, and politically inadequate state system. This one-sidedness, according to Eboe Hutchful (1991), was reflected at the level of state–society relations as well as in terms of intrastate relations. Colonists established and used the state for the explicit and unambiguously ruthless plunder and extraction of human labor and wealth, which, to a large extent, benefited Western societies over a period of several hundred years (Rodney 1974).

Colonial military structures, fashioned after the systems of the colonizing society in class and racial terms, operated on behalf of the state. These structures expressly sought to accumulate wealth through the waging of war and deployed rampancy against the bodies and sexualities of African women in particular,

thereby laying the basis for the furtherance of such practices during this particular moment of neocolonial class rule.[4]

To acknowledge this fact in its most radical implications would require a
major shift in the kinds of analytical approaches adopted and the kinds of proposals drawn from studies of the state on the continent. It would also require an
acknowledgment of the kinds of deep-seated inequalities in terms of race, class,
gender, and other identities that characterize the relationship between the
bourgeois liberal state in the West and its citizens. Such an acknowledgment
would have major repercussions for future intellectual and activist agendas in the
Western and African academy. As Hutchful explains:

> The primarily administrative and extractive relationship between the
> colonial state and society, emphasizing the element of coercion and
> command, left large areas of state/society relations undefined. The
> transfer of the modern state form was both institutionally and culturally
> selective. . . . In particular, the colonial state failed to instill notions of
> the legitimate purpose and limits of state action, of acceptable proce-
> dures for gaining and maintaining power, and of the place and rights of
> the individual in the political system . . . or to elaborate effective sym-
> bolic support for state authority based on concepts of the utility, rele-
> vance and distinctiveness of the state. The reason for this of course was
> that the colonial state was not a "political" state in the normal sense of
> deriving its sense of legitimation and authority from society or being
> concerned with the representation and pursuit of a "national" interest.
> (1991, 185–186)

Everywhere, the fundamental elements of the colonial state as a vehicle of plunder and class privilege, as well as the means of suppression and violation of the
working people—through the use of legal and extralegal coercion and force—were
retained, reentrenched, or redressed in a language of liberal inclusive rhetoric
and universal embrace (Alexander 2002; Mafeje 1992; Hutchful and Bathily 1998;
Hansen 1987).

We must recognize that what became the neocolonial state in Africa (and
elsewhere in the former colonies) not only served the purposes of colonial conquest and surplus extraction but continues to operate primarily on behalf of
global and national class, gendered, and raced interests. Everywhere on the continent, without exception, special arrangements were made and deals were
hashed out between those who eventually had to hand over the state and those
who inherited it.

In Zimbabwe, for example, after a long and bitter war of liberation,
the"warring parties" composed of, on the one hand, the Rhodesian regime
led by Ian Smith, supported by the United Kingdom of Great Britain, and on the
other, the liberation movements ZANU and ZAPU,[5] led by Robert Mugabe and

Joshua Nkomo, respectively, entered into a deal, enshrined in the Lancaster Agreement, that came to serve as the independence constitution of Zimbabwe. The primary function of this agreement was to ensure access to the state by an impatient aspirant group of black men whose class anxieties could only be assuaged by the acquisition of wealth and the exercise of political power in celebration of independence. Most important for Smith and his flock of white settlers, the agreement guaranteed protection of their immense wealth in land, control over mineral and forest resources, and maintenance of a lifestyle second only to that enjoyed by whites in South Africa. It was only in 1998, with the threat of the political displacement of Mugabe and the ZANU Patriotic Front by the working poor of Zimbabwe through their occupancy of white-controlled or white-owned land, that the crisis around property and white privilege erupted in Zimbabwe—a crisis exacerbated by Tony Blair's alleged duplicity in fulfilling the terms of the agreement in favor of the new black ruling class (see McFadden 2005; Hammar, Raftopoulos, and Jensen 2003).

In South Africa, a similar agreement was worked out among the African National Congress and the governments of the United States, the United Kingdom, and various Scandinavian countries, culminating in the Sunset Clause within the independence agreement. This agreement assured not only that white property and wealth would be protected by the incoming black rulers but that the military would continue to play the dominant role it had assumed under apartheid. Most importantly, the agreement forestalled a repeat of the Zimbabwe scenario whereby white property would be "confiscated" by an "unruly rogue state" (Alexander 2002; Campbell 1998; Sanders 2006).

In countries such as Angola and Mozambique, the socialist project had served well in mobilizing the rural and urban working communities to support the liberation struggles against Portuguese colonialism. However, wars of attrition and destabilization, initiated mainly from apartheid South Africa and Namibia (then an apartheid-controlled territory), were launched against the governments and people of these newly independent countries in order to achieve what Chester Crocker quaintly referred to as "constructive engagement"—code for the reentrenchment of white-settler, U.S., and other imperial interests and privileges in the Southern African region at the moment of independence, 1975–1994 (Crocker 1992; Hanlon 1991; Minter 1994).

By acquiring property and wealth, as in countries like Zimbabwe and South Africa, for example, those who occupy the state have been able to exert control and surveillance over the populace, particularly with regard to the public expression of resistance and agency by those groups that have historically been kept farthest from a direct relationship with the state. The exceptionally brutal, racist, gendered, and homophobic ideology and practice of the white colonial state on the continent specifically reinforced the already existing feudal hierarchies within African societies. In so-called sub-Saharan Africa, this patriarchal cocktail created a moment of mutually beneficial contact and collusion, particularly through the intersection of race, class, and gender, thereby entrenching the essential features that define neocolonialism in its present form across most of the continent (Meena 1992; Imam, Mama, and Sow 1997; McClintock 1993).

This dual scenario of complicity between emerging black elites and privileged white settlers around property and maintenance of the status quo in some instances (South Africa, Zimbabwe, and Namibia), and the attempt to restructure the state and property relations as part of a socialist program on the other (Angola and Mozambique), ultimately resulted in situations that have left the working people of all these countries economically and politically excluded. In each case, the military has been increasingly strengthened and well positioned within the state, at the behest of those who rule (Collins 2006).

However, due to a mutually reinforcing relationship between the dominant Western academy and the media, especially at this time of the so-called war on terror, the rhetoric and stereotypes replicated by both of these powerful sites in the United States and Europe had until recently acquired an almost sacrosanct quality. The hegemony of conservative and often vitriolic propaganda about the "Other" and "their moral flaws" was overwhelming and deeply perturbing to many radicals in the academy as well as in the wider civil society.

Thus, the devastation of African societies through long wars, initially of resistance to colonialism and apartheid, and later as a consequence of the realignment of forces to serve Western military and consumer interests, has been casually represented in various media as something inherent to Africans and their social realities. Much of what is offered as intellectual argument and empirical "truth" about the continent largely regurgitates the familiar partialities that characterize the views of people who perceive themselves as better than the rest of the world. Martin Meredith's *The Fate of Africa: From the Hopes of Freedom to the Heart of Despair* (2005) represents a typical example of voyeuristic journalism that churns out tirades that fit nicely into the media stereotypes while claiming to represent a liberal viewpoint on Africa. Similarly, in "Why Is Africa Still Poor?" an article reviewing Meredith's book in the *Nation,* Andrew Rice begins with a slogan he claims can be found "all over Africa" (this in itself is hyperbolic), which reads, "NO CONDITION IS PERMANENT." He then proceeds to debunk this obvious truth by claiming that "this is true, but some are recurring. Tyranny in Zimbabwe, famine in Niger, a constitutional coup in Togo, rampant corruption in Kenya, protesters shot in Ethiopia, an epidemic in Angola, civil war in Sudan—these are this year's headlines, but if you think you've heard it all before, you have" (2005, n.p.). In one fell swoop, he not only suggests that he has said everything about an amazingly diverse and dynamic continent, but he flattens the political, economic, cultural, social, and linguistic landscape. This dual dismissal provides the U.S. public, mostly young readers, with their daily dose of narrow-minded, exoticized, patronizing half-truths, which serve as the source of "knowledge" about Africa and the world outside the West for millions of U.S. citizens.

The op-ed pieces that regularly appear in newspapers like the *New York Times* and in magazines like the *New Yorker* reflect much of the same liberalism, repeating the tired racist-inspired diatribes. They refuse to delve further into the historical and financial forces that continue to exert so much dominance over the lives of Africans and sabotage, increasingly through militaristic means, any efforts to break out of the stranglehold of neoimperial control and exploitation. Silvia Federici explains why so few scholars and journalists in the West see the links between the various weapons that have been used to occupy and exploit the societies of the South, particularly on the African continent, among which are structural adjustment programs, trade liberalization, privatization, and intellectual property rights. She argues that "a further reason why the marriage between war and globalization, the form that imperialism takes today, is not more evident is that most of the new 'globalization wars' have been fought on the African continent, whose current history is systematically distorted by the media which blame every crisis on the Africans' alleged 'backwardness,' 'tribalism' and incapacity to achieve democratic institutions" (Federici 2005, n.p.). Michael Parenti aptly summarizes what has been described as the "dumbing down of America": "The difference between what US citizens think their rulers are doing in the world and what these rulers actually are doing is one of the great propaganda achievements of history" (2006, iii).

Radical Western Traditions of Scholarship on the State in Africa

Radical scholarship on Africa in the United States and Europe arises from a long and admirable tradition of critical analysis about the colonization and plunder of the human and material resources of Africa (and other societies of the South). An ongoing critique of imperialism, in its most current form as globalization, is growing stronger, particularly as the United States and the countries of the European Union, which are engaged in wars in Afghanistan and Iraq, sink even deeper into the quagmire of inevitable defeat. The links between war/militarism and economic imperial restructuring of the world (globalization), through World Bank–and International Monetary Fund–driven structural adjustment programs (SAPs) and policies imposed on and or accepted by virtually all African governments over the past two decades, have been made by outstanding radical scholars such as Jean-Francois Bayart (1999), Walden Bello (1994), Atilio Boron (2005), James Petras and Henry Veltmeyer (2005), and numerous other scholars whose radical credentials are well established in the Left academy internationally. On the African continent, Ghana provides an excellent example of "voluntary restructuring," while Mozambique is an equally good example of "coerced restructuring."

However, like most radical males, these writers make scant reference to the critical significance of feminist analysis within the Western academy, let alone give any indication that African feminists have opinions or thoughts about the struggles in which their societies are engaged. Interestingly, feminist scholars in the Western academy, particularly those who come out of the radical Left traditions of socialist/Marxist scholarship, have developed an important discourse around the notions and practices of international relations, diplomacy, national security, and militarism (Tickner 1992, 2001; Peterson 1992; Enloe 2000).

Silvia Federici's current work, which brilliantly analyses the intersections among neoimperial agendas, the restructuring of African economic and wider social environments through SAPs, and the globalization of war in its various new forms, reflects the emergence of a deeper and more activist-oriented analysis and understanding of the world and what needs to be done by those who seek political transformation in the United States and Europe in particular. She concludes her article "War, Globalisation and Reproduction" by arguing that we must go beyond the acknowledgment that death, disease, hunger, and destruction are daily realities for the majority of people on the planet:

> More than that, structural adjustment, the most universal program in the Third World today, the one that, in all its forms (including the African Growth and Opportunity Act), represents the contemporary face of capitalism and colonialism, is war. Thus, the program of the anti-war movement must include the elimination of structural adjustment in all its many forms if war, and the imperialistic project it embodies, is to finally come to an end. (Federici 2005, n.p.)

However, Federici does not reference a single text by African feminists. Nor does she refer to the extensive work of African feminists and other gender/civil society activists who are challenging the state and its related institutions, critiquing notions and practices of hegemonic masculinity (Obano 2005; Salo and Lewis 2002; Isis-Wicce 2005), questioning the normalization of war, and escalating military budgets in various countries, and proposing alternatives to militarization through debates and conversations about peace and postconflict reconstruction. Therefore, although a traditional radical political economic analysis of war, imperialism, and globalization reveals emerging expressions of political consciousness in a general sense, the lack of a critical feminist analysis and the failure to recognize its existence, particularly on a continent where imperial jingoism is intensifying,[6] miss a crucial element in the visioning of transformational discourses and activities. It is partly as a response to the wider inadequacies of political analyses about Africa, as well as in recognition of the existence of a radical African feminist critique concerning the state, militarism, and citizenship on the continent, that this chapter was conceptualized and crafted.

Radical but Partial African Scholarship on the State and Militarization

Discursive continuities exist between established Western approaches to the African state and the production of a rich and diverse genre of political-economy analyses, most of which reflect the specific historical and neocolonial experiences and debates about the state on the continent. This well-established tradition of African scholarship (which is at least a century old, beginning during the early twentieth century among the most eloquent of the anticolonial nationalists) encompasses a range of perspectives and imaginaries largely unknown or unacknowledged in the narratives of most scholarship within the U.S. academy in particular.

Many African male scholars on the continent still adopt and apply the analytical frameworks crafted by Africanists on the state and the military without the necessary critically diverse gaze that an anticolonial consciousness ought to have invoked half a century after independence for most of their societies.[7] However, it is important to note the distinctions between Western "Africanist" scholarship on the "African state" and a flourishing, often vibrant, and impassioned discourse that has emerged out of the African academy, also reflected in the United States within African studies departments, which merits recognition and affirmation in its own right (Nzongola-Ntalaja and Lee 1997; Mandaza 1999; Martin and West 1999).

The latter scholarly tradition is remarkably insightful and reflective both of the narratives of theoretical contestation within the liberation movements of eastern, central, and southern Africa in particular (Mafeje 1992; Nzongola-Ntalaja and Lee 1997; Mamdani 1996; Mandaza 1999; Ake 1978; Shivji 1991) and of the often direct encounters that many African male scholars experienced in their particular societies during the first years of independence. Of particular interest is the profusion of research and analysis that has been undertaken on the contentious relationships among the state, constitutionalism, and the military in numerous societies of the continent over the past half century (Shivji 1991; Oloka-Onyango and Peter 2004; Hutchful and Bathily 1998). Such scholarship presents the state in Africa as a complex, dynamic, crisis-driven, deeply contested site—a site onto which hundreds of millions of Africans have extrapolated their dreams and visions for a better life, especially in those societies where people had to engage in liberation wars in order to initiate the process of independence and establish a semblance of democratic institutions.

Societies like those of Kenya, Namibia, Zimbabwe, Angola, Mozambique, Guinea Bissau, and South Africa—where long, brutal wars against colonial terror and occupation were fought and many Africans lost their lives—have become archetypal examples of the deepening contestations between state-positioned elites and citizens who are demanding a more democratic relationship with the state as the controller and assumed custodian of national wealth and institutional resources (Macamo 2005; Alexander 2002; Nyamnjoh 2006).

Nevertheless, although numerous research and tertiary institutions in various countries of the continent support gender research, none have positioned themselves as openly in support of feminist scholarship or of women's radical political ideas concerning the state in Africa and the manner in which ruling classes occupy and deploy the state against the majority of Africans who are women. Some male scholars, especially younger male researchers, claim to be engaged in feminist analysis of African politics, but generally they have not had the courage to undertake feminist analyses or adopt radical/critical approaches to politics and power beyond the mainstreaming of gender as a notion and practice related to identity and culture. A recent attempt by the Council for the Development of Economic and Social Research in Africa (CODESRIA) to position its work as feminist failed dismally on closer inspection and sadly reflected more of a backlash against feminist radical analysis and activism rather than ideological progress on the part of these CODESRIA scholars.[8] Therefore, in general, African male scholarship on the state and the various issues that swirl around this deeply contested notion and political site of power remains largely Western-liberal influenced in terms of the issues that it situates as having critical value in understanding the state on the continent. The predominance of discussions about electoral systems, political parties, constitutionalism, and militarism within narrowly defined hetero-normative notions of masculinity and power, and the almost total neglect of gender as a vibrant and critical construct that transforms social analysis, have deeply undermined the ability of African male scholarship to break new ground and expand the analysis of the state and militarization on the continent.

A rare, albeit limited, exception has been the work of Horace Campbell (2003) and Eboe Hutchful (1989, 1991), two black male political scientists whose attempts to expand the parameters of the debate on the state in Africa bear particular mention. The former's work reflects a courageous application of the language and uses of feminist critical analysis in a study of patriarchal state occupancy and plunder in the context of Zimbabwe. The latter's analysis of the exclusionary features of the neocolonial state provides interesting and important insights into my own work on the historical processes and deliberate distancing of African women from the idea and practice of citizenship, especially during the colonial period (McFadden 2007).

Focusing on the theorization of the colonial state and the limitations of this transplanted "bourgeois constitutional state" onto the colonies for the explicit service of white settlers' needs and entitlements, Hutchful exposes the inadequacies of the colonial state as a foundation for the practice of constitutional democracy and popular participation in the future politics of African societies. He identifies the problem of a lack of "state–society relations" and argues that "the lack of an organic and elaborated connection between state and society created a large area of vacancy and ambiguity in relations between these two spheres. Late colonial and post-independence constitutionalism may thus be seen as a process of 'filling in' these spaces and developing appropriate linking mechanisms between state and society" (Hutchful 1991, 186).

Hutchful does not speak specifically to issues of race and gender, and makes only passing mention of women's rights and civil society. Nonetheless, his analysis opens up interesting windows of opportunity in terms of stimulating a more

reflexive consideration of constitutions as contested sites of power that are routinely appropriated by militaries in their desire to occupy the state and consolidate power in the neocolonial period. The examples of Ghana, Togo, Guinea, and
particularly Nigeria have informed a wide-ranging debate on the state, issues of
constitutionalism, and the military across the continent (Hutchful and Bathily
1998).

By exposing the conceptual and structural limitations of the liberal constitutional model, so ubiquitous to colonialism and so widely bemoaned as a
"wasted legacy" by most Western scholars of Africa, Hutchful exposes the
limitations of what he calls "constitutional engineering" and proposes what is an
unusually radical solution to the problem of the state in Africa. "What is
required is the reconstruction of the entire economic, social, and normative
foundation of the state, a task which goes much beyond constitutional engineering" (Hutchful 1991, 189).

Studies on the role and persistence of militarism in Africa since independence have shown how the colonial state incorporated militarization as part of the
colonial practice in every instance of occupation. These studies further uncov-
ered the exclusionary character of the colonial state in relation to the majority of
African people, who were treated as subjects and as mere inputs of production
rather than as active agents who had the capacity to engage with the state and to
participate in civic life (Mamdani 1996).

Intersections of Critical Feminist Discourse
on the State, Militarism, and Class

Most recent, and significantly more interesting in terms of the development of an
alternative "canon," is the emergence of an African feminist epistemological and
activist politics, which is straining against the more parochial Western-
influenced notions of a (peculiar) yet conventional patriarchal state in Africa.
This alternative perspective problematizes and scrutinizes contestations and
power struggles within the state around issues of constitutionalism and militarism. It accomplishes this by interpolating a notion and practice of popular
agency into the process of crafting new and different relationships between those
who occupy and deploy the state for the realization of specific class or secular
agendas and those who are demanding a fulfillment of their identities as citizens
in the transitional moment to postcolonial societies across the continent.

I argue that African women scholars and activists, in particular, feminist
scholar/activists, whose radical political agencies have maintained an unrelent-
ing pressure on the boundaries of the state, are slowly forcing a shift in the institutional and sociocultural definitions and practices of politics within the state
and in the wider social contexts of the African continent. This scholarship resists
the monopolization of scholarship on Africa by Westerners and by African male
scholars at the same time that it makes a critical theoretical intervention in

thinking about present-day neocolonial state practice in Africa (Lewis 2004; Andrade 2002; Hassim 1999).

I situate my analysis of the state in Africa and its deployment of rampancy and plunder in relation to women's demands for citizenship within the emerging feminist genre of radical analysis. This genre critiques the neocolonial state and its excesses regarding the plunder and privatization of national wealth, and increasingly links both debates and activist responses to a nascent but crucial reconceptualization of citizenship and rights for women in their respective societies across the continent.

In particular, I find the work of Amina Mama (1998, 2001) especially insightful in this "political recrafting" of the politics of the continent, and specifically of the state as a critical phenomenon within the epistemological project of African feminist theorization. She argues:

> A feminist analysis of post-colonial states links the violent and destructive manifestations of modern statecraft with the persistence of patriarchy in all its perversity. It approaches authoritarianism in a manner that draws on the insights of feminist studies, building on work that begins to explore the complex resonances and dissonances that occur between subjectivities and politics, between the individual and the collective. It offers a powerful rethinking of national identity and opens up possibilities for imagining radically different communities. (1998, 16–17)

It is critical, therefore, that a feminist perspective on the state and its deployment of militarism as a violence-driven means of accumulation be expanded and actively pursued. Of even greater urgency is the fact that the majority of debilitated Africans whose lives are ruptured and destroyed by the intensification of militarism across the societies of the continent are women, yet this reality remains excluded from the mainstream progressive African intellectual enterprise.

To instigate this conceptual and ideological shift, I suggest that feminist scholars, particularly on the continent, reinterpret the notion of *rampancy* in relation to *violation* as a state-embedded, state-enabled patriarchal relationship of power. By imbuing the notion of rampancy with political weight in terms of its use as a gendered and supremacist practice within militarism, and by associating this notion with state-facilitated plunder, we can begin to show how militarism facilitates class consolidation and accumulation, which results in the gendered exclusion of women and working communities in Africa and around the world. This is particularly the case where the state is engaged in wars of plunder and accumulation, largely because states on the continent still do not consider women complete citizens (McFadden 2005).

Such a deployment of the state enables males to transform themselves in class terms (into members of a ruling class), and in Africa—where competition for resources has been intensified by the seemingly insatiable needs of neoimperialist states for oil, diamonds, and other critical resources—the imperative of class reproduction is even more intense. To quote Federici: "In this context of generalized economic bankruptcy, violent rivalries have exploded everywhere among different factions of the African ruling class who, unable to enrich themselves through the exploitation of labour, are now fighting for access to state power as the key condition for the accumulation of wealth" (2005, n.p.). Repositioning the notions of *violation* and *impunity* in relation to the practices of plunder and accumulation by military means shifts the discourse on how working women in particular, and their communities, are affected by wars of plunder across the African continent.

My arguments are embedded in a feminist tradition of critical political writing and activism that is at least three decades old, emerging out of a sense of frustration at the inability of African male scholars who, despite their rhetorical intention of creating a more inclusive political discourse on the state and citizenship, have failed dismally in embracing the more radical, inclusive notions and practices crafted through feminist intellectual production (Osinulu and Mba 1996; Obbo 1986; Meena 1992; Imam, Mama, and Sow 1997).

Side by side with a persistently masculinist, liberal-informed discourse on the state and militarism is a different set of questions and theoretical challenges on the state raised by feminist scholars. These analyses question the capacities of existing formulations of the state to encompass the entitlements and demands of women and working communities beyond the already recognized structuralist and or class-biased inadequacies so well reflected in the work of scholars like Hutchful and Campbell. Feminist scholarship highlights the necessity of a more intersectional analysis of the systems and practices that should become foundational to the emerging postcolonial African state (Selolwane 1997; Mama 2005; Gqola 2001; Ahkire 2004).

Therefore, by reposing the existing constructions of the state as a preeminently militarized relationship between those who occupy it and those who are most affected by the deployment of militarism—experienced as violence, plunder, and exclusion from a life of dignity and safety—it is possible to insert conceptually and in activist terms the often unrecognized or unacknowledged agency of women to restructure the state (as a relational experience) and begin to transform their lives and their societies. Such a stance also challenges the generalized perception of the violation experienced by women and unarmed people in sites of conflict as *peculiarly* African.

The flouting of human dignity and civil protections by those who use violence to access and acquire immense wealth so as to consolidate class status is deeply entrenched in the very character of the state, in Africa and everyplace where the state has emerged as a vehicle for generating and protecting patriarchal class privilege. Through violence and impunity, both of which are gendered and supremacist practices, working women in particular on the continent continue to be excluded from a direct relationship with the state. This circumstance has significant gendered and class implications and consequences for the struggle to acquire citizenship for the majority of Africans who are women. Existing discourses on the state in Africa are disrupted through an interpolation of political claims, made by women of all classes, into the public as a site of contestation over citizenship and the demand for accountability on the part of those who occupy the state.

It is at this intersection of ideology and structure, where patriarchal power is exercised, that the notions of rampancy (as violent masculinist impunity) and plunder (as the process of primitive accumulation necessary for the ensconcement of a class to be able to rule) acquire a specifically feminist and radical appeal. Faced with the imperative of acquiring a ruling-class identity in order to consolidate power, and given that most neocolonial rulers on the continent derive from working-class or peasant backgrounds and consequently did not own or control wealth, positioning themselves in the state and using state structures to acquire material and political clout becomes an unavoidable exigency.

The notion of rampancy thus conceptualized allows for the imagining of a theoretical relationship between the militaristic, often impunitous behavior and the practices of those who occupy the state and who exercise or facilitate the violation of women's bodily and sexual integrity as an expression of "reclaimed" African masculinity. Re-positioning the notion of plunder in relation to class mobility enables the reinsertion of economically motivated imperatives into the conceptualization of class formation, militarization and the consolidation of power within the parameters of the state.

I contend that the most realistic possibilities for change on the continent will emerge from a more radical understanding of the state as a vehicle of class plunder and political repression whose military rampancy can only be resisted and overcome through the recentering of politics in the struggles and agencies of women, particularly those of working women, whose lives represent a mirror image of the need for political, economic, sociocultural, and juridical transformation.

The practice of rampant militarism, which facilitates the plunder and accumulation of wealth, also reentrenches the exclusionary practices that have kept the majority of working people at a distance from the state. The expulsion of communities from their homeland and historical location enables militarized males of various kinds (soldiers, mercenaries, bandits, and louts) to rampage with impunity over the bodies and the lives of women and girls, of children and the elderly—the majority of society in many instances—and requires this majority to live without the protections and obligations that the state owes them as citizens.

War and genocide raged in Rwanda, South Africa, and Namibia barely a decade ago, and not so long ago in Sierra Leone, Liberia, Angola, Mozambique, Burundi, Eritrea, and the Democratic Republic of Congo. Still ongoing are wars and conflicts in the north of Uganda, Somalia, Chad, Côte d'Ivoire, northern Nigeria, southern Sudan, Somalia, and Equatorial Guinea. The list seems endless, the number of African lives countless. Across the continent, the rampancy of militarization seems unstoppable, largely as an expression of national class rule. This rampant militarism is entrenched in burgeoning military budgets, the holding of "weapons fairs" in countries like South Africa, the increase in military loans and sale of arms to Africa by the U.S. military, and the proliferation of small arms deeper into communities across the continent as merchants of death respond to the marketing of Africa as an "emerging military market" (Majavu 2006; Amoa 2006). The United States and Europe have stepped up implementation of the so-called AFRICOM—a U.S.-European neoimperial initiative intended to "help the US military focus on a continent that is essential to our national security," according to Democrat Russell Feingold, one of the most liberal members of the U.S. Senate who also chairs its subcommittee on Africa (Lobe 2007). Victoria Holt, who is described as a "peacekeeping expert at the Henry L. Stimson Center," cautions that "there are some sophisticated military thinkers who know that it's not just guns. . . . They've spent enough time in Africa to understand some fundamental challenges, such as peacekeeping and governance. . . . If we don't have a countervailing civilian presence, we risk sending the signal that our engagement with Africa is primarily military, and that's not a signal we want to send" (as quoted in Lobe 2007, n.p.).

Such blatant imperial long-range militarism in relation to the continent should ring alarm bells for all who are dedicated to the creation of inclusive and participatory societies on the continent and everywhere else (Butterfield 2006). Feminist scholars have to scrutinize more closely the practices and policies that neocolonial states have adopted in consolidating militarism and extending militarized institutions and systems, often into the civic domain, as is the case after coups d'état as witnessed in Nigeria, Ghana, Gabon, Zaire (now the Democratic Republic of Congo), Ethiopia, Somalia, and the Sudan, for example.

The deliberate crafting of a critical notion of the state as a site of class accumulation and as a vehicle of control and surveillance over the lives and bodies of African women offers an alternative perspective of the forces and factors that have shaped this tremendously powerful phenomenon. It also enables imagining women positioned in new and empowering ways in relation to the state and its various apparatuses. Having traveled the distance between the margins of colonial society, wherein African women were considered the private property of black men, and the public as a space of engagement and conscientization, largely through the creation of a women's movement, African women can no longer be represented as either absent or sexualized objects, as they were generally portrayed in colonial literature. Nor can African women be treated as narrowly defined gendered beings, whose ideas and demands are ignored and or neatly categorized as issues of gender.

Large numbers of Africans have been brutally murdered or driven from their communities and homelands, with unspeakable acts of genocidal impunity and misogynistic violence being committed on and through the bodies of young girls, children generally, older people, and women (United Nations Security Council

2001; Coomaraswamy 1999). Nonetheless, imperial aggressors such as Britain, France, and the United States have often simply restructured their relationships with newly ensconced regimes, and or have installed preferred regimes, under-lining always the necessity for the West of maintaining economic power and the extraction of critical resources, increasingly through the further militarization of neocolonial regimes.

In central Africa, the case of the Democratic Republic of Congo (DRC) has been most instructive. Among the wealthiest countries on the continent, the DRC is a classic example of rampancy and plunder, conducted through imperial collusion with local despot Mobuto, who was installed by the United States and Belgium after the assassination of Lumumba in 1961 (De Witte 2001; Nzongola-Ntalaja 2002; Baregu 1999). Over the past forty-five years, the former Belgian Congo, which became known as Zaire at independence and has now been renamed the DRC, has lurched from one crisis to the next, and since 1995 has been embroiled in a brutal war that claimed the lives of at least five million African peo-ple. The war has been conducted mainly in the eastern DRC, where, according to the United Nations Security Council, "three categories of products were of primary consideration: (a) mineral resources, primarily coltan, diamonds, gold, and cassi-terite; (b) agriculture, forests and wildlife, including timber, coffee and ivory; and (c) financial products, mainly in regard to taxes. Copper, cobalt, livestock, gorillas, okapis, tobacco, tea, palm oil and land allocation" (2001, 4). According to this UN Security Council report of April 2001, countries directly involved in the "conflict" in the DRC between 1995 and 2000 were Angola, Burundi, Namibia, Rwanda, Uganda, and Zimbabwe; so-called third parties were Belgium, Cameroon, China, Denmark, France, Germany, the World Bank, the International Monetary Fund, the World Trade Organization, and a host of other institutions based mainly in the West (United Nations Security Council 2001).

In Sierra Leone and Liberia, war was about diamonds; in Angola it was about oil; in Nigeria it continues to be about oil and land; in Sudan it has always been about oil and land. Across the continent, the emergent bourgeoisie has systema-tically and ruthlessly colluded with established capitalist classes that controlled the key resources of each country at the moment of independence, negotiating deals and waging war when required, to establish itself as a ruling class at the moment of ascendancy into the neocolonial state.

More recently, feminist analyses have also focused on the consequences of militarism for the environment and other natural ecosystems, showing how destructive and pervasive patriarchal vandalism has become (Seager 1999) and how the pernicious intrusion of militarism into the daily lives of communities globally poses an urgent challenge to transnational feminist initiatives and solidarities. As stated by Feminist Dialogues,

> Militarism, taken as a system of belligerent domination of society, goes
> beyond military insubordination, excess in functions assigned to the

armed forces or civil disobedience. It is the penetration and influence of its norms and culture in the norms and culture of society. The logic of keeping power by force and the violent resolution of conflicts is often accompanied and promoted by civilians who support or promote military policies. (2007, n.p.)

Conclusion

Any discussion of the state must take into consideration the reality of the state as a dynamic force in the human political, cultural, and social universe. From the earliest recollections of state formation, a clear and unambiguous link has existed between the maintenance and expansion of state power and the growth and use of militarism as an expression of that state power. Militarism has also been central—conceptually and empirically—to the deployment of the state as a site of accumulation by various ruling classes throughout history, as well as a vehicle of repression, surveillance, and exclusion of the majority of people, particularly women, the young, and the elderly in working communities.

Thus, on the one hand, those who occupy the state in Africa face the imperative of making it into a viable state—in economic, legal, and political terms—in an era that is defined and constrained largely by an aggressive, predominantly U.S.-driven neoimperialism, manifest in military, cultural, media, and economic expansion across the world. On the other hand, the African state is confronted with the persistent demands of its people as they continue to struggle for their entitlements as citizens. These demands for an *entitled citizenship* pose a major threat to the consolidation of black ruling-class privilege and control in all the societies of the African continent.

At the moment of independence, the new black ruling class steps into this conundrum as it tries to negotiate the voracious class (and raced) agendas and interests of national, continental, and imperial imperatives of state and class consolidation. It must simultaneously manage the demands and rising political consciousness of its people, represented mainly through the activism of the civil society movements, among which are women's movements, which bring power and new political ideas and visions to the national agenda. This amazing performance of new history is reflected in the ongoing debates and public engagements, which characterize a profusion of civil society movements, directly challenging the tyranny and presumptions of the ruling classes everywhere on the continent.

My argument therefore is that the challenges posed—particularly by women's organizations and feminist analysis and activism against state power and practices of impunity, by demands for accountability for the use and abuse of public resources, by the rejection of regionalized and continental systems of exploitation and economic exclusion, and by the challenge to states on issues of militarism and resource allocation—are all expressions of a political agency that is becoming the primary marker of African political resistance to militarism and plunder. Whereas at a global level, all progressive intellectuals must of necessity analyze and critique the pernicious implication of state and social militarization, it is as important, if not more critical, to understand the ways in which this outrageous militarization of our societies anticipates the emergence of a more unpretentious, fascistic global state, one that will be managed and utilized by a globalized ruling class whose racial and gendered features seem to encompass fewer and fewer of the contradictions and tensions that have differentiated such oppressive classes in past history.

NOTES

1. During the 1990s, a series of arguments erupted within the U.S. academy about the hegemony of white, predominantly older male intellectuals over the definition and orientation of African studies. The collection *Out of One, Many Africas,* edited by Martin and West (1999), reflects the gist of these contestations.

2. The quotation "do not imagine that the exploration ends, that she has yielded all her mystery or that the map you hold cancels further discovery" is excerpted from Gwendolyn MacEwen's "The Discovery."

3. As the work of scholars like Basil Davidson and R. Pankhurst (in Ethiopia), David Hochschild, and Paul T. Zeleza, among several excellent African historians, can attest, such ahistoricism is peculiarly European.

4. It is exceptionally difficult to find historical narratives on the experiences of African women with militarism or the colonial army, although many anecdotes and allusions exist which attest to black women's experiences with rape and sexual violation generally in all the societies that where colonized and settled by white males of various nationalities. Even the interesting work of Anne McClintock on women in early South African history focuses specifically on the experiences of white (*boer*) women, which is a peculiar slant given the context and the well-documented rampancy of white armies across that region.

5. The Zimbabwe African National Union (ZANU) and the Zimbabwe African People's Union (ZAPU) were merged soon after independence into the ZANU Patriotic Front, controlled by Robert Mugabe and ZANU.

6. The U.S. military has established what are described as "forward bases" in several African countries, the key ones being Egypt, Sudan, Eritrea, Djibouti, and Kenya on the northeast African coast, in addition to the United States' occupation of the island of Diego Garcia. On the West African coast, the main collaborating countries are Senegal, Ghana, Benin, Mali, Gabon, and Nigeria, with Malawi, Namibia, South Africa, Mozambique, and Ethiopia. By 2007, it was expected that forty-seven African countries would be part of the U.S. military command for sub-Saharan Africa. For details on U.S. military involvement in Africa, see the Association of Concerned Africa Scholars' Web site: http://www.prairienet.org/acas/military/military06.html.

7. The referencing patterns and epistemological arguments made in an anthology like *The Military and Militarism in Africa,* edited by Eboe Hutchful and Abdoulaye Bathily (1998), reflect this essentially liberalist political tendency regarding the state in Africa.

8. This particular publication by CODESRIA (2006), which is a special issue titled "The African Woman," is particularly disappointing because it reflects the shift toward a more conservative use of the notion of gender by the institution itself (as can be read in the introduction, which quotes Mamphela Rampele, who works for the World Bank and is most definitely not a feminist).

REFERENCES

Ahkire, Josephine. 2004. "Towards Women's Effective Participation in Electoral Processes: A Review of the Ugandan Experience." *Feminist Africa* 3. http://www.feministafrica.org/03-2004/03-2004/josephine.html (accessed May 13, 2007).

Ahmad, Eqbal. 2000. *Confronting Empire: Interviews with David Barsamian.* Cambridge, MA: South End Press.

Ake, Claude. 1978. *Revolutionary Pressures in Africa.* London: Zed Press.

Alexander, Neville. 2002. *An Ordinary Country: Issues in the Transition from Apartheid to Democracy in South Africa.* Pietermaritzburg, South Africa: University of Natal Press.

Amoa, Baffour Dokyi. 2006. *WAANA, Pambazuka News* 270. September 25.

Andrade, Susan. 2002. "Gender and 'The Public Sphere' in Africa: Writing Women and Rioting Women." *Agenda* 54.

Baregu, Mwesiga. 1999. *Crisis in the Democratic Republic of Congo.* Harare: SAPES Books.

Basedu, Matthias, Gero Erdmann, and Andreas Mehler. 2006. *Votes, Money, Violence: Political Parties and Elections in Sub-Saharan Africa.* Uppsala, Sweden: Nordic Africa Institute.

Bayart, Jean-Francois. 1999. *The Criminalization of the State in Africa.* Oxford: James Curry.

Bello, Walden. 1994. *Dark Victory: The United States, Structural Adjustment and Global Poverty.* London: Pluto Press.

Boron, Atilio. 2005. *Empire and Imperialism: Critical Reading of Michael Hardt and Antonio Negri.* London: Zed Books.

Butterfield, Greg. 2006. "Africa: Threat of US/NATO Military Intervention Grows." April 9. http://www.workers.org/2006/world/africa-0413/ (accessed May 13, 2007).

Campbell, Horace. 1998. "The Popular Demand of the Dismantling of the Apartheid Military Machine and Problems of Conversion of the Military Industrial Complex." In *The Military and Militarism in Africa*, ed. Eboe Hutchful and Abdoulaye Bathily, 541–588. Dakar: CODESRIA.

——. 2003. *Reclaiming Zimbabwe: The Exhaustion of the Patriarchal Model of Liberation.* Trenton, NJ: Africa World Press.

CODESRIA (Council for the Development of Economic and Social Research in Africa). 2006. "The African Woman." Special issue. *CODESRIA Bulletin, nos.* 1 and 2.

Collins, Carole J. C. 2006. "Mozambique's HIV/AIDS Pandemic: Grappling with Apartheid's Legacy." Paper no. 24. New York: United Nations.

Coomaraswamy, Radhika. 1999. "A Question of Honour: Women, Ethnicity and Armed Conflict," Lecture delivered at the Third Minority Rights Lecture, Geneva. May. http://www.sacw.net/Wmov/RCoomaraswamyOnHonour.html (accessed May 13, 2007).

Crocker, Chester. 1992. *High Noon in Southern Africa: Making Peace in a Rough Neighbourhood.* New York: W. W. Norton.

Davidson, Basil. 2001. *African Civilization Revisited.* Trenton, NJ: Africa World Press.

De Witte, Ludo. 2001. *The Assassination of Lumumba*: London: Verso.

Engel, Ulf, Annamaria Gentili, and Patrick Chabal. 2005. *Is Violence Inevitable in Africa: Theories of Conflict and Approaches to Conflict Resolution.* Leiden, The Netherlands: Brill Academic Publishers.

Enloe, Cynthia. 2000. *Maneuvers: The International Politics of Militarizing Women's Lives.* Berkeley: University of California Press

Federici, Silvia. 2005. "War, Globalization and Reproduction." July 29. http://libcom.org/library/war-globalisation-reproduction-silvia-federici (accessed May 13, 2007).

Feminist Dialogues. 2007. "Democracy and Militarism." January 17. http://feministdialogue.isiswomen.org/index.php?option=com_content&task=view&id=57&Itemid=106 (accessed May 13, 2007).

Gqola, Pumla Dineo. 2001. "Ufanele Uqavile: Blackwomen, Feminisms and Postcoloniality in Africa." *Agenda* 50:11–22.

Hammar, Amanda, Brian Raftopoulos, and Stig Jensen, eds. 2003. *Zimbabwe's Unfinished Business: Rethinking Land, State and Nation in the Context of Crises.* Avondale, Harare, Zimbabwe: Weaver Press.

Hanlon, John. 1991. *Mozambique: Who Calls the Shots.* Bloomington: Indiana University Press.

Hansen, Emmanuel. 1987. "The State and Popular Struggles in Ghana, 1981–86." In *Popular Struggles for Democracy in Africa*, ed. Peter Anyang' Nyong'o. London: Zed Books.

Hassim, Shireen. 1999. "From Presence to Power: Women's Citizenship in a New Democracy." Special issue on Citizenship. *Agenda* 40:6–17.

Hutchful, Eboe. 1989. "Military and Militarism in Africa: A Research Agenda." Working Paper 3/89. Dakar: CODESRIA.

——. 1991. "Reconstructing Political Space: Militarism and Constitutionalism in Africa." In *State and Constitutionalism: An African Debate on Democracy*, ed. Issa Shivji, 183–201. Harare: SAPES Books.

Hutchful, Eboe, and Abdoulaye Bathily, eds. 1998. *The Military and Militarism in Africa.* Dakar: CODESRIA.

Imam, Ayesha, Amina Mama, and Fatou Sow, eds. 1997. *Engendering African Social Sciences.* Dakar: CODESRIA.

Isis-Wicce. 2005. "Women's Voices on Armed Conflict." *Women's World Newsletter*, nos. 39 and 40.

Lewis, Desiree. 2004. *African Gender Research and Postcoloniality: Legacies and Challenges.* Dakar: CODESRIA.

Lobe, Jim. 2007. "Africa to Get Its Own US Military Command." February 1. http://www.antiwar.com/lobe/?articleid=10443 (accessed May 13, 2007).

Macamo, Elisio Salvado. 2005. *Negotiating Modernity: Africa's Ambivalent Experience.* Dakar: CODESRIA.

Mafeje, Archie. 1992. *In Search of an Alternative: A Collection of Essays on Revolutionary Theory and Politics.* Harare: SAPES Books.

Majavu, Mandisa. 2006. "Merchants of Death." *FAHAMU/Pambazuka News*, September 21. http://www.pambazuka.org/en/category/comment/37271.

Mama, Amina. 1998. "Khaki in the Family: Gender Discourse and Militarism in Nigeria." *African Studies Review* 41(2): 1–18.

——. 2001. "Challenging Subjects: Gender and Power in African Contexts." In *Identity and Beyond: Rethinking Africanity.* Discussion Paper 12. Uppsala, Sweden: Nordic Africa Institute.

——. 2005. "'Gender Studies' for Africa's Transformation." In *African Intellectuals: Rethinking Politics, Language, Gender and Development*, ed. Thandika Mkandawire, 94–116. London: Zed Books.

Mamdani, Mahmood. 1996. *Citizen and Subject: Contemporary Africa and the Legacy of Late Colonialism.* Princeton: Princeton University Press.

Mandaza, Ibbo, ed. 1999. *Reflections on the Crisis in the Democratic Republic of Congo.* Harare: SAPES Books.

Martin, William G., and Michael O. West. 1999. *Out of One, Many Africas: Reconstructing the Study and Meaning of Africa.* Bloomington: University of Indiana Press.

McClintock, Anne. 1993. "Family Feuds: Gender, Nationalism and the Family." *Feminist Review* 54 (Autumn): 69–79.

McFadden, Patricia. 2005. "Becoming Postcolonial: African Women Changing the Meaning of Citizenship." *Meridians: Feminism, Race, and Transnationalism* 6(1): 1–18.

———. 2007. "African Feminist Perspectives on Post-Coloniality." *Black Scholar: Journal of Black Studies and Research* 37(1): 36–42.

Meena, Ruth, ed. 1992. *Gender in Southern Africa: Conceptual and Theoretical Issues.* Harare: SAPES Books.

Meredith, Martin. 2005. *The Fate of Africa: From the Hopes of Freedom to the Heart of Despair: A History of Fifty Years of Independence.* New York: Public Affairs.

Minter, William. 1994. *Apartheid's Contras: An Inquiry into the Roots of War.* Johannesburg: University of the Witswatersrand.

Nyamnjoh, Francis B. 2006. *Insiders and Outsiders: Citizenship and Xenophobia in Southern Africa.* Dakar: CODESRIA.

Nzongola-Ntalaja, Georges. 2002. *The Congo: From Leopold to Kabila: A People's History.* London: Zed Books.

Nzongola-Ntalaja, Georges, and Margaret Lee, eds. 1997. *The State and Democracy in Africa.* Harare: AAPS Books.

Obano, Ana Elena. 2005. "Masculinity, Peace Processes, Impunity and Justice." *Pambzuka News,* January 20.

Obbo, Christine. 1986. *African Women: Their Struggle for Economic Survival.* London: Zed Books.

Oloka-Onyango J., and Chris Maina Peter, eds. 2004. *Constitutionalism and Transition: African and Eastern European Perspectives.* Nairobi, Kenya: Kituo Cha Kitabu.

Osinulu, Clara, and Nina Mba, eds. 1996. *Nigerian Women in Politics: 1986–1993.* Lagos, Nigeria: Malthouse Press.

Parenti, Michael. 2006. Introduction to Gregory Elich's *Strange Liberators: Militarism, Mayhem and the Pursuit of Profit.* Coral Springs, FL: Lumina Press.

Peterson, V. Spike, ed. 1992. *Gendered States: Feminist (Re)Visions of International Relations Theory.* Boulder, CO: Lynne Rienner Publishers.

Petras, James, and Henry Veltmeyer. 2005. *Empire with Imperialism: The Globalizing Dynamics of Neo-Liberal Capitalism.* London: Zed Books.

Rice, Andrew. 2005. "Why Is Africa Still Poor? *Nation,* October 24. http://www.thenation.com/doc/20051024/rice (accessed May 14, 2007).

Rodney, Walter. 1974. *How Europe Underdeveloped Africa.* Washington, DC: Howard University Press.

Said, Edward. 1994. *Culture and Imperialism.* New York: Vintage Books.

Salo, Elaine, and Desiree Lewis. 2002. "Democracy, Citizenship and Gender." *African Gender Institute Newsletter* (Cape Town), July 10.

Sandbrook, Richard. 2000. *Closing the Circle: Democratization and Development in Africa.* London: Zed Books.

Sanders, James. 2006. *Apartheid's Friends: The Rise and Fall of South Africa's Secret Service.* London: John Murray Publishers.

Seager, Joni. 1999. "Patriarchal Vandalism: Militaries and the Environment." In *Dangerous Intersections: Feminist Perspectives on Population, Environment, and Development,* ed. Jael Silliman and Ynestra King, 163–188. Cambridge, MA: South End Press.

Selolwane, Onalenna Doo. 1997. "Gender And Democracy in Botswana: Women Struggle for Equality and Political Participation." In *The State and Democracy,* ed. Georges Nzongola-Ntalaja and Margaret Lee, 25–41. Harare: AAPS Books.

Shivji, Issa, ed. 1991. *State and Constitutionalism: An African Debate on Democracy.* Harare: SAPES Books.

Tickner, J. Ann. 1992. *Gender in International Relations: Feminist Perspectives on Achieving Global Security.* New York: Columbia University Press.

———. 2001. *Gendering World Politics: Issues and Approaches to the Post–Cold War Era.* New York: Columbia University Press.

United Nations Security Council. 2001. *Report on the DRC.* S/2001/357. April 12.

9

==

Because Vieques Is Our
Home: Defend It!

Women Resisting Militarization
in Vieques, Puerto Rico

KATHERINE T. McCAFFREY

The women of the Alliance have decided that Vieques is our house and therefore we will defend it. For too long, our house, Vieques, has been raped, robbed, burned, mutilated, mistreated by military forces, which brought damage to the population for 60 years. This is why we are determined and unafraid to put our house in order. I want to [invite] all of you women who hear this message to unite in one voice, to unite your voices with ours, because the only requirement that you need to belong to the Alliance, to be part of this blessed struggle, is to be a woman, to have the desire to be free and above all to want to live in peace. For this, in the name of all the women of Vieques, thank you, thank you very much. We move forward together declaring in unison: Ni un tiro más, ni una bomba más para Vieques! (Not one more shot, not one more bomb for Vieques!) (Sobá 2000, n.p.)

Vieques is a fifty-one-square-mile island municipality of Puerto Rico, located six miles off its southeast coast. For roughly six decades the U.S. Navy controlled more than two-thirds of the island's land and used Vieques for live-fire practice, air-to-ground bombing, shelling, artillery fire, ship-to-shore bombing, and maneuvers. Conflict simmered between the U.S. Navy and the 10,000 island residents, who lived wedged between an ammunition depot and a maneuver area. After years of tension and periodic protest, a social movement coalesced when a stray bomb killed a civilian security guard. Four years of mass mobilization, thousands of arrests for civil disobedience, and international political pressure and media attention halted live-bombing exercises on Vieques Island in 2003.

Women emerged as new leaders in the Vieques protest, organizing behind the banner of the Vieques Women's Alliance (Alianza de Mujeres Viequenses). This organization rallied opposition to the live-bombing exercises by emphasizing the health and security threat that military forces and training practices represented to islanders. Although conflict between Vieques residents and the U.S. Navy extended back to the 1940s, and protest spanned decades, it was only in 1999 that women first organized along gender lines and asserted a distinct female voice in protest.

In this chapter I explore why Vieques women decided to organize as women to resist militarization. Baldez notes that "women do not inevitably organize as women simply because they are women," but when "women mobilize as women, they tap into common knowledge about gender norms that portray men and women as categorically different" (2002, 15). Vieques Women's Alliance activists embraced an ideology that celebrated women's roles as housewives as they struggled for a Vieques "clean" of the navy. Banging pots and pans, distributing white ribbons for peace, and demonstrating with megaphones at the gates to the base, Vieques women declared that they were acting in defense of their homes: "Vieques is our home, we want it clean, we want it neat, we want it in peace. . . . Navy get out!"

Mobilizing along lines of gender requires a common vision of what it means to be female. On the surface, the vision of women's identity embraced by the Vieques Women's Alliance seemed to emanate from conservative, even essentialist, notions of women's roles and potential: the woman as housewife. But the Vieques Women's Alliance cannot neatly be dismissed as a "feminine" mobilization, concerned only with defending women's roles as mothers and wives rather than resisting inequality. The Vieques women's movement follows a path of Latin American grassroots feminism that collapses the difference between "feminine" and feminist agendas, mobilizing "traditional" roles while forging new political spaces and collective identities for women (see, e.g., Schirmer 1993; Stephen 1997, 2005). The Vieques Women's Alliance suggests the fluidity between so-called feminine and feminist movements, and the diversity of perspectives within grassroots mobilizations. The movement also demonstrates how women's participation can expand and contribute to the success of social mobilization. The Alliance succeeded in rallying new segments of the Vieques population to take political action and contributed to the dramatic expansion of Vieques' movement to end military occupation and destruction of the island.

In this chapter I consider first how women's protest in Vieques was rooted in subsistence struggles. I then briefly explore the history of the conflict between Vieques residents and the navy, and how the intensification of weapons testing sparked protest. The decision to organize along gender lines was in part a strategy to assert the primacy of bread-and-butter issues and avoid more complicated debates over Puerto Rican sovereignty. Women's identification as homemakers created a space in which they could contest military policy without appearing politically subversive or embroiling themselves in controversies over colonialism. The Women's Alliance emerged in the context of the resurgence and broadening of the antinavy movement in a post–cold war context. Women brought new energy and vision to the struggle and helped mobilize new sectors to protest. "Feminine" rhetoric fused with fiery sentiment to establish women as a forceful presence in the limelight of Vieques' ongoing struggle.

Women's Protest and the Material Basis of Discontent

Conflict in Vieques has its foundation in the material conditions of everyday life. The U.S. Navy has had an overwhelmingly negative effect on the island's economy, social life, and ecology. The municipality of Vieques is one of the poorest in all of Puerto Rico, with 65 percent of the population living below the poverty level (U.S. Census Bureau 2000). Health indicators are poor, with high rates of cancer and infant mortality as compared to the rest of Puerto Rico. In 2001, the Puerto Rican Department of Health reported that death rates from cardiac illness, diabetes, HIV/AIDS, strokes, hypertension, liver disease, and cancer were substantially higher than on the main island of Puerto Rico (*Caribbean Business* 2004). A 1999 special commission to the governor of Puerto Rico concluded that the navy's control of land, water, and island resources caused high unemployment and economic stagnation on the island (Special Commission for Vieques 1999).

Scholars have noted that women are often radicalized by threats to subsistence (Corcoran-Nantes 1990, 1993; Kaplan 1982; Moser 1987; Safa 1990; Susser 1992; Nash 1990). Indeed, men and women in Vieques historically have mobilized around issues of subsistence, environment, and health. A protest movement in the 1970s crystallized around the claims of local fishermen. Intensified naval maneuvers had damaged coral reefs and fish in an already fragile marine environment. Increased ship traffic was severing buoy lines from the traps they marked, effectively destroying fishing gear and the financial investment the traps represented. Fishermen rallied against the navy's encroachment into prime fishing grounds and the destruction of traps. Women were involved in this mobilization, but their leadership on a local level was circumscribed, and their participation was largely auxiliary to men.

In 1999, however, Vieques women for the first time formed a separate women's organization to challenge military occupation and live-bombing practices. Baldez argues that gender-based protest is politically strategic: "Mobilizing as women provides a rhetorical frame that permits women with diverse substantive interests to engage in collective action to pursue their ends under the rubric of having access to political decision making" (2002, 15). Organizing specifically along gender lines, the Vieques Women's Alliance developed a grassroots coalition among longtime female activists and previously apolitical Vieques women from varying backgrounds—teachers, housewives, secretaries, and retired grandmothers. On an island deeply divided by partisan politics, the Alliance transcended political divisions and united women from different political affiliations.

The Vieques Women's Alliance allowed women to assume new leadership in social mobilization and contribute to shaping the ideology and tactics of the broader Vieques movement.

Embracing an ideology of domesticity was important to claiming a public voice. It allowed women to confront military authority while shielding themselves from accusations of subversion by claiming for themselves a "traditional" woman's role. This strategy echoes other women's mobilizations against military power, such as the Mothers of Plaza de Mayo in Argentina, who defied the military dictatorship while identifying themselves as concerned mothers (Bouvard 1994). In the United States more recently, Cindy Sheehan emerged as one of the most powerful critics of the Bush administration and the Iraq War by mobilizing her status as the grieving mother of a fallen soldier.

In Puerto Rico, confronting the military is often regarded as subversive and anti-American. Puerto Rico's status as a nonsovereign U.S. territory complicates political debate. Although a vocal minority advocates independence by radicalizing political discourse and tapping into widespread cultural nationalism (Ayala 2003, 217), the large majority of the Puerto Rican population is politically moderate, preferring continued political and economic ties with the United States even while maintaining a profound sense of Puerto Rican identity (Dávila 1997; Duany 2000, 2002; Morris 1995).

Conflict with the U.S. military exposes the ambivalence about citizenship, sovereignty, and national identity that are at the heart of Puerto Rican society (see Flores 2000; Negrón-Muntaner and Grosfoguel 1997). As both a potent symbol of American influence and a powerful actor in island affairs, the U.S. military evokes charged debates over loyalty and identity. In general, opposition to the military is viewed as part of the anticolonial movement. The dilemma in Vieques is that the navy is not only a symbol of colonial power but also a very real actor that has caused material harm to the community.

Protest in Vieques is framed by this tension. Viequenses object to the military on material grounds, citing restrictions on economic opportunity, denial of access to natural resources, destruction of the environment, and degradation of public health. Merely raising these grievances is a highly charged political act. The navy interprets criticism as a threat to national security. The commonwealth government avoids confrontations that could jeopardize its relationship with the United States, particularly as they affect ongoing debates about potential statehood or a modified form of association. Activists from Vieques and Puerto Rico who are concerned specifically about military actions become embroiled in debates over sovereignty. Thus, what is peculiar about Vieques' struggle is the way residents have struggled to assert specific material grievances resulting from Puerto Rico's political domination by the United States and its armed forces while avoiding the delicate issue of sovereignty.

By rallying behind a collective identity as homemakers, Vieques women sidestepped complicated questions of national identity and loyalty, and approached the problem of the navy from an elemental female identity. This strategy legitimized women's activism and created a space for women's politicization and protest outside of paralyzing debates over Puerto Rican sovereignty.

Background: Growing Threat of Military Exercises

During and after World War II, the U.S. Navy expropriated three-quarters of Vieques Island to establish a major military installation in the Caribbean. Over time, this base evolved into one of the key U.S. naval training installations in the Western Hemisphere. A resident civilian population of about 10,000 ended up wedged between an ammunition depot and a maneuver area. The navy's control of land, air, and water resources set up fundamental obstacles to stable civilian life. The sugar industry that once completely dominated the local economy was liquidated by the military. The island's development as an ammunition depot and theater for war games failed to generate regular employment, and the military was overtly hostile to the development of Vieques' civilian economy. Huge maneuvers were periodically scheduled on the island, and tens of thousands of sailors would flood the small town on pass, drinking and carousing, looking for women. Most of the year, however, residents struggled to survive, always anxious that the navy would seek to usurp the entire island and evict the remaining residents.

Culebra, a ten-square-mile island municipality of Puerto Rico to the north of Vieques, also existed under the grip of the U.S. Navy. Culebra and Vieques formed a strategic triangle with the Roosevelt Roads Naval Station on the eastern coast of the Puerto Rican main island. The navy launched amphibious assaults on Vieques and concentrated naval and aerial bombardments on Culebra. The U.S. military's shift to missile technology in the late 1950s intensified the bombardment of Culebra and pushed tensions over the edge in both Culebra and Vieques.

Recognizing the incompatibility of civilians living at the center of territory used mainly for live-fire practice, the navy secretly took steps in the 1960s to forcibly remove and relocate the civilian populations of Culebra and Vieques. The Puerto Rican government resisted, and ultimately President Kennedy intervened to block the navy from evicting the residents (see Fernández 1996; Meléndez López 1989). The navy continued its maneuvers, with nearly 600 residents of Culebra and 9,000 residents of Vieques captive to increasingly overwhelming military exercises.

Culebrenses, in particular, lived under a surreal set of circumstances. The U.S. Navy owned one-third of the ten-square-mile island and its entire coastline. A bombing range and bomb-laden harbor circled the civilian sector. Low-flying helicopters and planes and extensive firing practice besieged residents. In a single year, 1969, Culebra was under fire by naval gunnery for 123 days and pounded by direct missiles for 228 days. Planes made between 35,000 and 40,000 target runs on the island that year. There were a series of misfires and wild shots, with bombs landing yards from private homes and mortar rounds sweeping waters where children frolicked in the surf (Schemmer and Cossaboom 1970; Schemmer et al. 1970).

By the late 1960s, a militant antinavy movement led by the Puerto Rican independence movement emerged (see Delgado Cintrón 1989; McCaffrey 2002). In the context of struggles against the Vietnam War and the strengthened anticolonial movement in Puerto Rico, Culebra became the cause célèbre of the Puerto Rican independence movement. The Puerto Rican Independence Party (PIP) and the Puerto Rican Socialist Party (PSP) were instrumental in leading a direct action campaign against the naval presence. The PIP defined the battle as one of "pacific militancy" and organized demonstrations on beaches used for target practice, blocking ship-to-shore missile fire with human chains of protesters. Ultimately, Culebra activists were successful in halting military exercises and forcing the navy off the island. Culebra's success, however, became Vieques' problem.

Although the navy was instructed to find an alternative training site to Culebra, and Congress authorized funds for the transfer, the navy simply shifted its bombardments to existing facilities in Vieques (U.S. Congress 1994). By the midseventies, it was apparent that Vieques had received the brunt of the Culebra "solution" in the form of increased bombing, maneuvers, and restrictions, which sparked a confrontation with local fishermen. Emphasizing concerns about livelihood—the destruction of traps and fishing gear by navy boats on maneuvers and the restrictions on the use of prime fishing grounds—fishermen led a grassroots community movement. Positioning themselves in the direct line of missile fire, local fishermen succeeded in interrupting international military maneuvers. Pickets, demonstrations, and a campaign of civil disobedience put Vieques' grievances on an international stage.

But by the late 1970s, when the Vieques protest erupted, the political setting was dramatically different from that of Culebra. Cold war tensions peaked with the Soviet invasion of Afghanistan and revolutions in Iran and Nicaragua. The Puerto Rican anticolonial movement had weakened, and local Vieques activists were reluctant to link their specific grievances against the navy with an unwinnable battle against U.S. colonialism.

Vieques' fishermen-led movement emphasized that their concerns were not about politics but about the "authentic" problems of the Vieques people—the concrete, material needs of the people that seemed to be ignored by the maneuverings of politicians and activists with broader agendas. Fishermen were important to the success of the movement because they characterized it as based on issues of quality of life and economic opportunity as opposed to broader anticolonial concerns. A focus on local grievances was effective in building consensus in a politically conservative populace. It was also a way of keeping Viequense leadership at the helm and preventing the movement from becoming merely a platform for the embattled cause of Puerto Rican independence or a tool of political interests.

On a local level, however, the focus on fishermen and male leadership limited women's participation in the movement. Vieques women were involved in the mobilization, but their participation was often auxiliary. They picketed, demonstrated, wrote pamphlets, and cooked rice and beans for protesters but did not give press conferences, travel lecture circuits, or rise to leadership positions. Circumscribing the participation of half of the population limited potential sources of creativity and solidarity in that women often play instrumental roles in community-based mobilizations, especially when they perceive threats to their internalized domestic or caretaking roles (Kaplan 1982, 1990). The focus on fishing traps rather than live-bombing exercises, however, inhibited the growth of what Temma Kaplan (1982) has called "female consciousness."

Vieques' fishermen-led movement won several important concessions from the navy but ultimately did not succeed in shutting down the base. Heightened cold-war tensions constrained the effectiveness of the movement (see McCaffrey 2006). For the next fifteen years, the community lived with military exercises. In the 1980s and 1990s, the navy trained an average of 180 days per year and dropped or fired an average of 1,464 tons of bombs and explosives annually on Vieques (Shanahan and Lindsay-Poland 2002, 2). In 1998, the last year before protests interrupted maneuvers, the navy dropped 23,000 bombs on the island, the majority of which contained live explosives (Fallon and Pace 1999).

Shifts in technology meant that risk to the civilian population from bombing practice was greatly magnified. High-speed jets flew from increasingly high altitudes, magnifying the probability of a fatal error. A pilot's miscalculation of ten seconds could land a bomb dead center on Vieques' capital. In fact, a string of training errors raised residents' anxieties. In October 1993, an FA/18 Hornet flying at 1,300 mph dropped five 500-pound bombs one mile from Vieques' capital. Then, in 1995, two bombs destroyed military installations on the firing range. In 1996, bombs fell near fishermen off the southern coast of Vieques. Finally, in 1997, a National Guard unit strafed a school bus and a police car parked near the town dump with M-16 bullets (Giusti-Cordero 2000).

In addition to the growing threat of training errors during military exercises, residents became increasingly concerned about contamination from military practices. A study in the late 1980s documented high levels of residual explosives in Vieques' drinking water. Because Vieques' water is piped in from Puerto Rico, the study hypothesized that significant bomb residues were airborne and were traveling downwind to the civilian population (Cruz Pérez 1988). Residents began to recognize what studies later confirmed: the island's cancer rate was soaring.[1] Within the small island's tightly knit community, everyone had a friend, relative, or neighbor with cancer.

The collapse of the Soviet Union in the early 1990s created a new political space in which renewed protest could develop. As U.S. military priorities shifted and dozens of bases were closed, activists in Vieques rallied to seek the closure of their base. They mobilized local support by emphasizing the health and security threat that the military installation represented. Also, grassroots organizers galvanized concern about the sudden surge in cancer rates among the island population and linked the cancer increases to the intensification of military training on the island. When a civilian employee was killed on base by a misplaced bomb, residents' fears of the navy threat were confirmed. A new·movement was catalyzed.

On April 19, 1999, during a routine training mission, two navy jets missed their mark by a mile and a half. Flying between 500 and 1,300 miles per hour, they dropped two 500-pound bombs not on the live-impact range but on the barbed-wire-ringed observation post from which the navy surveyed the shelling. The navy's range control officer and three security guards inside the observation post were injured by fragments of shattered glass and concrete. David Sanes Rodríguez, a thirty-five-year-old civilian security guard on patrol outside, was knocked unconscious by the explosion and bled to death from his injuries.

Sanes's death sparked a new movement to remove the navy from Vieques. In the days following his death, demonstrators entered the heart of the base, erecting tents on the live-impact range. They staked crosses to commemorate Sanes's death and those of residents who had died of cancer. Protesters built settlements to fortify their claims to the land and to block bombing exercises. They positioned themselves as human shields on the navy's bombing range and halted military training exercises for over one year.

In 1999, a proliferation of groups rallied behind the Vieques cause: church and ecumenical groups, independence organizations, students, horseback riders, federal employees, as well as various Puerto Rican regional associations. Puerto Ricans in the diaspora and U.S.-based politicians rallied behind Vieques' cause. This revitalized movement of 1999 had a much wider base than the mobilization of the 1970s, with a symbolic framework broader in scope. Rather than a hierarchical movement controlled by fishermen and run by the political left, this new movement operated as a coalition, with power distributed horizontally rather than vertically.[2] The broadening of the Vieques movement coincided with the emergence of the first women's organization to back the struggle, the Vieques Women's Alliance.

The Founding of the Vieques Women's Alliance

"We decided to organize a group for women because we were concerned about the lack of voice for women in the movement," explained Judith Conde, thirty-two years old and cofounder with Gladys Rivera of the Vieques Women's Alliance.[3] The women's campaign emerged on the Vieques political landscape a month after the death of David Sanes. Conde, a home economist at the agricultural extension, and Rivera, a forty-two-year-old social worker, wanted to contribute to the burgeoning movement and provide a space for women to articulate their concerns. Both Conde and Rivera worked with women in Vieques at the grassroots level and worried that neither their own voices and experiences, nor those of the other women, were represented in existing organizations. Conde and Rivera wanted to join the movement and project a "women's perspective": "The men tend to emphasize the economic and political aspects [of the military presence]. We [emphasize] the emotional and psychological aspects. How we are affected on the individual level as wives and mothers trying to raise families. It's a more sentimental, emotional approach," Conde explained.

Rivera remarked that her own work in the community had demonstrated to her the profound emotional damage the military had inflicted on children and adults. She described the pictures that children drew of navy boats and fighter jets, superimposed over images of Vieques dripping with blood. Conde and Rivera wanted to create a forum where women could express how the military presence affected them as wives and mothers trying to raise families on Vieques and to mobilize women from that shared experience. They organized a meeting one evening in mid-May. "We issued an invitation to women to come to a meeting. It was a simple letter that said the following: Vieques is our home. We want it clean. We want it neat. We want it in peace. Let us women meet at 7:00 PM at the Fortín Conde de Mirasol" (Suárez Toro 1999, n.p.). Twenty-five women turned out.

This first gathering brought together long-term activists with women who had never before been politically involved. Some of the women were the wives of leading male activists and had participated in rallies and pickets, written letters, helped produce leaflets, boarded visitors in their homes, and provided demonstrators with food and drink, but they had never risen to positions of leadership themselves. "The women were interested in expressing themselves and were looking for an opportunity to speak," remembered Rivera. Women were attracted to a supportive environment in which their voices were heard. "I felt called to join as a woman and as a Viequense," remembered Miriam Sobá, a thirty-nine-year-old teacher and founding member of the Women's Alliance. "I felt called as a woman, one among others, to join with the struggle. We feel like 'little fish in the water.' [Here] someone was going to let us talk, someone was going to listen to us." Sobá characterized this first gathering as "an oasis, a space for relaxation. This was a therapy session."

The overriding concern women expressed at the first meeting involved health, in particular, the island's soaring cancer rate. Conde and Rivera listened to the women's concerns about cancer and the health of their families and suggested new ways of thinking about Vieques' health problems. "We told them that just as we want our homes clean and safe to raise our children, we want the same for Vieques," explained Conde. Conde and Rivera believed women would be able to connect and relate to metaphors of domesticity. Cleaning house, as Conde and Rivera conceptualized it, meant confronting the major power broker on the island, the U.S. Navy. This challenge, however, was not one of political defiance but domestic necessity. "Obviously, the navy has to go since they are causing damage," Conde asserted. She emphasized to the women that the navy was a menace to community health and that military training exercises negatively affected the women's families.

Although women were motivated by concerns about cancer and the danger that the navy posed to the community, they were initially hesitant to speak out. They were afraid that they might lose their food stamps or that they would jeopardize their own or their husbands' jobs. "Many women were afraid that the municipal government would block them from working," Conde noted. These concerns were not ill founded: in Puerto Rico, partisan politics are fierce, and in Vieques, politics are local. Moreover, in Vieques and throughout Puerto Rico, the government sector is a major source of employment. Taking a minority political position can have concrete ramifications: a pothole in front of your house is not repaired; your job application is "misplaced"; you are let go from your office job at the public school. Organizing women to confront the navy meant overcoming working-class women's reluctance to risk their economic security.

The surging cancer rates and a series of military mishaps and accidents, including the accidental bombing that killed David Sanes, contributed to a climate of overwhelming insecurity on Vieques Island. Painstaking grassroots organizing over the course of six years transformed these grievances into the basis for a social movement. The activists' focus on the threat of bombing exercises and military contamination encouraged women to risk speaking out against the navy's live-fire exercises. Conde was heartened by the transformation of women who initially had hesitated to mobilize against military bombing exercises.

Taking to the Streets

> The sentiment of the woman, of the mother, is what brings us to the street, is what gets us involved. We have a sixth sense when it comes to danger. The woman gets involved to defend her family and other women see her and she creates a network and the idea that this is something partisan disappears and they unite and they are going to create consciousness. (Sobá 2000, n.p.)

The Vieques Women's Alliance organized its first public action in June 1999, roughly two months after protesters entered the bombing range and set up a civil disobedience encampment. "The navy said it would resume bombing in June," explained Conde; "we convoked a caravan—over a hundred cars came." The caravan traveled all over the island before stopping in front of the gates of Camp García, the main entrance to the navy's eastern maneuver area. The protesters, mostly women and children, blocked traffic and banged on pots and pans. They sang antinavy songs and attached white ribbons to the chain-link fence demarcating military terrain. Conde announced that the group would continue to attach white ribbons to the fence until it was completely covered as a testament to Viequenses' desire for peace. "The caravan was a great success," she assessed.

"We were newly formed and didn't expect many people would turn out. We saw that we had the power to convoke a meeting and involve people who would never have participated in the struggle before."

The response to the ribbons was so great that the Women's Alliance started distributing white ribbons and encouraging supporters to wear them as a symbol that "Vieques wants peace." The Women's Alliance encouraged people to continue to tie white ribbons onto the chain-link gates of Camp García as a petition for peace and an end to the bombing. So many people tied white ribbons to each honeycomb of chain link that the fence soon appeared as a tattered white sheet, dancing in the wind.

On July 4, 1999, the Women's Alliance sent a contingent to demonstrate in front of the gates of Roosevelt Roads in Ceiba, Puerto Rico. Roosevelt Roads, the heart of naval operations in Puerto Rico, was more physically intimidating than Vieques' decommissioned Camp García. To protest the navy on the main island took greater courage and a commitment to travel there. The women held a spirited demonstration. Conde noted that the same women who had expressed reluctance to protest now marched with placards in front of the base.

> The reality is that they are at the front lines. I feel so happy. Women who told me they didn't want to get involved are picketing in front of the base at Ceiba. They say, "I'm raising my child in Vieques, so all of this affects me." Now they say they are going to the target range, that they are prepared to be arrested. (Laughing) I have created a monster!

The newly formed Vieques Women's Alliance not only put women on the front lines of protest but also encouraged them to ascend the ranks. Carmen Valencia, a fifty-nine-year-old retired schoolteacher, assumed new leadership in the Alliance. Valencia had long been active in the movement to evict the navy but in the past her role had been largely supportive: she had cooked for demonstrations; she had taken care of leading activist Ismael Guadalupe's children.

Through her involvement in the Women's Alliance, however, Valencia moved from the sidelines into the limelight. In February 2000, Valencia traveled to Washington, D.C., to take part in a Capitol Hill press conference followed by a noisy demonstration outside of the White House. In March 2000, she traveled to Springfield, Massachusetts, to meet with a support group and promote solidarity for Vieques' struggle for peace. In May 2000, she visited the office of Vermont senator Patrick Leahy in an effort to promote solidarity with a senator who had "played a role in fighting for world peace." Valencia had speaking engagements at Dartmouth College, and participated in public forums in Burlington and Montpelier, Vermont. She carried with her photos of a little girl who was dying of brain cancer to dramatize islanders' concerns about rising cancer rates. In this way she demonstrated the Alliance's particular approach of emphasizing the personal, the individual story, the struggle women faced to raise their children on the island, and the health risks the navy caused. Yet while "defending her house,

Vieques," she had traveled far from home to advance the struggle, away from the kitchen and into the center of political action. Her photo appeared on the front page of regional newspapers, and she was quoted extensively by the press.

Conde reflected on the emergence of women's leadership: "Look how far we've come. It's not a movement of supporting husbands, backing husbands, cooking meals. The women are on the frontlines. They are doing projects, going to conferences, coordinating activities. We don't have a particular ideology; it's the experience of living here that motivates participation."

Women's Contributions to Grassroots Mobilization

The work of the Alliance made ripples throughout the varying groups that comprised Vieques' movement. Although the white ribbon campaign was well received, Conde noted that a number of men had problems with women's leadership. Still, the Women's Alliance forced other grassroots organizations, such as the Committee to Rescue and Develop Vieques (Comité pro Rescate y Desarrollo de Vieques or CPRDV), to focus on the role of women within the movement. The CPRDV started shifting public attention away from leading male activists, to emphasize the voice of Nilda Medina in press conferences and press releases. It began to highlight women's lead in various demonstrations and activities. In fact, women had a slight majority in the Vieques movement, but it was the Alliance that gave them greater voice.

One of the most significant, if unplanned, contributions of the Alliance was to develop a community presence at the gates to Camp García. With its pot-and-pan protest and ribbon campaign at the gates to base, the Alliance effectively opened another front in the battle and broadened Vieques' struggle. "Not everyone can be so macho, not everyone can be out at the bombing range," Conde noted. She felt that male leaders valorized the initial strategy of setting up encampments on the bombing range. Living for days, weeks, even months on a no-man's-land of scorching sun, with no access to food and water, and thousands of unexploded bombs, was a dramatic but extreme strategy that most community members were not prepared to emulate.[4] The Alliance focused attention on another space where protest could develop, a site that was more accessible to a broader range of people.

This presence was institutionalized in December 1999 when demonstrators locked the gates to the Camp García and planted themselves squarely at the entrance. They built an encampment they christened the Peace and Justice Camp. This camp would prove crucial to the expansion and continuity of the movement. "The Peace and Justice Camp became like the center of town for those of us who couldn't be on the bombing range," reflected Myrna Pagán, a Vieques resident who participated in Alliance events. Many elderly people, who could not handle the arduous journey and terrain of the bombing range, took up regular positions at the gates. Women with small children and residents who could not leave their jobs or family passed through the encampment. Importantly, the

Catholic Church, which shared with the Women's Alliance a common vision of Vieques' movement as a grassroots struggle for peace, started holding Saturday night prayer vigils at the gates. Activists rented a house across the street from the encampment, and tapped into electric and water lines to maintain the camp. Miriam Sobá reflects on the significance of the encampment:

> The Peace and Justice Camp, which is located in front of the gates to Camp García, the civil disobedience camp, has earned the title "The Women's Camp" because of our active participation. This blessed camp teaches us, not only the women but all of our people, that there are no chains that can hold back Viequenses who struggle. Not a people who have decided to be free. It is teaching us that we can struggle without limits, that there is no difference between men and women in struggle. (2000, n.p.)

After protesters were evicted from the bombing range in May 2000 and the Peace and Justice Camp was dismantled by the navy, protest simply shifted across the street from Camp García. The house that had provided electricity and water became the command center, with computers, phone lines, and fax machines broadcasting Vieques' struggle to the world. New structures were erected, banners were strung from fences, and tents were staked on the hill. The prayer vigils, the meals of rice and beans, the domino games, the music and pickets continued in the face of a wall of riot police. The Peace and Justice Camp allowed the Vieques movement to continue, even after it lost the encampments that had focused and defined the movement for over a year.

Again, the Peace and Justice encampment was not specifically the project of the Women's Alliance, although members of the Alliance participated in activities and prayer vigils held outside the gates to Camp García. Rather, the camp demonstrated the way in which the work of the Women's Alliance contributed to the expansion and continuity of the Vieques struggle.

Mobilizing Women: Ideologies and Tactics

> In life, there are things that we learn only when we women experience them. We have learned a lot about what fear is, sadness, misery and suffering through the death of our loved ones because of cancer. We ourselves suffer from cancer in our bodies. We have seen our sons and daughters leave for the big island, as we affectionately call it, and to other countries because there are no opportunities to study or work in Vieques. We feel the pain of not being able to give birth in our beautiful "Little Girl Island." Most importantly, we long for the right to live in peace and the liberty which belongs to us and our loved ones. (Sobá 2000, n.p.)

Judith Conde, an avowed *independentista* and feminist, contends that most members of the Alliance would not identify themselves as feminist: "There are some *compañeras* [fellow activists] who aren't comfortable with the Alliance calling itself feminist, because the perception still exists that feminists are lesbians. They would prefer to belong to a group of women that works for women's issues, but is not feminist." Interviews with Alliance members and participant observation at Alliance-sponsored events, however, suggested a complex reality both in terms of how women viewed themselves and the militancy with which they championed their cause.

For example, some Alliance members saw no contradiction between feminist principles and their domestic identities. When asked if she would consider herself a feminist, fifty-five-year-old Alliance activist Zaidy Torres responded:

> Of course! I was raised by a single mother. I believe women have to be strong. I'm not a feminist in the sense that I'm a radical extremist. But in terms of believing that women can get ahead, that they don't need a man to survive, sure I'm a feminist. I believe we are strong, we know how to administrate; we know how to take charge. We can do a lot of things; it doesn't have to be a man in charge.

It was precisely Zaidy Torres's confidence in the private, domestic sphere that made it natural for her to assume leadership in a women's mobilization: "If we can run a house, of course we can run a movement," she explained. Torres was motivated to join the Alliance to bring about social change for her grandchildren. A retired nurse, Torres had never before joined grassroots struggle against the navy. Torres's husband worked as a plumber for the navy on Camp García for twenty-seven years, which bought her silence, she explained, for over twenty years. In 1997, however, Torres lost her seventeen-year-old daughter to leukemia after a difficult two-year battle. In Vieques, residents largely accept that cancer is the unquestionable consequence of over sixty years of military practices, but the death of her child inspired Torres to speak out against the navy. "I want changes for my grandchildren," she explained. "It's my obligation to the memory of my daughter. For over twenty years I kept quiet, and didn't get involved before because of my husband's job. Now I think of my four grandchildren and realize I want to do more. I'm going to defend my family." Torres clearly felt justified in speaking out. As a grieving mother, she was unconcerned with charges of radicalism or extremism. She was acting as a mother, to fight for her daughter's memory. As a woman who knew how to manage a household and job, she was fully confident in her leadership abilities. The Alliance allowed Torres to draw on these dual aspects of her female identity, grieving mother and competent manager, as she spoke out against the naval presence.

Lynn Stephen (2005) argues that it is important to distinguish between the public face and the internal dynamics of grassroots organizations. To gain support from outsiders, the Women's Alliance needed to craft a message that would appeal to popular sensibilities in Puerto Rico about women's role and place. Nonetheless, "the political necessity of projecting 'sameness' does not . . . explain how a movement operates, what it means to those involved, or what it is able to accomplish. It is also not evidence of shared consciousness or identity" (Stephen 2005, 66).

Miriam Sobá clearly distinguished between her own feelings and the outward symbolism of the Women's Alliance. The white ribbon campaign, one of the Alliance's most successful aspects, promoted the imagery of pretty white ribbons, of women as defenders of the domestic and as emotional, sentimental protectors of peace. Sobá rolled her eyes when asked about the campaign. "Everyone *loves* the ribbons," she moaned. Then, shrugging her shoulders, she explained, "We in Puerto Rico operate on symbols. On the surface, the white ribbon seems innocent, feminine, and nice. It's appealing. Everyone says, 'Give me a ribbon. I'll wear that.' But the more people see the ribbons, the more they think of Vieques. It raises consciousness."

Alliance organizers had a clear sense of the strategic utility of mobilizing certain symbols and identities. As much as Conde and Rivera struggled to find appropriate symbols and rhetoric to connect to the women, they also consciously manipulated symbols and maintained a somewhat ironic perspective on their import. For instance, despite the initial meeting at which women expressed their concerns about health issues and cancer, Conde and Rivera elected to emphasize women's concerns for peace in their rhetoric and imagery. Proving that the navy caused cancer on the island was more difficult, Rivera explained, whereas peace was a universally recognized basic human right.

When asked if the women's group contributed something unique to the mobilization of Vieques, Zaidy Torres was absolute: yes. She felt this difference was most apparent on the lecture circuit:

> There's a big difference when a woman speaks and when a man speaks. When the men spoke, the audience gave them their attention. When the women spoke, they made the presentation very different. They drew on their own personal experience in the family. They presented their perspective as mothers, wives, and all the effects the navy has had on our families. People understand that more.
>
> In Philadelphia, we went to a workshop. What we said wasn't different from the men. But we expressed it with more emotion. When women speak of their experience as wife and mother, people feel the experience more. It's more from the heart than the head. We speak of the same issues, but the emotion we bring is different.

In a sense, what women brought to the Vieques mobilization was *testimonio,* a Latin American literary tradition of bearing testimony, particularly in relation to human rights abuses and injustice. Latin American women such as Carolina María de Jesus, Domitila Barrios de Chungara, and Nobel Prize–winning Guatemalan activist Rigoberta Menchú exemplify this tradition. George Yúdice defines *testimonio* as

an authentic narrative, told by a witness who is moved to narrate by
the urgency of a situation (e.g. war, oppression, revolution, etc.).
Emphasizing popular, oral discourse, the witness portrays his or her own
experience as an agent (rather than a representative) of a collective
memory and identity. Truth is summoned in the cause of denouncing a
present situation of exploitation and oppression or in exorcising and
setting aright official history. (Yúdice as quoted in Gugelberger and
Kearney 1991, 4)

Alliance activists tended to highlight their personal experiences as women
and mothers living on an island dominated by military forces. "Our work is not
only [about] the political action to get them out. We are organizing to bring attention to the social and psychological effects of the presence of the navy here,"
explained Judith Conde (Suárez Toro 1999, n.p.). In practice, this meant that at
speaking engagements, when male activists chronicled the history of Vieques'
domination by the U.S. Navy and the island's subjugation to broader political
forces, women activists gave highly emotional presentations about their suffering
and abuse at the hands of the navy, and about their struggles to keep their families intact, healthy, and functioning. When Miriam Sobá spoke at a conference at
the University of Puerto Rico, she was both vehement and emotional:

How do the children feel, how do they perform in the classroom, how do
they respond day by day? How did the women feel when 2000 Americans
came to town and you had to protect your house, you couldn't go out
because it was dangerous, you could lose your life and your dignity as a
woman . . . and many did and many kept quiet. I believe that the situation in the town was that [the marines] believed it belonged to them, the
Americans thought it was theirs, they thought the people of Vieques
belonged to them and they could do and destroy whatever they wanted.
It is the woman who carries all of these experiences, because it is we who
keep in our hearts the feeling that, in a certain sense, our privacy and
our liberty were violated, our peace. It's an incredible indignation. (Sobá
2000, n.p.)

The organization of the Women's Alliance and its symbolic framework
allowed room for the expression of fiery sentiment and provided space for the
emergence of women's leadership in a way that non-gender-based organizations
did not. At a July 4, 2000, rally at the gates of Camp García, women picketed in
front of a human wall of Puerto Rican police in riot gear. Tensions were high.
Federal marshals had dislodged protesters from the bombing range after a year of
civil disobedience. Residents were angry that the governor had ordered heavily
armed Puerto Rican police to guard navy boundaries.

Yet the women were not deterred. Conde rallied protesters with a bullhorn.
She read a declaration of U.S. hypocrisy in which she pointed out that the United

States was celebrating its independence while Puerto Rico languished as its colony. She iterated demands for freedom and justice. Women marched in a lively picket line, interrupted only when bursts of tear gas were inexplicably fired on them.

By embracing the idea of woman as housewife and defender of the home, the Alliance was able to allow the emergence of strong female leadership and involvement in the movement. The rhetoric of women protecting their homes legitimized women's participation in protest and sidestepped partisan politics and the specter of anticolonialism. The Vieques Women's Alliance celebrated women's domestic roles while asserting a public voice for women and challenging one of the most powerful expressions of U.S. colonialism in Puerto Rico—the U.S. military. The Women's Alliance successfully avoided the issue of Puerto Rican sovereignty, while implicitly, and sometimes explicitly, challenging colonial domination by the United States.

Conclusion

The women of Vieques embraced private, domestic identities to assert a powerful public voice in protest of the navy's sixty-year occupation of Vieques Island. Joining a coalition movement united by the theme of peace and tactics of nonviolent civil disobedience, the Vieques Women's Alliance mobilized new sectors of the public and expanded the vision of the movement. Women's new participation and leadership in grassroots struggle were crucial elements in the shutting down of military operations on Vieques Island. The Vieques movement succeeded in halting live-bombing exercises and forcing the military to withdraw, although the navy's toxic legacy remains very much a problem on the island.[5] The Vieques movement points to the power of locally based social movements that are linked to broader goals, visions, and alliances. Rather than seeking total social transformation, these small movements focus on more specific, concrete, everyday concerns and grievances. The Vieques mobilization marks a "refusal to accept" (Holloway 2002) injustices of state power. By organizing as a coalition movement and by accepting a multiplicity of voices rather than asserting the primacy of a particular, dominant voice, the movement expanded. The reconstituted Vieques mobilization of 1999 allowed for the participation of new sectors of the population and the emergence of new leadership.

The work and history of the Vieques Women's Alliance offer implications for broader social movement theory on the nature of women's participation in protest. Vieques follows a pattern of women mobilizing around subsistence issues by drawing on their identities as mothers, wives, and homemakers to rally support for their cause. What the Vieques case makes clear is that women's organizing framework—in this case, the defense of the domestic sphere—does not necessarily limit the scope or aspirations of participants. In fact, in Vieques, it was through asserting their domestic role that women were able to assume leadership and assert themselves forcefully in the public sphere. The agenda of the Women's Alliance influenced the tactics and priorities of the broader movement as a whole. Ideologies of domesticity and women's traditional place allowed women to envision themselves as part of a social movement that had often been identified with fishermen's struggles and land rescues, or what Conde described as the "macho" tactics of men. The Women's Alliance also created a space for protest that sidestepped paralyzing debates on colonialism, dramatically expanding Vieques' grassroots mobilization. In sum, by drawing on gender-based experience, women in Vieques demonstrated that women everywhere have the potential to broaden bases of social protest and strengthen the effectiveness of movements for social change.

ACKNOWLEDGMENTS

This chapter builds on long-term ethnographic and documentary research in Vieques, Puerto Rico. Parts of this chapter are drawn from *Military Power and Popular Protest: the U.S. Navy in Vieques, Puerto Rico* (McCaffrey 2002) with the permission of Rutgers University Press. Other parts are based on new documentary and ethnographic research. My thanks to the women of the Alianza de Mujeres Viequenses, especially Judith Conde, Gladys Rivera, Miriam Sobá, Carmen Valencia, Myrna Pagán, and Zaidy Torres for the time they took to speak to me. Thanks also to my husband, Howard Fischer, for his sharp editorial skills and patience. It is with sadness that I note that Gladys Rivera died of cancer on February 13, 2007. I dedicate this essay to her memory and legacy.

NOTES

1. Dr. Cruz María Nazario Delgado, principal investigator of the Epidemiological Study of Cancer in Vieques, sponsored by the Puerto Rican legislature, analyzed the 2005 Puerto Rican Health Department statistics. Dr. Nazario concluded that the average incidence of cancer in Vieques for the five-year period of 1980–1984 was 266 per 100,000. During 1995–1999 the cancer incidence was 359 per 100,000. The risk of developing cancer in Vieques was approximately 1.35 times greater in 1995–1999, compared with the risk in 1980–1984 (Nazario 2005).

2. In this way, Vieques' revitalized movement follows the pattern of social movement organizing, seen in Seattle in 1999, in which the structure is one of a decentralized, non-hierarchical network of antiglobalization activists.

3. Judith Conde, Gladys Rivera, Miriam Sobá, Carmen Valencia, Myrna Pagán, and Zaidy Torres are quoted throughout this chapter. If a citation is not given for a quotation, the reader should assume the statement comes from the interviews I conducted with these women in Vieques during the summers of 1999, 2000, and 2006.

4. One of the major challenges of the movement was sustaining the activists who were living out on the encampments. Fishing boats made daily trips to bring water and food to the protesters camping on the bombing range.

5. See *Centro Journal* (2006), a special issue partially devoted to Vieques' current struggles for demilitarization, decontamination, development, and return of military-controlled land.

REFERENCES

Ayala, César. 2003. "Recent Works on Vieques, Colonialism, and Fishermen." *Centro* 15(1): 212–225.

Baldez, Lisa. 2002. *Why Women Protest: Women's Movements in Chile.* Cambridge: Cambridge University Press.

Bouvard, Marguerite Guzman. 1994. *Revolutionizing Motherhood: The Mothers of the Plaza de Mayo.* Wilmington, DE: Scholarly Resources.

Caribbean Business. 2004. April 15.

Centro Journal. 2006. Vol. 18, no. 1 (Spring).

Corcoran-Nantes, Yvonne. 1990. "Women and Popular Urban Social Movements in Sao Paulo, Brazil." *Bulletin of Latin American Research* 9(2): 249–264.

——. 1993. "Female Consciousness or Feminist Consciousness? Women's Consciousness in Community-Based Struggles in Brazil." In *Viva: Women and Popular Protest in Latin America,* ed. Sarah A. Radcliffe and Sallie Westwood, 136–155. London: Routledge.

Cruz Pérez, Rafael. 1988. "Contaminación producida por explosivos y residuos de explosivos en Vieques, Puerto Rico." *Dimensión* 8(2): 37–42.

Dávila, Arlene. 1997. *Sponsored Identities: Cultural Politics in Puerto Rico.* Philadelphia: Temple University Press.

Delgado Cintrón, Carmelo. 1989. *Culebra y la marina de Estados Unidos.* Río Piedras, Puerto Rico: Editorial Edil.

Duany, Jorge. 2000. "Nation on the Move: The Construction of Cultural Identities in Puerto Rico and the Diaspora." *American Ethnologist* 27:5–30.

——. 2002. *The Puerto Rican Nation on the Move: Identities on the Island and the United States.* Chapel Hill: University of North Carolina Press.

Fallon, Vice Admiral William, Commander, U.S. Second Fleet, and Lieutenant General Peter Pace, Commander, U.S. Marine Corps Forces, Atlantic. 1999. "The National Security Need for Vieques: A Study Prepared for the Secretary of the Navy." July 15.

Fernández, Ronald. 1996. *The Disenchanted Island: Puerto Rico and the United States in the Twentieth Century.* New York: Praeger.

Flores, Juan. 2000. *From Bomba to Hip-Hop.* New York: Columbia University Press.

Giusti-Cordero, Juan. 2000. "One Stop Shopping for Navy Facts: A Response to the Navy's Vieques Website." http://www.vieques-island.com/board/navy/navyfacts.html (accessed March 30, 2007).

Gugelberger, Georg, and Michael Kearney. 1991. "Voices for the Voiceless: Testimonial Literature in Latin America." *Latin American Perspectives* 18(3): 3–14.

Holloway, John. 2002. *Change the World without Taking Power: The Meaning of Revolution Today.* London: Pluto Press.

Kaplan, Temma. 1982. "Female Consciousness and Collective Action: The Case of Barcelona, 1910–1918." *Signs: Journal of Women in Culture and Society* 7(3): 545–566.

——. 1990. "Community and Resistance in Women's Political Cultures." *Dialectical Anthropology* 15:259–264.

McCaffrey, Katherine T. 2002. *Military Power and Popular Protest: The U.S. Navy in Vieques, Puerto Rico.* New Brunswick, NJ: Rutgers University Press.

——. 2006. "Social Struggle against the U.S. Navy in Vieques, Puerto Rico: Two Movements in History." *Latin American Perspectives* 33(1): 83–101.

Meléndez López, Arturo. 1989. *La batalla de Vieques.* Río Piedras, Puerto Rico: Editorial Edil.

Morris, Nancy. 1995. *Puerto Rico: Culture, Politics, and Identity.* Westport, CT: Praeger.

Moser, Caroline. 1987. "Mobilisation Is Women's Work: The Struggle for Infrastructure in Guayaquil, Ecuador." In *Women, Human Settlements and Housing,* ed. Caroline Moser and Linda Peake, 166–194. London: Tavistock Publications.

Nash, June. 1990. "Latin American Women in the World Capitalist Crisis." *Gender and Society* 4(3): 338–353.

Nazario Delgado, Cruz María. 2005. "Analysis of the Most Recent Statistics on Cancer in Vieques." June 29. http://pr.indymedia.org/news/2005/06/8736.php (accessed March 30, 2007).

Negrón-Muntaner, Frances, and Ramón Grosfoguel, eds. 1997. *Puerto Rican Jam: Essays on Culture and Politics.* Minneapolis: University of Minnesota Press.

Safa, Helen. 1990. "Women's Social Movements in Latin America." *Gender and Society* 4(3): 354–369.

Schemmer, Ben, and Bruce Cossaboom. 1970. "Culebra Act II: House Panel Reschedules Hearings." *Armed Forces Journal*, June 6, 16–20.

Schemmer, Ben, Clare Lewis, et al. 1970. "Culebra: Navy Focus on Cinclant's Bull's-Eye Is Way off Target, but May Be Coming into Range." *Armed Forces Journal*, May 23, 28–39.

Schirmer, Jennifer. 1993. "The Seeking of Truth and the Gendering of Consciousness: The CoMadres of El Salvador and the Conavigua Widows of Guatemala." In *Viva: Women and Popular Protest in Latin America*, ed. Sarah A. Radcliffe and Sallie Westwood, 136–155. London: Routledge Press.

Shanahan, John, and John Lindsay-Poland. 2002. "Vieques: Is It Needed by the Navy?" Vieques Issue Brief. Fellowship for Reconciliation. Winter. http://www.prorescatevieques. org/doceng/VIEQMILBRIEF.PDF (accessed March 30, 2007).

Sobá, Miriam. 2000. "Una voz de mujer en el deseo compartido de vivir en paz." Third keynote address, at the conference From Vieques to the University: Lessons and Needs of the People of Vieques in Their Struggle for Peace and Development." UNESCO University of Education for Peace and Development. University of Puerto Rico, Río Piedras. February 24. http://unescopaz.rrp.upr.edu/act/Lecciones/tercera/3raSoba.html (accessed March 30, 2007).

Special Commission for Vieques. 1999. "Report to Puerto Rican Governor Pedro Rosselló." June 25.

Stephen, Lynn. 1997. *Women and Social Movements in Latin America: Power from Below.* Austin: University of Texas Press.

———. 2005. "Gender, Citizenship and the Politics of Identity." In *Social Movements: An Anthropological Reader*, ed. June Nash, 66–77. Malden, MA: Blackwell Publishing.

Suárez Toro, María. 1999. "Alianza de Mujeres Viequenses on FIRE." September. http://www.fire.or.cr/etaesept.htm (accessed March 30, 2007).

Susser, Ida. 1992. "Women as Political Actors in Rural Puerto Rico: Continuity and Change." In *Anthropology and the Global Factory*, edited by Frances A. Rothstein and Michael Blim. New York: Bergin and Garvey.

U.S. Census Bureau. 2000. "Demographic Profile of Social, Economic, and Housing Characteristics. Percent of Population under Poverty Level in 1999." http://www.gobierno.pr/Censo/CensoPoblacionVivienda/Censo2000/PerfilDemograficoCaracteristicasSociales/ (accessed January 9, 2008).

U.S. Congress. House of Representatives. Subcommittee on Insular and International Affairs of the Committee on Natural Resources. 1994. *Vieques Land Transfer Act of 1994: Hearings on H.R. 3831.* 103d Cong., 2nd sess.

PART III

============================

Localizing Militarization in the United States

10

===

Manhood, Sexuality, and Nation in Post-9/11 United States

BONNIE MANN

You don't prevent a war with words. But speaking was not necessarily a way of changing history; it was also a certain way of living it.

–Simone de Beauvoir, *The Mandarins,* 1960

After September 11, 2001, the Bush administration and the nation embarked on a strange and fated project of "manning up." We recognize here an old quest for invulnerability, one that finally was to make up for the feminizing loss of the Vietnam War (Jeffords 1990; Boose 1993). Fated, like any quest for absolute invulnerability, the Bush administration's policy of preemptive war led to the toppling of two governments and the death, disability, and displacement of thousands of Iraqi and Afghan citizens—which is to say the policy is, at this writing, still fostering an ever-growing number of people who have deeply personal and immediate reasons to hate the United States.[1] Each week, more U.S. soldiers are killed or disabled as well, and the lies of the administration regarding the reasons for these sacrifices grate on the patriotic nerves of even conservative U.S. citizens. As leaked details of the National Intelligence Estimate (Office of the Director of National Intelligence 2006) confirmed, the project of "manning up" has created more vulnerability, not less, in a global climate of intensified disgust for the world's one remaining superpower.[2]

"Manning up" is also a strange project. U.S. national manhood is reconstituted through an exotic stew of stories that do not seem, at first, to belong together. Each of the two preemptive wars was tied to a racialized project of women's liberation (explicitly in Afghanistan, implicitly in Iraq) by the Bush administration itself—we might say the administration took up and occupied the discursive site of a global Western (and Christian) "feminist" subject who set out to free the oppressed Muslim woman—whose supposed "liberation" reinvigorated, at the same moment, good old-fashioned masculinist protectionism. From the beginning, documents associated with the war effort have deployed complex

narratives of racialized homoerotic violence,[3] and in the midst of our masculiniz-
ing military adventures, the use of torture by U.S. troops became an international
scandal. The dominant images of this scandal from Abu Ghraib prison featured
white women sexually humiliating Iraqi men—even while the strategies of torture
and humiliation included the racialized homosexualizing of the prisoners, who
were forced to simulate fellatio with one another and photographed with anuses
exposed. As the pictures hit our evening news, the panic that had been building
domestically over the prospect of legal gay marriage crescendoed into a flurry of
right-wing activism, resulting in more than a dozen new state constitutional
amendments defining marriage as "between one man and one woman."
American "tolerance" of homosexuality was claimed by right-wing pundits to be
the cause of terrorism at home (Knight 2004), and warnings circulated, in the
form of colorful pamphlets for voters, that the legalization of gay marriage would
lead to the systematic sexual abuse of children, renewed terrorist attacks, and the
downfall of civilization itself.

If writing is, as Simone de Beauvoir suggests, a way of living through history
(1960, 602), then this writing is no more nor less than the attempt of one lesbian
feminist philosopher to make sense of the pastiche of narratives of manhood,
sexuality, and nation that continue to proliferate in post-9/11 America. Here I am
moved by two observations. One is that the rebuilding of American national
identity after 9/11 relies on what we generally consider to be postmodern sensibilities to reinforce what we generally consider to be modern notions of imperial
power and sovereignty. The second is that the style of national manhood under
reconstruction in post-9/11 United States is a big part of what, for too long, made
the wars make sense to many U.S. Americans.

Another way of stating this second observation is to say that the sense that
the wars made, and continue to make for a good number of people, is primarily
aesthetic.[4] By this I mean that the process of making sense is more bodily than
conceptual, carried by stories and images more than by argument or reason. The
powerful commitments associated with the aesthetic of manhood that prolifer-
ated after 9/11 function first beneath rational argument, as the motivational base
for things like argument and opinion, so that support for the war is an intentional
posture lived viscerally, a matter of *who we are* as a nation rather than a thoughtful commitment to the justice of a cause. As I have noted elsewhere, the association of an aesthetic of manhood with war is not new. It is to be found both in
Kant's early work on aesthetics and in William James's 1910 essay "The Moral
Equivalent of War." James argues that the manly aesthetic that war both expresses
and produces could find some other cultural point of purchase that would both
preserve masculine "hardihood" and be less catastrophic for humanity. The association of manhood with war has been a theme of feminist criticism for generations. Virginia Woolf's brilliant antiwar treatise *Three Guineas* (1938) is a notable
example (Mann 2006, 148–149).

Contemporary events challenge us to reopen the question of the relation between politics and aesthetics because the aesthetic continues to found the political in sometimes astounding ways.

Imagining Gender: The Primacy of the Aesthetic

To begin, I borrow another beginning, the opening of a well-known and important feminist essay on war written by Carol Cohn just after the first Gulf War. The essay, "Wars, Wimps, and Women: Talking Gender and Thinking War" (1993), is Cohn's account of her study of the gendered speech of foot soldiers, drill sergeants, and defense intellectuals. Cohn begins her account like this: "I start with a story, told to me by a white male physicist." By beginning with a story, she already moves us into the realm of the aesthetic, but the story is also the story of an aesthetic experience:

> Several colleagues and I were working on modeling counterforce attacks, trying to get realistic estimates of the number of immediate fatalities that would result from different deployments. At one point, we remodeled a particular attack, using slightly different assumptions, and found that instead of there being thirty-six million immediate fatalities, there would only be thirty million. And everybody was sitting around nodding, saying, "Oh yeah, that's great, only thirty million," when all of a sudden, I heard what we were saying. And I blurted out, "Wait, I've just heard how we're talking—only thirty million! Only thirty million human beings killed instantly?" Silence fell upon the room. Nobody said a word. They didn't even look at me. It was awful. I felt like a woman. (227)

After that, Cohn's physicist adds, he was much more careful.

Cohn is concerned here to show how the policing of the boundaries of masculinity plays its part in the militarization of sectors of the social world, in the training of soldiers, the strategizing of physicists. She wants us to recognize how thinking itself is constrained by gender boundaries and the fear they generate. By the content and tone of his expression, Cohn's physicist has impulsively entered a region of affect and care that has been rigidly zoned as feminine. He has committed a kind of violation; his fellow physicists avert their eyes, embarrassed for him, unable or unwilling to look at him. He finds himself literally unmanned by the experience, which is to say his felt sense of his own gender identity is temporarily but deeply shaken.

The physicist does not say, "I realized I sounded like a woman," nor "I was given to understand that the others thought my outburst was inappropriately feminine," but "I *felt* like a woman," which I take to mean "my subjective experience became that of a woman," or "I found myself being the wrong sort of subject." On my reading, what the physicist had violated was a certain aesthetic style that might be described as "masculine" or even "masculinist," as long as we keep in mind that this is a *particular* style of masculinity.

Let me insist from the outset that masculinities, like femininities, are multiple, complex, contradictory, and under constant cultural revision. Let me insist as well that they are identifiable, cohesive in sometimes intransigent ways, and take more or less dominant, even hegemonic forms in particular places and at particular times. On my account, then, masculinities are neither biological essences nor a set of culturally introjected characteristics empirically discoverable in the psychologies of individual men—although they are embedded in our relations to both biology and psychology. Masculinities, and genders more broadly, are primarily lived *aesthetically*. This is not to say that gender is separate from politics or violence; on the contrary, the whole point of opening the question of the aesthetic is to find a way to talk about how gender operates in politics, and how gendered violence can seem, to the powerful, to be self-justifying.

It is important to note that masculinities tend to fuse with race in practices of sexuality promoted or enforced in the context of nationalism, so it is necessary to speak of racialized masculinities (and femininities) in the plural. I am following the work of Maria Lugones here, who argues that "heterosexism is a key part of how gender fuses with race in the operations of colonial power" (2007, 186). Lugones presses for an understanding of how gender arrangements and sexuality in colonial contexts are differentiated "along 'racial' lines" (190), so that what she calls "the light side of the colonial/modern organization of gender" is marked by "biological dimorphism, heterosexualism, and patriarchy," while the "dark side" of the colonial/modern organization of gender may be very differently marked (190). As we shall see later in the chapter, the aesthetic of manhood that is reconstituted in the rise of U.S. nationalism after 9/11 relies in certain contexts on a fusion of race, gender, and sexuality.

When I claim that gender is primarily lived in the realm of the aesthetic, I do not mean that it is superficial; nor do I mean that it is art (although it certainly involves a good deal of artifice). Nor do I mean that gender is only aesthetic. It is appropriate to talk about racialized masculinity in relation to economic structures, political institutions, kinship structures, and systems of belief. These are the aspects of masculinism that can be observed, studied, and documented empirically. The point here is that when we look at how gender is lived by both women and men, the aesthetic dimension has a certain primacy that has often been neglected. On this level, racialized gender does its work more through the body than through the mind, although it is never radically distinct from mental processes, since our bodily awareness will be the foundation for cognitive commitments. The aesthetic produces our felt sense of orientation or disorientation, of rightness or wrongness, in the sexual, racial, and moral order of things.

The aesthetic works at the level of the imaginary, but I want to understand the imaginary in a particular way. We might take the imaginary to be a domain in the subjective life of an individual person, what makes it possible for her to live in relation to what does not yet exist, and thus hope for a future different than this present (Sartre 2004). The imaginary might be viewed as the force of the image of myself in the mirror, or in the eyes of others, which makes it possible for me to imagine myself as a singular, unified "I" despite evidence to the contrary (Lacan 1966, 1975). But we might also understand the imaginary to be a structure of sociality in a grander sense, what enables us to imagine ourselves in relation to others whom we have never met yet with whom we stand together in some particular way; we are a community consisting of believers in this religion, practitioners of certain rituals in this culture, or fellow citizens of this nation (Anderson 1983; Taylor 2004). If we take these different imaginaries to be distinct modalities of the same capacity, we get closer to the understanding of the imaginary at work here; it is what makes it possible for humans to live the relations between subjective experience, intersubjective entanglements, and broad social identities. I understand the aesthetic to be the net that binds bodily awareness and social meaning, and the imaginary to be the acrobat that climbs back and forth between them.

In order to say why, I want to think two very different notions together: the phenomenological notion of "style" most fully developed in the work of Merleau-Ponty (1962, 1993a, 1993b) but recently appropriated by feminists as a way of talking about gendered experience (Heinämaa 1996, 2003); and the notion of the "social imaginary," which is Charles Taylor's (2004) reworking of Benedict Anderson's (1983) idea that the nation is an "imagined community." I am interested in understanding how gender gets to be both a deep, personally lived identity commitment and a site of the production of broad, almost impersonal, yet extremely powerful social meanings. As Cynthia Cockburn puts it, "identity processes matter because they are second only to force as the means by which power is effected in oppressive and exploitative systems" (1998, 10). "The notion of nation always suggests a project of power," she notes (55), and all nationalisms appeal to identity as a source of power, "hailing us, flattering us, holding us hostage" (11). A feminist reading of our contemporary political situation needs to understand the particular entanglement of lived gender, racialization, and sexuality. These entanglements change form, sometimes with stunning speed, but often find their most virulent and direct expression in the context of state violence. The current U.S.-sponsored wars are no exception, of course. The actual events of the war have been accompanied, since the beginning, by the inundation of U.S. cultural "airspace" with images and words whose work seems to be to both seduce and reconstitute the national imagination.

Anderson, in his classic definition of the nation as an "imagined political community," argues that communities are to be distinguished by "the style in which they are imagined" (1983, 15). He does not mean to imply by this that nations are mere fictions but rather that nationalism and national identity depend on a process of imagining and creating. This process builds "a deep horizontal comradeship," he argues, "a fraternity." "Ultimately," Anderson claims, "it is this fraternity that makes it possible, over the past two centuries, for so many millions of people, not so much to kill, as willingly to die" in the interest of nationalism (16).

Taylor's "social imaginary" expands Anderson's work to include other kinds of imaginary formations that mobilize broad social meanings. By "the social imaginary" he does not mean a set of ideas or a theory, but meanings that are carried in stories, images, and legends (2004, 106). This "largely unstructured and inarticulate understanding" (106) is how we make sense of the practices of our society. The social imaginary denotes "the ways in which people imagine their social existence, how they fit together with others, how things go on between them and their fellows, the expectations that are normally met, and the deeper normative notions and images that underlie these expectations" (106). The social imaginary grounds a widely shared sense of legitimacy that makes our common practices possible. It gives us an "implicit map of social space" (25), which allows us to orient ourselves in the social world without consulting a map or rulebook (26).

Although Taylor calls the social imaginary "an inarticulate understanding," I suggest that it is not yet an understanding at all but rather a felt sense of legitimacy, normalcy, rightness—and their correlates, illegitimacy, abnormality, wrongness—broadly but not monolithically or seamlessly shared. Multiple social imaginaries cross and entangle in the lived identities of individuals, communities, and nations. Taylor is interested in the sense of moral order that emerges in the social imaginaries of modernity, whereas I am interested in the sense of sexual order that is under constant construction and reconstruction, and has been under intensive reconstruction since September 11, 2001, in the United States. The social order that emerges is one that engages and organizes meaning along multiple axes of power, so that race, religion, and nation become fused with gender and sexuality. At key moments, as we shall see later in the chapter, race/religion becomes the axis along which gendered power/sexuality reinvents itself, although it is just as certain that gender/sexuality becomes the axis along which racialized power reinvents itself as well. These reinventions entangle themselves with the "identity processes" (Cockburn 1998, 10) of U.S. nationals by animating more or less successfully the deeply felt and personal sense of such things as "manhood," "womanhood," or "nation" that all of us carry in some deeply embodied way, even if we resist such notions instead of affirming them. This felt sense is the seat of more or less deeply held commitments that legitimate themselves through stories, images, and legends that cross borders (between the modern and postmodern, for example), mix messages (women's liberation and masculinist protectionism, heterosexual purity with violent homoeroticism), and reinvent U.S. national identity.

Taylor neglects the workings of the social imaginary in the body. The notion of style, developed in certain strains of existential and feminist phenomenology,[5] by contrast, will bring the body into the center of our reflections. At the same time, *style* in this tradition has generally not been explored in its relation to the broader social imaginary.

When I speak of *style* here, I do not mean a style of art or painting, although lived, embodied style will bear a strong resemblance to these. I don't mean to refer to a "fetish of the commodity market" (Singer 1993, 234)—to what makes us choose our clothes in the morning or trade in our cars for something trendier. Yet *style* in the phenomenological sense is intimately related to those kinds of choices. In the words of feminist phenomenologist Linda Singer, "style emerges from and appears as an expressive gesture, which is an extension of the body's basic capacities to intentionally intertwine with the world" (1993, 238).

The body stylizes through gesture, both lived from the inside and recognized by others. We are immersed in our own style in such a way that it is not simply transparent to us. We walk without having an image of how we walk and recognize ourselves on film only after a strange effort. Yet others recognize my walk from a distance, at a glance, before they are able to see my features. Merleau-Ponty recounts the story of Matisse, who was utterly startled by a film of himself painting, by the strangeness of seeing his own habitual gestures from the outside (1993b, 82–83). We are haunted when we meet someone new who reminds us of someone else we have known, in their gesture, voice, movement. In Beauvoir's words, the "body is first of all the radiation of a subjectivity" (1952, 267); it radiates significance in and through and as style (Singer 1993). For Merleau-Ponty, the "lived body is unified by its style" (Singer 1993, 241). "I have received with existence a manner of existing, a style. All my actions and thoughts stand in relation to this structure" (Merleau-Ponty 1962, 455). In his view, even objects have style (450). A stiff wooden chair demands a particular posture, but also a particular mood, whereas an overstuffed chair demands not only a different posture but a different mood.

What we need is to bring the notions of the social imaginary and style together and put a hinge between them in good Merleau-Pontian fashion. I will call the hinge *gender* for now, recognizing that it can and does have many other names. On a broad social scale, the stories, images, and legends that are produced and deployed, cited, reiterated and revised, *carry* gender. The physicist's embarrassed admission, "I felt like a woman!" shows that he carries gender too, unselfconsciously for the most part and then suddenly as a shameful, almost unbearable burden. Gender is also the hinge, a structural feature of both psyche and social world, that connects the two levels of life in experience, so that *how* gender is carried by one *hinges on* the other. Otherwise said, the aesthetic relation I am calling gender is the hinge that connects the individual imagination to the social imaginary.

This structural feature allows the imaginary to continually reinvent broadly social gendered interests through deeply personal gendered commitments, but not in any simple or determinate way. And here it is useful to compare gendered style to a style of music or painting, both identifiable and open, both radically individual (each individual artist creates a different jazz, a different impressionism), and deeply social (jazz is jazz, until it becomes rock and roll;

impressionism is impressionism until Van Gogh pushes it over some unspeakable border). Each musician, each painter, belongs in relation to a stylistic movement, in and through her own style.

Similarly with gender. As Beauvoir pointed out, "to go for a walk with one's eyes open is enough to demonstrate that humanity is divided into two classes of individuals whose clothes, faces, bodies, smiles, gaits, interests, and occupations are manifestly different" (1952, xx–xxi). This may be a little less true in some places today, but only slightly. Although each individual man or woman both embodies and produces his or her own style of gender, we still tend to be deeply disturbed when gender identity is questioned or ambiguous. I have in mind the continued visceral efficacy of gender slander in the lives of children and adults alike, so that calling a boy or man a "bitch" or "pussy" or "fag" or "little girl" still seems to inspire a deep fear of nonexistence that is constitutive of the experience of coming to manhood for so many. Such misattributions need not be intentional to evoke a powerful response. This phenomenon is often described and, to choose the most extreme example, has been key to the actual legal use of, and also analyses of, what is called the homosexual panic defense.[6] Here men have defended themselves against charges of committing hate crimes against gay men who supposedly flirted with or propositioned them by arguing that their own sense of gender identity was so severely threatened by the sexual attentions of another man that the ensuing violence was, psychologically considered from the perspective of the perpetrator, self-defense. Certainly there are those who live in cultural enclaves in which a conscious and sustained resistance to binary gender diminishes the effect of discomfort or fear, but clarity about binary gender identity is still linked to deep fear in the larger social imaginary.

National Manhood from Vietnam to 9/11

Consider the images that played and replayed on and after 9/11. Two erect towers are penetrated over and over again by aircraft used as weapons. These images have many meanings, of course, but Carla Freccero asks us to focus on how the images call up "the spectacle of the pierced and porous male body, a male body riddled with holes" (2002, 453). Consider as well the political cartoons that circulated after 9/11, many of which turned on themes of penetration, such as images of Osama bin Laden sodomized by a U.S. bomb, or the caption "bend over Saddam." Freccero asks, "what does it mean that a certain US cultural imaginary associates this attack with being sodomized and sodomizing in return?" (454). We come to understand that this imaginary reads the attack on the twin towers as a simultaneous act of penetration (the images of the towers being penetrated by the planes plays over and over again) and castration (the towers collapse), when we attend to the subsequent images of missiles poised to anally penetrate Saddam Hussein (or think of the slogan "USA: Up Saddam's Ass"), or see a photo of soldiers spray painting a missile with the words "Highjack This Fags." A symbolic effort to reassert the power of the American phallus is only necessary if the attack is read as an assault on that power. Why does this attack get read not just as a criminal act of violence reprehensible in its inhumanity but as sexual violence, as the unmanning of America?

The events gave rise immediately to presidential assurances of American manhood, of the "quiet, unyielding anger" of the nation (Bush 2001a, 1). "Our country is strong," Bush assured us, "our military is powerful and prepared," "our financial institutions remain strong" (1). The motivation for the attacks was named that very evening: "America was targeted for attack because we're the brightest beacon for freedom and opportunity in the world" (1). It is "our way of life, our very freedom" that has come under attack and must be defended (1). Again and again in the days following 9/11, and more recently on the fifth anniversary of the attacks, the administration claimed that the terrorists hate "who we are" (2001b, 1), they hate "our way of life" (2006, 4). But the terrorists have found a willing and manly opponent in the United States, we are assured: after all, "America has stood down enemies before,"[7] and although "these attacks shattered steel, they cannot dent the steel of American resolve" (2001a, 1). Yet the steel of American resolve was already dented, and U.S. citizens know this. The Vietnam War has long taken its place in our social imaginary as the story of the first great unmanning of America (Jeffords 1990; Boose 1993).

Lynda Boose (1993) claims that two separate gender-marked antiwar narratives circulated and consolidated themselves after the loss of the Vietnam War. One narrative concluded that the war was a bad war because we lost, and called on America to "man up." The second concluded that it was a bad war because it was wrong, and promoted a different sort of masculinity altogether.

The second narrative emerges in the seventies, along with "an ethic outside of the claims of patriotic nationalism" (Boose 1993, 70). This antiwar position relied on the promotion of values that were not traditionally masculinist. "It was a set of ethics that, by the very nature of its self-reflexivity, its internalization of guilt, and its antimilitarist, antiviolence ethos, had asserted—and for a time successfully promoted—an identifiably 'feminized' structure of values" (70). Yet these values were promoted as values *for men* and were at the very heart of the emergence of an alternative masculine aesthetic, as well as ethic, at the time. "While the long hair, flowers, and flowing robes disappeared from post-Vietnam male popular culture, what did not so readily disappear was the potential for an ethically reconstituted masculinity," Boose claims (70).[8]

The other antiwar narrative, which understood the war to be bad because we lost, rejected this more complex and self-reflective masculinity in favor of an ethic of absolute certainty, indomitable will, and total invulnerability. This narrative embraced a return to a hypermasculine aesthetic. Here, "reconceived at a safe distance from images of either napalmed Vietnamese children or returning American body bags, the problem of Vietnam was no longer the excessive deployment of militarized values but the failure to deploy them strongly enough" (Boose 1993, 72). This narrative produced the language of a war fought "with one hand tied behind our backs," a war lost because of politicians "kowtowing to liberals" (72); it produced "an obsession with a manhood imagined as having been abandoned by US 'withdrawal' (a term that itself connotes masculine shame)" (75).

We have, throughout the Reagan era, the cultural reassertion of American masculinity in its invulnerable form, the emergence of the "fortress-like" masculine body in children's action figures, film, and fitness centers (Boose 1993, 74). Boose argues that America's shame, and reassertion of masculinity, expresses itself most explicitly in film (76). In other words, it gets worked on aesthetically through the hypermasculine cinematic action figure, the "symbol-laden depiction of the male body" (76). *Rambo: First Blood Part II*, in particular, mythologized the return to an indomitable and manly America, with Stallone's "fortress-like" body and single-handed dominance of an enemy who had defeated, and thus feminized, the entire U.S. military and consequently the nation itself.

The film places the blame for the defeat on the politicians who would not let our boys win and mythologizes American will as the vehicle for restoring the manhood of the nation. As Susan Faludi points out, "Winning—that first principle of manhood in the American Century—would be reaffirmed and encapsulated in a famous exchange. . . . Rambo demands of his commanding officer, Colonel Sam Trautman, who has ordered the hero back to Vietnam, 'Sir, do we get to win this time?' 'This time,' Trautman assures him, 'it is up to you' " (Faludi 1999, 364). The will to win this time penetrates the enemy's defenses; houses, villages, and bodies are literally pierced and torn apart. These acts of violence restore American masculinity and the "enemy's" effeminacy at the same time. When the twin towers are penetrated and collapse, then, the social imaginary that demands a reading of that event as homoerotic violence is already set up. The response, a hypermasculine reassertion of invulnerability, is already set up as well.

There is something both grotesque and comic, frightening and adolescent, about images of manhood such as that of John Rambo. "As the masculine icon has undergone . . . literal inflation, the representation of maleness and the narrative in which it is imagined—which together constitute a set of culture-specific dreams, desires, and fears—has become progressively less adult as a projection and more and more the cartoon image of a little boy's fantasy of manhood" (Boose 1993, 74). Such images have appeared with renewed vigor since 9/11.

There is perhaps no better illustration of Boose's point than a poster of President Bush as Uncle Sam, a bestseller at the Conservative Political Action Caucus in 2005.[9] Here, Bush appears as a "beefcake" action figure dressed in the stars and stripes, rolling up his right sleeve to reveal prominent veins throbbing away; bulging biceps and billowing flag link the cartoonish, larger-than-life manhood of the president with the identity of a nation. Yet this image is merely the cartoon version of another that indisputably played an important role in solidifying what we might call the dominant aesthetic of the Bush presidency. The administration's staged landing on a military aircraft carrier featured Bush decked out in full military combat gear, a pronounced genital bulge, and a victorious swagger. Here was the president as a manly war hero returned from the battlefield to announce a U.S. victory. That this image itself has become more and more cartoonish as the much trumpeted "victory" continues to elude the administration and the military is perhaps too obvious to mention.

Yet, even so, these images were meant to be constitutive of a social imaginary that would bolster continued support for the war. They turn on a fantasized hypermasculine power capable of complete invulnerability, expressive of absolute sovereignty. For these images to do their work, they must both engage a broadly shared cultural aesthetic of gender and animate deeply personal gender commitments in the imaginaries of individual citizens. Certainly they have not met with unmitigated success in this regard, but neither have they met with unmitigated failure.

The narrative that calls for the return of a manly and invulnerable nation draws on modernist notions of sovereign power, imperial conquest, and global dominance. In contemporary life, however, such narratives risk becoming mere comic parodies of themselves. A deeply sedimented skepticism about such forms of power is as much part of our contemporary social imaginary as Bush on his aircraft carrier in combat gear, and in fact a great many of us found the stunt tragic/comic rather than epic/heroic. In order to contend for a place of power in the social imaginary, the manly/heroic nation depends on other kinds of narra- *Obama* tives to make it palatable to a postmodern sensibility. The obvious example is the Bush administration's claim to be liberating the women of Afghanistan and Iraq. Laura Bush herself became the spokeswoman for this strange women's liberation, asserting in a Thanksgiving radio address in 2001 that "the fight against terrorism is also a fight for the rights and dignity of women" (n.p.). But matters are a good deal more complex than even this odd juxtaposition of a beefcake Bush wrapped in the flag with a supposed commitment to the liberation of women would lead us to suspect.

"Gender Bending to the Breaking Point": Three Stories from Abu Ghraib

Fast forward to spring 2004. Two wars are under way to make the United States invulnerable to penetration by the enemy. The Iraq War has been initiated on a model of "shock and awe"—through which defense intellectuals had promised the American public a spectacle of violence so complete it would ensure the immediate capitulation of "the enemy."[10] We have been told that both wars are fought, in part, for the freedom of women. But that spring, U.S. soldiers start e-mailing home pictures of the sexualized torture and murder of Iraqi prisoners in Abu Ghraib prison.[11]

There are many pictures, tied to many separate events of torture, and many stories. Some of these become culturally enlarged, particularly the images of racialized homoerotic violence, and those of the women. Lynndie England, Megan

Ambuhl, and Sabrina Harmon are all implicated by their youthful, happy smiles: Lynndie England with a prisoner on the ground on a leash; Sabrina Harmon beaming, thumbs up, over the corpse of Manadel al Jamadi, who had been captured a few hours earlier and beaten to death, then packed in ice; Harmon again, with a male officer posing behind a pyramid of Iraqi men, stripped and hooded, anuses exposed. America is shocked, and fascinated, by the role of its women as perpetrators of the torture. Other images, for example, one of male soldiers, penises exposed, standing over a naked, bound, and kneeling Iraqi woman, don't even make the news.

Ellen Goodman called it "gender bending to the breaking point" (2005, 1). Somehow the pictures manage to reinforce the message that the war is a war for women's liberation, since the United States has clearly freed its women to the point that they too represent the manhood of the nation—but who can affirm a women's liberation that looks like this? Here white women are given the proverbial military phallus; they preside over the homosexualizing and feminizing of the male prisoners, who are forced to simulate fellatio with one another and to be photographed with anuses exposed to the camera. In the weeks and months that follow, the pictures give rise to a complicated set of stories about racialized sexual hierarchy. Three stories stand out: one is a story about Muslim men, another is about homosexuality, and the third is a family story.

The first story is especially focused on the images of Lynndie England and naked Iraqi men, but the theme of the story is Muslim men in general, and the story is told across the political spectrum. Robert Knight, a political commentator from the extreme right, argues that "the photo of an American female soldier leering at naked Iraqi men could not have been better designed to enrage Muslims" (2004, 1). Charles Krauthammer of the *Washington Post* comments that "one could not have designed a more symbolic representation of the Islamist warning about where Western freedom ultimately leads than yesterday's *Washington Post* photo" (he refers to England), "a pictorial representation of precisely the lunatic fantasies that the jihadists believe" (2004, 1). And Barbara Ehrenreich from the feminist left agrees. "You could not have staged a better image to galvanize misogynist Islamic fundamentalists around the world," she writes (2004, 1); "here in these photographs ... you have everything that the Islamic Fundamentalists believe characterizes Western culture, all nicely arranged in one hideous image—imperial arrogance, sexual depravity ... and gender equality" (2). Of course the image of England, cigarette butt dangling from her smirking lips, hands and fingers made into a pretend gun pointing at the genitals of nude, hooded Iraqi men, is not an image of gender equality at all, and Ehrenreich knows this. What we have here is a renewed form of racialized gender hierarchy, where the axis of power that is eroticized is gendered race rather than gendered sex. As Linda Burnham so succinctly put it, "In her role as dominatrix over Iraqi men England exposed the sexualization of national conquest. As a participant in the militarized construction of the masculine she inaugurated a brand new, frightening archetype: dominant-nation female as joyful agent of sexual, national, racial and religious humiliation. How's that for liberation?" (2004, 1).

But Burnham's story is very different from the strange stories most commentators told after the photos were released. They did not analyze the images they saw in relation to what they might tell us about us about a culture that is honing sadistic hypermasculinity and rewarding its representatives with governorships and presidential reelection.[12] There are no warnings here about gender equality being redefined as racialized sexual violence. Instead, we get an American fantasy of a Muslim fantasy about what's wrong with Western democracy. We get a highly racialized story of the Muslim fundamentalist's sexual nightmares, as if the photos themselves were designed by the fantasies of the Muslim clerics. The narratives connect the photos to something that is wrong about Muslim fundamentalism. Somehow, these narratives seem to reaffirm the sense of legitimacy that continues to define these wars as wars for women's freedom and Western values. As Krauthammer reminded us, "For the jihadists, at stake in the war against the infidels is the control of women. Western freedom means the end of women's mastery by men" (2004, 1). The torture photos, remarkably, tell a story about the Muslim fundamentalist man's perverted views on women, not about U.S. policies or practices.[13]

The second story is a story about homosexuality. Recall again the images of Osama bin Laden, anus exposed to a U.S. missile. Recall the images of U.S. soldiers preparing missiles to launch into Afghanistan, and then Iraq, by spray painting them with messages like "Highjack This Fags!" and "USA: Up Saddam's Ass." Recall the pyramid of Iraqi prisoners, stripped, anuses exposed to the camera. As Carla Freccero points out, contemporary notions of homosexuality in the West do not really allow for defining the one who is penetrated as gay and the one doing the penetrating as heterosexual. Although the use of sexual violence by men against men in war is nothing new, what is new is that we live at a time when broadly shared cultural beliefs require an understanding of such actions that implicates the perpetrator in the act, that is, defines the act of penetration of one man by another as homosexual for both parties (Freccero 2002, 454). Indeed, if the act is forced, it may be only the perpetrator who is implicated. Yet the contemporary social imaginary affirms the virility of the nation through a violent, top/bottom, homoerotic rape narrative.

At the same time, gay marriage panic spreads across the country. Bush proposes a federal constitutional amendment to ban gay marriage, and state amendments proliferate. In November 2004, eleven states (joining two others that already have such amendments) pass constitutional legislation defining marriage as a relation between one man and one woman.[14] Some on the far right claimed that events in Abu Ghraib were the result of liberalism taken to its natural and logical conclusion, and Robert Knight went so far as to connect gay marriage to the rise in danger from terrorists: "Imagine how those images of men kissing men outside of San Francisco city hall after being 'married' play in the Muslim world.

We couldn't offer the mullahs a more perfect picture of American decadence. This puts Americans at risk all over the world" (2004, 2).

The flurry of activism against gay marriage crescendoes at a time when nation building requires the dominance of a hypermasculine, invulnerable national aesthetic. Acceptance of gay marriage would seem to disrupt this project (we can't have American men penetrating other American men, and smiling about it, if we want to recuperate our national manhood). Civilization itself is at stake, or so slick fliers promoting the Oregon amendment and left on my front porch claimed. Homoeroticism belongs between nations at war, not citizens in love, and what matters most is who is penetrating whom.

The third story generated by the Abu Ghraib photographs is a family story. What happens to the white women soldiers at Abu Ghraib when they come home? Lynndie England is tried in the United States for her crimes, but the stories generated about England and the trial are astounding. The *New York Times* headline of May 10, 2005, reads, "Behind Failed Abu Ghraib Plea, a Tangle of Bonds and Betrayal," and the version reprinted in the *International Herald Tribune* makes the story line even more explicit: "For 3 Lovelorn GIs, a Soap Opera Triangle at Abu Ghraib." Kate Zernike, the reporter, describes Abu Ghraib as "more college fraternity house than military prison" (2005, 1). Of course even if it is "more college frathouse" for the soldiers, which one has to doubt, it is certainly not that for the prisoners, but this headline manages to replace the images of cruel moral depravity with one of privileged white college boys on a lark. There is a return, here, from the brutal sexualized power of whiteness, which the torture photos presented so blatantly, to another cultural trope of whiteness: whiteness as innocence.

Similarly, England's attorney decides on what Ellen Goodman calls the "wronged woman" or "girl defense," and the photos play along (Goodman 2005, 1–2). Charles Graner, the army reservist and specialist at Abu Ghraib prison who is generally considered to have directed much of the abuse and has been convicted in the scandal, is presented as the traditional, selfish, two-timing man. Lynndie the dominatrix is replaced by Lynndie the scorned woman, eight months' pregnant, and then holding her seven-month-old baby. England is returned to the fold of a more traditional white womanhood through these narratives; young and innocent, a devoted mother, and duped by her older male lover, she is suddenly a pathetic figure, deserving of sympathy, rather than a figure for all that is wrong with U.S. foreign policy. We learn that Staci Morris, the ex-wife of specialist Charles Graner, has befriended England. We learn of Graner's marriage to Megan Ambuhl, another defendant in the case, and we are given to understand that the two of them got involved before Graner broke things off with England (Zernike 2005). As Ellen Goodman points out, this focus on the "chains of love" removes the focus from the "chains of command" that authorized torture at the prison (2005, 2). A story with which we are all too familiar, young and naive woman scorned by no-good man, displaces our interest in U.S. policy.

Racialized gender is carried in each of these three stories, and the power of each hinges on the deeply personal gender and race commitments that are broadly shared in U.S. American culture. But these commitments are not seamless, and neither are the stories. We could not have a successful revival of masculinist protectionism without women's liberation hanging in the balance. We could not stomach the affirmation of homoerotic violence as the practice of a manly nation confronting an exotically/erotically different and dark "other" without ensuring that our domestic institutions are purified of the homosexual menace. A post-modern return to modernist imperial arrogance requires that the narratives switch and alternate, that the stories nourish and contradict one another.

Conclusion

Stories of manhood and sexuality animate American nationalism because gender is a hinge between the inner life of an individual citizen and the social imaginary of the nation. The nation gets into the most deeply felt commitments of its citizens *as* gender (and as other things, including most obviously race). And the nation gets from these intimately lived personal commitments that strange energy we call patriotism.

Gender is lived in the body as style, and style is the answer to the question "Who is she (he)?" Certainly when faced with this question our tendency is to respond with facts: She is a university professor or a school bus driver; she is tall or plump or aging; she has children or she does not. But all of these facts are ways of talking around style. The question "Who?" is most deeply intertwined with the question "How?" "Do you know her?" can only be answered in the affirmative if I have been in the presence of and grasped something of her style, of *how* she is who she is. Indeed, if I have never seen how she moves across a room, nor heard the pitch and intensity of her voice, nor encountered the particular slouch of her body in a chair, it is hard to claim that I know her at all—even though I may have a great deal of information about her, know the most troubling facts about her intimate personal life, have read every word that she has written. Which is to say, style is primary. The bodily presence/practice/awareness that is style is always beneath or behind thinking, deciding, choosing, arguing, doing.

Personal style is hinged to the social world, and with luck for the nationalists, it is hinged to national style. National style is the felt sense of rightness, wrong-ness, of who we are as a nation, which comes before and founds things like rational justifications for preemptive war. The administration was so successful, for so long, in animating the support of so many U.S. citizens for the war in Iraq, not because they provided compelling reasons for the war. Indeed, support for the war lasted much longer than the "reasons" did (connections to al Qaeda, weapons of mass destruction), although these reasons are still reiterated today. They are reiterated, I suspect, not because anyone is still likely to believe them but because they fulfill a certain aesthetic purpose. These are the kinds of reasons that a nation like us *would* have, in the stories we tell about ourselves, in the legends we make. If Bush finds it necessary to continue to insist that what is at stake in the war on terror is "our way of life"—that is, who we are as a people—it is because those who can still be provoked to patriotism can only be so provoked by an appeal to deeply held identity commitments that one would *always* have reason to defend.

Although a person's style is infused by gender, it is not exclusively infused by gender, nor is it in any way exhausted by gender. Yet gender saturates style. And this is why gender is one of the ways that the social imaginary animates deeply held personal commitments. Images of beefed-up male bodies in combat boots or wrapped in American flags, images of white women with big smiles orchestrating the sexual humiliation of Iraqi men, and enormous billboards proclaiming "marriage = one man, one woman" agitate in the intimately personal and broadly social spaces of lived experience where personal style and national style collude and collide—the spaces of the imaginary, the spaces of the aesthetic.

If there is one thing that antiwar movements since Vietnam have not adequately understood, it is that the aesthetic dimensions of resistance do more than just accompany the political struggle. Indeed, these dimensions found struggle in the lived experience of the persons who are the movement. When a certain aesthetic commitment, such as the post-9/11 promise of hypermasculine invulnerability, becomes hegemonic to the point that both major political parties merely compete to fill its shoes, and there is no culturally viable counter-aesthetic in broad circulation, the struggle is lost whether or not the arguments against the war are won. Congress, including far too many in the Democratic Party, will continue to vote "tough-on-terrorism" laws such as the detainee legislation that strips prisoners at Guantánamo of the right to habeas corpus and extends Bush's powers to evade the judicial realm yet again.

The terror of "feeling like a woman" that Cohn's physicist experienced permeates the realm of the political as long as it retains its sovereignty in the realm of the aesthetic. If feminism has always been necessary to a politics of peace, it is more so now than ever. It is this aspect of the movement that is capable of revealing the tragic/comedic adolescent masculinity that infuses our times for what it is. But even this is not enough. Feminists must ask: What other manhood, what other womanhood, is to take the place of American national manhood in post-9/11 United States? How shall it announce itself? What stories must it tell?

NOTES

1. The recent declassification of a small portion of the April 2006 National Intelligence Estimate confirms that the war in Iraq has produced more "terrorists" whose main enemy is the United States (Office of the Director of National Intelligence 2006).

2. As Judith Butler writes in the introduction to her post-9/11 essays, "I would suggest . . . that both our political and ethical responsibilities are rooted in the recognition that radical forms of self-sufficiency and unbridled sovereignty are, by definition, disrupted by

the larger global processes of which they are a part, that no final control can be secured, and that final control is not, cannot be, an ultimate value" (2004, xiii). And further, "Mindfulness of this vulnerability can become the basis of claims for non-military political solutions, just as denial of this vulnerability through a fantasy of mastery (an institutional fantasy of mastery) can fuel the instruments of war" (29). See also Cynthia Enloe's "Masculinity as a Foreign Policy Issue" (2003), especially p. 286.

3. See Mann (2006) for a reading of one of these documents, the 1996 National Defense University publication *Shock and Awe*.

4. To clarify, I do not mean to imply that the primary motivational structure for the decision makers in this process is aesthetic. At this level material interests are in play in an extremely important way, although the aesthetic is certainly in play as well. For the rest of us, on the other hand, material interests would seem to push toward an antiwar position, yet support for the war remained very high, for a very long time, even after Abu Ghraib, even after the Downing Street Memo. It is here that the aesthetic seems to play a primary role.

5. This notion can be found in the work of Merleau-Ponty and Simone de Beauvoir, as Sara Heinämaa (2003) points out. Linda Singer (1993) has also played a role in the recuperation of this notion.

6. For a feminist and philosophical analysis of this "disorder," see Sedgwick (2002); see also Comstock (1992).

7. In the 9/11 fifth anniversary speech, this language is repeated: "America has confronted evil before, and we have defeated it" (Bush 2006, 3).

8. A question Boose does not explore is that of the relation between this counter-aesthetic and the ethics of a less grandiose masculinity. It is important to wonder whether the ethics actually depended in some important way on the aesthetics.

9. See Michelle Goldberg's *Salon* article on the 2005 Conservative Political Action Conference, "Among the Believers." The image in question initially appeared with this article but is no longer available at the Salon site; I encourage readers to view the image through Google Images, at http://images.salon.com/news/feature/2005/02/19/cpac/cover.jpg (last accessed January 6, 2008).

10. See my analysis (Mann 2006) of the National Defense University document *Shock and Awe: Achieving Rapid Dominance* (Ullman and Wade 1996).

11. See Walsh (2006).

12. Linda Burnham, again: "The soldiers at Abu Ghraib pulled back the curtain on their perverse enactments so that we may see who we are. Do we have the courage to look? Do we have the will to change?" (2004, 2).

13. It is as if, if the images were reversed, American men would not be particularly humiliated by the sexual torture of U.S. (male) soldiers by Iraqi women.

14. At this writing, twenty-seven states have passed constitutional amendments limiting marital relationships to heterosexual couples. Most other states have state laws that accomplish the same thing.

REFERENCES

Anderson, Benedict. 1983. *Imagined Communities: Reflections on the Origin and Spread of Nationalism*. London: Verso.

Beauvoir, Simone de. 1952. *The Second Sex*. New York: Knopf.

——. 1960. *The Mandarins*. New York: Meridian Fiction.

Boose, Lynda E. 1993. "Techno-Muscularity and the 'Boy Eternal': From the Quagmire to the Gulf." In *Gendering War Talk,* ed. Miriam Cooke and Angela Woollacott, 67–106. Princeton: Princeton University Press.

Burnham, Linda. 2004. "Sexual Domination in Uniform: An American Value." *CounterPunch,* May 22–23. http://www.counterpunch.org/burnham05222004.html (accessed April 12, 2007).

Bush, George W. 2001a. "Statement by the President in His Address to the Nation." White House, Washington, DC. September 11. http://www.whitehouse.gov/news/releases/2001/09 (accessed October 10, 2006).

———. 2001b. "Radio Address of the President to the Nation." White House, Washington, DC. September 15. http://www.whitehouse.gov/news/releases/2001/09/print/20010915.html (accessed October 10, 2006).

———. 2006. "President's Address to the Nation." White House, Washington, DC. September 11. http://www.whitehouse.gov/news/releases/2006/09 (accessed September 29, 2006).

Bush, Laura. 2001. "Radio Address by Mrs. Bush." White House, Washington, DC. November 17. http://www.whitehouse.gov/news/releases/2001/11/20011117.html (accessed April 12, 2007).

Butler, Judith. 2004. *Precarious Life: The Powers of Mourning and Violence.* New York: Verso.

Cockburn, Cynthia. 1998. *The Space between Us: Negotiating Gender and National Identities in Conflict.* New York: Zed Books.

Cohn, Carol. 1993. "Wars, Wimps, and Women: Talking Gender and Thinking War." In *Gendering War Talk,* ed. Miriam Cooke and Angela Woollacott, 227–246. Princeton: Princeton University Press.

Comstock, Gary. 1992. "Dismantling the Homosexual Panic Defense." *Law and Sexuality* 2:81–102.

Ehrenreich, Barbara. 2004. "What Abu Ghraib Taught Me." *Women's Human Rights Net,* May. http://www.whrnet.org/docs/perspective-what_taught.html (accessed October 26, 2005).

Enloe, Cynthia. 2003. "Masculinity as a Foreign Policy Issue." In *After Shock: September 11, 2001/Global Feminist Perspectives,* ed. Bronwyn Winter and Susan Hawthorne, 284–289. Vancouver: Raincoast Books.

Faludi, Susan. 1999. *Stiffed: The Betrayal of the American Man.* New York: W. Morrow.

Freccero, Carla. 2002. "They Are All Sodomites!" *Signs: Journal of Women in Culture and Society* 28(1): 453–455.

Goldberg, Michelle. 2005. "Among the Believers." *Salon,* February 19. http://archive.salon.com/news/feature/2005/02/19/cpac/index.html (accessed March 30, 2007).

Goodman, Ellen. 2005. "The Downside of Equality." *Boston Globe,* September 30. http://www.boston.com/news/globe/editorial_opinion/oped/articles/2005/09/30/the_downside_of_equality/ (accessed October 26, 2005).

Heinämaa, Sara. 1996. "Woman—Nature, Product, Style? Rethinking the Foundations of Feminist Philosophy of Science." In *Feminism, Science, and the Philosophy of Science,* ed. Lynn Hankinson Nelson and Jack Nelson, 289–308. Dordrecht: Kluwer Academic Publishers.

———. 2003. *Toward a Phenomenology of Sexual Difference: Husserl, Merleau-Ponty, Beauvoir.* Oxford: Rowman and Littlefield.

James, William. 1910. "The Moral Equivalent of War." New York: American Association for International Conciliation.

Jeffords, Susan. 1990. *The Remasculinization of America: Gender and the Vietnam War.* Bloomington: Indiana University Press.

Knight, Robert. 2004. "Iraq Scandal Is 'Perfect Storm' of American Culture." *WorldNetDaily,* May 12. http://www.worldnetdaily.com/news/article.asp?ARTICLE_ID=38462 (accessed October 16, 2005).

Krauthammer, Charles. 2004. "Abu Ghraib as Symbol." *Benador Associates,* May 7. http://www.benadorassociates.com/article/4068 (accessed April 12, 2007).

Lacan, Jacques. 1966. "Du 'Trieb' de Freud et du desir du psychanalyste." In *Ecrits.* Paris: Seuil.

———. 1975. *Le séminaire XX: Encore.* Ed. Jacques-Alain Miller. Paris: Seuil.

Lugones, Maria. 2007. "Heterosexualism and the Colonial/Modern Gender System." *Hypatia* (22)1: 186–209.

Mann, Bonnie. 2006. "How America Justifies Its War: A Modern/Postmodern Aesthetics of Masculinity and Sovereignty." *Hypatia* 21(4): 147–163

Merleau-Ponty, Maurice. 1962. *Phenomenology of Perception.* London: Routledge and Kegan Paul.

———. 1993a. "Eye and Mind." In *The Merleau-Ponty Aesthetics Reader,* trans. and ed. Michael B. Smith, 121–150. Evanston, IL: Northwestern University Press.

———. 1993b. "Indirect Language and the Voices of Silence." In *The Merleau-Ponty Aesthetics Reader*, trans. and ed. Michael B. Smith, 76–120. Evanston, IL: Northwestern University Press.

Office of the Director of National Intelligence. 2006. "Declassified Key Judgments of the National Intelligence Estimate 'Trends in Global Terrorism: Implications for the United States' dated April, 2006." http:www.dni.gov/press_releases/Declassified_NIE_Key_Judgments.pdf (accessed October 6, 2006).

Sartre, Jean-Paul. 2004. *The Imaginary: A Phenomenological Psychology of the Imagination.* London: Routledge.

Sedgwick, Eve Kosofsky. 2002. "The Beast in the Closet: James and the Writing of Homosexual Panic." In *The Masculinity Studies Reader*, ed. Rachel Adams and David Savran, 57–74. Boston: Blackwell Publishing.

Singer, Linda. 1993. "Merleau-Ponty on the Concept of Style." In *The Merleau-Ponty Aesthetics Reader*, trans. and ed. Michael B. Smith, 76–120. Evanston, IL: Northwestern University Press.

Taylor, Charles. 2004. *Modern Social Imaginaries.* Durham, NC: Duke University Press.

Ullman, Harlan K., and James P. Wade. 1996. *Shock and Awe: Achieving Rapid Dominance.* Washington, DC: National Defense University Press.

Walsh, Joan. 2006. "The Abu Ghraib Files." *Salon,* March 14. http://www.salon.com/news/abu_ghraib/2006/03/14/introduction/index.html (accessed March 30, 2007).

Woolf, Virginia. 1938. *Three Guineas.* New York: Harcourt, Brace.

Zernike, Kate. 2005. "Behind Failed Abu Ghraib Plea, a Tangle of Bonds and Betrayals." *New York Times,* May 10, 1. Also published as "For 3 Lovelorn GIs, a Soap Opera Triangle at Abu Ghraib." *International Herald Tribune,* May 11, 2005. http://www.iht.com/articles/2005/05/10/news/abuse.php (accessed April 12, 2007).

11

===

The Citizen-Soldier as a
Substitute Soldier

Militarism at the Intersection of
Neoliberalism and Neoconservatism

LEONARD C. FELDMAN

President George Bush's stint in the Texas Air National Guard during the Vietnam War became an issue in the presidential election of 2004 when critics contended that Bush used connections to secure a cushy position and avoid combat duty in the Vietnam War. It is one of the deep ironies of Bush's decision to invade and occupy Iraq that the administration's plans relied on the National Guard and reserves to an unprecedented degree. This reliance prompts questions of both explanation and evaluation. How did the U.S. military come to rely on its citizen-soldiers in a war on foreign soil? Does such reliance promote democratic norms of military accountability, or does it constitute a pernicious form of substitution?

Who is the contemporary citizen-soldier? According to a 2005 Office of Army Demographics report, women make up 12.8 percent of the Army National Guard, 14.3 percent of the active-duty army, and 23.2 percent of the army reserves. Nonwhite soldiers (defined by the army as "black, Hispanic, Asian and other") make up 26 percent of the Army National Guard, 39.2 percent of the active army, and 40.9 percent of the army reserves (Maxfield 2005). Some 30 percent of the nearly 140,000 U.S. troops in Iraq in 2005 were members of the National Guard and reserves (Finer 2005). Furthermore, a *USA Today* investigation found a higher casualty rate (35 percent higher) for Army National Guard soldiers than active-duty, full-time members of the army (Moniz 2004). A higher death rate for National Guard soldiers is unprecedented. The investigation concludes with the following comment from Richard Stark, a senior fellow at the Center for Strategic and International Studies in Washington: "It's a changed paradigm. We have completely crossed the line in terms of what it is to be a citizen-soldier" (Moniz 2004).[1]

As I show in this chapter, reliance on National Guard and reserve forces can be traced to the fallout from the Vietnam War. Furthermore, this reliance attempts to cover over deeper tensions concerning military obligations in a liberal, "contractarian" society. The National Guard and reserves incorporate aspects of both liberalism (military service as voluntary) and civic republicanism (military service as an aspect of citizenship). However, this combination does not work well. The National Guard and reserves are considered citizen-soldiers, but the status "citizen-soldier" is an elective, voluntary one, not an obligation of citizenship. By combining the rhetoric of patriotic sacrifice and instrumental market rationality, the United States, in its reliance on National Guard and reserve forces, partly reflects and reinforces the intersection of the two main currents of New Right ideology: neoliberalism and neoconservatism. The citizen-soldier has traditionally been a racialized and gendered category (Snyder 1999), and the "volunteer" soldier has traditionally been a volunteer partly by virtue of class inequities (the poor fighting in place of the wealthy). Such markers persist; what is new, however, is the intersection of these two political rationalities, which rearticulates the citizen-soldier as a voluntary, "market-rational" substitute. The citizen-soldier is, in a sense, a substitute soldier, a substitute soldier shaped by neoliberal imperatives of governmental efficiency and privatization.

Liberalism, the All-Volunteer Army, and the Substitute Soldier

A variety of liberal political theorists wrote during and after the Vietnam War, critiquing conscription or defending the right of conscientious objection (Carter 1998). The political theorist who has done the most to explore these issues is Michael Walzer. In his 1970 collection, *Obligations*, Walzer tackles head-on the morality of conscription with a thought experiment about choice:

> Native-born young men are not obviously different from young aliens. . . .
> Before they are conscripted, then, they ought to be asked, as aliens traditionally were, whether they "intend" to become citizens, that is, whether they intend to exercise their political rights. If they say no, then we must at least consider the possibility that they be allowed, like aliens again, to avoid the draft and continue their residence, that is, to become *resident aliens at home,* acknowledging their obligation to defend society against destruction, but refusing to defend or aggrandize the state. (1970, 112)

Native-born males might elect the package of rights and obligations of citizenship or elect to give up both. This would make the citizen-soldier ideal, as it is putatively realized in conscription, consistent with a liberal norm of voluntary consent. Walzer ultimately rejects this approach for a couple of reasons. First, asking a young person to make a once-for-all-time choice to renounce his political rights is placing too heavy a burden on him. Second, Walzer asserts, "there is something repugnant in the spectacle of a group of men denied political rights because of a decision made in their late adolescence or early manhood" (116). Walzer instead suggests that such "alienated residents" should, like conscientious objectors, be exempted from conscription but not deprived of political rights. This holds true except in the case of a fundamental threat to the political community's survival.

The distinction between wars fought for the survival of the community and elective wars fought for other reasons is central to Walzer's account of obligations. Walzer concludes his analysis with the argument that conscription is inappropriate for military adventurism. Conscription is "morally appropriate" only when the very existence of the political community is threatened—for the self-defense of society. "Military conscription," Walzer writes, "for any other purpose—for political crusades, foreign interventions, colonial repressions, or international police actions—is virtually certain to be unjust to many individuals, even if the war itself is entirely justified" (1970, 118). And, in general, Walzer says that the state should always rely on volunteers (118). But where do such volunteers come from? Where are they found, or how are they made? This issue has bothered liberal political theorists in their attempts to reconcile the necessity of defense with robust practices of individual liberty. It is my argument that liberal, contractarian arguments have relied on poverty and class inequality as naturalized facts about a political community to effect this reconciliation.

Hobbes: Individualism, Substitution, and Conscription

Poverty, I suggest in this section, needs to be assumed by Thomas Hobbes, who, in *Leviathan,* presents us with the figure whom we might call the "substitute soldier." Historically, practices of substitution introduced a market logic into conscription—a kind of hybrid practice combining conscription and market liberty. In such a substitution, conscription is combined with a provision allowing the conscripted to pay another person to stand in his place. Although substitution and buyout provisions were a product of the feudal order as Margaret Levi describes (1997, 80), the practices persisted into the nineteenth century, with justifications concerning the utility of elites serving their country in more valuable ways than with their bodies in battle. Furthermore, the substitute soldier has a deeper place in political orders than arguments from utility would indicate. During the Civil War, such a provision for the furnishing of a substitute existed in the conscription law for the Union army. It was subsequently replaced with a state-regulated buyout provision. (The flat fee commutation provision was viewed by its designers as an egalitarian measure since it "would place a ceiling on the price of a substitute and bring exemption within the reach of poor men" [Bernstein 1990, 9].) In the United States, the practice of substitution and buyouts was shaped by class, ethnicity, and race. As Bernstein writes, "There was no explicit mention of race in the Conscription Act, but because the law pertained to 'able-bodied male *citizens* of the United States' ... only whites were subject to the draft" (1990, 9). As Michael Sandel argues, both substitution and the buyout provision are ways of incorporating some market logics of individual choice into the practice of conscription (1998, 109). However, it is interesting that although substitution allows for a voluntary exchange within the person-to-person realm of civil society, the flat-fee exemption transforms this trade into a state-directed exchange.

A seemingly marginal figure, the substitute soldier, I argue, is the hidden linchpin of the social contract tradition, an unsettling rejoinder to civic republicanism's tradition of the citizen-soldier. For instance, Thomas Hobbes introduces the substitute soldier in chapter 21 of *Leviathan* on the "liberties of subjects." Here, Hobbes's account of robust sovereign power seems to undo itself through the sheer consistency of Hobbesian logic. Hobbes makes the audacious claim—audacious to those defenders of absolute royal power—that a subject might legitimately disobey the sovereign's command to commit a dangerous act, such as going into battle. Hobbes would seem to be reintroducing the hornet's nest of individual judgment of the sovereign and conflicts over interpretation with these words. But he goes on to specify some examples of such legitimate refusal: "Upon this ground a man that is commanded as a soldier to fight against the enemy, though the sovereign have right enough to punish his refusal with death, may nevertheless in many cases refuse without injustice, as when he substituteth a sufficient soldier in his place; for in this case he deserteth not the service of the commonwealth" (Hobbes 1994, 21/16). Hobbes thus asserts that if the sovereign demands one of his subjects to fight in defense of the commonwealth, it is permissible for that subject to substitute another person in his place. Hobbes does not say more about how this swap works, but one imagines that a binding contract and the exchange of money would be involved.[2]

The introduction of the substitute soldier leads to a two-track system of political obligation, with those who are commanded to fight by the sovereign having a lesser obligation than those who have volunteered, contracting either with the government or with an individual: "When armies fight, there is, on one side or both, a running away; yet when they do it not out of treachery, but fear, they are not esteemed to do it unjustly, but dishonourably. For the same reason, to avoid battle is not injustice, but cowardice" (Hobbes 1994, 21/16). On the other hand, "he that enrolleth himself a soldier, or taketh imprest money, taketh away the excuse of a timorous nature, and is obliged, not only to go to battle, but also not to run from it without his captain's leave" (21/16).

Why is this allowance for a substitute soldier necessary? Hobbes does not explicitly tell us, but he provides some fairly strong clues. Hobbes does not endorse pride, whether it be of an individual or collective nature. Hobbes suggests that pride can only lead to conflict. Nor does Hobbes see courage as an especially valuable attribute, since it undermines the fear of death. This is evident when he discusses the natural (but very gendered) timidity of human beings, which he attributes "to women (of whom no such dangerous duty is expected), but also to men of feminine courage." Such "natural timorousness," a result of our fear of death, means that "to avoid battle is not injustice, but cowardice" (21/16). It should not be a surprise that Hobbes makes allowances for the fear of death. Fear of violent death gets us out of the state of nature, so it is not really a passion to be undermined. If anything, the fear of violent death needs to be accentuated in order to consolidate a political subject's sense of the necessity of robust sovereign power. As Lawrence Berns argues, both diffidence (fear of violent attack) and acquisitiveness are causes of conflict in the state of nature, but they are also passions that can induce a desire for peace (fear of death and desire for commodious living). It is only the third cause of conflict in the state of nature—pride—that has no peace-directed corollary. Berns writes:

> fear of death and desire for comfort are present both among the inclinations toward peace and among the causes of enmity; vanity, or the desire for glory is absent from [the] former group. The task of reason then is to devise means of redirecting and intensifying the fear of death and the desire for comfort, so as to overpower and cancel out the destructive effects of the desire for glory, or pride. (1987, 375)

Indeed, Hobbes argues that

> desire of ease and sensual delight disposeth men to obey a common power, because by such desires a man doth abandon the protection might be hoped for from his own industry and labour. Fear of death and wounds disposeth to the same. . . . On the contrary, . . . men that are ambitious of military command, are inclined to continue the causes of war and to stir up trouble and sedition. (1994, 11/4)

The desire for glory is thus a passion to be limited.

Furthermore, courage itself is not a desirable trait for the population as a whole. In *Behemoth*, Hobbes explicitly distinguishes between the virtues of soldiers and of the nonsoldier subjects: "Fortitude is a royal virtue; and though it be necessary in such private men as shall be soldiers, yet, for other men, the less they dare the better it is both for the commonwealth and for themselves" (1990, 45). Hobbes does not want his political order to mold the passions of its subjects such that "natural timidity" is eliminated; indeed, natural timidity is a prerequisite of political order. This explains the potential need for substitute soldiers in the Hobbesian political system. But from where does the substitute soldier come? If the Hobbesian sovereign has succeeded in dampening pridefulness, the substitute soldier will not be motivated by the desire for glory. And how is one to ensure that courage—that daring fortitude—is limited only to those private subjects who are called upon to fight? If the sovereign has succeeded in accentuating the natural fear of death, the substitute soldier's courage will necessarily be inflected by a risk assessment and a continual calculation concerning his own risk of violent death and the political community's chances of survival.[3] What is left is the desire for commodious living. My reading suggests that Hobbes's substitute soldier is paid to fight in place of the timid, and he accepts this role, and this risk, for money, out of necessity. Hobbes's substitute soldier has made a strategic wager—placing the desire for "commodious living," the desire to escape poverty, ahead of the fear of violent death—betting that he will not suffer a violent death but rather return to civilian life more comfortable than when he left it.

If, as I suggest, the substitute soldier is a key, rather than marginal, figure in the social contract, two further interesting points emerge. First, the biopolitical social contract (preserving life itself), resting on a necropolitical foundation (the willingness to lay down one's life for the security of the political community), requires some sort of market system to secure the voluntary consent of soldiers; and second, it requires economic inequality and economic vulnerability in order for some to be induced to take the necropolitical wage(r).

Civic Republicanism: Conscription and the Citizen-Soldier Ideal

Liberal or protoliberal social contract theorists such as Hobbes introduce the substitute soldier, I argue, because some market principles must take the place of an ethos of patriotic sacrifice realized in compulsory military service. Conscription poses less of a difficulty, by contrast, for the civic republican tradition in which citizenship is not understood as merely an instrumentality for the preservation of individual life. For theorists such as Machiavelli and Rousseau, the citizen-soldier ideal was key to the promotion of civic virtue and patriotism (Snyder 1999). From the civic republican perspective, an all-volunteer army and the reliance on any kind of substitution provision both corrupt our practices of citizenship and lead to politically dangerous results. Some form of conscription, national service, and/or the revitalization of the citizen-soldier ideal offers the possibility of nurturing more robust forms of citizenship and civic virtue, containing militaries to their proper role of self-defense, and generating active forms of citizen engagement with military issues and public accountability of political elites.

From the perspective of civic republicanism, broad-based conscription encourages civilian control of the military. It knits civil society and military together in a way that helps to prevent the military from becoming detached from society as a whole. The argument here is that participation helps to nurture accountability. As David Kennedy writes in the *New York Times,* "the tradition of the citizen-soldier has served the indispensable purposes of sustaining civic engagement, protecting individual liberty, and guaranteeing political accountability" (2005, A19). Kennedy makes a related but more explicitly instrumental argument: that conscription, or some form of compulsory national service, nurturing denser citizen involvement in defense, will help to prevent imperialist adventures. The disconnect between the military and the citizenry with a volunteer professional force, Kennedy writes, "is, among other things, a standing invitation to the kind of military adventurism that the founders correctly feared was the greatest danger of standing armies." Some working within the civic republican approach also make the case that the citizen-soldier ideal helps to nurture links between civil society and the military, beyond ones of civilian accountability—including, in the opposite direction, greater military influence. As an Air Force War College report states, "The existence of the citizen-soldier helps to ensure military legitimacy. As both a civilian in the community and a member of the military structure, he serves as a bridge between national policy and the population" (Meyer 1996, 11).

Furthermore, from the civic republican perspective, conscription and the citizen-soldier ideal help ensure that the military is representative of society as a whole. Critics point to several problems with the unrepresentativeness of the current military, including, most prominently, that economic and political elites are shielded from the realities of war. Because the elites who make the decision to go to war are shielded from its direct effects, making the decision is that much easier. That conscription makes the military more representative of society as a whole was a prominent justification offered by Rep. Charles Rangel when he introduced a bill to reinstitute the draft before the start of the Iraq War. Representativeness invokes a principle of democratic equity, but furthermore, the demand of shared sacrifice might also induce a more cautious approach to the use of military force. Although he supported conscription to promote "more equitable representation," Rangel also asserted that "those who make the decision and those who support the United States going into war would feel more readily the pain that's involved, the sacrifice that's involved, if they thought that the fighting force would include the affluent and those who historically have avoided this great responsibility" (CNN 2003).

At the deepest level, however, the civic republican argument for conscription is moral and constitutive, not strategic and instrumental: conscription and the citizen-soldier ideal realize a thicker version of citizenship and civic virtue. As R. Claire Snyder writes, " 'citizens' are not pre-existing entities who then choose whether or not to engage in political action. Instead, citizens are actually *produced* through engagement in civic and martial practices" (1999, 46). Similarly, for Michael Sandel, representativeness is not the key issue, nor the reality of poverty that might force some to "voluntarily" enlist. Although these are legitimate objections for Sandel, more fundamental is the problem that a volunteer army, or conscription with a substitution or buyout provision, corrupts citizenship by introducing market logics where they don't belong:

> If the Civil War system is objectionable on the grounds that it allows people to buy their way out of a civic obligation, isn't the volunteer army objectionable on similar grounds? . . . All three policies—the Civil War system, the volunteer army, and the mercenary forces—offend the republican conception of citizenship. Our unease in each case is best articulated and justified by the argument from corruption, which presupposes in turn the republican ideal of citizenship. (Sandel 1998, 114)

Whether or not one is persuaded that the language of corruption is the most suitable for framing the issue, Sandel's republican critique points to the affinities between various market or voluntaristic practices. In the next section I argue that contemporary military practices, including reliance on National Guard troops, and the use of expedited citizenship as an inducement to resident aliens to enlist, might best be described, critically, not in the language of voluntarism but in the perhaps more archaic, but also critical, vocabulary of substitution.

The civic republican defense of active citizen participation in collective self-defense does not necessarily mean a simple embrace of a draft. For instance, Snyder distinguishes between the citizen-soldier ideal and the U.S. draft: "Despite its emphasis on the military obligations of all male citizens, the Selective Draft Act of 1917 does *not* in fact represent the epitome of the Citizen-Soldier tradition, because it does not link military service to participatory citizenship." However, for Snyder, conscription seems to be at least part of the citizen-soldier ideal, just not the whole deal. Simple conscription is the "less democratic half" of the citizen-soldier ideal (Snyder 1999, 68). The draft does not situate military service within a broader context of civic membership and other practices of democratic citizenship. In a similar vein, Andrew Bacevich seeks a revival of the citizen-soldier ideal through various inducements short of conscription, the goal being that "the burdens (and benefits) of service to the commonweal should fall evenly across all sectors of society" (2005, 219).

Although civic republican critiques may become fuzzy when it comes to the proposed remedy to rectify the problems with an all-volunteer, professional military, two deeper problems remain. First, it is not entirely clear how easily the instrumental and the constitutive arguments fit together. Reviving conscription to prevent or curtail an all-advised and nondefensive war entails the attempt to mobilize agonistic political energies that may flow from a liberal citizen's opposition to military obligation. Reviving conscription to promote a fuller practice of citizenship and civic virtue, on the other hand, is premised on an exclusively republican vision of patriotism. Second, the civic republican critique of the current military fails to address the status of the National Guard, which is promoted in precisely the same civic republican language but involves, I argue in the next section, a practice of substitution. I turn to the ambiguous position of the National Guard in the next section.

The Contemporary Citizen-Soldier Is a Substitute Soldier

The same political turmoil surrounding conscription during the Vietnam War, which prompted political theorists such as Michael Walzer to write so powerfully about political obligations, also changed military practices, raising new and different questions about the morality of conscription and its alternatives. As Bacevich asserts, "Vietnam demolished the notion of military obligation and brought the tradition of the citizen-soldier to the verge of extinction" (2005, 99).

The path of this demise is complex, however. Not only has there been a reluctance to institute a draft after Vietnam, but military reforms have increased the role of military reserves. Developed by army chief-of-staff Creighton Abrams after the Vietnam War, these reforms tied together reserve and active units, meaning that a combat operation would require the activation of reserve units. It was hoped that by requiring the engagement of reserves, the Abrams Doctrine would make it more difficult for civilian leaders to enter a war. As Bacevich puts it: "In effect, no president could opt for war on any significant scale without first taking the politically sensitive and economically costly step of calling up America's 'weekend warriors'" (2005, 39). The Abrams Doctrine, or what later was called the Total Force policy, was at the time actually designed to tap into the long-standing citizen-soldier tradition: "Proponents of the Abrams Doctrine contend that dependence on [reserve components] serves as an extra-Constitutional tripwire on the presidential use of military power. Citizen-soldiers, they would provide a strong bond between the military and civil society. Any large-scale mobilization of Reserves would affect communities throughout the country and engage the American people" (Carafano 2005, n.p; see also Meyer 1996). This doctrine, ironically, was not the attempt of civilian leaders to reassert control over the military; it was rather a military elite's attempt to rein in civilian leaders, to prevent them from waging war without the active support of the American public. The National Guard is also more white and more male as compared to the active-duty army.

Much of political theory's engagement with issues of military service has been, however, oriented toward a pre-Total Force, pre-Abrams Doctrine situation. For instance, when questions surrounding military service have been raised, they have been oriented toward the issue of conscientious objection. Justice, however, seems to make two different claims on us. On the one hand, if the United States is to fight nondefensive wars, then it seems unjust for these to be prosecuted through a conscripted army. Individual rights are violated when citizens are forced to fight in anything but a war to defend the political community itself. On the other hand, the cause of limiting war to defensive action seems to be best pursued by instituting conscription or by encouraging a revival of the citizen-soldier and wider citizen participation in national defense, and as a result encouraging civic engagement on questions of war and peace. As Bacevich argues, "Persuading at least some among the sons and daughters of the elite to serve will elevate the risk of domestic blowback if interventions go awry, inducing presidents to exercise greater caution in making decisions that put Americans at risk in the first place" (2005, 220).

Liberal commitments lead to the conclusion that conscription is unjust in the prosecution of anything but those defensive wars that are fought for the very survival of the political community, whereas civic republican commitments lead to the view that conscription or some sort of national service is the best way to ensure that nondefensive wars are not fought. The National Guard and reserves have been positioned to respond to both of these demands, but the current situation indicates that they may be ill prepared to fulfill those tasks. In other words, our current way of managing this dilemma—by the use of the National Guard and reserves as citizen-soldiers whose role will limit war makers and revitalize public accountability while simultaneously retaining our liberal commitment to a nonconscripted force—has proven inadequate for responding to either side of the dilemma. The Total Force policies constitute an unstable fusion of the substitute-soldier/volunteer of liberal contractarianism with the citizen-soldier of the civic republican tradition. Indeed, one might well describe the National Guard and its role in terms of civic republicanism in ideology but neoliberal in practice.

Mark Meyer, in an Air Force War College report, asserts that "beyond the contribution that the National Guard makes providing combat ready forces, the National Guard first maintains consistency with the long tradition in the US of a citizen army" (Meyer 1996, 3). The Army National Guard's own Web site presents the Total Force policy as a way to connect the military and civil society, thereby reaping the benefits of the citizen-soldier tradition:

> Following the experience of fighting an unpopular war in Vietnam, the 1973 Total Force Policy was designed to involve a large portion of the American public by mobilizing the National Guard from its thousands of locations throughout the United States when needed. The Total Force Policy required that all active and reserve military organizations of the United States be treated as a single integrated force. A related benefit of this approach is to permit elected officials to have a better sense of public support or opposition to any major military operation. This policy echoes the original intentions of the founding fathers for a small standing army complemented by citizen-soldiers. (U.S. Army National Guard n.d.b, n.p.)

However, while this Total Force policy seems to tap into the civic republican, citizen-soldier ideal, it also reflects its demise. The Total Force policy was not only a response to the way the United States entered Vietnam without public support but was also a response to the ending of conscription. An all-volunteer professional army would require extensive support from National Guard and reserve forces. And if the goal of the Abrams Doctrine, in requiring National Guard activation for any military deployment, was to trigger a kind of public accountability of civilian leaders in their decision to go to war, it is far from clear that it has worked. As Carafano argues, "There is . . . scant evidence that the employment of the Reserves has served to constrain presidential decision-making" (2005, n.p.).

What remains is a liberal (or, more accurately, neoliberal) logic of cost cutting and substitution. As the Total Force policy bound the National Guard to the active-duty military, citizen-soldiers increasingly came to take up tasks formerly carried out by professional soldiers. The increased involvement of the National Guard was not simply a way then to keep alive the torch of the civic republican tradition; it was also a way to cut costs and maintain sufficient forces without conscription. As Carafano writes, "the additional costs of recruiting and retaining volunteers and simultaneously pressure to reduce defense spending made reliance on the Reserves a virtual prerequisite." (Carafano uses the term *reserves* to apply to both the Army National Guard and the army reserve.) The Total Force policy was "a means to provide sufficient troops for the nation's security needs without the costly burden of maintaining a large standing-army" (Carafano 2005, n.p.).

Thus, the citizen-soldier is also, in a sense, a substitute soldier, a substitute soldier shaped by neoliberal imperatives of governmental efficiency and privatization. The citizen-soldier, viewed from the perspective of civic republican ideology, enacts the values of patriotism and a military embedded in civil society. The citizen-soldier viewed from the perspective of neoliberalism is one more form of cost-effective substitution, joining the ranks of corporate subcontractors and private security firms.

In addition to the Total Force policy and its reliance on reserve troops, another logic of substitution is worth noting. The U.S. government actively promotes enlistment by resident aliens by offering them expedited citizenship in exchange for serving in the military. In 2002, President Bush issued the following order:

> In order to provide expedited naturalization for aliens and noncitizen nationals serving in an active-duty status in the Armed Forces of the United States during the period of the war against terrorists of global reach, it is hereby ordered as follows:
>
> For the purpose of determining qualification for the exception from the usual requirements for naturalization, I designate as a period in which the Armed Forces of the United States were engaged in armed conflict with a hostile foreign force the period beginning on September 11, 2001. Such period will be deemed to terminate on a date designated by future Executive Order. Those persons serving honorably in active-duty status in the Armed Forces of the United States, during the period beginning on September 11, 2001, and terminating on the date to be so designated, are eligible for naturalization in accordance with the statutory exception to the naturalization requirements, as provided in section 329 of the Act. (Bush 2002, n.p.)

This order allows those noncitizens "serving honorably" after September 11, 2001, to waive the usual three-year waiting period before applying for citizenship (Wallace 2002, n.p.). For civilian resident aliens, the waiting period is, and remains, five years. Before this order, the waiting period for green card holders in the military had been three years (Rhem 2002, n.p.). Noncitizens who die in battle are awarded "posthumous citizenship," which "does not convey any benefits under the Immigration and Nationality Act to any relative of the decedent" (U.S. Citizenship and Immigration Services 2006, n.p.).

The patriotic sacrifice of the non-citizen-soldier may also be a strategic wager, however. This wager involves a set of calculations that have been shaped by the U.S. government's encroachment on the rights of noncitizen resident aliens, including subjecting some to mass detentions immediately after 9/11, secret military tribunals for noncitizens accused of terrorism, and forced deportations of those convicted of a felony. In other words, the reward of the status of citizenship for noncitizens serving in the military needs to be read against the backdrop of the increasing insecurity of the status of noncitizen. As Deborah Sontag reports in the *New York Times:*

> It has really been since 1996, though, that the government has been pitiless toward immigrants who break the law. In that year, new laws made even relatively minor missteps—shoplifting, cocaine possession—cause enough for a permanent legal resident of the United States to forfeit his membership in American society. . . . Congress greatly expanded the grounds for deportation and made immigrants and refugees deportable retroactively for crimes that were not deportable offenses when committed. It also took away, in many if not most cases, their right to go before an immigration judge and petition for their deportations to be waived on the basis of their rehabilitation or family ties or military service. . . . Noncitizen immigrants and refugees became a class of American residents ineligible for forgiveness or even for individual consideration by our judicial system. No matter how long they had lived in this country, if they broke the law, they were once again aliens, criminal aliens. (2003, 14)

The U.S. government's assault on the civil and political rights of noncitizens provides an additional inducement to enlistment, with its promise of expedited citizenship, but, as Pilar Marrero reports, non-citizen-soldiers also face, statistically, a greater risk: the likelihood of combat death is higher for noncitizens in the aggregate as a result of their overrepresentation in infantry divisions, exclusion from officer ranks, and denial of security clearances. Doubly exposed, the noncitizen is more likely to be on the front lines in the military and is vulnerable to deportation in civilian life (Marrero 2003, n.p.). Where Walzer once asked if native-born men ought to have the chance to become "resident aliens at home," current military practice asks resident aliens if they want to become citizens abroad. The fruits of this policy have been evident in Iraq.

Another way to think of this citizen-soldier/substitute soldier blend is in terms of the combination of neoconservatism and neoliberalism. In making this claim, I do not mean to suggest that neoconservatism is a simple equivalent of civic republicanism nor that the liberalism of Hayek and Friedman can stand in for the liberal tradition as a whole. Nevertheless, neoconservatism's embrace (at least at the level of rhetoric) of patriotism as a fundamental value and neoliberalism's emphasis on the privatization of a wide range of state functions come together in the "cost-effective" reliance on substitute citizen-soldiers. These two ideologies or political rationalities, which together guide the New Right and play such a central role in contemporary U.S. politics, run at cross-purposes, however. As Wendy Brown argues, "the upright, patriotic, moral, and self-sacrificing neo-conservative subject is partially undone by a neoliberal subject inured against altruism and wholly in thrall to its own interest: the neoliberal rationality of strict means-ends calculations and need satisfaction . . . clashes with the neoconservative project of producing a moral subject and moral order against the effects of the market" (2006, 699). Nonetheless, as Brown persuasively argues, neoliberalism and neoconservatism do not simply conflict; they also reinforce each other: "the moralism, statism, and authoritarianism of neoconservatism are profoundly enabled by neoliberal rationality" (702). Brown emphasizes the antidemocratic aspects of both neoliberalism and neoconservatism, and describes neoliberalism as "preparing the ground" for neoconservatism.

The contemporary citizen-soldier reflects these two political rationalities. In advertisements on television and National Guard recruiting Web sites, citizens are invited to become citizen-soldiers. As one recruiting Web page puts it (U.S. Army National Guard n.d.a),

As a citizen-soldier who trains part-time in the Army National Guard, you can:

- Serve Your Community and Country
- Earn great benefits (including educational benefits)
- Earn Money for College
- Earn an Additional Paycheck
- Find Career Opportunities
- Find Adventure and Challenge

The mixture of selling points here reflects this unstable combination of logics. The first benefit—service to the political community—is of a different order than the others, which are about individual material rewards or less materialistic, but no less individualistic, personal fulfillment goods. The unstable combination of logics is further reflected in the fact that the citizen-soldier is an elective status, not a constitutive feature of membership: *soldier* modifies *citizen* as a result of an act of individual choice. But it is an elective status viewed by some as fulfilling the same vital functions as those of the older citizen-soldier ideal. The unstable combination of neoliberalism and neoconservatism is also manifest in the expedited citizenship policies for non-citizen-soldiers. Those policies treat citizenship itself as a neoliberal good—a commodity to be gained through the risky endeavor of enlistment.

In sum, the National Guard is called to respond to two demands: first, that a group of soldiers carry forth the citizen-soldier ideal, and second, that the National Guard meet the needs of an imperial army at a time of neoliberal streamlining of government, in the name of efficiency and market logic. Indeed, there are numerous forms of substitution in operation: a volunteer army fighting for the U.S. citizenry, and an estimated 25,000 private armed security personnel, contracting in a "public/private partnership" with the U.S government, and substituting for the U.S. military in such activities as guarding U.S. compounds in Iraq (Bergner 2005, 29). The United States' reliance, for the past several years, on the National Guard for some of the most dangerous missions in Iraq is another such substitution. However, it is unique insofar as this substitution also implicates the citizen-soldier ideal of the civic republican tradition. It is necessary for political theory to move beyond liberal critiques of conscription and civic republican defenses of the citizen-soldier ideal to grapple with the complexities of current practices of substitution and citizenship.

ACKNOWLEDGMENTS

My thanks to Julie Novkov, Barbara Sutton, and Deborah Baumgold for helpful suggestions and Brian West for outstanding research assistance.

NOTES

1. Reliance on National Guard and reserve forces decreased in 2006 (Alvarez and Lehren 2007).

2. Hobbes is more explicit about these dynamics than Locke, who may have simply assumed a version of the substitute soldier, without articulating a defense of substitution in his theory. As April Carter writes about Locke, "a class analysis does seem plausible here—that Locke is implicitly assuming the propertied classes . . . consent to pay for the maintenance of an armed force, but the unpropertied are expected to fight" (1998, 73). This focus has left liberal theory ill-prepared to deal with a different problematic: the ethical status of a professional, "volunteer" army—what I am suggesting be described in the more archaic language of "substitution."

3. Walzer writes that "risking one's life is not the same as losing it, and it might be said even of Hobbesian men that they can be bound . . . to take certain limited and foreknown risks for the sake of a secure social life" (1970, 83).

REFERENCES

Alvarez, Lizette, and Andrew Lehren. 2007. "3,000 Deaths in Iraq, Countless Tears at Home." *New York Times,* January I, A-I.

Bacevich, Andrew. 2005. *The New American Militarism: How Americans Are Seduced by War.* Oxford: Oxford University Press.

Bergner, Daniel. 2005. "The Other Army." *New York Times Magazine,* August 14, 29.

Berns, Lawrence. 1987. "Thomas Hobbes." In *History of Political Philosophy.* Ed. Leo Strauss and Joseph Cropsey, 396–420. Chicago: University of Chicago Press.

Bernstein, Iver. 1990. *The New York City Draft Riots.* New York: Oxford University Press.

Brown, Wendy. 2006. "American Nightmare: Neoliberalism, Neoconservatism, and De-Democratization." *Political Theory* 34(6): 690–714.

Bush, George W. 2002. "Expedited Naturalization Executive Order." White House, Washington, DC. July 3. http://www.whitehouse.gov/news/releases/2002/07/20020703–24.html (accessed March 27, 2007).

Carafano, James Jay. 2005. "Total Force Policy and the Abrams Doctrine: Unfulfilled Promise, Uncertain Future." Foreign Policy Research Institute. February 3. http://www.fpri.

org/enotes/20050203.military.carofano.totalforcepolicyabramsdoctrine.html (accessed
March 27, 2007).

Carter, April. 1998. "Liberalism and the Obligation to Military Service." *Political Studies*
46:68–81.

CNN. 2003. "Rangel Introduces Bill to Reinstate Draft." January 7. http://www.cnn. com/
2003/ALLPOLITICS/01/07/rangel.draft/ (accessed March 27, 2007).

Finer, Jonathan. 2005. "U.S. Toll Rises by 4 in Iraq; Reserves Hit Hard in Recent Attacks."
Washington Post, August 5, A6.

Hobbes, Thomas. 1990. *Behemoth.* Chicago: University of Chicago Press.

——. 1994. *Leviathan: With Selected Variants from the Latin Edition of 1668.* Indianapolis: Hackett
Publishing.

Kennedy, David M. 2005. "The Best Army We Can Buy." *New York Times,* July 25, A19.

Levi, Margaret. 1997. *Consent, Dissent and Patriotism.* Cambridge: Cambridge University Press.

Marrero, Pilar. 2003. "Noncitizens in the Line of Fire." Pacific News Service. http://www.alter-
net.org/story.html?StoryID=15671 (accessed March 27, 2007).

Maxfield, Betty D. 2005. "US Army Demographics Report FY05." Office of Army Demographics.
http://www.armyg1.army.mil/hr/demographics/FY05%20Army%20Profile.pdf (accessed
March 27, 2007).

Meyer, Mark P. 1996. "The National Guard Citizen-Soldier: The Linkage between Responsible
National Security Policy and the Will of the People." https://research.au.af.mil/
papers/ay1996/awc/meyer_mp.pdf (accessed March 27, 2007).

Moniz, Dave. 2004. "Rate of Guard Deaths Higher." *USA Today*, December 13. http://www.
usatoday.com/news/world/2004–12–13-guard-deaths_x.htm (accessed March 27, 2007).

Rhem, Kathleen T. 2002. "President Lifts Citizenship Wait for Military Aliens." American
Forces Press Services. http://federalvoice.dscc.dla.mil/federalvoice/020911/citizen.html
(accessed March 27, 2007).

Sandel, Michael J. 1998. "What Money Can't Buy: The Moral Limits of Markets." Tanner
Lectures on Human Values. http://www.tannerlectures.utah.edu/lectures/sande100.pdf
(accessed March 27, 2007).

Snyder, R. Claire. 1999. *Citizen-Soldiers and Manly Warriors.* Lanham, MD: Rowman and
Littlefield.

Sontag, Deborah. 2003. "In a Homeland Far from Home." *New York Times Magazine,* November
16, 14.

U.S. Army National Guard. N.d.a. "College Bound Network." National Guard. http://www.
collegebound.net/arng/ (accessed April 17, 2007).

——. N.d.b. "Constitutional Charter of the Guard." National Guard. http://www.arng.
army.mil/constitution.aspx (accessed April 20, 2007).

U.S. Citizenship and Immigration Services. 2006. "Application for Posthumous Citizenship."
http://www.uscis.gov/portal/site/uscis/ (accessed March 27, 2007).

Wallace, Kelly. 2002. "Bush Speeds Citizenship for Military." July 3. http://www.cnn.
com/2002/US/07/03/bush.military.citizenship/ (accessed March 27, 2007).

Walzer, Michael. 1970. *Obligations: Essays on Disobedience, War and Citizenship.* Cambridge:
Harvard University Press.

12

I Want You!

The 3 R's: Reading, 'Riting, and Recruiting

KAREN HOUPPERT

The U.S. Army Recruiting Command has a motto: "First to contact, first to contract" (U.S. Army 2004, 3). In the 2004 school recruiting handbook the army hands to the 7,500 army recruiters it has trawling the nation these days (Gilmore 2005),[1] the motto crops up so often it serves as a stuttering paean to aggressive new tactics—tactics that target increasingly younger students.

To make sure they *are* the first folks to contact students about their future plans, army recruiters are ordered to approach tenth, eleventh, and twelfth graders repeatedly. Army Recruiting Command spells out the rules of engagement (U.S. Army 2004). Recruiters are to dig in deep at their assigned high schools: to offer their services as assistant football coaches—or basketball, track, wrestling, or baseball coaches (but, interestingly, not softball or volleyball coaches); to "be chaperon or escort for homecoming activities" (5) (although not thespian ones); to "deliver donuts and coffee for the faculty once a month" (5); to visibly participate in Hispanic Heritage and Black History month activities; to "get involved with local Boy Scout troops" (5) (Girl Scouts aren't mentioned); to "offer to be a timekeeper at football games" (6); to "serve as test proctors" (6); to "eat lunch in the school cafeteria several times each month" (5); and to "always remember secretary's week with a card or flowers" (5). They should befriend student leaders and school staff: "Know your student influencers. . . . Identify these individuals and develop them as COIs [centers of influence]" (3, 5). After all, "some influential students such as the student president or the captain of the football team may not enlist; however, they can and will provide you with referrals of those who will enlist" (3). Cast a wide net, recruiters are told. Go for the Jocks, but don't ignore the Brains. "Encourage college-capable individuals to defer their college until they have served in the Army" (7), commanders write.

Army brass urges recruiters to use a "trimester system of senior contacts" (3), reaching out to high school seniors at three vulnerable points in fall, winter, and spring. Their future looms largest in the spring. "For some, it is clear that college is not an option, at least for now" (3), the handbook says. "Let them know that the Army can fulfill their college aspirations later on" (3).

Finally, recruiters must follow the vulnerable to college: "Focus on the freshman class [there] because they will have the highest dropout rate. They often lack both the direction and funds to fully pursue their education" (9). (Apparently, this is one of the ways in which decreasing federal funds for college complement recruiters' goals.)

"The good high school program is a proactive one," the sloganeering commanders remind. "The early bird gets the worm" (9).

Junior ROTC—A Vital Feeder Stream

The army, which in 2005 missed five of its monthly recruiting quotas for active duty troops[2]—and fell short of its quotas for nine months running with the Army National Guard (Tice 2005)—is getting desperate. Stepping up the pressure, army brass added a thousand new recruiters between September 2004 and September 2005 to pound the pavement—or linoleum hallways. New Junior Reserve Officer Training Corps (JROTC) programs are being introduced in high schools across the country, and lately, kids as young as eleven are being invited to join pre-JROTC at their elementary and middle schools. The army increased its advertising budget by $500 million in the summer of 2005, bringing total recruiting campaign spending to $1.3 billion, and introduced a new ad campaign emphasizing patriotism in September of that same year (Herskovits 2005). (In the past, it has focused on job opportunities and personal growth—a harder sell these days, with the Iraq War going on.) The army has also announced a slew of new signing bonuses designed to raise today's average enlistment bonus from $14,000 to $17,000—with some recruits getting as much as $30,000 for hard-to-fill specialties and some reenlistment bonuses spiking as high as $75,000 (Tice 2005, 8).

Times are tough. Disaffected teens are plentiful—but skeptical. And the army is getting creative about recruiting and retention. On the sly it cut some corners, with recruiters helping high schoolers cheat on entrance exams, fudge their drug tests, and hide police records, as the *New York Times* reported in May 2005. The *Times* exposé revealed that the army investigated 1,118 "recruiting improprieties" in 2004 ranging from coercing young people to lying to them. It substantiated 320 of them (Cave 2005a).

But even on the up and up, the military is marching double time. Recruiters' access to college campuses has been protected under the Solomon Amendment since 1996—and the military is taking full advantage of this provision. Although some schools are fighting the "equal access" recruiters are guaranteed under this amendment, which ties federal funding to access (Lane 2005), the military recruiting effort has continued apace at most schools, especially community colleges, where students with fewer choices are more likely to consider a military career. And now the military has gained open access to high schools as well under a little-known clause in the No Child Left Behind Act. Here, nestled among floral tributes to educational reform and clunky legalese, is a brief passage stating that all public schools are required to share students' names, addresses, and telephone numbers with recruiters.

Armed with this information, recruiters begin their search for good candidates. "They have unrestricted access to kids in the schools, in cafeterias and classrooms," says Hany Khalil, an organizing coordinator at United for Peace and Justice, a national antiwar coalition, who describes a by-any-means-necessary mentality. Most schools have no rules on the books regarding recruiters on campus and give them free rein. "They've even brought humvees onto campuses to make the prospect of going to war seem sexy and exciting."[3]

And it works. Not necessarily for the white doctor's son in the suburbs—who can see both Princeton and a Porsche in his future—but for the low-income urban youth who is struggling. In fact, the fewer alternatives a young person has the better. "The military recruiters are especially targeting working-class youth and communities of color," says Khalil. "These are the communities that don't have access to good schools or good jobs so it's easier to take advantage of them." Indeed, these are not just the words of a counter-recruiting activist. They are backed up by Department of Defense population studies showing that most recruits are drawn from lower socioeconomic backgrounds; that 43 percent come from the South, where the schools are generally poorer (whereas only 15 percent come from the more populous Northeast); and that only 8 percent of new recruits come from families with a father or mother in the "professions" (U.S. Department of Defense 2000).

Looking to build on its strengths here, the military is turning up the tempo on its Junior ROTC—a longtime recruitment tool particularly popular in the South and in urban minority communities. Describing JROTC as "adventure training," the military crowed about plans to introduce JROTC to 91 new high schools in 2006 (U.S. Army Cadet Command 2005). But JROTCs were already an integral part of the formal curriculum in 1,555 high schools in every state in 2005. Taught by retired military—who may or may not have a college degree—the instructors bring "discipline, leadership training, military history, marksmanship and rifle safety" to 273,000 high-school JROTC "cadets" today, up from 231,000 cadets in 1999 (U.S. Army Cadet Command 2005, 7). Of those who participate, 45 percent typically enlist after the experience. The military particularly likes to sell its JROTC programs to troubled inner city schools, where the student body is composed largely of people of color and where key words like *discipline* are meant to appeal to administrators and parents exasperated with unruly students.

Junior ROTC is described as training teens to be good citizens, and the cost of JROTC teachers' salaries is shared by the military and the school district.[4] It's a win–win situation: cash-strapped schools get a bargain-rate teacher for a slew of additional elective courses; the military gets inside the schools for one-on-one contact with potential recruits. In some overburdened public school systems, students are involuntarily placed in the program. Teachers and students in Los Angeles, for example, have complained that high school administrators are enrolling reluctant students in JROTC as an alternative to overcrowded gym classes.

ASVAB—No Child Left Untested

To help high school students find "their rightful place," the army employs its standard recruiting tool, the Armed Services Vocational Aptitude Battery (ASVAB). High school juniors and seniors are encouraged to take this test to "identify and explore potentially satisfying occupations" (ASVAB Career Exploration Program n.d., n.p.). The army, which encourages high school career counselors to administer the test—ideally, making it mandatory for all juniors or seniors—has stopped spelling out the acronym in the last few years. Many parents and students don't know what it stands for. Carefully described in literature and on Web sites simply as a "career exploration program," the ASVAB, according to the army, is "specifically designed to provide recruiters with a source of prequalified leads" (U.S. Army 2004, 7). Further, "it gives the recruiter the students' Armed Forces Qualification Test scores, military aptitude composites and career goals. It identifies the best potential prospects for recruitment that allows recruiters to work smarter" (7). It also provides the recruiter with "concrete and personal information about the student" (7)—the better to contact him or her repeatedly.

"My son scored in the top 1 percent of the ASVAB," says Lou Plummer of Fayetteville, North Carolina. "When the recruiters got the scores we got almost nightly calls for a while from the air force, the marines, the army, and the navy." Plummer, an army veteran himself, encouraged his seventeen-year-old son, Drew, to heed the recruiters' call and become the fourth generation in their family to serve in the armed forces. "He was an obviously very bright kid, but a slacker who was never into school," Plummer says. "I thought this would be a good opportunity for him to learn a lot." Plummer cosigned, since Drew was underage, and just weeks before the terrorist attacks of September 11, Drew joined the navy. Drew has since left the navy. After telling a reporter that this was a "war for oil" but that he would do his duty and fight, he was disciplined for "disloyalty" because of the comment. He finally became so disgusted with the repercussions of speaking his mind that he went AWOL in 2004 and was "discharged other than honorably" in March 2005. Lou Plummer has become an outspoken antiwar activist, and he bristles when he continues to get calls from recruiters for his eighteen-year-old daughter. His advice to similarly harassed parents? "Tell recruiters your child is gay or lesbian," Plummer says. "I've heard that works pretty well." [5]

Meanwhile, confusion swirls around the rules for recruiters. Although parents can sign an "opt-out" form that prevents schools from giving out information about their kids to recruiters, most schools don't publicize this alternative; many administrators don't even know the option exists. And students themselves are further confused when offered—or ordered—to take the ASVAB. Just as the advanced placement kids are encouraged to take SATs, the vocational kids are encouraged to take the ASVAB to "discover your possibilities." According to Arlene Inouye, a speech and language specialist in the L.A. Unified School District and a cofounder of Coalition against Militarism in Our Schools, it's not unusual for students to be strong-armed into the taking the test. "It's a voluntary test but students don't know that," she says, describing a situation in 2005 in which students at Fremont High in South Central Los Angeles didn't realize it was a military test until they walked in the room and saw the uniformed proctors.[6] Nine students refused and were suspended. Later, under pressure, administrators reconsidered and reinstated the students (Knopp 2005). "A lot of people here are concerned about the issue," Inouye says, "but don't know what to do about it."

Even those inside the military are worried about recruiters' aggressive tactics, with critics suggesting that in the army's rush to fill its ranks, it is recruiting those who are not well qualified. And weeding out those poor-performing recruits during basic training just got a lot harder; in spring 2005, army brass moved the decision for discharge up the chain of command from those in closest contact with new soldiers to more senior brigade commanders—a transparent effort to stop the costly hemorrhaging of marginal recruits (Schmitt 2005). But the army insists it is holding steady. "No, we haven't lowered the enlistment standards in any way," says army spokesperson Douglas Smith. And indeed, according to army figures, which measure in broad categories, the quality of recruits over time has remained fairly constant. In 1999, 90 percent of active duty recruits were high school graduates, 63 percent scored in the top half of the ASVAB, only 2 percent scored in the lowest acceptable ASVAB category. In 2005, 90 percent were still high school grads, 71 percent scored in the top half of the ASVAB, and the same 2 percent were drawn from those with the lowest acceptable ASVAB scores.[7]

Harder to pinpoint is just where in that "upper half" recruits scored and whether the test itself has remained consistently vigorous. In my admittedly unscientific survey, I had my son take the army's online sample ASVAB test to see if he met the educational requirements for enlistment. He did, scoring a perfect 100 percent; he is eight years old.

Playgrounds and Parade Grounds—A Youthful Cadre

Today, Chicago is the military's rising star. In 2005 it cemented its reputation as having the public school system with the largest military program when the program grew to include 10,000 teen "cadets" in the city's elementary, middle, and high schools (Moody 2005). Joining Florida and Texas in offering military-run after-school programs to sixth, seventh, and eighth graders, the Chicago program drills its youngsters with wooden rifles as they chant time-honored marching cadences ("I used to date a high school Queen; Now I lug an M-16," etc.).

In Chicago, however, as in other cities and towns across the country, a coalition of indignant parents, concerned teachers, and savvy activists have joined together to draw attention to the issue. "The local school council was asleep at the switch when the military after-school program was proposed at Goethe Elementary School," says current Goethe school council member Jim Rhodes, who successfully spearheaded a drive to eliminate the program this year. "It didn't raise any red flags until one of the teachers wrote an impassioned letter about how they were marching with wooden guns and showing how attractive and fun the military could be to influence these kids to go into JROTC when they got to high school and then hopefully enlist after that." Beyond the program's efforts to seduce kids into the military, Rhodes worried about its educational value. "It was sold to the parents in a presentation as a citizen and leadership program," he said, "but it ended up just being about obedience." [8]

Undaunted by opposition to the military's presence in the schools, the Chicago school board opened the city's third military academy for high school students in September 2005. In these academies, students typically are uniformed, military bearing and discipline are required, and JROTC attendance is mandatory. Chicago's new Senn High Naval Academy is the thirty-ninth such JROTC Career Academy that the Defense Department, in partnership with the U.S. Department of Education, has established in mostly urban areas across the country (Robyn and Hanser 1995). These schools, marketed as promoting discipline, citizenship, and values among troubled students, are seen as solutions to a problem for school districts and as a pool of potential recruits for the armed services.

JROTC spokesperson Paul Kotakis is quick to clarify that the initiative to create such academies does not come from the military. "In some instances, some academic institutions have decided that JROTC is so worthwhile that they have made it mandatory," he explains. "So when all the students attending the school are required to attend JROTC, the 'academies' are created—and that is a decision made by the individual school, not the army." [9]

Although school administrators, school boards, and politicians may be drawn to the discipline of the JROTC academies, some parents make it a hard sell. When parents in Chicago got wind of school board plans to open the aforementioned military career academy for six hundred students at a North Side high school in 2004 to be run jointly by the navy and the city—they mounted a campaign to stop it. Troubled by press reports indicating that 18 percent of students in Chicago's three military academies join the armed services upon graduation (Grossman 2004), hundreds of parents and high school students crammed into a school board meeting to protest. But the school board held firm. They had the support of Chicago mayor Richard Daley. "I don't know why people are so upset about this idea of discipline and this idea of military service," Daley told the

Chicago Sun-Times in December. "I believe in military academies all over this city" (Spielman 2004, 12).

Recruiters are also being dispatched in increasingly larger numbers to colleges and universities. There, a different set of tactics is employed. "My son's recruiter told us that his student loans would be paid in full if he joined the army," says Kathy Allwein, an administrative assistant in Lebanon, Pennsylvania, whose twenty-one-year-old son was in his third year of college and constantly worried about the $19,000 student loan he carried when recruiters approached him in 2003. Relieved by the promise of financial help, he immediately signed on the dotted line. After serving ten months in Iraq, he learned the army would not be paying his loans because, although they were procured through the Pennsylvania Higher Education Assistance Agency, they were not, technically, government loans. "We didn't even realize the difference, to be honest," says Allwein. "For a long time the recruiter just told us to be patient and the loans would be paid for. We've been very patient but when the bill collectors start knocking on the door, it gets a little scary."[10]

Deceived and disillusioned, the Allweins then began getting mail from recruiters trying to sign their sixteen-year-old daughter in 2005. Fortunately, Allwein, who opposes the Iraq War and is still furious that her son hasn't received army money for his student loans, has yet to answer the phone and find a recruiter on the other line. "I would tear them from limb to limb," she says.

Recruiting Parents—The Army's New Headache

Meanwhile, whether the army solicits younger recruits who require a parent's signature before enlisting (seventeen-year-olds) or those who've reached the age of majority, parents—or "adult influencers" as they're dubbed in army parlance—are proving a serious obstacle to recruiting goals. According to a November 2004 Defense Department poll, only 25 percent of parents said they would encourage their teens to enlist, compared to 42 percent two years ago (Cave 2005b).

"For the first time our recruiters are having to really work not only with the applicant but with their family members," says Army Recruiting Command spokesperson Douglas Smith, "to explain why enlisting is important not only for the applicant but for the country." Pressed about the issue of safety by parents, Smith told me in summer 2005 that recruiters are always forthright. "What they can say is the young man or woman enlisting is going to receive very good basic and advanced training from the army. And that army basic training is designed to prepare every soldier with basic combat skills so they are trained to protect themselves and their fellow soldiers if they're called upon." Recruiters reassure parents that even though the nation is at war, the army hasn't reduced training or taken any shortcuts with gear or weaponry. "But it's an emotional issue," Smith acknowledges. "And we can't give any guarantees of safety. And we can't say anything to lead someone to think there is such a thing as a truly safe occupation in the army." In the end, a plea to patriotism seems best. "Ultimately, there is no answer to parents but 'service to country,'" says Smith.[11]

On the army's recruiting Web site (goarmy.com), parents' concerns are also addressed, but the conversation unfolds somewhat differently. Here, the campaign offers reassurance and mock dialogues for parents. To the hypothetical youth who worries, "It's dangerous," the army responds, "There's no doubt that a military career isn't for everyone" (the faint-of-heart, for example). With a straight face, the army downplays the deaths of truck drivers, mechanics, supply officers, and the like to reassure parents, "But you and your young person may be surprised to learn that over 80 percent of military jobs are in non-combat operations" (U.S. Army n.d., n.p.).

Thus the army's recruiting command both tiptoes around the issue of a dangerous war in Iraq and simultaneously insists that American parents need to face the facts and ante up their youth. "What I think we've got to do is articulate to the nation that we're at war, and this is a global struggle, this is a generational struggle," Defense Department spokesperson Col. Gary Keck told the *Army Times* in June 2005. "It's not going to be over in two years. It's going to be with us for many years" (Naylor 2005).

Of course, this message is the opposite of the one the Bush administration has been sending. After all, until Bush's June 2005 speech at Fort Bragg—where he first pled for recruits by reminding "those watching tonight who are considering a military career [that] there is no higher calling than service in our Armed Forces" (Bush 2005)—he had spent a lot of time downplaying the sacrifices this war would exact from Americans. So, although the military would like him to turn up the volume by regularly reminding potential recruits and their parents of the need for patriotic investment over time, the administration has historically worked to dispel that notion.

Consider one telling linguistic debate. During summer 2005 the Bush administration haggled about whether to continue calling this our "war on terror" (President George W. Bush) or to shift to broader, less militaristic terms like "the global struggle against violent extremism" (then defense secretary Donald Rumsfeld). Although the latter term was clunky, it reflected Rumsfeld's scramble to address the war's decreasing popularity (and perhaps his own). This way, the Iraq War was recast as one aspect of an international "struggle" against not just al Qaeda but all "Islamic extremists." The use of the term *struggle* had the bonus of sounding less violent and more inclusive of nonmilitary tactics. But just as Rumsfeld hoped to fudge things—we're not "at war" per se, just "struggling"—a casualty rate, that in fall 2005 already exceeded 18,000 dead and wounded American soldiers, made it harder to bury the cost of this "struggle."[12] Ultimately, the inability to bury the costs of this protracted and poorly orchestrated war led to Rumsfeld's ouster in November 2006.

Historically, what has made Americans willing to make this sacrifice—or let their children make this sacrifice—is the certainty that it was both unavoidable and served some achievable greater good. Bush has tried to make this point. "We live in freedom because every generation has produced patriots willing to serve a cause greater than themselves," he said to the troops at Fayetteville's Fort Bragg and to a television audience in June 2005 (CNN 2005). But the ongoing "struggle" in Iraq is a hard sell, and the ongoing "struggle" to meet recruiting goals reflects that.

ACKNOWLEDGMENTS

A version of this chapter was first published in the *Nation* as "Who's Next?" on September 12, 2005. Reprinted with permission from the *Nation* and the author.

NOTES

1. According to the cover sheet of the *School Recruiting Program Handbook*, "this pamphlet provides a single-source document for the School Recruiting Program" and is "applicable to all elements of the United States Army Recruiting Command" (U.S. Army 2004, 1).
2. Department of Defense, e-mail to the author, July 11, 2005.
3. Hany Khalil, telephone interview with author, July 13, 2005.
4. Paul Kotakis, telephone interview with author, July 18–19, 2005.
5. Lou Plummer, telephone interview with author, February 7 and July 13, 2005.
6. Arlene Inouye, telephone interview with author, July 13, 2005.
7. Douglas Smith, telephone interview with the author, July 18–19, 2005.
8. Jim Rhodes, telephone interview with the author, July 19, 2005.
9. Kotakis, telephone interview.
10. Kathy Allwein, telephone interview with the author, July 12, 2005.
11. Smith, telephone interview.
12. See http://www.defenselink.mil/ (accessed July 2005). In July 2005 readers could scroll down the right bar on the U.S. Department of Defense Web site to "casualty reports" and click on it to download the latest figures. Here, to come up with a proper total, one could add the figures from Operation Enduring Freedom and Operation Iraqi Freedom, including the columns on "total deaths," "wounded-in-action and returned to duty," and "wounded in action and not returned to duty." If the math were done correctly, the number should have been higher, sadly.

REFERENCES

ASVAB Career Exploration Program. N.d. http://www.asvabprogram.com (accessed May 7, 2007).

Bush, George W. 2005. "President Addresses Nation, Discusses Iraq, War on Terror, Fort Bragg, North Carolina." June 28. http://www.whitehouse.gov/news/releases/2005/06/20050628-7.html (accessed May 7, 2007).

Cave, Damien. 2005a. "For Army Recruiters, a Day of Rules, and Little Else." *New York Times*, May 21, A8.

——. 2005b. "Growing Problem for Military Recruiters: Parents." *New York Times*, June 3, A1.

CNN. 2005. "Transcript: 'We Accept These Burdens.'" June 28. http://www.cnn.com/2005/POLITICS/06/28/bush.transcript/index.html (accessed May 7, 2007).

Gilmore, Gary G. 2005. "Army Recruiters Stand Down to Refocus on Values." Press release. U.S. Department of Defense. May 20.

Grossman, Kate N. 2004. "Foes of School Say It Steers Kids to Military." *Chicago Sun-Times*, October 29, 26.

Herskovits, Beth. 2005. "Army Nearly Doubles Budget for Upcoming Recruitment Campaign." *PR Week* (U.S.), June 27, 1.

Knopp, Sarah. 2005. "Battle in an LA School." *Socialist Worker Online*, March 4. http://www.socialistworker.org/2005–1/533/533_09_LosAngeles.shtml (accessed May 7, 2007).

Lane, Charles. 2005. "Court to Review Military Recruiting at Colleges; Law Schools Challenge Rule Requiring Universities to Give Equal Access or Risk Losing Funding." *Washington Post*, May 3, A2.

Moody, Bruce. 2005. "Chicago Public Schools to Get Naval High School." *Source for Navy News*, July 23.

Naylor, Sean D. 2005. "An Army of Want: Americans Won't Sign up if They Don't Sign on to War, Officers Say." *Army Times*, June 20. http://www.armytimes.com/legacy/new/0-ARMYPAPER-907320.php (accessed May 7, 2007).

Robyn, Abby, and Lawrence M. Hanser. 1995. *JROTC Career Academies' Guidebook*. Santa Monica, CA: RAND Corporation. http://www.rand.org/publications/MR/MR573/ (accessed May 7, 2007).

Schmitt, Eric. 2005. "After Lowering Goal, Army Falls Short on May Recruits." *New York Times*, 8 June, A9.

Spielman, Fran. 2004. "Military Discipline Is Good For Young People: Daley." *Chicago Sun-Times*, December 1, 12.

Tice, Jim. 2005. "Get Thousands More to Re-up, but Don't Delay." *Army Times*, June 18, 8.

U.S. Army. 2004. *School Recruiting Program Handbook*. Army training pamphlet, USAREC Pamphlet 350–13. Distributed by United States Army Recruiting Command in Fort Knox, KY. September.

——. N.d. Go Army Web site. http://www.goarmy.com/for_parents/index.jsp?hmref=tn (accessed July 14, 2005).

U.S. Army Cadet Command. 2005. "JROTC Overview." Power Point presentation.

U.S. Department of Defense. 2000. "Population Representation in the Military." Washington, DC.

13

===

Living Room Terrorists

CATHERINE LUTZ

War always comes home, even when it seems safely exported. We now have indications that the new wars of preemption and empire building are bleeding back already onto our shores. The evidence is not just in the 10,000 ill and mangled soldiers returning from combat but in troubling new clusters of domestic violence in the military as well as ongoing efforts to shield military batterers from justice. Just as individuals, families, public infrastructure, and the international reputation of the United States will be paying the price of the ongoing debacles in Iraq and Afghanistan for decades, women partnered with soldiers will face increased rates and levels of violence far down the road.

The spotlight was focused on this problem during 2002, when the bodies of five women, each the current or recently separated wife of a soldier at the army's Fort Bragg, were discovered in Fayetteville, North Carolina. Shalamar Franceschi had her throat slit; Marilyn Griffin was stabbed seventy times and her trailer set on fire; Teresa Nieves and Andrea Floyd were shot in the head; and Jennifer Wright was strangled. They are only a few of the hundreds of women who have been killed or permanently disabled by soldiers—often their husbands or partners—in recent years around the approximately 1,600 domestic and overseas U.S. military bases. Even in the best of times, rates of domestic violence are three to five times higher among military couples than among comparable civilian ones. Yale University researchers reported their finding that male veterans who had been in combat (a relatively small subset of all veterans) were more than four times as likely as other men to have engaged in domestic violence (Prigerson, Maciejewski, and Rosenheck 2002).

Despite the prevalence of such crimes, the murders in North Carolina became objects of intense media attention: reporters and film crews flew in from all over the country and from as far afield as Japan and Denmark. The attention was in part because the killings were clustered tightly together, but also because several of the killers had recently returned from the war in Afghanistan. But the media have now moved on to other things, and the many murders and murderous assaults around the country that have followed those at Fort Bragg have been ignored.

Many in the general public and media wondered if the murders might have resulted from combat trauma suffered by the perpetrators. Army brass immediately suggested that the stress of deployment was to blame, particularly because it created what the army called marital problems. This argument had the advantage of supporting the army's requests to Congress for more money for a larger military, while also maintaining the hygienic fiction about combat, a required fiction if the military was to reach its recruitment goals. In both media and military accounts, the soldier was the victim, and his murdered wife in one sense was the sign of his sacrifice and pain. After the murders, army officials ordered an investigation. Its conclusions: the couples suffered from marital discord and family stress. At most, gender appeared briefly in the analysis when it was noted that soldiers, perhaps qua men, have difficulty "asking for help" from service providers available on installations like Fort Bragg.

In an earlier formal directive to military commanders, Deputy Secretary of Defense Paul Wolfowitz had said that "domestic violence is an offense against the institutional values of the Military" (2001, 1). But from the ritualized abuse at the navy's Tailhook convention to the ubiquitous and virulent misogyny of everyday "humor" in the military to the 1993 public testimony of dozens of women cadets raped at the Air Force Academy (fifty-six rapes are currently under investigation there), all the instances indicate that domestic and other forms of violence against women are not anomalies. Rather, they are at the center of the rationale and methods of war. The military as an institution promotes the idea of heterosexual male supremacy, glorifies power and control or discipline, and suggests that violence is often a necessary means to one's ends. Taking a life already requires that soldiers violate the most basic precept of human society. In a military increasingly forced or even willing to bend international codes of conduct in prosecuting wars, soldiers may absorb an attitude that they are above the law at home as well.

Alternative, more adequate explanations come from those who work daily to provide services to women attacked or threatened by their partners and from the battered women themselves. They focus on what should be obvious—that there is no workplace more supportive of a masculine identity centered in power, control, and violence; that there is little institutional incentive to rid the service of men who batter, since the military puts its war-making mission above all others; and that the military's toxic effects on rates of violence against women continue apace in "peacetime" as well as in wartime. Moreover, the military attempts to retain soldiers despite their crimes when they see them in terms of training costs that can range from $100,000 to $500,000 and more per person.

The Miles Foundation and STAAMP (Survivors Take Action against Abuse by Military Personnel) are the two organizations working most visibly on the issue of military domestic violence at the national level, while virtually every domestic violence shelter and service provider in the country deals with women who have been assaulted by active-duty soldiers or veterans. These groups know that the immediate pre- and postdeployment periods are the most dangerous for women: their partners fear losing control as they prepare to leave and attempt to reassert it when they return. Christine Hansen of the Miles Foundation has said that her group could "tell what units were being deployed from where, based on the volume of calls [for help] we received from given bases" (pers. comm. with author). She notes that soldiers may also attempt to exert control at home in response to their workday experiences: they are among the most supervised and tightly controlled workers in the United States.

The military has worked hard to learn of, count, and root out same-sex, private sexual behavior in the services, but for some reason it is stymied when it comes to the much more visible problem of domestic violence. The army in 2000 reported that 1,213 domestic violence incidents had been recorded by their military police during that year. This figure is a drastic undercounting of the actual incidence of this crime, given the strong disincentives to report it. Victims fear retaliation by the perpetrator, of course, but many also believe that reporting the crime will "destroy his career" or, paradoxically and apparently much more realistically, that it will not be taken seriously. Of the more than 1,200 cases, the army reported that only 29 resulted in court-martial or civilian court prosecution of the accused. They have no record of what happened in 81 percent of the military police reports, or in any of the 12,068 violent incidents reported to the post's family services that same year.

An investigative report in the *Denver Post* by Amy Herdy and Miles Moffeit (2003) that examined military and civilian documents, including hospital, police, and court records, showed that all branches of the military have systematically ignored the problems of domestic violence and rape. They have failed to investigate or prosecute offenders, failed to provide protection to the women involved, and in fact often intimidated or even prosecuted the victim herself. Batterers are often given light administrative punishments, such as anger management classes, and go on eventually to be promoted and given honorable discharges.

Even men who murder their partners have not been pursued. When Tabitha Croom was killed and her body found at Fort Bragg in 1999, investigators had strong probable cause that her special forces boyfriend, Forest Nelson, was the perpetrator. (He was the last person seen with her before she disappeared; a neighbor saw him load a large sheet-covered object in his trunk that night; he failed a polygraph test; and he had a previous history of attacks on her and on a former wife.) But Sergeant Nelson continued to work in a psychological operations battalion for the next two and a half years, at which point he separated from service. The case was closed mere months after the multiple Fort Bragg murders and after assurances that domestic violence prevention was a key army goal. Croom's case was only reopened after the attention brought to it by the *Denver Post*, and murder charges were finally filed against him in 2004. Nelson's military unit works under the banner "Win the Mind, Win the Day," which is clearly the military's strategy not only for engaging the "enemy without" but the "enemy within." That enemy is any woman (or anyone else) who threatens the recruitment, "unit cohesion," and budget goals of the U.S. military.

The Department of Defense has consistently failed to respond to congressional directives meant to deal with domestic violence, a problem that has been evident for several decades now. In 1988, for example, the department was told to report crimes committed by soldiers to the FBI; it has not yet complied. Even after the Fort Bragg murders, the Pentagon continues to stonewall efforts to raise awareness about the problem of domestic violence in the military and its cover-up.

Domestic violence in this country typically is defined by the boundary of the heterosexual family, although as conceptions of family and appropriate sexuality have shifted in most parts of society, that boundary has expanded to include intimate partners. The military, however, lags behind in this area. During my visits to U.S. military base communities in several Asian-Pacific countries over the last several years, many women activists in these communities told me about the problems of prostitution, rape, and other forms of violence, and about the local government's and the U.S. military's tolerance or support of it. The intent of this complicity, Suzuyo Takazato of Okinawan Women Act against Military Violence told me, has been to deflect violence from "good" local women onto the "bad" ones, who, as a result of poverty and other forms of coercion, become prostitutes. In 1992, however, hundreds of thousands of Koreans rallied in protest around the Internet-circulated image of the desecrated body of a woman prostitute, Yoon Kum-I, who had been killed by a GI. Since then, the National Campaign for the Eradication of Crime by U.S. Troops in Korea has kept a list of offenses perpetrated by members of the U.S. military, although it does not categorize assaults on women by their relationship to the man who attacked or killed them.

In the United States we find that desperately underfunded civilian public services—from shelters for victims of domestic violence to courts and hospital emergency rooms—do not have the money to deal with the injured and dead women or the returning troops. The military adventure in Iraq has created further problems for women in at least three ways: it has taken funds away from prevention and treatment of domestic violence; it has increased the demand for such services in the ways just mentioned and through a general militarization and masculinization of the culture; and it continues to legitimate a huge military and an atrophied sense of the public interest—something further exacerbated when the military siphons off several million, often working-class men and women who receive the health and educational benefits that a more fully socialized system of public care would provide for all.

Since the *Denver Post* articles, there have been yet more calls for reform of the military's methods for preventing and handling domestic violence and for more congressional hearings. Virginia Republican John Warner held hearings of the Senate Armed Services Committee in 2004 but restricted them to the problem of rape at the Air Force Academy. An aide to a key member of that committee claimed that hearings after the Fort Bragg murders had established that in those cases, "there were problems in the marriage either before he left or while he was gone that served as a catalyst [for murder] rather than him just coming home and freaking out," repeating the army's findings that the murders were not part of a pattern of masculine control and militarized abuse. With every failed attempt to get justice for the victims of violence, however, more people may recognize that the problem is in fact war itself and the system of patriarchy and profit it is meant to defend.

The catchphrase "Support our troops" is on many lips these days, and the courage and endurance of military family members are widely celebrated. Few in government or media, though, suggest that this notion means anything more than beaming them all good feelings. The Bush administration has cut back on some veterans' benefits, while the tangible and often violent costs of being in a military family continue apace. Like earthquakes, however, moments of tectonic social change often expose buried objects as the ground shifts and opens. So the unprecedented level of military mobilization and interventionism that has gone on in the last several years has suddenly revealed the problem of "normal" military violence against women. It is especially striking that it began to garner that attention in 2002 and 2003, when the issue to which our attention seemed fixed was official state-sanctioned violence in mortal contest with unsanctioned non-state violence, or "terror." But terror is a homegrown tactic of patriarchy; its victims are not random at all but our sisters, mothers, and friends. Tens of thousands of these women are working bravely against such terror every day.

ACKNOWLEDGMENTS

A version of this chapter first appeared in the *Women's Review of Books* 21(5): 17–18. Reprinted by permission of the author.

REFERENCES

Herdy, Amy, and Miles Moffeit. 2003. "Betrayal in the Ranks." *Denver Post*, November 16, 17, and 18. http://extras.denverpost.com/justice/tdp_betrayal.pdf (accessed April 1, 2007).
Prigerson, Holly G., Paul K. Maciejewski, and Robert A. Rosenheck. 2002. "Population Attributable Fractions of Psychiatric Disorders and Behavioral Outcomes Associated with Combat Exposure among U.S. Men." *American Journal of Public Health* 92(1): 59–63.
Wolfowitz, Paul. 2001. "Memorandum for Secretaries of the Military." November 19. http://www.ncdsv.org/images/Att5LetterfromWolfowitz.pdf (accessed March 10, 2007).

===============================

PART IV

Demilitarization, Pedagogy, and Culture

14

==

Militarizing Women in Film

Toward a Cinematic Framing of War and Terror

JANELL HOBSON

What is most disturbing to me about Paul Greengrass's 2006 film *United 93*, which dramatizes the events of September 11 aboard the doomed titular flight, is the way it begins. The opening bears an uncanny resemblance to the first scene in the horror classic *The Exorcist* (Friedkin 1973), which starts off ominously with the sounds of an Islamic chant before we witness a scene of an archaeological dig in Iraq, where we first encounter the ancient presence of the devil. Although *United 93* shows no desert landscape filled with mysteriously veiled women and turbaned men, it evokes the same racialized otherness in its opening shots by depicting Middle Easterners (the infamous September 11 hijackers) who prostrate themselves in prayer before an open Koran that historic morning. When we consider that both movies are concerned with the overwhelming forces of evil—the unforeseen terrorist attacks in the 2006 film and the grotesque scare tactics of the devil in the horror film—it is difficult to overlook the demonization of Islam, which has become such an acceptable trope in Hollywood cinema.

When we move away from "First World" cinema and its various "tropes of empire" to assess oppositional narratives in what Ella Shohat and Robert Stam term post–Third Worldist cinema, we encounter different worldviews and aesthetics "often rooted in non-realist, often non-Western or para-Western cultural traditions featuring other historical rhythms, other narrative structures, other views of the body, sexuality, spirituality, and the collective life" (Shohat and Stam 1994, 292). In this chapter, through an exploration of such cinema, I assess how themes of war and terror unfold beyond Eurocentric or U.S.-centric discourse. Further, as a way of showcasing the pervasiveness of militarization and its impact on everyday life, I examine how women become central to these narratives. Unlike Cynthia Enloe, who mostly focuses on the mundane effects of daily militarization in women's lives—from buying a can of soup to buying clothing that copies the camouflage attire of soldiers (see Enloe 2000)—the makers of post–Third Worldist films often explore the immediate effects of war violence.

Because of these global North–South differences, I use critical race and post-colonial feminist theories to address embodiment issues in the context of war and terror; I then analyze how women's bodies come to the fore in films and function as sites for national, cultural, and sexual struggles. My film analysis is grounded in a theoretical framework on embodiment that helps to advance decolonized understandings of women's embodiment in relation to militarized violence. I start with a discussion on embodied resistance before delving into analysis of the selected films: Nelofer Pazira's *Kandahar* (Makhmalbaf 2001), Mani Ratnam's (1998) *Dil Se*, and Santosh Sivan's (1999) *The Terrorist*. All precede the September 11 events and thus illuminate how late twentieth-century post–Third Worldist concerns of war and terrorism predate American interests in these global issues. The politics of global film distribution have prevented these films from receiving wider circulation in the United States and, hence, from finding a transnational audience that could weigh in on global debates from an alternative cultural viewpoint that is not dependent on state rhetoric. To that end, I conclude this chapter by considering the viability of cinema for addressing foreign policy issues.

Embodied Resistance

Somewhere between "war" and "terror" lies resistance. By resistance, I refer to theories and practices that challenge institutional power, often upheld by state-initiated violence, and that function beyond the extremist operations of antigovernment and guerrilla units, which fail to envision nonviolent means to social change. The resistance that occupies the space between war and terror questions systems of violence without normalizing one form while demonizing another. As Neloufer de Mel explains, we condemn acts of "terrorism," versus acts of "war," because the former is perceived as operating

> *outside* the mainstream "legitimate" violence unleashed by a military force. That "legitimate" violence, which includes set battles and strafing that cause enormous destruction of civilian life and livelihoods, is not regarded as immoral in the course of war points to how normalized these forms of violence have become through the process of [militarization] in which fashions of camouflage dress to merchandising of toy weapons, advertising, and popular culture [glamorizing] military images, film, and literature play their part. (de Mel 2004, 76–77, emphasis in original)

By refusing to distinguish between war and terrorism, a resistance stance challenges the ideology of domination that frames both sides.

Functioning much like the in-between space of resistance, the "space between the legs," as M. Nourbese Philip describes, mediates the private space of female power (in its creation of life and locus for sexual pleasure) and the public space of violence, which renders that same site of power as vulnerable space (1994, 76). It is also the site for biological and political control. This "space between" determines whether one can enter the streets after a certain hour or receive harassment at any given hour. As Philip further observes, those of us who carry power within are rendered powerless when male space is equated with public place, with war and terrorism: "[He] walks / as if / he owns the earth / steps into his boat . . . his fighter jet / his idea / his war / as extensions of his / very self . . . no memory of murder / in his walk" (89).

Despite Philip's reliance on heteronormative gender constructions in her critique of men's and women's embodied experiences, we should not ignore her main point: social and cultural meanings of gender and sexuality are already inscribed onto these bodies and, hence, confine women's mobility and positionality. Because women are subject to the violable space of the public—whether in the streets or in wars—we have learned to adapt our bodies to this dominance, recreating what Foucault has termed "docile bodies," in which the body is regulated by institutions of power. It is thus "manipulated, trained . . . obeys, responds, becomes skillful and increases its forces [through reproduction]" (Foucault [1977] 1995, 136).

This experience is especially true for women of color, who—when operating within a white supremacist system—are recast through what Evelyn Brooks Higginbotham calls the "metalanguage" of race, which "not only tends to subsume other sets of social relations, namely gender and class, but it blurs and disguises, suppresses and negates its own complex interplay with the very social relations it envelops" (1992, 255). This metalanguage is further exacerbated by colonialist discourse, which encourages a paternalistic attitude toward women's struggles in the global South, or what Chandra Mohanty calls Western feminism's attribution of "Third World difference" in non-Western women's lives (1991, 72). As such, these intersectional relations among race, class, gender, and nation complicate what constitutes a "docile body." Moreover, given the geographical and historical contexts, the raced/classed/gendered body is either a protected body or a rapeable one. If we fear rape in peacetime, it becomes policy in wartime, and certain bodies are never protected at any time. And yet these same bodies have learned to resist their expected docility.

Because of these embodied conditions, women come to know what postmodern artist Barbara Kruger once famously proclaimed on an art poster for a 1989 pro-choice march on Washington: "Your body is a battleground." Borrowing the sentiment from Kruger's poster, I offer a different configuration of this battleground in which women's bodies become the site for more than battles about reproductive rights. For if women are the battlegrounds on which war and terrorism play out struggles for power, what choices do women have in forging their own national identities? Moreover, if their nationalism is also tied to their sexuality, what spaces of resistance exist for feminist consciousness?

These questions especially hold resonance for global feminism, which has yet to build successful coalitions across nations and cultures that can sustain a planetary women's movement. Such coalition building is especially critical when we understand how our own governments, namely, the United States and its own coalition forces in Afghanistan and Iraq at present, exercise their superpower status by controlling affairs of state around the globe. When our nation acts with this kind of power, it absolutely behooves U.S. feminists to resist the same colonizing worldview in promoting *all* women's liberation. In other words, uncritical patriotism hinders global feminist consciousness.

Too often, U.S.-centered and Eurocentric feminists fail to articulate an antiwar feminism that benefits women on different sides of war and occupation. For instance, the Revolutionary Association of Women in Afghanistan (RAWA) opposed the rule of the misogynistic Taliban—as did the U.S.-based Feminist Majority—but unlike the Feminist Majority, RAWA also opposed the United States' "war on terror," waged in retaliation for the attacks of September 11 and through the discourse of the liberation of burqa-covered Afghan women. The body-as-battleground resurfaces in these global spheres of politics and militarism. However, mainstream U.S. feminists, like the Feminist Majority, have yet to fully incorporate the discourse of women of the global South most impacted by these policies; nor have they developed a "curious feminism," as Cynthia Enloe advocates, to inquire about international politics in ways that can strengthen global feminism and "make the global workings of unequal power fully visible" (2004, 305). The globalizing forces of war and terror necessitate that we become curious about each other's lives and the effects of global policies on our bodies, not to better understand our "enemies" but to forge future alliances.

A Curious Feminist Odyssey

The curious feminism that Enloe advances is perhaps best exemplified in Afghan-born Canadian journalist Nelofer Pazira's *Kandahar*, a film she made in collaboration with Iranian filmmaker Mohsen Makhmalbaf (2001), which debuted at the 2001 Cannes Film Festival shortly before the events of September 11 and the subsequent war in Afghanistan. Unfortunately, most commentators viewed and celebrated the film through a veneer of the savage, Orientalist East and not through an antiwar sensibility, which is its underlying premise. The film is based on Pazira's factual account of leaving Canada and returning to Afghanistan in a quest to locate her childhood friend—referred to as her sister in the narrative—who had written her a suicide note in 1998, having despaired after her injury by a land mine and the solidification of the oppressive Taliban regime.

Kandahar blurs distinctions between nonfiction and fiction through its narrative, which weaves documentary-style reportage with storytelling. Filmed around the Iran–Afghanistan border, *Kandahar* captures the despair of a war-torn country as witnessed through the journalistic eyes of Pazira, who revisits her homeland and reacts with culture shock. We experience with Pazira the devastation of war: of the numerous land mines that litter the landscape and maim civilians; of the lack of education for young girls and the indoctrination of young boys, who are trained to link Islam with militarism; of the severe famine and lack of drinkable water, which has transpired during the course of continuous warfare; of lawlessness and border patrols; and of the ubiquitous and enforced burqa, which at first "suffocates" Pazira and the myriad faceless women in the film but then provides her with "safety" and comfort from the many dangers she encounters.[1]

Under their full cover, the burqa-clad women defy this enforced invisibility by asserting their individuality and beauty throughout the film. They apply lipstick, paint their nails, wear noisy bangles, advocate for their children's schooling, chant funereal dirges or sing wedding songs, and display colorful burqas, which Pazira herself calls breathtakingly beautiful in her film commentary. In these subtle depictions, we see Afghan women performing embodied resistance by insisting on their right to be seen *and* heard, even though we cannot view their faces.

Significantly, the film begins its journey into Afghanistan with a familiar image, reminiscent of *National Geographic*'s 1985 cover photo of the "Afghan girl," whose piercing eyes revealed to us the unspeakable horrors of war. At the point where Pazira crosses the Afghan border on foot, the camera pans to show numerous Afghan girls, who return the camera's gaze with their own stares defiant enough to rival any *National Geographic* cover. They are receiving an important lesson on how to avoid land mines, which has already disfigured the eye of one of the young girls present. In this poignant shot, we recognize the colonizer/ethnographer's gaze and the ways in which the film subverts the colonial narrative to "heal our imperialized eyes" (Bambara 1992). When we consider, however, that the "Afghan girl"—now named to the world as Sharbat Gula—merely grows up to be pictured in full cover of the burqa, as offered in the 2002 update of *National Geographic*, and that these young girls will also don such invisibility when they become women, we witness the difficulties in creating Third World female subjectivity in global narratives of war. In these ways, *Kandahar* plays to and counters this dominant representation, but most importantly, it projects the (female) body politic onto the nation-state.

In another poignant scene, we observe men, who have been maimed by land mines, walking with crutches, gathering at a Red Cross camp in search of spare prosthetics, and desperately chasing after a plane flying over their heads, which has parachuted down to the camp various pairs of prosthetic legs—feminized in appearance. Having already viewed an earlier scene depicting an Afghan man arguing with one of the white female medical volunteers at this camp for "suitable" legs for his maimed wife—because the available pair are too masculine—we might interpret, in our globalization of Rosemarie Garland Thomson's feminist disability theory, that war renders the orderly spheres of gender, nation, and the able body meaningless. This nationalized disability, recognized in Western contexts as "the messiness of bodily variety," merely reflects the messiness of war (Thomson 1997, 24). Such disruptions extend further into queer subtext, whether as men desperately donning feminine prosthetic legs to become able-bodied or—in another scene—as a man attempting to escape his perceived militant threat as a masculine subject by cross-dressing in a burqa when passing by border patrol.

In yet another subversive rendering of the body politic, the film dramatizes Pazira's encounter with an African American man posing as a local physician. Through this character, we are reminded of a specific history in the 1970s that connected Black Power movements in the United States with Third World and Marxist liberation movements, during which time our exiled American joined a Muslim sect in Afghanistan, fought in the local wars, and remained behind to provide humanitarian services. That this same man could then blend in as an Afghan, even though he must don a fake beard—because of the Taliban's enforced codes of masculine presentation—further questions the fixed categories of race, ethnicity, and nationality. Again, war and border crossings destabilize such identities.

Unfortunately, while embarking on this "curious feminist odyssey," Pazira fails to rescue her friend/sister from her "suicide mission." However, we may be able to capture something of the pain and despair of this subaltern figure—whom we never meet—through the sobering images offered both in *Kandahar* and in *Return to Kandahar*, Jay and Pazira's (2003) follow-up documentary, which examines how the U.S. war in Afghanistan has exacerbated decades of fighting, which first began with the Soviet Union and then continued with ethnic conflicts. The suicide of Pazira's friend—named Dyana in the documentary—can be interpreted as embodied resistance against the unlivable conditions produced by wars, not unlike the martyrdom enacted by female suicide bombers, minus the perpetuation of mass bloodshed. Although this conclusion may seem problematic in the wake of such a violent death, this drastic measure nonetheless serves as a performative protest that counteracts state assertions of the necessity of war.

Romancing the Subaltern

The story of the female suicide bomber has been retold in such Indian films as the 1998 Bollywood movie *Dil Se* and the 1999 art film *The Terrorist*; neither film, however, fully articulates her desires or her political zeal without scripting sexual difference onto her body. In the case of *Dil Se*, the militant Meghna eventually succumbs to love at the end of the film, thus embracing her lover as her bomb-laden vest explodes in the interest of the heterosexual romance rather than in the interests of her militant group. In *The Terrorist*, Malli, our titular heroine, seems to have a change of heart about her suicide mission when she learns she is pregnant.

Both characters allude to Dhanu, the twenty-five-year-old female member of Sri Lanka's infamous Liberation Tigers of Tamil Eelam (LTTE), who martyred herself in the assassination of former Indian prime minister Rajiv Gandhi in 1991 by garlanding him just before detonating the bomb on her suicide vest. Nevertheless, both filmmakers are unable to envision the female "terrorist" carrying out her orders. Subsequently, these representations "invariably twin her body to sexuality. It is a scripting that ... undermines ... her historicity and socio-political role in the liberation struggle she dies for" (de Mel 2004, 79). They also reinscribe silences of the subaltern, who has not yet been able to speak, to paraphrase Gayatri Spivak (1988).

Dil Se concerns a typical yet unconventional Bollywood romance between Amar (played by international star Shahrukh Khan), a young radio journalist for New Delhi's All India Radio, and Meghna (played by Manisha Koirala), the mysterious, beautiful woman from the countryside with whom Amar falls hopelessly in love. Eventually, Amar discovers that his beloved is in the service of an underground militia group and is prepared to carry out a suicide-bombing attack at India's 1997 Republic Day ceremony marking the fiftieth anniversary of colonial independence from Great Britain. In a pivotal scene, which depicts Amar confronting Meghna about her true identity, the film effortlessly weaves competing narratives of heterosexual romance and obsessive love and of state dominance, militaristic force, and the fight for state independence. Although the film's presentation of Meghna's frustrated romance with Amar perpetuates her sexualization, it is important to note the ways that Meghna does not participate in the fantasies of romance—usually expressed and elaborated in the musical sequences of popular Hindi cinema.

Meghna is thus a complex figure who serves as contrast to another important female character in the film: Preeti Nair (played by Preity Zinta). In the latter half of the film—after he has lost track of the elusive Meghna—Amar resigns himself to heartbreak and eventually agrees to his family's arranged marriage to Preeti, an army officer's daughter and thus an appropriate partner for his nationalist loyalties. We may see the first half of the film, which is preoccupied with Amar's unsuccessful pursuit of Meghna, as representing the fantasy or the myth of love, whereas the latter half—with the introduction of Preeti—as focusing on the realities of courtship, as when the audience is confronted with the reality of Meghna's militant plans. Amar reconstructs Meghna in his idealized image of the beloved either in need of rescue, as imagined in the musical number "Dil Se" (With all my heart)—never imagining that she is the one who poses the violent threat—or as a divine figure who is to be worshipped, as fantasized in the Ladakh desert in the musical number "Satrangi Re" (Oh, seven-colored one).

In this particular sequence, we interpret the meaning of the song through the numerous colorful outfits that Meghna wears while signifying on religious poses of Hinduism, Buddhism, and Islam in the choreography. Her dance further alludes to Amar's desire in worshipping his mythologized beloved and also highlights India's cultural diversity and idyllic landscape. In addition, this musical number segues from a voyeuristic moment in which Amar spies Meghna bathing in a private room. Meghna, however, returns his gaze and is thus "granted a visual, counter-narrative agency to refuse this subject position" (Kabir 2003, 151).

During the "realist" segment of the film, another scene mirrors this situation. We witness Preeti, who prepares for their engagement ceremony, accidentally spying Amar in the shower. However, there is no lingering gaze between the couple, no defiant return of the voyeur's stare. Instead, Preeti screams in embarrassment at having seen her fiancé's nudity, apologizes profusely for this "transgressive" act, and swears that she "has not seen anything." This comical rendering lays bare the gendered differences between the two scenes in which the female gaze is not permitted the same erotic intrusion and possession of the male body; it also suggests a reversal of their gender roles, since Preeti pursues Amar and will eventually, like Amar in his pursuit of Meghna, meet with heartbreak.

To some extent, Preeti defies the stereotypes that Westerners construct of the South Asian woman as submissive, demure, and a "victim" of arranged marriage, a custom we have pathologized as an antiquated ritual incompatible with the demands of modernity and individualistic pursuits of love and sexual desire. Preeti's approach to her arranged marriage to Amar, however, does not fit our Western perceptions. Not only does she negotiate this custom with her own growing desire for Amar, but she is assertive and talkative in their courtship. She admits to having had previous relationships; she boldly inquires about Amar's virginity (mimicking—through her role reversal as interrogating lover—masculinist desires for female chastity while simultaneously dismissing its importance when she tells him that he does not have to answer); and she remains completely unselfconscious about eating (and subsequently making a mess of herself) in front of him.

Most importantly, Preeti is permitted her own realm of fantasy in the musical sequence "Jiya Jale" (My soul burns), an erotic number that allows her to imagine sexual desire for Amar in anticipation of their upcoming nuptials. Yet, as Ananya Jahanara Kabir (2003) notes in her essay, Meghna remains exclusively in the realm of realism and politics, unable to fantasize for herself a vision for either love or state independence. This situation is especially dramatized when her history is revealed to us in a flashback that recalls her experience of warfare, the destruction of her home and the death of loved ones, and, most importantly, her rape by soldiers. This scene thus grounds Meghna in a "realist" documentary style that establishes her story as explanation for the recruitment of young women into terrorist units. Kabir also notes how Meghna's only lyrical lines and flight of fantasy occur in the musical sequence "Satrangi Re," in which she chants the refrain, "Love cannot be forced," a theme that reverberates throughout the film in a foreboding and haunting manner.

This sentiment is especially troubling when we reach the end of the film, and Amar, who has abandoned Preeti, his family, and by all means his nationalist responsibility—when he refuses to turn in Meghna to the authorities—still forces the issue of their "love." Perhaps we can interpret this film, as Kabir argues, as a political allegory on war and terrorism and consider that the nation (symbolized by the lover) that forces union with resisting states (the resistant beloved) at the expense of the coalescing states (the fiancée in his arranged marriage) will cause destruction for all, as the nation implodes with the conflicts between hegemonic and marginalized forces, just as Amar and Meghna literally and figuratively implode at the end. Their deadly consummation leaves behind an anguished Preeti even while offering viewers what is perhaps the most intense symbolic orgasm one will ever witness in a filmic genre that forbids on-screen kissing.

Can the Female Suicide Bomber Speak?

Although *Dil Se* reinforces certain silences of the female suicide bomber, the film is in line with other films ultimately invested in redeeming this subaltern figure and—unlike the Hollywood examples, which tend to be Orientalist in their ethnocentric depiction of people and cultures in the Middle East, South Asia, and East Asia—in reframing her in the context of a normative femininity: one that can accept a woman's sacrifice of her life for romantic love and motherhood rather than for her guerrilla beliefs. Nowhere is the argument for normative femininity more upheld than in the subsequent film, *The Terrorist*, directed by Santosh Sivan, who served as the cinematographer on *Dil Se*. In having Malli (played by Ayesha Dharker) discover in the line of duty that she is pregnant, Sivan envisions his heroine developing a crisis of faith, even as we are to also imagine that, at the moment of her assigned execution, she will abandon her suicide mission and nurture instead the life growing inside her.

Perhaps as an attempt to elaborate on the character of Meghna, Sivan—clearly troubled by the actions of the real-life Dhanu—imaginatively struggles to realign this problematic historical figure with acceptable womanhood. As the filmmaker admits, "I used to wonder, how would someone do something like this? And what possibly would make her *not* do it? . . . Supposing she got exposed to all the laws of nature that a woman normally confronts" (Walsh 1998, emphasis in original). Sivan, more so than Ratnam, cannot imagine the cinematic Dhanu acting solely in the interests of war and politics. However, such chauvinistic sentiments underestimate women's desires and ability for carnage, thus reinforcing a militarization staunchly in support of men on the battlefield and women in the domestic sphere tending to love, marriage, and motherhood.

To his credit, Sivan recuperates the demonized figure of the female suicide bomber by representing the terrorist as a young woman who could be anyone's daughter, sister, or girlfriend were it not for the forces of warfare that have ensnared her into accepting guerrilla-like ideologies. The opening shots present a montage of different young women bravely, yet fanatically, spouting militant rhetoric. Each is prepared to sacrifice herself for the cause of their militant group; each willingly volunteers to be the next assassin—a martyrdom role that fills each trained soldier/warrior with honor and pride, even if those of us outside this guerrilla community recoil at what is presumed to be an evil task. Malli accepts her assassination assignment with eagerness—casually recognizing a portrait of her target, whom she has seen in newspapers—and subsequently journeys toward her fateful appointment.

Even as the film depicts different scenarios that document her status as a guerrilla soldier—she brutally murders a man who gets in her way—we are reminded of her maternal potential. In flashbacks, we witness the way she cradles her lover, a fellow guerrilla fighter (and possibly the father of her unborn child), before he dies. We also witness her ability to express compassion when she caretakes a young boy—who is a victim of the same war that she is resisting through her militarized role. Without knowing much about the war, we may surmise that the film's context is the Sri Lankan fight for autonomy against India. We are not told the details of this war and who is the target of Malli's assassination, but Sivan concerns us only with the possible salvation of Malli and, by extension, the cinematic rewrite of Dhanu's history, which reinscribes this terrorist figure back into the normative script of mother and daughter.

It is significant that while Malli is hiding out at an elderly couple's home—where she pretends to be a student in need of room and board—her relationship strengthens with the old man (his wife is comatose), and he alerts Malli to her pregnancy after she displays signs of morning sickness. Her identity as "daughter" within this new family unit seems to erase Malli's bonds with her militant community, even though the film never considers the violent consequences that await Malli were she to break ranks with her guerrilla group and not carry out her suicide-assassination orders. The ending—which depicts Malli's hesitation in pressing the button on her bomb-laden vest—refutes Dhanu's history even as it imagines that a woman's biology would alter such history.

Although these films envision female militants trapped by their sexual bodies, such narratives necessarily force a complex dialogue on issues of nationalism, terrorism, and conflicts of war without drawing facile lines between "us" and "them." Perhaps it is precisely in their roles as women that their dialogue becomes complicated, since women are traditionally viewed as mothers, wives, daughters, and sisters of the nation, or as enemy women to be raped—and certainly not as being in a position to defend themselves, let alone carry out mass carnage. We still await a cinematic image beyond the Orientalist or male gaze that can view the militant woman as a self-assured, disciplined, driven—and, yes, fanatic—individual capable of resorting to violence to avenge herself, her family, and her nation. This assertion is not to morally defend the role of the female suicide bomber, who is just as problematic as her male counterpart in perpetuating violence. However, our inability to recognize women—cinematically or on the battlefield—beyond their "docile bodies" allows such women to strategically function in surprise attacks in the first place. Because we continue to underestimate women's militaristic and violent actions, they will likewise continue to maintain the element of surprise in war and terror.

Conclusion

What should intrigue us about these cinematic worldviews are the ways that war-weary women, who protest militaristic imperialism and patriarchy through their bodies—to the point of self-destruction—illuminate the horrors of war that we can neither visualize nor tell. As such, the silences surrounding the absent suicide victim of *Kandahar* and reinforced by the cinematic Dhanu in *Dil Se* and *The Terrorist* speak louder than the cacophonous pronouncements by public officials who justify perpetual warfare, even as we understand what Spivak has concluded: "The subaltern cannot speak because the subaltern cannot be heard" (1988, 308). She is always already spoken for.

Nonetheless, if the subaltern could speak a cinematic language, what are the barriers that would prevent our hearing her words? After all, it is difficult to measure the impact on our own worldviews of non-Western films that address global and transnational concerns. For instance, do films like *Kandahar*, *Dil Se*, and *The Terrorist* inform our understanding of the globalizing world in which we live? Do they change how we listen to the news of terrorist attacks in faraway places, such as the Mumbai train bombings in 2006 or the various attacks in war-torn Afghanistan or Iraq? Can we view such films and have a deeper impression of the lives that people live across the globe, of gendered relations and the ways that women enact their power, whether as young women entering marriage or making a pact to carry out warfare? Moreover, had we been given mainstream access to such films, which debuted a few months or a few years before September 11, would we be as confused about the world and the reason why terrorism exists?

Although the world of cinema is confined by the imaginations of producers, performers, and audiences, it provides significant commentary on real-world politics and policies. Even if our post–September 11 worldview has been shaped by the sudden realization that we can no longer be comfortable perpetuating the United States' indifference to global affairs, the "us" versus "them" ideology that has dominated much of our foreign policy discourse seems just as inadequate in addressing these issues. Perhaps we can challenge both isolationist and dichotomous stances by embracing a multiracial and transnational worldview that can start on the most personal level, such as watching and analyzing movies in different languages. Fortunately, the films assessed in this essay are available on DVD, but we have yet to demonstrate—as a U.S. viewing market—any significant desire for such films, which might be featured at our art house theaters but might not reach our multiplexes.

Enloe advocates not only "curious feminism" but a feminism that "listens" to other feminists and different feminist messages around the globe. What better way to listen to each other than by engaging in our cultural texts—books, music, art, and films? How can we also listen effectively so as to challenge both the meta-language of race and colonialist discourses that might skew the way we hear each other's gendered narratives?

I close this chapter by offering the example of another film, one that is con-sciously post–September 11 in its critique of war and pro-resistance in its politics. I also argue that it maintains a feminist stance, although the filmmaker has never made any statements toward this sensibility. Mexican filmmaker Guillermo del Toro (2006) presents his Spanish-language film *Pan's Labyrinth* as a realist fantasy that follows the travails of a young heroine, Ofelia, who is forced to live with her cruel stepfather, Captain Vidal, in the fascist, post–civil war world of 1940s Spain. Fortunately for her, the woods nearby include a magical, underground labyrinth, where she encounters an ancient and mythical figure, the Faun. Incidentally, these same woods also provide shelter for an underground resistance group, aided by Captain Vidal's maid, Mercedes, and his physician.

As these two narratives intertwine, we recognize how an underworld existence—often presented as the terrain of the devil, who is himself rewritten as a morally ambiguous, indigenous, and pre-Christian trickster god—provides sus-tenance for childhood fantasies, female and folk wisdom, and resistance from patriarchal and fascist oppressions. The film also invites us to consider the fan-tasy tale as a metaphor for cinema and the realist tale as a reflection of the real world. (After all, could we not interpret post–civil war Spain as a metaphor for the present-day United States–dominated global village?) Interestingly, both Ofelia and Mercedes bring about Captain Vidal's downfall in fantasy and reality, for he continues to dismiss feminine power and the ways that women and girls rely on subterfuge in a militarized sphere.

Unlike *The Exorcist*'s devil, the Faun in *Pan's Labyrinth* exists not to terrorize and control a young girl's mind but to liberate it and complicate her worldview as she transcends the dark forces of war to find a mythical world of peace. As with the other films examined here, these cinematic framings of war and terror remind us that the categories of good and evil are not so clear-cut and, when viewed through a non-U.S.-centered framework, challenge our global conscious-ness and values for social justice. Most of all, they remind us that women's embodied resistance in a militarized world should never be discounted.

NOTES

1. The words in quotations come from Pazira's running commentary on the DVD version of the film.

REFERENCES

Bambara, Toni Cade. 1992. Preface to Julie Dash's *Daughters of the Dust: The Making of an African American Woman's Film*. New York: New Press.

del Toro, Guillermo, dir. 2006. *Pan's Labyrinth* (film). Perf. Sergi López, Ivana Baquero, Doug Jones, Maribel Verdú, Ariadna Gil. Warner Brothers.

de Mel, Neloufer. 2004. "Body Politics: (Re)Cognising the Female Suicide Bomber in Sri Lanka." *Indian Journal of Gender Studies* 11(1): 75–93.

Enloe, Cynthia. 2000. *Maneuvers: The International Politics of Militarizing Women's Lives.* Berkeley: University of California Press.

——. 2004. *The Curious Feminist: Searching for Women in a New Age of Empire.* Berkeley: University of California Press.

Foucault, Michel. [1977] 1995. *Discipline and Punish: The Birth of the Prison.* Trans. Alan M. Sheridan. New York: Vintage Books.

Friedkin, William, dir. 1973. *The Exorcist* (film). Perf. Max von Sydow, Ellen Burstyn. Warner Brothers.

Greengrass, Paul, dir. 2006. *United 93* (film). Perf. Daniel Sauli, Lewis Alsamari, J. J. Johnson, Gary Commock, Polly Adams. Universal Pictures.

Higginbotham, Evelyn Brooks. 1992. "African American Women's History and the Metalanguage of Race." *Signs: Journal of Women in Culture and Society* 17(2): 251–274.

Jay, Paul, and Nelofer Pazira, dir. 2003. *Return to Kandahar* (film). Bullfrog Films.

Kabir, Ananya Jahanara. 2003. "Allegories of Alienation and the Politics of Bargaining: Minority Subjectivities in Mani Ratnam's *Dil Se.*" *South Asian Popular Culture* 1(2): 141–159.

Makhmalbaf, Mohsen, dir. 2001. *Kandahar* (film). Perf. Nelofer Pazira. Avatar Films.

Mohanty, Chandra. 1991. "Under Western Eyes: Feminist Scholarship and Colonial Discourses." In *Third World Women and the Politics of Feminism,* ed. Chandra Talpade Mohanty, Ann Russo, and Lourdes Torres, 51–80. Bloomington: Indiana University Press.

Philip, M. Nourbese. 1994. *A Genealogy of Resistance and Other Essays.* Toronto: Mercury Press.

Ratnam, Mani, dir. 1998. *Dil Se* (film). Perf. Sharukh Khan, Manisha Koirala. Eros International.

Shohat, Ella, and Robert Stam. 1994. *Unthinking Eurocentrism: Multiculturalism and the Media.* New York: Routledge.

Sivan, Santosh, dir. 1999. *The Terrorist* (film). Perf. Ayesha Dharker. Shringar Films.

Spivak, Gayatri. 1988. "Can the Subaltern Speak?" In *Marxism and the Interpretation of Culture,* ed. Cary Nelson and Lawrence Grossberg, 271–313. Urbana: University of Illinois Press.

Thomson, Rosemarie Garland. 1997. *Extraordinary Bodies: Figuring Disability in American Literature and Culture.* New York: Columbia University Press.

Walsh, David. 1998. "An Interview with the Director, Santosh Sivan, and Leading Actress, Ayesha Dharker, of *The Terrorist.*" World Socialist Web site, October 9. http://www.wsws.org/arts/1998/oct1998/int-009.shtml (accessed June 20, 2006).

15

===

Army of None

Militarism, Positionality, and Film

CINDY SOUSA AND RON SMITH

War is only a symptom of international militarism, racism, and imperialism and an unworkable capitalism which makes the rich richer and the poor poorer.

> –Public Enemy, "Pump the Music, Pump the Sound," 2005

When we stand here today, it is not enough to simply be for peace, we have to be for social justice, the fact is that right now, even as we are talking, people are being murdered by U.S. imperialism throughout the Middle East and throughout the world. . . . If there is going to be any peace on earth, it is going to come as a consequence of our people uniting to defeat U.S. imperialism, once and for all.

> –Paris, "Sheep to the Slaughter," 2003

Previous chapters in this volume propel us from a feminist and social justice lens, toward antimilitarism as a hopeful alternative for security. The potential exists for a multifaceted antimilitarism movement that brings together communities of color, labor, faith, students, military members and their families, and the more mainstream "liberal" Left in this country. What happens, however, when the hopes for a diverse antimilitarism movement are threatened by the replication or reinforcement of the pillars of militarism, such as sexism, racism, classism, and elitism? How can social justice work challenge these columns and confront the oppressive dynamics by merging theory and practice, the academy and the street, researcher and subject?

This chapter provides analysis of these questions through a case study. It describes our journey, which is far from over. Here, we examine the positionality of activist researchers responding to the dual commitments of academic research and democratic participation for social justice. Though our exploration, we argue for scholars and community organizers to ground their work in these commitments. Our work follows the tradition of Paulo Freire (1983) and others who engage in praxis, the continual circular process by which theory and practice meet to create something better than either is alone.

We situate these insights through an analysis of our film project *Army of None: What the Military Recruiters Aren't Telling You* (Smith and Sousa 2005).[1] In reflecting on our experiences with this project, we look at how the gender, race, class, and social group memberships of researchers and practitioners inform, hinder, and aid in the process of interviewing veterans for a documentary and engaging in counter-recruitment activities and coalitions. Using these lessons, we dissect the implications of this process for organizing, theorizing, and educating around militarism in a multicultural context. We also examine the group politics present in today's antimilitarization or antiwar efforts in the United States and outline essential steps for activists, particularly white activists, in order to contribute in conscious and conscientious ways. Drawing from the fields of gender studies, peace studies, anthropology (especially feminist anthropology),[2] and social work, we provide an example of the reflection necessary for effective activist scholarship around gender, race, and militarism.

We first focus on the ethical issues surrounding our work with the vulnerable population of young veterans of the first and second U.S. wars in Iraq, and the subsequent occupation, for the production of our film *Army of None*. Second, we discuss feminist theory, critical whiteness studies, and critical race theory and their implications in antiwar community organizing, specifically countermilitary recruitment, which is also grounded in our experiences with the film.[3]

Historical and Methodological Contexts of *Army of None*

Army of None is a sixteen-minute video documentary highlighting the voices of young soldiers and veterans, most of whom have recently returned from Iraq and all of whom oppose the war. Interviewees educate youth about the realities of the military and speak openly about their experiences. *Army of None* uses hip-hop music, thoughtful interviews, and fast-paced editing to reach out to young people in hopes of countering military recruitment propaganda. By providing education on the realities behind the recruiters' propaganda, the video counters the tools they use to enlist young people. It emphasizes that service contracts are eight-year commitments, debunks the myth that the military provides easy and good college funding and job training, and talks about the psychological impact of war on soldiers. The video comes with a discussion guide and resource packet that we created to help youth or adult facilitators and educators to use the video as an educational tool.

In March 2005, we traveled to Fayetteville, North Carolina—home of Fort Bragg, one of the largest military bases in the United States—to attend a protest planned for the second anniversary of the most recent U.S. invasion of Iraq. Video documentary has long been a venue for us to engage in complex work around intense issues, and we saw this event as an opportunity to use our film production skills to contribute to the U.S. social movement challenging military recruitment. While in Fayetteville, we conducted several interviews with veterans of the U.S. war in Iraq, and these interviews form the bulk of our finished video project, *Army of None*.

In *Army of None*, like our past research and film projects, we had no pretension of creating an objective or even balanced study. Our philosophy as producers, academics, and organizers is that we are responsible to effect change with our work where possible. Film has been a venue to bridge theory and reality and to help to build community-organizing efforts. Although the production of a film is an undertaking in its own right, the continual reflection on the practical uses of the *Army of None* film project has been as important as its production.

Working with veterans provides many ethical challenges, regardless of the goal or method of research. In the case of *Army of None*, we were working with a particularly vulnerable population: veterans who had served in the U.S. invasions and occupation of Iraq who then voiced their opposition to the war. Essentially, we were hoping to work with individuals who had been multiply marginalized. Knowing this, we approached this project with an insistence on challenging the biases that could inhibit the partnerships we sought to create. These veterans were marginalized in U.S. society by class and racial divisions, marginalized from the Left during their time serving the U.S. military, then marginalized by the military establishment when they returned and refused to continue their service or spoke out upon completion of their service.

Research with vulnerable populations is particularly tricky when you are committing interviews to film, and even more so when the distribution of the film is a part of the project. Because we recognized the vulnerability of the people we interviewed, we established some protections for them. First and foremost, we ensured voluntary participation through establishing both verbal and written consent after providing a clear explanation of ourselves and the project, including how it would be used. In conducting the actual interviews, the interviewer explained to participants that we could stop the camera whenever they felt like it and that our intention was not for them to be unnecessarily vulnerable or to be taken to any emotional place with which they were uncomfortable or to which they didn't want to go. Moreover, we actively sought to avoid the commodification of veterans' experiences, especially violent ones. We refrained from asking questions that might lead participants to talk about brutality and actions that may constitute war crimes. This decision to steer away from the tendency to use veterans' intimate stories to simply advance a cause or organization, or to market a book or film, has taken on even more importance as work with war resisters and young Iraq veterans has intensified in this country, often to their potential detriment, as subsequent conversations with Iraq War veterans have elucidated for us.

We also asked all participants how they wanted to be identified for the film, and we went through a university's Human Subjects Review process, consulting with colleagues at the university about the potential ethical issues.

Positionality: Gender and *Army of None*

The Gender, Race, and Militarization conference at the University of Oregon in October 2005 provided us with an opportunity to reflect on own participation in the *Army of None* film project. Our analysis here draws on our reflection on the project with the students, faculty, and community organizers in the audience of our presentation. Although this project was a collaborative effort, we each approached it as an individual, with a distinct social position.

RON: I realized that I had something in common with many of the participants in the video in that I, too, was a member of a military family. This revelation came to me during a question-and-answer session after the screening of *Army of None*, when a student claimed that it was easy to decide to not participate in military service and that she considered the participants stupid for volunteering for military service. She identified herself as a feminist and an activist. Her comment demonstrated a limited understanding of feminist thought, which excluded a deep examination of the complexities of power and privilege.

CINDY: Her response further ingrained in me the imperative for critical feminist theory that does not limit itself to the analysis of women but examines the creation of gender in society, for men, women, and for those not accurately described by the male/female binary. An active consideration of the relationship between gender and militarism should take on an increased urgency in this post-9/11 world, but in a highly critical manner, and the film project certainly did this for me as it deepened my conception of solidarity. Through reflecting on her comment and the underlying sentiments and biases, I was impelled to consider the personal and political complexities of working with soldiers, most of whom were men, to make this film. I had to consider my own position of both privilege and of vulnerability in conducting the interviews. I say vulnerability because as a woman, I personally felt both solidarity with and fear of the people who had been in the military, especially the men, with whom we worked on this project. However, this film was a moment of deep personal and professional growth as I found myself in the precarious place of understanding that the creation of manhood, while victimizing women, takes a toll on men to a magnitude that we scarcely consider, unless perhaps we raise boys. I certainly took away from this project a deeper appreciation for the real denial of humanity that occurs with the construction of gender under militarism.

RON: In responding to that student's statement, I realized something about my own past and its relationship to identity, especially the relationship between manhood and militarism. When I was sixteen years old, I was attending public schools in Nashville, Tennessee. It was the era of Desert Shield and Desert Storm, the 1990 U.S. invasion of Iraq, a time of great patriotic fervor. Since I found myself marginalized in Nashville society, and was raised not as an American Jew but as an Israeli living in U.S. society, it seemed like a logical step to join the Israeli military. It seemed like a fast out of my social situation and a rapid means of achieving respect. After a summer trip to Palestine with an American Jewish tour group much like Birthright, I saw some particularly heinous aspects of the Israeli occupation of Palestine and chose not to join the military.

In reflecting on the conception of manhood in my life, it is essential for me to understand manhood as I absorbed it, which is distinct for someone raised as an Israeli. In essence, military service was attractive to me in that it could propel me into manhood, bypassing the travails of adolescence. When I answered the student, I felt that I drew very specifically from my experiences growing up in a military family, and I felt that I could, just for a moment, very clearly understand what would lead young people to risk their lives and their futures pursuing nebulous promises of freedom, adventure, and righteousness in the military. Manhood is a powerful motivator.

The irony of the pursuit of manhood in the military is that military command structure today encourages a certain stunting of personal development. This was made clear to us through our discussion with Desert Storm veteran Dennis Kyne, who taught himself psychological methodology as a means of coping with his own post-traumatic stress disorder and other psychological maladies directly related to his military service. Dennis explained clearly the psychological impacts of military service, from boot camp to active duty, particularly the subjugation of soldiers' natural human development. In a sense, according to Dennis, although the army promises manhood, it actually functions to stunt development in both a larger, psychological sense and a practical day-to-day manner as well.

Once a soldier enters the military, the military prioritizes and rewards quick responses to commands, not individual thought. After four or eight years of service, soldiers can find it difficult to make an immediate transition to civilian life, where the soldier's peers have a head start. In addition, soldiers encounter practical difficulties dealing with the necessities of life. According to Dennis, soldiers leaving military service don't have basic skills. They don't know how to interview for a job or fill out an application. They don't know how to find an apartment. The army has no interest in teaching these skills, so veterans are forced to fend for themselves. Discussion of this process in our film delegitimizes the platform of the military's Army of One recruitment campaign (the campaign that provided the inspiration for the name of our film), which promises individual empowerment through joining the army. In reality, the military wants nothing resembling personal empowerment while soldiers are in the service or when they leave. Instead it relies on groupthink and control to accomplish the mission. This is the crux of the complex relationship between manhood and militarism, and we see it played out with public military resisters, who are castigated and sometimes imprisoned for thinking for themselves, and whose manhood is challenged by mainstream media and the public when they challenge the military.

Positionality: Elitism, Militarism, and *Army of None*

A growing aspect of the antiwar movement in the United States in the twenty-first century is the empathy expressed for troops, at least in the rhetoric of antiwar work. Even with this empathy, however, many among the Left, including the two of us, still stand in resistance of those who knowingly commit crimes in the service of empire. Thus, our own potential discomfort with and biases against military veterans, including our dissociation with the militarism within our own families, generated an additional hurdle for us in making the film. In planning the project, we could not ignore the ideological divide between ourselves as anti-imperialist activists and our subjects as participants in the U.S. military, even though they now situate themselves as critics.

We examined the overlapping concepts of class and elitism, and especially the impact of education on class mobility in our lives as compared to those of our participants, as one important part of our positionality related to our engagements with veterans. In addition to education as it pertains to class, we critically considered the elitism that can pervade social movements that appear to be segregated along lines of privilege, such as the antiwar movement (Martinez 2003). We were interviewing veterans who tended to come from working-class families with limited options for higher education. In contrast, both of our families assumed that we would attend college and possibly graduate school. The individuals we interviewed had finished high school but joined the military for its promises of further educational options that seemed unavailable without military service. Although the consideration of elitism arises in most of the film projects we undertake, it took on a special dimension with *Army of None* because of the elitism prevalent in what some consider the "mainstream peace movement." The establishment of common ground and attention to humility, therefore, took on increased importance to us throughout production and distribution.

The Search for Common Ground

Army of None humanized U.S. soldiers for us in a way that nothing else could have. We produced the film primarily to aid in countermilitary recruitment efforts by providing education to high-school-age students about the realities of the military. Unexpectedly, the film serves to humanize U.S. soldiers to

audiences and has had a warm reception outside of the venues for high schoolers that we had initially targeted. We came to this project viewing military personnel as the foot soldiers of imperialism (Butler 1935). Spending time in serious
conversation with participants allowed us to critically differentiate the individual soldier from the overall policy demanded by the command, while maintaining an understanding of individual responsibility. This tension between
sympathy and critical evaluation of the current rules of engagement is a central
dynamic of work with soldiers and veterans, and adds a constant complexity to
the relationship between activists and soldiers. The partnerships that we established and that continue to grow between us as producers/activists and military
refusers have deepened the scope of our participation in the antimilitarism
movement.

The film has also had some surprisingly positive unanticipated consequences for members of the military. For one thing, we began to notice that the
process of the interviews, while exhausting, offered a venue for the participants
to interact with young people whom they could imagine watching the film and to
sum up their reflection for these young audiences, whether to implore them to
avoid the choice that some veterans said will haunt them for the rest of their lives
or to plead with young people simply to examine all of their alternatives before
signing up. Without exception, we believe that the most compelling and ener-
getic parts of the interviews are the final questions, when we asked the participants what they would like to tell young people who are considering joining the
military. Participants responded emotionally and directly, explaining that viewers should avoid making the mistake of unquestioningly listening to recruiters or
signing up without fully understanding the realities of war. One very young participant stated: "You might be watching that list of causalities and see someone
from your school." Another reflected: "Someone should be held accountable and
literally be held liable for the lies I was told."

Besides offering a way for participants to talk directly to youth, our film has
had another unplanned outcome. We have shown this film to many people who
are either still in the service or are now veterans, and from talks with them we
realize that they seem to take away a decreased sense of isolation as they listen to
the soldiers' stories that reflect what they also feel or experienced. One striking
comment came from Camilo Mejía:

> You go in there and you get in one firefight, and you see at the end of the
> firefight that most of the insurgents got away, if not all of them, most of
> the soldiers survived, if not all of them, and you look at the middle
> ground, and you see a bunch of dead civilians—you know, children
> included, women, elderly, you name it. And this is not just an isolated
> event, you know, this is a pattern. It doesn't happen because soldiers are
> bad people, it doesn't happen because insurgents want to kill their own
> citizens, it happens because that is the nature of war.

As if they were in dialogue with each other, another participant, Charlie Anderson, somberly concluded during his interview: "No amount of religion, no amount of atonement . . . will make up for the lives that I helped shatter in Iraq." The willingness of the project participants to open up to unknown audiences astounded us. Also, while wholly unanticipated because they were not our intentioned audience, the responses of current soldiers and combat veterans have certainly been one of the highlights of the film for us as filmmakers.

Wrapping Up Production

Although the inadvertent success of the film in reaching formerly unintended audiences is wonderful, the planned measures of success of *Army of None* have always lain in the work of tying the project into community-organizing efforts. We are explicit that people using the videos for political-organizing purposes are free to distribute the film in any useful way, as long as it is distributed free of charge. The film also comes with a discussion guide and supplemental materials.

Army of None exists within the context of activism and partnership. We have both sought contact with local counter-recruitment organizations in Seattle and are now both involved with the national G.I. Rights Hotline, an organization committed to helping soldiers out of the military. By maintaining a grassroots activist component, we maintain a true praxis, and the film *Army of None* will continue to represent our political goals for the project. Our preparation in feminist and anti-imperialist scholarship, especially feminist anthropology and social work, has propelled us to employ informed praxis of engaged scholarship with the distribution of the film.

Army of None in the Community:
Whiteness, Racism, and the Antiwar Movement

Organizers will call for peace around the world but "when it comes to people of color here, they just want Peace on the Plantation." (Participant in a "Hard Knock Radio" program with hip-hop activists, KPFA [Pacifica] Berkeley, as quoted in Martinez 2003)

Antiwar organizing after September 11, 2001, has been both exhilarating and exhausting. Although the resurgence of groups mobilizing has been a real strength, and people are discovering new and exciting tactics to decrease militarization of youth and the larger society, the problems of racism within community organizing and antiwar activism cannot be underestimated. In particular, countermilitary recruitment movements have emerged around the country. It was in this context that we conceived of and completed the film *Army of None*. Military recruitment itself is obviously fraught with issues around power and privilege. An essential lesson from the *Army of None* project as we took it to communities was that effective community organizing cannot limit itself to simply addressing the military's targeting of poor youth or youth of color. After completion of the film project, during engagement in counter-recruitment efforts, we realized that white countermilitary recruiters must consider the implications of our own privilege and the racist dynamics within ourselves and our communities, and our coalitions or efforts, on this work. Would it have been enough to simply complete the film and distribute it? Perhaps, but as Minh-ha states, "the relation between filmmaker, filmed subject, and the film viewer becomes so tightly interdependent that the reading of the film can never be reduced to the filmmaker's intentions" (1991, 109).

The problem of privilege and entitlement as it relates to power in movements is acute in the counter-recruitment movement, as many groups, including those not truly rooted in the communities they enter, rush around from school to school, following the military to "save" youth from their lies. To what extent does our film further these dynamics? This remains an important question. We had hoped to represent a wide diversity of participants, a goal we did not adequately meet. Even so, where we did succeed, does representation in a film and a discussion of issues of racism in recruitment practices relieve white antiwar activists of the analysis of dynamics of privilege in community organizing itself? Does it relieve activist filmmakers of the responsibility for supporting or demanding a thoughtful use of the tool?

Many wise activists discuss and consider the phenomenon of white folks aligning themselves with issues without a thorough analysis of oppression. In "An Open Letter to Activists Concerning Racism in the Anti-War Movement," the authors note: "Apparently, it hasn't occurred to this activist that his/her 'whiteness,' along with class privilege, both enables and influences the luxury of choosing on which issues s/he will focus" (Bloom et al. 2003, n.p.). The risk of the "peace movement" is that in organizing against war abroad, activist/scholars from a privileged standpoint can forget the race- and class-based luxury of not already seeing domestic militarism and oppression, such as the privatization of the schools, police brutality and unjust prison systems, poverty and the war on the poor, and the damaging effects of globalization. For community organizers to effectively counter issues of war and militarism, we need to build a movement that more accurately reflects the realities of militarism and the people who have the most to lose from it. It is because of this dynamic that we have maintained a commitment to our participants and our intentions in the trajectory following the completion of the film, which included immersing ourselves in organizing efforts led by military and faith-based groups.

Feminist organizers have long criticized oppressive modes of organizing. All organizing practices could inadvertently perpetuate imperialism, patriarchy, empire building, and white supremacy through their meeting structures, "coalitions," campaigns, and practices. Taking *Army of None* to the community coalitions working on counter-recruitment on the West Coast was no different, and in fact was not the ideal experience we had anticipated, largely because of some of the unrecognized dynamics of position and privilege within a few key groups working against the war. Through the two years of distribution of the film, we have found that *Army of None* may fail, then, in that it could inadvertently contribute to a movement against the war that is permeated by elitism, classism, sexism, and racism. For example, we were not able to secure interviews from veterans who would more accurately represent the people serving in the military, especially in war zones. As filmmakers and community workers, our experience of the entire process further underscored the imperative of staying grounded in an understanding of the personal relationship of the researcher to the project. It also highlighted the necessity to understand that tools created as part of a (albeit powerful and urgent) social movement can end up perpetuating oppressive dynamics instead of challenging them. Such movement tools can serve either to strengthen or weaken the movement's integrity. We have reflected on what would have been a more ideal way to undertake the venture. The reminder of the chapter describes some of the results of this deliberation.

Two Years Later: Where Does the Film *Army of None* Go from Here?

The process of making an engaged film to connect young Iraq War veterans with civilians and with youth was complex and energizing. The subsequent work of using it within the counter-recruitment and antiwar movements has proven to be equally complex. The number of public Iraq War resisters in the year following our film's release has increased significantly. The politics of coalition building in order to support both resisters and the counter-recruitment effort has strengthened our resolve to examine our own positionality within our work, both in the academy and in our communities. We offer the following thoughts and suggestions arising from our experience of moving toward antiracist and anti-elitist engagement in bringing *Army of None* to community-organizing efforts within antiwar movements.[4] Considering the film project as part of a much larger effort, not led by us, to build bridges between soldiers and the Left, and between segregated communities that are all dealing with increased militarization of our youth, we have reached these conclusions in the two years since *Army of None* was officially released.

Relationships

One of the main critiques we have heard over the years from radical organizers of color is that white folks tend to jump in too soon, put product before process, and define getting work done very narrowly. Through the relationships we have built during work on and after completion of the film, with military members and families, as well as with people within faith communities, we have heard similar criticisms of what could be labeled the "traditional" Left within antiwar work. Mary

Beth Maxwell, a national organizer with Jobs with Justice, writes: "In Jobs with Justice we often say that it takes a long time to build relationships and a short time to ruin them . . . people need face-to-face time, experience overcoming conflicts, the kind of trust that only develops over time because I see what you actually *do*, not just what you say in a meeting" (2002, 77). Perhaps some of the challenges we experienced with the film could largely have been circumvented if, from the inception of the project, we had established more of a partnership with veterans and communities who most suffer from militarism.

Militarism as a Holistic Concept

The work of countering militarism is not simply about war or peace. It is about our schools, the prison industrial complex, police brutality, and much more. Society is increasingly militarized through racism and xenophobia. Personally, we are learning again and again that as white antiwar activist filmmakers, we must understand how our own internalized racism, as well as institutionalized racism, plays into militarism. Chomsky points out that "the criminal justice system increasingly is becoming a system for targeting the poor and minorities, who are being turned into people under military occupation" (2002, 191). Many would argue that the poor and people of color have been under occupation since before the beginning of this country. As white antiwar activists, we must consider the occupation at home and work in solidarity with this cause. We must not use our antiwar activism to ignore the racism and targeting of people of color and poor communities at home, or to ignore our own privilege. An "antiwar" film project and counter-recruitment efforts contribute most when they are linked with groups or emerge organically from groups that are already working with youth on the many institutional risk factors youth face, including but not limited to military recruiters.

It is only logical to be strategic about our time and energy and where we focus it. But choosing to focus is different from tunnel vision. Understanding militarism comprehensively (including its connections to police brutality, globalization, war, imperialism, sexism, racism, homophobia, militarization of schools, and the political hegemony of the U.S. ruling class throughout the rest of the world) is a powerful way to avoid single-issue politics.[5] Another film project provided a natural avenue for understanding the intersections of labor and militarism in our day in Colombia, where, as of the year 2000, over two thousand labor leaders have been murdered, in collusion with militarization largely supported by the United States (Smith forthcoming). Palestinian organizations in the United States, as groups that have experienced more than four decades of organizing under occupation, can also be models for work related to the U.S. occupation of Iraq. Although *Army of None* is deliberately disciplined in its narrow focus, we aimed to include a discussion of the political economy of recruitment and the politics of race and class within today's militarization of youth. *Army of None* also exists as part of a larger portfolio of film and activist work that engages with the complex overlapping of issues related to oppression and imperialism both in the United States and around the world. It is not a perfect balance, but we aimed for this breadth of analysis.

Accountability

After the completion of *Army of None*, we took the film into community efforts to counter the military recruitment in schools, attending many meetings in an attempt to be a part of what were sometimes optimistically referred to as "community coalitions." We soon recognized that the dynamics of meetings and the ways that privilege and power shape them ran against the principles of engaged activism at which we had aimed with this project. For example, we realized that both *Robert's Rules of Order* and consensus decision-making, if overtaken by an individualist sentiment or a manipulated process, can silence people and inhibit authentic community engagement, compromising the accountability that forms the foundations of coalitions. Landsman and Krasniewicz (1990) make this point in their case study on intercultural participation.

Accountability was a major tenet throughout the making and distribution of *Army of None*, including within our local community. It has meant that, in addition to working ethically with participants, we must continually ensure that we offer the project in true partnership, that we solicit and digest feedback, and that we live up to our responsibilities, both ethically and practically. It also means that we have to know to whom we are accountable, locally, nationally, and even internationally, and that we withdraw from unalterable efforts that conflict with the paramount ethical obligations of this project. Since beginning work with the G.I. Rights Hotline in the year following the making of *Army of None*, we have realized that becoming G.I. rights counselors has added a layer of ethical responsibility and a clarity of purpose, moving our work away from the usual Left and toward more of a partnership with those who have a bigger stake in militarism than we could imagine. Above all, we are still ruminating on the complex questions that arose before, during, and well after filming *Army of None*, because they are the larger questions related to positionality that underpin the tensions between insider/outsider and scholar/activist that exist in much feminist, anti-imperialist, anti-oppression coalition building.

Conclusion

In this chapter, we have examined the dynamics of organizational politics and explored our own positions and the impact they have on effective community-based work, using our film project *Army of None: What the Military Recruiters Aren't Telling You* as a case study. In this project we have worked with a commitment to destroy artificial barriers between academic research and social action. Through recognition of our own positionality, we have explored the process of interviewing veterans, working toward antiracism within the antiwar movement, and contributing to the field of community organizing with sound theories built around insights about oppression and power. We have certainly faltered in our attempts, but opening our research and work to public scrutiny enables the opening of dialogue with others within, without, and straddling the borders of academia.

As the fields of community-based practice, social work, anthropology, feminist theory, critical race theory, and whiteness studies continue to evolve, we will have an increasingly powerful base of theory on which to build our work. Such evolution, however, requires deep examination of the politics of privilege and the ways in which these politics undermine coalitions and movement building, ultimately maintaining the underpinnings of social injustice rather than establishing common ground toward authentic security apart from militarism.

NOTES

1. Other films by Ron Smith include *Resistance as Democracy* (2000) and *Regalo del Cielo* (forthcoming).

2. Edward Said's (2000) and Linda Tuhiwai Smith's (1999) critiques of anthropology and frameworks for academics to carry out engaged research were important to our analysis.

3. We discuss critical whiteness studies as developed by theorists such as Karen Brodkin (1999), Ruth Frankenberg (1993), Janet Helms (1992), Cheryl Hyde (1995), Noel Ignatiev (1997), David Roediger (1991), Mab Segrest (1994), Beverly Daniel Tatum (1997), Thandeka (1999), Maggie Potapchuk et al. (2005), and Tim Wise (2005). In terms of the particular issues of racism and antiwar organizing, the work of Elizabeth (Betita) Martinez (2003) and the writers of "An Open Letter to Activists Concerning Racism in the Anti-War Movement" (Bloom et al. 2003) were invaluable in our research.

   Our critical and self-critical exploration is a continual process, and we in no way wish to convey that we consider ourselves somehow "done" reflecting on ethical and engaged scholarship or organizing. Precisely for this reason, this work must be considered in the context of Ché Guevara's insistence that self-criticism is at the heart of revolutionary activity. We, the authors, are ourselves highly imperfect, but we cannot allow these imperfections to paralyze us and keep us from participating in social change, nor can we participate in social change that is void of critical reflection.

4. This reflection was greatly aided by the work of theorists and organizers such as the Anti-Racist Alliance (n.d.), Gloria Anzaldúa (1981, 1990), Challenging White Supremacy Workshop (n.d.), Chris Crass (n.d.), Beverly Guy-Sheftall (1995), Patricia Hill Collins (2000), bell hooks (1994), Sharon Martinas (1998), Elizabeth Martinez (2003), Joanie Mayer (1997), Tema Okun (n.d.), the Prison Activist Resource Center (n.d.), Felix Rivera and John Erlich (2001), Bernice Johnson Reagon (1983), Fred Rose (2000), and many more.

5. The classic works by Franz Fanon (1968), Albert Memmi (1965), and Ngugi Wa Thiong'o (1993) greatly aided the anti-imperialist analysis that informed our work.

REFERENCES

Anti-Racist Alliance. N.d. "Anti Racist-Alliance: A Web Based Curriculum on Whiteness." http://www.antiracistalliance.com (accessed March 31, 2007).

Anzaldúa, Gloria. 1981. *This Bridge Called My Back.* Cambridge, MA: Persephone Press.

——. 1990. *Making Face, Making Soul: Creative and Critical Perspectives by Feminists of Color.* San Francisco: Aunt Lute Books.

Bloom, Steve, Jean Carey Bond, Humberto Brown, Saulo Colón, Bhjairavi Desai, Cherrene Horazuk, Randy Jackson, Hany Khalil, Ray Laforest, Ngô Thanh Nhàn, René Francisco Poitevin, Merle Ratner, Liz Roberts, Juliet Ucelli, and Lincoln Van Sluytman. 2003. "An Open Letter to Activists Concerning Racism in the Anti-War Movement." February 13. http://www.cwsworkshop.org/pdfs/WIWP_Analysis/14Open_Letter_to_Activists.PDF (accessed March 31, 2006).

Brodkin, Karen. 1999. *How Jews Became White Folks and What That Says about Race in America.* New Brunswick, NJ: Rutgers University Press.

Butler, Smedley. 1935. *War Is a Racket.* Los Angeles: Feral House.

Challenging White Supremacy Workshop. N.d. http://www.cwsworkshop.org (accessed April 1, 2007).

Chomsky, Noam. 2002. *Understanding Power: The Indispensable Noam Chomsky.* New York: W. W. Norton.

Collins, Patricia Hill. 2000. *Black Feminist Thought: Knowledge, Consciousness, and the Politics of Empowerment.* New York: Routledge.

Crass, Chris. N.d. " 'Forging a Movement on Shifting Ground': Reflections on Anti-Racism as a Catalyst for Global Justice Organizing." http://colours.mahost.org/articles/crass9.html (accessed February 27, 2006).

Fanon, Franz. 1968. *The Wretched of the Earth.* New York: Grove Press.

Frankenberg, Ruth. 1993. *The Social Construction of Whiteness: White Women, Race Matters.* Minneapolis: University of Minnesota Press.

Freire, Paulo. 1983. *Pedagogy of the Oppressed.* New York: Continuum Publishing.

Guy-Sheftall, Beverly, ed. 1995. *Words of Fire: An Anthology of African-American Feminist Thought.* New York: New Press.

Helms, Janet. 1992. *A Race Is a Nice Thing to Have: A Guide to Being a White Person or Understanding the White Persons in Your Life.* Topeka: Content Communications.

hooks, bell. 1994. *Feminist Theory: From Margin to Center.* Boston: South End Press.

Hyde, Cheryl. 1995. "The Meanings of Whiteness." *Qualitative Sociology* 18(1): 87–95.

Ignatiev, Noel. 1997. "The Point Is Not to Interpret Whiteness but to Abolish It." Presentation at the Making and Unmaking of Whiteness Conference, University of California, Berkeley, April 11–13.

Landsman, Gail, and Krasniewicz, Louise. 1990. " 'A Native Man Is Still a Man': A Case Study of Intercultural Participation in Social Movements." *Anthropology and Humanism Quarterly* 15(1): 11–19.

Martinas, Sharon. 1998. "Shinin' the Lite on White Privilege." http://prisonactivist.org/cws/sharon.html (accessed January 30, 2006).

Martinez, Elizabeth Betita. 2003. "Looking for Color in the Anti-War Movement." *Z Magazine,* November. http://zmagsite.zmag.org/Nov2003/martinez1103.html (accessed April 1, 2007).

Maxwell, Mary Beth. 2002. "Coalition Building: Lessons from the Jobs with Justice Model." In *The Global Activist's Manual: Local Ways to Change the World,* ed. Mike Prokosch and Laura Raymond, 72–77. New York: Thunder Mouth Press/Nation Books.

Mayer, Joanie. 1997. "Barriers to Organization between Anti-Racist White People." Anti-Racist Agenda. http://www.cwsworkshop.org/resources/ARAgenda.html (accessed March 31, 2007).

Memmi, Albert. 1965. *The Colonizer and the Colonized.* Boston: Beacon Press.

Minh-ha, Trinh T. 1991. *When the Moon Waxes Red.* New York: Routledge.

Okun, Tema. N.d. "White Supremacy Culture." http://prisonactivist.org/cws/dr-culture.html (accessed February 27, 2006).

Paris. 2003. "Sheep to the Slaughter." *Sonic Jihad* (studio album). Oakland, CA: Guerrilla Funk Recordings.

Potapchuk, Maggie, Sally Leiderman, Donna Bivens, and Barbara Major. 2005. *Flipping the Script: White Privilege and Community Building.* Baltimore: MP Associates and the Center for Assessment and Policy Development.

Prison Activist Resource Center. N.d. http://prisonactivist.org/cws/dr-culture.html (accessed March 31, 2007).

Public Enemy. 2005. "Pump the Music, Pump the Sound." *Rebirth of a Nation* (studio album). Oakland, CA: Guerrilla Funk Recordings.

Reagon, Bernice Johnson. 1983. "Coalition Politics: Turning the Century." In *Home Girls: A Black Feminist Anthology,* ed. Barbara Smith, 356–368. New York: Kitchen Table Press.

Rivera, Felix, and John L. Erlich. 2001. "Organizing with People of Color: A Perspective." In *Tactics and Techniques of Community Intervention,* ed. John E. Tropman, John L. Erlich, and Jack Rothman, 254–269. Itasca, IL: F. E. Peacock.

Roediger, David. 1991. *The Wages of Whiteness: Race and the Making of the American Working Class.* London: Verso.

Rose, Fred. 2000. *Coalitions across the Class Divide: Lessons from the Labor, Peace and Environmental Movements.* Ithaca, NY: Cornell University Press.

Said, Edward. 2000. "Representing the Colonized: Anthropology's Interlocutors." In *Reflection on Exile and Other Essays,* 293–316. Cambridge: Harvard University Press.

Segrest, Mab. 1994. *Memoir of a Race Traitor.* Boston: South End Press.

Smith, Linda Tuhiwai. 1999. *Decolonizing Methodologies.* New York: St. Martin's Press.

Smith, Ron, dir. 2000. *Resistance as Democracy* (film). Portland, OR: activ8media.

——. Forthcoming. *Regalo del Cielo* (film). Portland, OR: activ8media.

Smith, Ron, dir., and Cindy Sousa, assoc. prod. 2005. *Army of None: What the Military Recruiters Aren't Telling You* (film). Portland, OR: activ8media. http://www. activ8media.org/army-page.html (accessed April 1, 2007).

Tatum, Beverly Daniel. 1997. *Why Are All the Black Kids Sitting Together in the Cafeteria?* New York: Basic Books.

Thandeka. 1999. *Learning to Be White.* New York: Continuum Books.

Wa Thiong'o, Ngugi. 1993. *Moving the Center: The Struggle for Cultural Freedoms.* London/Portsmouth: Currey/Heinemann Books.

Wise, Tim. 2005. "Membership Has Its Privileges: Thoughts on Acknowledging and Challenging Whiteness." In *White Privilege: Essential Readings on the Other Side of Racism,* ed. Paula S. Rothenberg, 119–123. New York: Worth Publishers.

16

Teaching about Gender, Race, and Militarization after 9/11

Nurturing Dissent, Compassion, and Hope in the Classroom

SIMONA SHARONI

Manipulation of the tragedy of 9/11 by both the U.S. government and the mainstream media has left its mark on academia. An unprecedented number of students have sought to enroll in Middle Eastern studies as well as peace and conflict studies courses, while scholars critical of U.S. foreign policy have come under attack from outside academia, especially when we question conventional interpretations of 9/11 (Bird 2002; Doumani 2006). September 11 has served as a pretext for acceleration of the U.S. government's empire-building plans and for the overt remilitarization of both the United States and the global community (Eisenstein 2004; Roy 2003). This remilitarization has not bypassed college campuses. According to Margaret Stetz, "college campuses have been militarized—in some cases, re-militarized—under our noses" (2003, n.p.).

Refusing to be intimidated and silenced and recognizing both the privilege and responsibility that come with inhabiting an institution of higher learning, I have made militarization a central theme in my teaching. My scholarly work on gender and militarization in the past two decades notwithstanding, my investment in the topic is not merely intellectual. It is fueled by a passion to create a space in my classrooms for students to critically reflect on contemporary issues, engage in critical conversations, and feel empowered and motivated to get involved in struggle for social and political change. When I have designed courses on militarization, I have drawn on my knowledge of and commitment to feminist critical pedagogy, and therefore pay as much attention to the experience I want to create for students as to the written syllabus, which often tends to become the blueprint for teaching.

I decided to use militarization as a focus in courses because of its pervasiveness in our lives. I was intrigued that many people around me were unaware of the ways that we, in our personal lives, are implicated in current wars. In addition to addressing this topic in every class I have taught since 9/11, I have designed and

taught three courses on three different college campuses that focused on the relationship among gender, race, and militarization. While designing course materials and outlining the process for the classroom experiences, I had several
objectives in mind:

1. to inspire my students to think critically about militarization by learning to
   recognize its presence in our everyday lives;
2. to distinguish among the military as an institution, soldiers as people who
   serve that institution, and militarization as a process that blurs the distinction between military and civilian life;
3. to highlight the commonalities and differences among militarism, sexism,
   and racism as systems that play a role in forming and transforming people's
   individual and collective identities; and
4. to examine alternatives to militarization and strategies to challenge it
   effectively.

In this chapter, I reflect on the materials and the pedagogy I have used in my
teaching about gender, race, and militarization. I pay particular attention to students' reactions to the classes by drawing on their written work as well as their
formal and informal evaluation of the class. Finally, I discuss some new ideas and
examine various resources designed to inspire faculty to integrate teaching about
militarization into both graduate and undergraduate teaching.

Situating Myself: Critical Pedagogy and the Politics of Location

It makes perfect sense to me that I have to tell you about myself before I tell you
what I taught and how my students responded. Yet, because the practice of teachers and scholars speaking or writing explicitly about themselves is not yet common in academia, I draw on critical pedagogy and feminist theory to explain why
situating myself is integral to my teaching and scholarly work in general and to
this project in particular. I also hope that teachers who have shied away from this
practice will embrace it.

I was introduced to critical pedagogy in 1984 by reading Paulo Freire's semi-
nal work *Pedagogy of the Oppressed* (2002). Critical pedagogy has come to be used
as an umbrella term for a range of more specific educational practices such as
feminist pedagogy, antiracist pedagogy, emancipatory pedagogy, and democratic
pedagogy. All these educational practices have been informed by discourses that
explicitly question and challenge existing knowledge claims and power relations.
Further, they have as their basic purpose the empowerment and social better-
ment of marginalized, disadvantaged, oppressed, and exploited groups in society.
For critical educators, the classroom is a microcosm for the interrogation of
unequal relations of power and privilege, and the structures that uphold them.
Along these lines, critical pedagogy is both a process and a strategy designed to
develop analytical skills and consciousness among the students/ learners and

to empower them to join struggles for social and political change. Critical education creates opportunities for people to rethink who they are and consequently
has the potential to transform the lives of both students and teachers. Feminists
have adopted critical pedagogies and often refer to the unique blend of philosophy and teaching strategies we use in the classroom as feminist critical pedagogy
(Gore 1998; Luke and Gore 1992; Weiler 1991).

According to Parker Palmer (1998), teaching should not be informed primarily by one's knowledge of a subject matter, nor by a set of teaching techniques.
Instead, he suggests that good teaching originates from the identity and integrity
of the teacher. For Palmer, "good teachers possess a capacity of connectedness.
They are able to weave a complex web of connections among themselves, their
subjects, and their students so that students can learn to weave a world for themselves" (1998, 11).

These ideas have inspired much teaching and learning in women's studies.
In our efforts to link content and process and to bridge the artificial divide
between theory and practice, feminists have embraced two key concepts: social
location and situated knowledge. According to Kirk and Okazawa-Rey, "social
location is a way of expressing the core of a person's existence in the social and
political world" (2007, 71). The concept of situated knowledge stems from the
feminist claim that our social locations shape our relationship to knowledge.
Contrary to the pretenses of neutrality and objectivity that have been used to
legitimate social scientific knowledge since the nineteenth century, feminists
have argued that knowledge claims are always partial and informed by the social
locations and relationships among all the subjects involved in the process of
knowledge production and dissemination (Haraway 1988; Harding 1991).

As a first-generation college student, an activist, and a relentlessly honest
person, I found that situating myself made a lot of sense to me, even before I had
the theoretical justification to back up my pedagogy. When teaching about gender, race, and militarization, I draw on several aspects of my identity and experiences. I tell my students that my perspective on gender and its intersections with
race is informed by feminist theory and praxis, which is explicitly antiracist and
takes into account other relationships of power and privilege. My interest in and
research on militarization cannot be separated from my personal relationship
with militarization. Throughout my life, in Israel and in the United States, I have
been immersed in, observing, surviving, and resisting militarization and the
hegemonic and often racist and sexist conceptions of identity that it fosters. My
scholarly work on gender and militarism notwithstanding, only in recent years
have I begun to consciously and explicitly integrate into my teaching, when relevant, reflections on my own militaristic socialization, my mandatory military
service, and especially my own relationship with men whose masculinities get
militarized and demilitarized. I first became aware of the toll militarization takes
on soldiers during my mandatory military service in Israel in the late 1970s. I
became aware of the interplay between sexism and militarism at the age of

nineteen. I witnessed firsthand how sensitive boys are turned into tough guys, sometimes against their will, and had my first experience trying to challenge militarization.

Over the past twenty-five years, resisting militarization has been central to both my activism and my scholarly work. My research, writing, and teaching on gender, race, and militarization have been inspired by and grounded in my involvement with the women's peace movement in Israel and my solidarity work with Palestinian women to end the Israeli occupation of the West Bank and Gaza Strip. I have also had the privilege to work in the North of Ireland on several collaborative projects with Irish Republican political ex-prisoners and to gain a more complex understanding of the formation and transformation of militarized masculinities. In the United States, especially after 9/11, I have refused to let militarization go unnoticed in my community. From questioning a guest presentation by an armed policewoman to the children at my daughter's day-care facility, to protesting an exercise program called Body Combat at my gym and the use of the Port of Olympia to ship military equipment and supplies to Iraq, I remain relentless in resisting militarization. In the past two years, frustrated with government and media propaganda that represents critiques of militarization and war as coequal with lack of support for soldiers, I have reembraced my identity as a therapist, while delving into the literature on trauma and healing, with a special emphasis on veterans coping with post-traumatic stress disorder.

Critical educators who share their political views and experiences with their students are often accused of abusing their power with the intent to indoctrinate their students (hooks 1994, 2003). Contrary to this view, I believe that by situating myself openly and honestly I make myself vulnerable, and in doing so I contribute to reducing the power differentials between me and my students, and creating a more egalitarian atmosphere in the classroom. I believe that my identity, experience, and social location enhance my ability to create a meaningful and authentic experience for students interested in understanding the relationships among gender, race, and militarization.

Demilitarizing Minds and Hearts:
Notes on Curriculum Development and Implementation

In order to teach about gender and militarization in a manner that leaves a lasting impression on students and urges them to take action, I knew I needed to put a human face on the topics. I wanted to create opportunities for students to relate to and identify with people in different parts of the world who have been affected by and are resisting militarization and war. Toward this end, I looked for novels, guest speakers, and films that would address the course's themes. In choosing required texts, I sought readings that were accessible, that were written by authors who occupy different social locations, and that would take into account questions of power, privilege, and structured inequalities.

In the course Gender, Conflict, and Change in Political Context, which I taught in spring 2002 at Evergreen State College, I used the following nonfiction books: Cynthia Enloe's (2000) *Maneuvers*, Susan Faludi's (1999) *Stiffed*, and Betty Reardon's (2001) *Education for a Culture of Peace in a Gender Perspective*. In addition, I assigned Virginia Woolf's (1938) *Three Guineas* and two novels: Orson Scott Card's (1994) *Ender's Game* and Deborah Ellis's (2000) *The Breadwinner*.

Two years later in the class I taught at the University of Oregon under the title Race, Gender, and Militarization, I looked for recently published texts that addressed both post-9/11 realities and the U.S.-led attack on Afghanistan and Iraq from a global feminist perspective. After much research I adopted the following then new books: *Against Empire: Feminisms, Racism and the West* by Zillah Eisenstein (2004), *War Talk* by Arundhati Roy (2003), and *Worlds of Hurt* by Kali Tal (1996). I could not find a text that focused on militarization as a central theme, so I again assigned Enloe's *Maneuvers* and Virginia Woolf's *Three Guineas*. I did not assign any fiction in part because the course was taught in conjunction with a film series on gender and war. The film series, which I helped organize and facilitate, was designed to put a human face on the issues addressed in the course as well as to highlight the struggles of women (and men) around the world to survive and undo the damage of war. In addition, students reviewed a novel or a feature film that addressed a class theme.

When I taught this class in fall 2006 at Saint Martin's University under the title Gender, War, and Peace in Global Perspective, I again assigned Zillah Eisenstein's *Against Empire* and supplemented it with Mohanty's (2003) *Feminism without Borders* and a novel by Asne Seierstad (2004) titled *The Bookseller of Kabul*. I supplemented the texts with several journal articles, including a few articles I had written on masculinity and militarization and on changes that occur in conceptions of masculinity, femininity, and gender roles and relations in various political contexts. I also assigned several reports and policy documents pertaining to the history and current situation and struggles of women in Afghanistan and Iraq.

To encourage students to make connections between the texts and their lives and to encourage the application of theory to practice, I designed several unconventional assignments. In all three classes, students were asked to keep a media and popular culture journal. The journal had to include at least one entry per week in which they examined mainstream and alternative media items, including music, television shows and commercials, and Internet sites related to the course's themes. Students were asked to bring their journals to class every week, and during small-group work or as a "warm-up" activity at the beginning of each class session, they shared interesting items they had found.

In addition to explaining the assignment in my syllabi, I have spent considerable time in the classroom answering questions about the journal. In response to students' questions about what else can be included in the journal other than reflections on newspaper articles and television sitcoms, I offered that we become anthropologists in our own society. I used this opportunity to give a little background on the history of anthropology as a field of study, with a focus on the critiques of anthropological studies tainted by colonial assumptions. The lively class discussion in one course offered an excellent opportunity to integrate some of Zillah Eisenstein's arguments in *Against Empire*. Although the "data collection" part made sense to most students, some seemed unclear about how to summarize the journal and turn it in for evaluation. Students who were new to women's studies seemed particularly uneasy about the assignment. Therefore, I created an example of what a journal summary would look like. I made copies of my journal summary, and we discussed it in class the following week.

Here are some excerpts of what I wrote:

Field research in public bathrooms and beyond
Thursday, January 6, 2005

I have been thinking about how to structure the media and popular culture essay I promised you as an example of what such an essay should look like. Little did I know that my answer would come in the women's bathroom at the train station in Portland. As I washed my hands, I noticed a large flag with a "United We Stand" slogan on the soap dispensers. Intrigued, I looked closely, trying to discern what company is behind the nationalization of our public bathrooms. I resolved to find out more about the company: AIS. Interestingly enough, above the *United We Stand* slogan was another slogan, which I assume the company didn't find contradictory to the main one, or perhaps they did and they placed it there to provide balance. The company describes itself as "producing earth friendly products with you in mind for the 21 century." I wonder how many other people have noticed the political soap dispensers and further wonder how many notice me inspecting them and then reaching for my notebook to record what is written. In Orwell's *1984* Oceania is a place where the act of noticing and recording a phenomenon like this would be considered "a crime of independent thought." But I don't think that even there, efforts to create unity have resulted in companies *voluntarily* coming up with the "original" idea of nationalizing soap dispensers! And of course this phenomenon has its history—the slogan and the logo with the American flag were born after 9/11.

I used my essay to clarify what I meant when I asked students to be anthropologists in their own society:

As I was thinking about my observation I realized that what I am asking you to do is to be anthropologists in your own society. With this assignment, you are asked to step outside what we often take for granted and assume "normal" and to search for signs of militarization, sexism and racism in your everyday environment and culture. Read the newspaper, watch TV, listen to music, go about your daily life the way you usually do but always keep a notebook or pad of paper handy to record things that you notice. This is what anthropologists do when they embark on field research in far-away places, in *other* cultures. Like them, we are engaged in trying to understand how this particular society and culture work. Our dominant culture has become increasingly militarized and I am asking you to do field work in your own neighborhood, on your own campus, in your own town, so we can collectively try to identify the conditions, processes and practices that have played a role in the militarization of our culture. Equally important, is to pay attention to efforts to resist militarization and its effects.

In order to provide students with examples of what resistance to militarization may involve, I included the following in the essay I wrote:

In yesterday's *New York Times* (January 6, 2005), I read an op-ed piece written by Mark Danner [2004], author of a newly published book titled: *Torture and Truth: America, Abu Ghraib and the War on Terror*. I liked the provocative, yet very appropriate title of his op-ed (opinion) piece: "We Are All Torturers Now." Danner develops the case against Alberto Gonzales whose confirmation hearings to become Attorney General begin today. This discussion is particularly relevant to our course because Gonzales is a Latino man and his candidacy has been met with mixed feelings in the Latino community. Many feel a sense of pride that a member of the community has been nominated to such high office. But others feel uneasy with Gonzales' conservative stances that seem to echo the views of those who have power and privilege, not the immigrant community he came from.

I chose to provide another example, which involved an analysis of a political advertisement in order to broaden the range of items students may include in their journals as well as to provide another example of resistance to militarization.

Another item that caught my attention in today's *NYT* was a three-quarter-page ad sponsored by MoveOn.org, True Majority, Win Without War and Amnesty International. It pronounced in black bold letters with Gonzales' photo to its left and a photo of a hooded prisoner tied to electric wires on the left. The caption read: "you may not know Alberto Gonzales but we're sure you'll recognize the results of his work." I found particularly powerful the direct question to Gonzales, who was to be questioned as part of his confirmation hearings: "Of all the questions you'll face today, Judge Gonzales, this is the simplest: Will you sign our declaration to stop torture? Or Not?" This is a declaration that tens of thousands of Americans have signed. The header at the top of the slip that readers are asked to mail back to True Majority reads: "Help Us Make Sure Alberto Gonzales Knows: America Doesn't Stand for Torture." This timely ad campaign represents one act of resistance designed to reclaim America by refusing to accept torture as a pre-condition to our national security. It is an attempt to both de-militarize and to re-define such terms as "nation" and "security."

Another unconventional assignment, which the students seemed to enjoy, involved a visit to a local toy store. The assignment was designed as a group project to provide students with firsthand experience and an opportunity to critically examine the marketing and sales of militaristic toys and of gender-differentiated sexist toys. In addition, this was an opportunity for students to apply the vocabulary and analytical tools they had acquired through the readings to their field research. Students working in small groups engaged in participant-observations and field research at several toy stores in the area; they also examined closely the marketing and sales of toys on the Internet. The high-quality papers that resulted from this project were featured in a special issue of the summer 2002 *Peace Chronicle*, the quarterly publication of the Peace and Justice Studies Association. In her essay, Katie Falkoff remarked that

> The militarization of toys reflects the environment where young boys may be conditioned to support and in a sense participate in militaristic ideals. In contrast, the toys marketed to young girls at the Kay Bee store lacked any visually militaristic association. On the other hand, the Pepto-Bismol colored walls of fashion and beauty crazed Barbies and games that were organized around cooperation and care-taking reinforced the typical stereotypes of women as concerned with matters relating to the home. (2002, 12)

Falkoff also observed that if "the militaristic ideal of a strong man fighting off evil and protecting his property is exclusive to the male sex, then the female sex is left with 'other' duties. In a subversive way, the pink plastic theme in the girls toys is a result of militaristic attitudes among other things." Her conclusion was particularly powerful: "After visiting this toy store, it is clearer that one of the ways to really prevent war anywhere is to disrupt the socialization of children that is based on militaristic values" (2002, 12).

Because the results of the students' field research projects in commercial toy stores were fairly predictable and depressing from an antimilitarist, nonsexist standpoint, I wanted them to focus on alternatives as well. Upon my recommendation, a group of students took a close look at a family-owned local toy store in downtown Olympia. The following excerpts are from an essay by Savahn Rosinbum, who was part of the group:

The *Wind Up Here* toy store in downtown Olympia is a specialty toy store that makes a strong effort not to sell violent or gender-stereotyped toys. During our conversation, the owner remarked that the store serves a well-educated, mid to high-income population. Most of the toys in this store are different from toys found in mass market toy stores. Yet even the prices of cheaper toys are higher in this store than similar toys in mass market toys stores. This raises issues of the impact of class on raising children vis-à-vis gender roles and violence. Will upper class children be raised with less constricting gender roles? Are non–upper class children raised with more images of violence and militarization? What will be the repercussions of this? (2002, 14)

The questions that Savahn Rosinbum posed reflect a remarkable ability to examine militarization in its interplay not only with gender but also with other modalities of identity such as class and race. I was particularly excited to read this analysis because one of my objectives in teaching this class was to enable students to see these intersections. Rosinbum's awareness of systemic inequalities in general and of the interplay among race, gender, class, and militarization in particular are evident in her conclusion:

the awareness of the owners about gender stereotypes, violence, and diversity, which is reflected in a toy selection, helps to shape a new paradigm, even if only a small segment of society [is] exposed to it at the moment. Still, the messages that parents and children have internalized from commercialized pop culture and our militarized society seem stronger than the much needed alternative offered by this unique toy store. (2002, 15)

To elicit emotional responses from students through empathy and identification, I have incorporated guest speakers and documentary and feature films and film clips into all my classes. I made a particular effort to expose students to perspectives that are not easy to come by in the mainstream media. Along those lines, I tried to challenge essentialist stereotypes and binaries, including the association of women with peace and men with war, as well as viewing gender identities and roles as fixed. Because the curriculum included ample material by and about women, I made a special effort to put a human face on the interplay of militarism and masculinity, including highlighting men's transformation. The guest speakers my students had the opportunity to meet included Laurence McKewon, a former Irish Republican Army volunteer who had spent sixteen years in prison in the North of Ireland, Vietnam combat veteran Paul Gallegos, and Yehuda Shaul from Breaking the Silence, a movement of Israeli soldiers who call attention to the brutality of the Israeli occupation of the West Bank and Gaza Strip.

I have also designed field trips in an attempt to put a human face on the issues addressed in these courses and to create a lasting impression on students.

To accomplish one of the major theoretical objectives of the course—that of learning to distinguish among the military, militarization, and soldiers—I tried to organize a visit to a military base nearby. I began by contacting the public relations department for Fort Lewis, the largest of eight military bases in the state of Washington. Because I first approached the authorities on the base immediately after 9/11, I was not surprised that my initial efforts proved futile. The idea of a group of students from a college with a radical reputation roaming around the base and talking to people was not one that coincided with the educational priorities on the base.

About the time I was ready to give up, I received an e-mail from the same office that had rejected my initial request, inviting us to participate in Armed Forces Day—a yearly celebration of the base's relationship with the surrounding community. In retrospect and as my students' feedback (included later in this chapter) underscores, the new venue, even if part of a propaganda campaign, was more appropriate for the experience I sought to create for my students.

While crafting the curriculum for these courses, I made a conscious effort to balance critique with hope. I supplemented readings critical of U.S. foreign policy past and present, about militarized masculinities, or about rape as a weapon of war, with reports of individuals and groups working to undo the damage of unjust policies and practices and to put forth alternative visions.

Teaching Community: Power and Vulnerability in the Classroom

Professors and students engaged in critical pedagogy pay particular attention to the process by which teachers and students negotiate and produce meaning. According to this approach to teaching and learning, curricula and educational processes are examined in direct relation to the social and political relationships that characterize the dominant society. Critical pedagogy also takes into consideration how teachers and students are positioned within discursive practices and power/knowledge relations. Feminists have found many of the insights of critical pedagogy to be in line with feminist praxis, turning the classroom into an important site for critical thinking and social transformation.

I consciously use critical pedagogy in all my courses. I pay particular attention to my interaction with students and design the curriculum to take into account the students' own social locations, life experiences, and values. The readings I assign and our class discussions address disparities in power and privilege both in the classroom and in the "real" world. As a feminist teacher, a public intellectual, and a co-learner, I consciously and happily relinquish the pretenses of neutrality and objectivity and share my views on various issues from U.S. foreign policy and Middle Eastern politics to gender and race relations.

The level of honesty and vulnerability that I bring to my teaching have transformative qualities. I was long aware, from my earlier work with group dynamics and processes, conflict analysis and resolution, and consciousness-raising feminist groups that vulnerability is a key component of personal and intellectual transformation. To learn, we have to be human, that is, we have to embrace our uncertainties and approach new situations with questions rather than with set answers. To change, we have to be courageous enough to admit that there are gaps between how we see ourselves and how others see us and between who we are and who we want to become.

Although many teachers who practice critical pedagogy share my perspective on the crucial role vulnerability plays in transformation, few have been willing to make themselves vulnerable. In the past two decades, I have worked consciously and intentionally to create a safe space in my classroom in which students feel comfortable embracing their vulnerabilities and supporting one another in the process. I also have worked to perfect my teaching and expand my ability to work with students who become vulnerable, especially those who do so unintentionally as a result of their resistance to the issues as well as my approach to teaching.

Only in recent years, however, have I embraced my own vulnerability and come to see it as a creative teaching pedagogy. We can be aware of power relations in the classroom and work intentionally to create nonhierarchical interactions. Still, when students are expected to relate the course's subject matter to their own lives and the teacher holds back, the power hierarchy, no matter how subtle, gets reinforced. On the basis of my students' feedback, I am convinced that making myself vulnerable in the classroom gives students permission to make themselves vulnerable as well and to respond empathetically to their classmates' vulnerabilities. This approach also deepens their interest in the subject matter I teach. In retrospect, I do not see a way of approaching the topics of gender, race, and militarization that have been central to my personal, political, and intellectual journey without allowing myself to be vulnerable.

Although the practice of teachers' consciously relinquishing power and working to create an egalitarian atmosphere in the classroom is not new, it has not been widely practiced on conventional college campuses, at least in part because of the central role played by grading in mediating the relationship between students and faculty. For years I tried to stress the value of learning and to downplay grades. I have worked hard to get students excited about the subject matter, not the desired grade. This approach is part of why I have found it rewarding to teach at Evergreen State College, one of the few remaining colleges in the United States, and perhaps the world, where narrative evaluations are used in lieu of grades. As a result, the de-centering of grades was not an issue at Evergreen, but it was a challenge at the University of Oregon and Saint Martin's University. There I adopted an approach that I believe did not compromise the academic rigor of the class. I allowed students to turn in drafts of all written assignments and to resubmit anything they wrote; I provided students with very detailed feedback, focusing on the coherence of the argument and the evidence students provided to support it. In addition, I made it clear to students that they were not graded on their political perspective but rather on their analytical skill, their creativity, and their ability to articulate both their own as well as others' perspectives, including opposing viewpoints. At the conclusion of each course, students were asked to write me a note with the grade they expected for the class and a justification of why they were to receive the particular grade. With few exceptions, students gave themselves lower grades than the ones I had planned to give them.

The practice of downplaying grades as well as other pedagogical practices I used, which were new to many students, became topics of discussions in and outside of the classroom. Although grades were marginalized, I was explicit and intentional in my efforts to make learning exciting, and to nurture relationships and a sense of community in the classroom. I used small group work, art, music, creative writing, and food to instill a sense of community in the classroom. I consistently e-mailed or called students who missed class and encouraged classmates to do the same when they noticed someone missing. I could tell that my students were excited when they walked into class, and they were touched that someone noticed when they were not there. I made a special effort to cultivate personal relationships with students who entered the class identifying themselves as pro-war, especially if they were veterans or came from military families. I also worked to disarm and to befriend students who seemed resistant to the subject matters of the course and/or to my teaching pedagogy.

Listening to Students' Voices, Learning from Students' Feedback

Because of my personal and political investment in critical pedagogy, I have long been interested in the gaps between my students' and my own expectations. As a result, I have actively solicited students' reactions to the contents and processes that I bring to the classroom. I have come to rely on the solicited and unsolicited feedback that my students offer, both in official and unofficial evaluations, as an important measure that allows me to reassess my teaching materials, philosophy, and methods.

I often wonder which class materials leave a lasting impression on a student. Which texts, films, and field trips make a significant mark and are stored in their long-term memory? The answers to these questions are often unpredictable. Yet a careful review of students' feedback from the first course I taught focusing on gender and militarization, in spring 2002 at Evergreen State College, reveals that the visit to the military base left a lasting impression on most students. Experiential education provides students with ample opportunities to apply their analytical thinking to what they see and hear. When I designed the trip, I hoped that it would challenge stereotypes and highlight contradictions, and judging from my students' feedback, it accomplished these objectives and more. One student noticed right away that "peace" was defined differently on the military base: "It was amazing to me all the propaganda about peace, both in the army wives' seal, and in the various booths, as if peace is really the only motivation for war!

And in the booth for the army wives they offered cookbooks and needlepoint patterns for sale." Another student was surprised to find that selling cosmetics can contribute not only to stereotypical views about women but also to the war effort. She described one contradiction-filled encounter:

> The first encounter I had was with a Mary Kay woman who I think managed to talk to all of the women in our class. There was nothing unique about her approach, but I was amused to see the Mary Kay banner which read: "Mary Kay's mission is to enrich women's lives." I've never seen Mary Kay describe their efforts to sell beauty products as a "mission" and I thought that it was interesting that the Mary Kay booth was actually there amongst the tables of gun displays.

The same student described another encounter:

> At another table we spoke to a soldier who was displaying guns. Talking to him made me pretty sad because he said that he hopes to be deployed soon because he grew up in Washington and has never been able to travel. He said that he doesn't care where he gets sent, because every country has a different culture that he wants to learn about. We asked how he felt about killing the people in the countries that he's interested in, and he shrugged it off saying something about if there's a threat he doesn't mind.

One of my key motives in planning the trip was to make clear that a critique of militarization is not an attack on the soldiers who serve. It seems that most of my students got the point. Their face-to-face interactions with soldiers, many of whom were their same age, were intense and powerful experiences for the students (and, one would hope, for the soldiers as well).
One student wrote:

> I really benefited from talking to the soldiers, especially because since reading *Maneuvers* I've been really discouraged and upset about the military. The men that I talked to were genuinely likeable, as are my friends in the military, and I appreciate the reminder that not all soldiers are responsible for the actions of the military or the effects of militarization. I haven't come to any clear conclusions about this, and I have a million arguments swarming around my head, but I think that this was a great opportunity to enhance the reading with experience and to bring real emotions into the equation.

This quotation underscores that the trip to the military base was a good opportunity for students to apply the theoretical material and concepts they learned in the class. Another student began her reflection by stating that "it was cool to apply what we are talking about to the outside world." Some students took it upon themselves to engage soldiers in conversations and inquire about their experience in the military and the reasons that had shaped their decision to join. One student concluded that

> Many of the men I talked to had joined the military as an out from whatever life they previously had. Very few mentioned the college opportunities, but many said this gave them a chance to see what the world was like. Only a couple had any future goals in mind outside of military life— the common thread seemed to be there is nothing else out there for them. The idea I got from the men I talked to is that their skills levels were very low and only in the military did they have any expertise that meant anything. I guess that goes to say why so many stay in the military and retire there.

This conclusion seems to resonate with the statistics about military recruitment, especially in small rural communities, where the military is the only ticket out of poverty and away from limited career opportunities and predictable future prospects (Ensign 2004; Laufer 2006).

One of my students and I had a unique experience interacting with soldiers and their families because we brought our then three-year-old children along on the trip. Our kids helped us to blend in and gain some insights into family life on the military base. In fact, we were both mistaken for military wives. Here's how my student, who was accompanied by her son, summarized her experience:

> The trip humanized the military for me. It was a strong reminder that these people are families, fathers, mothers, children, and that they are no less loving to their kids. Perhaps their values differ somewhat from mine, but when it comes down to it they want their kids to be happy and healthy and smart as I do for my son. I spoke with other parents briefly, asking names, ages, making small connections as I do with parents in any given situation. They all smiled and spoke without any noticeable scorn or prejudice. Perhaps they did mistake me for a military wife, but I felt accepted, nonetheless. And I think that is an important aspect to being a military wife (and husband)—one has an immediate community. This is something everyone craves to some extent, and in the military it is provided. In some ways that is probably a good thing.

When I chose to integrate a visit to the military base, I did not do so to humanize the military as an institution but rather to humanize the soldiers who join and to shed light on their reasons. I confess that reading the positive reflections of my students left me a bit uneasy at first. I am now convinced, however, that humanizing soldiers is a crucial aspect of confronting militarization. In the same way that we stress the difference between the U.S. government and its citizens, we must recognize a difference between the Pentagon and its generals and a nineteen-year-old who joins the military to gain an education or see the world.

Because of logistical problems arising from a more traditional curriculum structure than the one at Evergreen State College, I was not able to include a field trip to a military base when I taught Gender, Race, and Militarization at the University of Oregon in Eugene. I tried, nevertheless, to create many opportunities for experiential learning in and outside the classroom. In their end-of-quarter anonymous questionnaire, in response to the question "What were the highlights of your learning experience?" or "Which books/films/subjects/speakers/left the most impact on you?" many students said the highlight was the guest presentation by Paul Gallegos, a Vietnam veteran. One student wrote: "The Vietnam veteran left the most impact on me. It was the first time I heard a veteran challenge the glorification of war and share his honest experiences. It was intense but amazing to hear his story." Another student remarked: "I loved listening to Paul because he was so connected and willing to present his whole experience as much as possible." Yet another student exclaimed: "I will never forget the Vietnam Vet who came and told us his story."

Students also commented that they liked the music that I wove into the curriculum. Many listed as a highlight the guest appearance of folk singers David Rovics and Robb Johnson. I had decided to invite the two because both David and Robb are different men—they truly represent demilitarized masculinities in the way they passionately fuse political protest with love songs. Here is one student's reaction: "David Rovics and Robb Johnson were awesome, their music was moving and wonderful. I listen to their music now."[1]

Several students commented positively on the critical pedagogy that I worked to reenact in the classroom. One said: "I loved the unconventional space and education technique. It's refreshing to see a form of education that is so freeing." Another student commented on the process and especially my downplaying of grades: "I enjoyed the course and your approach to teaching. I agree with the way you see grades and the process of grading. This class was refreshing because I like to get away from the stress of a grade and focus on getting the most out of the class." A few students addressed my direct critique of the war and U.S. foreign policy more generally. One student listed a class highlight as "the opportunity to be exposed to a professor who is *not afraid* to criticize our situation and present truths as they are. [It] encouraged me to do the same. This class would not have had half the impact it did had this element not been present" (emphasis in original).

Because I view feminist critical pedagogy as a tool that undermines militarization as a structure and as a process, I spend time in class elaborating on the process, especially the strategies I use for community building and interaction among students. Although the explicit attention to process is new to some students, many appreciate it. One student wrote: "I liked how you encouraged interaction between students. You made us all feel like equals, which allowed us to learn from each other." Another student noted that she liked "the structure of the class and your teaching style. It's great to have a teacher that feels so passionately about the subject they are teaching. Class interactions were great and it was a comfortable learning environment."

I was particularly moved to receive feedback from a student whom I had worked hard to keep engaged and get excited about the class. He chose to write his name on the anonymous questionnaire and gave me permission to share his story. He is an African American man who played sports for the school. I am aware that I invested considerable time and effort in this relationship because he was a minority not only in this class but in my classes generally. What I know about the systematic targeting of young African American males by military recruiters and what I learned about the academic achievement of this student indicate that if it hadn't been for his athletic skills, he could have ended up in the military rather than in college. A careful reading of the student's work and the many conversations we had as he worked on writing and rewriting the various assignments for the class suggest that it was the careful attention to race and popular culture coupled with my pedagogy that contributed to the positive experience he had in the class. Here are some of his comments:

> I like the fact that students as well as teacher have the freedom to speak their minds without holding back. I'm not a school person so it takes a lot to grab my attention and it's classes like this that do that for me. Thank you for your help, your attention, your shared experience, and your overall effort. I can tell you love what you do.

The overall feedback from the students at the University of Oregon was enthusiastic. Many provided detailed feedback on both the content and the pedagogy. The work that students submitted in this class coupled with their formal and informal evaluations and feedback suggest that for many of them the class was a transformative experience. One student described the class as "one of the most intellectually and personally stimulating classes of my education!" She added: "I now classify my views as before I took Simona's class and after I took Simona's class."

The students who enrolled in my Gender, War, and Peace in Global Perspective class at Saint Martin's University, most recently in fall 2006, appear the least enthusiastic about the class when compared to their counterparts at Evergreen State College and the University of Oregon. Students' feedback was extracted from the narrative part of their formal, anonymous, end-of-semester evaluations, which consisted of sentence completion. Here are some examples of how students completed the sentence "The course was good because . . ." One student wrote that the course "taught important perspectives." Another student mentioned that the course "related to life and the war." Several students saw as positive the fact that the course offered international perspectives. More specifically, they liked the course because "it offered views about globalization, gender and militarization in a wide spectrum" and because "it focused on gender themes and international perspectives." One response to this question stands out in that it calls attention to the transformative potential of the course. According to that student, the course was good because "it challenged my world views." The student further elaborated, stressing that the course challenged her or him "to read understand and write with a stronger voice that reflected strong critical thinking."

Feminist critical pedagogy seems to me to be an effective pedagogy for teaching about gender, race, and militarization, yet it may be doubly challenging for some students. Although some students noted my compassion and empathy, others were taken aback by my passion and direct engagement with and approach to conflicts in the classroom. One student completed the evaluation sentence "the instructor's teaching could be improved by . . ." with the suggestion that I should not be "so passionate [because] it sometimes interferes with the learning process." The student also added that I "started many conflicts with students." Although I was puzzled by this particular interpretation, because I couldn't recall a particular conflict that "I started," I interpret this feedback as an indication that the particular student was not comfortable with my style of welcoming conflicts and analyzing them in the classroom. Another student expressed uneasiness with my critique of the Iraq War, which had been woven into the contents of the class. The student suggested that my teaching would be improved if I were not "so rude in judgments of the current war."

The critical reactions of the students at Saint Martin's University to my teaching style can be attributed to the demographics of the college and to its conservative image, especially when compared to those of Evergreen State College. Saint Martin's University is a small, private, coeducational Roman Catholic university founded in 1895 as a school for boys by monks of the Benedictine Order. Saint Martin's began offering college-level courses in 1900, granting degrees in 1940, and accepting women in 1965. The women's studies program, of which my course was a part, was established in 2001 and currently offers an eighteen-credit minor. Both Saint Martin's University and Evergreen State College are situated in the same county, and students with progressive worldviews and an interest in critical thinking, social justice, and social and political change tend to gravitate toward the latter.

In addition, my class at Saint Martin's included more white men who had never taken a women's studies class before, compared to my classes at Evergreen State College and the University of Oregon courses. Over the years, I became particularly interested in the students who actively resisted critical pedagogy. My preliminary observations suggest that white men who have had no previous exposure to women's and gender studies or social justice studies tend to be more resistant to the contents of my teaching and especially to my pedagogy. In contrast, students from underprivileged or underrepresented groups—women, minority students, students from working-class families, international students, and students who are openly gay, lesbian, or bisexual—tend to feel validated and empowered in my classroom and therefore respond more positively to my teaching.

All in all, I think that the resistance to my pedagogy has had more to do with time constraints and the scheduling of my class than with the demographics of the particular college or university. It seems almost impossible to effectively teach about such complex issues as gender, race, and, militarization while under substantial time constraints.[2] By the time students settle in and are ready to engage the issues, there is little class time left. If a course is lecture-based, a one-hour class may work, but when a course challenges previously held assumptions about several interrelated issues and social and political structures, having more time for students to process information is essential.

Conclusion

In this chapter I have sought to encourage teachers in women's studies and gender studies programs as well as in other departments to adopt existing teaching materials and to develop new materials to address such issues as gender, race, and militarization. Teaching about these issues is both timely and necessary given the unfolding changes in the political context and its effects on our college campuses. My other objective in writing the chapter has been to suggest that militarization should become a central focus for women's and gender studies programs, especially as the curriculum incorporates global and transnational issues.

This chapter would have turned out differently if I had written it before 9/11. It is no doubt influenced by my new sense of urgency to speak out and to act, which I have felt both inside and outside the classroom since the tragic events in 2001 and the repressive reactions that followed. I have felt compelled to share my experiences in the classroom because, despite the lip service paid to academic freedom, teachers who have openly expressed their views on current events have been few. The 9/11 attacks and their mainstream interpretation have been used to justify the resurgence of a conservative approach to teaching and learning—one that upholds the pretense of neutrality and objectivity as the litmus test of academic legitimacy. The pressures to conform to this model of dispassionate teaching have increased in direct correlation to the erosion of academic freedom and the growing influence of David Horowitz (2006, 2007) and groups like Campus Watch. Ironically, Horowitz and his colleagues, under the charge of protecting students' so-called academic freedom, have engaged in a systematic campaign to intimidate and silence progressive scholars. Those listed on one of Horowitz's lists under the heading "the most dangerous professors in America" include feminist scholars as well as a host of public intellectuals who have been critical not only of U.S. policy abroad but of racism and discriminatory practices at home. All are lumped under the category "the cultural left" by conservative Dinesh D'Souza (2007) and accused of being "the enemy at home." These attacks on progressive academics and public intellectuals have many similarities to the targeting of university professors, administrators, trustees, and students during the McCarthy era (Schrecker 1986; Price 2004).

Academics who are critical of the new McCarthyism, however, often pride themselves on never having revealed their political views in the classroom. For them, the principles of neutrality and objectivity are essential building blocks for teaching and learning. The rationale behind this approach, which dominates the U.S. academy, is that teachers have the obligation to expose students to as many perspectives as possible so that they can make up their own minds. Accordingly, when we teachers share our views on a particular issue, it may be interpreted as an attempt to influence students' opinions. But how can we expect students to form their own views if we hide behind the pretense of neutrality and objectivity? How can we expect them to become passionate and involved with a particular issue if we shy away from difficult issues or address them in a dispassionate manner?

Echoing the sentiments of many critical educators, Roxanna Ng argues that "the role of the critical teacher is to bring into sharp relief the historical inequalities that have been entrenched in social structures and to facilitate the radicalization of students" (1995, 131). Ng further suggests that women and minority teachers are more likely to receive such criticism. She describes the case of a colleague, Susan Heald, who examined ninety-four student evaluations she received from a sociology course but found only three positive references to content on women and feminist issues. Ng points out that "most students considered her approach problematic and the issues she raised digressing from the formal curriculum." Some of the comments directed at Heald are similar to the hostile comments I have received from white men: she was accused of being "too opinionated" and having "a biased approach" to certain issues. Ng concludes that "a feminist perspective . . . is seen to be biased knowledge, vis-à-vis pure knowledge [and that] teaching from this critical perspective further undermines the credibility of a female teacher" (135). She urges us to examine students' resistance to critical pedagogy in the context of such broader social and political phenomena as sexism and racism, which are present in our classrooms, whether we acknowledge it or not.

Much like students with different learning needs and preferred styles, teachers too have different preferences; these are shaped not only by individual differences but by different social locations and political orientations. As an immigrant, an antiracist feminist, and a peace activist, I do not have the privilege of hiding behind the pretense of neutrality and objectivity. My work as a feminist peace activist in Israel and in the United States and my solidarity work and research in Palestine, Israel, and the North of Ireland are as important (if not more important) to my teaching on gender, race, and militarization as is my scholarly training. Although critics view these unique experiences as interfering with my teaching, I know that I am a better teacher because of my political experiences and commitments.

As is clear from most of my students' feedback, being an honest, authentic teacher, addressing current events in the classroom, and using critical pedagogy have the potential to create a dynamic, interactive, and political learning environment that is more reminiscent of the "real world," for which college is supposed to prepare students. The question for me then is not whether to use critical pedagogy in the classroom but rather how to best use my experiences and knowledge to create a critical learning environment, which will act as a springboard for political transformation.

I have embraced critical pedagogy since I first stood in front of a class as a teaching assistant in 1984 at Haifa University in Israel. This pedagogical approach has become part of my identity. Teaching about militarization and using critical pedagogy in the classroom in the United States in the aftermath of 9/11 are as much a survival strategy as a risk. When I use the word *survival*, I think about open resistance in the face of repression, the suppression of critical thinking by media propaganda, and assertions of blind patriotism. Public intellectuals who have chosen to speak out about the erosion of academic freedom and the militarization of college campuses and our students' minds have paid a price and are risking career advancement and job security. Our vulnerability is at least in part because of our relatively small number. We need to urge our colleagues to join us, and we need to broaden our support base among students. I hope this chapter contributes to this effort. By demonstrating how dissent, compassion, and hope can be used in women's studies classrooms to question the militarization of our daily lives, we exercise our rights as citizens and remind ourselves and others that another world is possible![3]

NOTES

1. David Rovics's Web site is http://www.davidrovics.com.
2. The course at Evergreen State College consisted on two weekly sessions of four hours each, and students earned eight credits for the course; the class at the University of Oregon consisted of one weekly session, which lasted three hours, and earned students three credits. In comparison, the Saint Martin's University class was taught twice a week in sessions that lasted only seventy minutes each.
3. "Another world is possible" is the motto of the international activist space embodied by the World Social Forum.

REFERENCES

Bird, Kenton. 2002. "Academic Freedom and 9/11: How the War on Terrorism Threatens Free Speech on Campus." *Communication Law and Policy* 74: 431–459.

Card, Orson Scott. 1994. *Ender's Game*. New York: Tor.

Danner, Mark. 2004. *Torture and Truth: America, Abu Ghraib, and the War on Terror*. New York: New York Review of Books.

Doumani, Beshara, ed. 2006. *Academic Freedom after September 11*. Cambridge, MA: MIT Press.

D'Souza, Dinesh. 2007. *The Enemy at Home: The Cultural Left and Its Responsibility for 9/11*. New York: Doubleday.

Eisenstein, Zillah. 2004. *Against Empire: Feminisms, Racism, and the West*. London: Zed Books.

Ellis, Deborah. 2000. *The Breadwinner*. Toronto: Groundwood Books/Douglas and McIntyre.

Enloe, Cynthia. 2000. *Maneuvers: The International Politics of Militarizing Women's Lives*. Berkeley: University of California Press.

Ensign, Tod. 2004. *America's Military Today: The Challenge of Militarism*. New York: New Press.

Falkoff, Katie. 2002. "Just Pretend: Popular Toys and the Militarization of Imagination." *Peace Chronicle* 1(3): 12.

Faludi, Susan. 1999. *Stiffed: The Betrayal of the American Man*. New York: Perennial.

Freire, Paulo. 2002. *Pedagogy of the Oppressed*. 30th anniversary ed. New York: Continuum.

Gore, Jennifer M. 1998. *The Struggle for Pedagogies: Critical and Feminist Discourses as Regimes of Truth*. New York: Routledge.

Haraway, Donna. 1988. "Situated Knowledges: The Science Question in Feminism and the Privilege of Partial Perspective." *Feminist Studies* 14: 575–599.

Harding, Sandra. 1991. *Whose Science? Whose Knowledge? Thinking from Women's Lives*. Ithaca, NY: Cornell University Press.

hooks, bell. 1994. *Teaching to Transgress: Education as the Practice of Freedom*. New York: Routledge.

——. 2003. *Teaching Community: A Pedagogy of Hope*. New York: Routledge.

Horowitz, David. 2006. *The Professors: The 101 Most Dangerous Academics in America*. New York: Regnery Publishing.

——. 2007. *Indoctrination U: The Left's War against Academic Freedom*. New York: Encounter Books.

Kirk, Gwyn, and Margo Okazawa-Rey. 2007. *Women's Lives, Multicultural Perspectives*. 4th ed. Boston: McGraw Hill.

Laufer, Peter. 2006. *Mission Rejected: U.S. Soldiers Who Say No to Iraq*. Chelsea, VT: Chelsea Green.

Luke, Carmen, and Jennifer Gore, eds. 1992. *Feminisms and Critical Pedagogy*. New York: Routledge.

Mohanty, Chandra Talpade. 2003. *Feminism without Borders: Decolonizing Theory, Practicing Solidarity*. Durham, NC: Duke University Press.

Ng, Roxanna. 1995. *Anti-Racism, Feminism, and Critical Approaches to Education*. Westport, CT: Bergin and Garvey.

Palmer, Parker. 1998. *The Courage to Teach: Exploring the Inner Landscape of a Teacher's Life*. New York: Jossey-Bass.

Price, David. 2004. *Threatening Anthropology: McCarthyism and the FBI's Surveillance of Activist Anthropologists*. Durham, NC: Duke University Press.

Reardon, Betty. 2001. *Education for a Culture of Peace in a Gender Perspective*. Teacher's Library. New York: UNESCO.

Rosinbum, Savahn. 2002. "Confronting Violence and Gender Stereotyping: The Tale of an Alternative Toy Store." *Peace Chronicle* 1(3): 14–15.

Roy, Arundhati. 2003. *War Talk*. Cambridge, MA: South End Press.

Schrecker, Ellen. 1986. *No Ivory Tower: McCarthyism and the Universities*. New York: Oxford University Press.

Seierstad, Esne. 2004. *The Bookseller of Kabul*. New York: Little Brown.

Stetz, Margaret. 2003. "Teaching 'Comfort Women' Issues in Women's Studies Courses—Military Sex Slaves." *Radical Teacher*, Spring. http://findarticles.com/p/articles/mi_moJVP/is_2003_Spring/ai_102119711 (accessed March 28, 2007).

Tal, Kali. 1996. *Worlds of Hurt: Reading the Literatures of Trauma*. Cambridge: Cambridge University Press.

Weiler, Kathleen. 1991. "Freire and a Feminist Pedagogy of Difference." *Harvard Educational Review* 61(4): 449–473.

Woolf, Virginia. 1938. *Three Guineas*. New York: Harcourt Brace.

Conclusion

SANDRA MORGEN

> Our belief in justice should give us cause for hope, but it should also give us
> cause for action.
>
> The Honorable Barbara Lee, U.S. Representative for Congressional
> District 9, California

The reader who has traveled with the scholars and activists whose words fill this book may well feel anguished, sometimes hopeless, in the face of the scale, the global breadth, and the human costs of militarization documented in these pages. As organizers of the conference and colloquia on which this book is based and as editors who have pored over drafts of these chapters, we sometimes experienced these feelings. Nevertheless, as so many chapters in this book attest, there is more to the analysis of militarization than understanding the scars it has left on the hearts of people, the damage it has inflicted on communities and the environment, and the holes it has caused in the budgets of governments and NGOs, as critically important as each of these are. In response to the pain, the injustice, the "rampancy and plunder" (Patricia McFadden's vivid phrase) of militarized violence and insecurity, activists, advocates, researchers, teachers, filmmakers, and others have challenged militarism and the classed, racialized, and gendered infrastructures, practices, and ideologies of militarization.

This resistance takes varied forms. The examples documented in this book are but a handful of the rich variety of individual and collective, local, national, and transnational efforts to challenge the militarization and injustice that exist and are documented in the larger literature. In her chapter, Gwyn Kirk encourages us to recognize the interconnected levels of "analysis and action" at which resistance takes place, ranging from the individual to the community, the institutional, and the transnational. In the preceding pages researchers have examined community-based political mobilizations, for example, against the U.S. Navy's live-bombing exercises on the island of Vieques, as well as transnational activism linking groups working across national borders to challenge militarism and militarized nation- and empire-building projects. Other chapters illustrate how filmmakers, professors, teachers, journalists, human rights lawyers and activists, and family members (for example, of *los nuevos desaparecidos, asesinados, y muertos*) are documenting and critiquing the harmful, sometimes deadly, consequences of militarization *and* envisioning demilitarized approaches to protecting and enhancing human security.

The three statements from activist groups included in chapter 4 exemplify the diverse political analysis that has emerged from and helped to inform women's global activism against militarization and for peace, justice, and human security during the twentieth and early twenty-first centuries. Two statements were produced for international meetings in The Hague. The first meeting, in 1915, was an international gathering of over a thousand women from Europe and North America. Eighty-four years later, the Gender and Human Security Network, representing "women from the Earth's five continents," at a meeting almost ten times as large as the earlier one, produced a statement that exemplifies late twentieth-century global feminist activism against militarization and for human security. The expanded national, racial, and ethnic diversity represented at this second gathering arises from the intensified globalization of both neoliberal capitalism and social justice activism. The final statement, from the Esperanza Peace and Justice Center based in San Antonio, Texas, was issued in the aftermath of the post-9/11 U.S. war on terrorism and military occupation of Iraq. Its opening words invoke the kind of broad coalition and political perspective that this group envisions as foundational for an effective twenty-first-century global movement for peace and justice:

> As
> people of color, as poor and working class people,
> as immigrant and native people, as women, men, old and young,
> queer and straight,
> as people moved by a vision of social justice,
> we denounce
> ACTS OF WAR.

As this chapter's epigraph, a quotation from Congresswoman Barbara Lee, reminds us, these stories and analyses of resistance to militarization are intended to inspire more than hope. They aim to catalyze action. We hope readers of this book will appreciate, in addition to the activism illustrated and analyzed herein, the possibilities offered by the action of developing a scholarship on militarization that takes seriously gender and race as interlocking systems of power and inequality and that recognizes how class, immigration status, sexuality, and national identities as well as locations within the global political economy condition the ways that different groups experience, interpret, participate in, and contest militarization. Gone are the days when essentialized notions of women as peacemakers and caretakers can suffice as a starting point for feminist theoretical analyses of women and militarization.

A long-standing debate about women's antiwar, peace, and antimilitarization activism focuses on whether women's near (if not) universal disproportionate responsibilities for care work produce a gendered ethics or politics opposed to violence, especially to war and militarism. Without going into the contentious history of these debates, we contend that research such as Katherine McCaffrey's on the Vieques Women's Alliance exemplifies the value of instead understanding as strategic women's *political* decisions to deploy traditional domestic identities as mothers and homemakers to challenge militarism. McCaffrey quotes and echoes Lynn Stephen's argument that in a social movement, "the political necessity of projecting 'sameness' does not explain … what it means to those involved. … It is also not evidence of shared consciousness or identity" (Stephen 2005, 66). Scholars' and activists' recognition that it is politics, rather than an essentializing naturalized care ethic, that impels women's diverse struggles against militarization is a more promising path of analysis. Women's activism is political, inflected by how racial, ethnic, national, and class identities and interests are framed, a perspective being developed increasingly by many scholars who study activism that challenges militarization.

This latter point is important, and we wish to amplify what this argument means both for scholars and activists. The growing body of scholarship on gender, race, and militarization encompasses a broad range of ways that militarization impacts women's lives and, consequently, an inclusive definition of what constitutes resistance to militarization and support of demilitarization. Under this broad umbrella, as this volume reflects, are issues that range from the growing reach of U.S. empire (including military bases and military exercises in communities in the global South), to war, the use of torture in the "war on terror," military recruitment, outsized military budgets, militarized conceptions of national security, security-legitimated immigration and civil liberties policies, and repressive state policies protected by the state's use of (or threats to use) force against its own people. How different struggles are conceptualized politically strongly influences whether and the extent to which different groups of women and men will support or become involved in particular campaigns.

For example, the enormity of the international protests against the threatened and then the actual U.S. invasion of Iraq in March 2003—with tens of millions of protesters in over eight hundred cities between January and April 2003 (Simonson 2003)—is not best understood simply as an expression of antiwar or pro-peace sentiment or politics. Many people were drawn to these protests because of their opposition to the arrogance, danger, and unilateral nature of the United States' imperial "pre-emptive strike" and the continuing occupation of a sovereign state. Here opposition to militarization is deeply intertwined with opposition to empire, demanding an analysis that goes beyond an "antiwar" or "pro-peace" frame.

Elizabeth Betita Martinez, in a powerful essay about the challenge of building an antiracist antiwar movement in the United States, argues that for many people of color, opposition to the war in Iraq is intimately connected to recognition that "the same capitalist empire-building forces that impose the wars abroad also impose the war at home. The main victims of both are peoples of color. Both are racist wars" (2003, n.p.). When white activists fail to make these linkages, the larger movement suffers. Ultimately, global, national, and local struggles against militarization increasingly commonly draw on and build an analysis that connects militarism to global economic, race, and gender injustice and that opposes empire building.

Our explicit goal in this book has been to affirm and exemplify the particular value of grounding scholarship about militarization in an analysis of intersectionality. And as Teresia Teaiwa reminds us in chapter 7, generalizations, especially universalizing generalizations, about the dynamics of gender, race, class, and militarization may well be complicated or belied by the particular histories of different countries. Counterposing the overrepresentation of racial minorities in the U.S. military today with the underrepresentation of ethnic minorities in today's Fijian military, Teaiwa recognizes that the particular "politics of inclusion and exclusion" in the militaries of different nations (with complicated implications for ideas about citizenship and belonging) will differ. She hopes to stimulate further "critical reflection on the following questions: In what circumstances might ethnicity, 'race,' gender, and militarization intersect in universal ways, and under what conditions might we find their intersections so historically and culturally specific as to defy generalization?"

Understanding the complex, situated dynamics of race, gender, class, and militarization is important for theory building and also for activism. Martinez argues that racism has often been relegated to the political margins of the peace movement in the United States, even as racist inclusions and exclusions have long histories in antiwar activism (2003). Despite this, women and men of color have been actively involved in and providing leadership to antiwar movements and campaigns. But, Martinez suggests, an explicitly antiracist antiwar movement would elicit greater participation from people of color and foster a more sophisticated understanding of the politics of militarization. In chapter 15, Souza and Smith discuss this explicitly (and self-critically) when reflecting on their creation and distribution of the film *Army of None* and the antiwar activism to which they saw their work on countermilitary recruitment intimately linked. Failure to examine race and racism has serious consequences for both scholarship and activism.

An example of the ways in which examining differences among women sharpens our understanding of women and militarization is illustrated by a closer examination of the gender gap, a concept used by scholars but one that has been mainstreamed into the mass media. The gender gap, defined as differences in political attitudes and voting patterns between men and women, is often described as in the following example from an American Political Science Association Web site by noted feminist political scientist Susan Carroll. Describing the gender gap in 2004 as representing, in part, different perspectives on the war on terror and the war in Iraq, Carroll explains: "While women and men see the same issues as most important, women have somewhat different perspectives than men on these issues. Women are less likely than men to think the U.S. is safer from terrorism now than it is was before 9/11, and women have more reservations than do men about our involvement in Iraq" (n.d., n.p.).

What happens when an intersectional perspective is brought to understanding the gender gap on militarization in the United States? In fall 2006 the results of a poll commissioned by the National Council for Research on Women (in the United States) strongly suggested that the gender gap masks significant differences between white women and women of color and among married mothers, single mothers, and single women.[1] A random-sample telephone survey of 2,097 registered voters polled between September 28 and October 9, 2006, conducted by Opinion Research Corporation of Princeton, found that 59 percent of women and 48 percent of men said they would be more likely to vote for a congressional candidate who favored troop withdrawal from Iraq within twelve months, an eleven-point gender gap (National Council for Research on Women 2006). Comparing the answers of white women, black women, and Hispanic women on this question revealed that 55 percent of white women, 68 percent of Hispanic women, and 83 percent of black women said they favored a candidate for Congress who supported withdrawing troops from Iraq within the next twelve months.[2] The poll also indicated a significant difference among married and single mothers and single women. Fifty-five percent of married mothers, 64 percent of single women, and 71 percent of single mothers said they would favor a congressional candidate whose position was one of support for troop withdrawal within twelve months. In both cases, the gap between white women and women of color and between single mothers and married mothers was greater than the (still significant) gender gap between men and women. Needless to say, documenting and understanding differences among women requires more than opinion poll data and more than the limited data provided by this poll. However, in the poll just discussed, a similar pattern of differences among women—with women of color and single mothers articulating the most oppositional perspectives—held true across a wide variety of foreign and domestic policy issues.[3] These data confirm our vision for this book and the arguments of its various authors—that feminist scholarship on gender and militarization will be greatly enriched by the analysis of race and class and other axes of difference among women.

Although about one-third of the chapters in this book concern militarization as it is experienced by women in the global South (recognizing that a number of these cases are highly conditioned by U.S. foreign policy), the majority of the book's authors are U.S. academics, politicians, or activists. The value of this work notwithstanding, it is vitally important that we work to create more forums for exchange between and among scholars from the global North *and* the global South. The chapters by Patricia McFadden, Roksana Bahramitash, and Teresia Teaiwa, for example, bring more than "cases" from Africa, the South Pacific, and the Middle East to the analysis of gender, race, and militarization. In each instance these scholars speak from (often complex) social locations outside North America and Europe, and they bring to the volume insights and perspectives that are influenced by intellectual debates and political investments quite different from those that have dominated the U.S. academy.

McFadden positions her arguments in the context of an "African feminist epistemological and activist politics" that explores the intimate connection between postcolonial state building in different African nations and militarism "as an expression of that state power," including the practices of rampancy and plunder. Unlike many of the other chapters, hers examines not just class but class conflict (and its role in African state-building projects) as central to the dynamics of militarization. For Roksana Bahramitash, the investigation of gender, race, and militarization encompasses both the subject matter of her chapter—the interweaving of Orientalist feminism, "Islamophobia," the "war on terror," and representations and (mis)understandings of the lives of women in Iran—and also her own post-9/11 experiences as an Iranian-born Canadian citizen who experiences "problems" when she travels across borders controlled by the United States. Bahramitash's intellectual border crossing includes an invaluable argument about how Orientalist feminism simultaneously drums up support for an interventionist, anti-Muslim foreign policy, legitimates racial profiling, and fosters and sanctions racist anti-Muslim ideologies and practices. In her chapter on militarized Fiji, Teresia Teaiwa takes the U.S. reader into a terrain of race and gender politics very different from what most non-Fijians understand. Beyond this analysis she explains how a "small South Pacific nation . . . experiences intensified processes of militarization as a result of decisions made by the president of the United States and the prime minister of Great Britain . . . that profoundly affect international movements of capital, investment, and labor." Her analysis challenges readers to reframe Fiji from an exotic travel destination "somewhere" in the South Pacific to a disproportionately large supplier of coalition forces in Iraq and workers in the privatized army of multinational security companies. The research of these scholars decenters Eurocentric assumptions and representations even as the centrality of colonial and postcolonial international relations firmly implicates the United States and Europe in the consequences of militarization in the nations of the global South.

We close this book less with a sense of finality than with a fortified enthusiasm for scholarship and advocacy that recognizes what many know but which was stated eloquently by Martin Luther King Jr. in a 1963 speech. His famous words defined peace not as the "absence of tension" but as "the presence of justice" (1963, n.p.). Drawing on this insight, Congresswoman Barbara Lee warns that the increasingly unpopular war in Iraq is not "an isolated [foreign policy] mistake"; instead, it exemplifies the larger problem of an aggressive, militarized foreign policy in the hands of an imperial superpower at odds with the basic concept of justice.

Contributors to this book insist that this Iraq war (indeed war in general) is only the tip of the iceberg of a deeply entrenched militarization that characterizes our age and saturates the domestic and foreign policies of the United States and many other countries. Like the glacial icebergs dangerously melting as a result of the complex human actions that cause global warming, the perilous military fortresses and ideologies beneath the tip of *this* iceberg will only be demilitarized by equally complex human actions and alternative visions of international, national, and human security.

We began this book holding ourselves and our readers accountable for the fact that "living in a time of war demands that we ask hard questions." Answers with any promise of leading to real solutions are most likely to emerge when they have been informed by solid research, accurate and accessible information, and robust, open, and inclusive public dialogue. These discussions will need to take place within and between nations, and involving all the diverse constituencies whose lives and livelihoods are at stake. We also need alternative visions of peace and security that recognize racism, gender oppression, extreme economic inequality, rapacious treatment of the environment and nonhuman species, and other forms of discrimination and marginalization as injustices historically and inextricably linked to the ideologies and practices of militarization.

Fortunately, such alternative visions are incubating and growing within an expanding international network of feminist activist organizations and NGOs, think tanks, political parties, schools, universities, writers, artists, filmmakers, journalists, cooperatives, religious organizations, and social movements. But it is easier to theorize than to sustain effective, democratic transnational feminist organizations, networks, and coalitions. The power inequalities among participants in transnational activist networks and coalitions, generated by geopolitical power differentials among their countries, as well as racism, gender subordination, and class divisions, often lurk below the radar, causing divisive conflict among even well-intentioned activists and scholars.

As transnational feminist activists and scholars are confronting the challenges of organizing across conflict zones, ethnic and racial differences, class inequalities, and national borders, they are imagining and developing practices of solidarity that can produce a politics of "mutuality, accountability, and the recognition of common interests as the basis for relationships among diverse communities" (Mohanty 2004, 7). Cynthia Cockburn and Lynette Hunter use the concept of transversal politics, an idea indebted to the work of Italian feminists involved in transnational peace activism, to envisage the process as one that seeks "commonalities without being arrogantly universalist, and . . . affirm[s] difference without being transfixed by it" (1999, n.p.).

Whether one uses this terminology is not important, but its political implications are. Annual global military expenditures exceeded $1.2 trillion in 2006, representing $177 in spending for *each* person in the world (Stockholm International Peace Research Institute 2006). In the face of such an expansive, entrenched, and profitable militarization, transnational activists cannot afford to presume but must actively build, solidarities, organizations, networks, and coalitions that promote real human security and social justice.

NOTES

1. Differences among married mothers, single mothers, and single women cannot be reduced to class. But extrapolating from what we know about the still-large salary and wage differential between men and women, single mothers and single women *as a group* likely have less wealth and lower incomes than many married mothers. These data confirm the importance of also examining class in an intersectional analysis.

2. Much of this data are available in the executive summary of the National Council for Research on Women (2006). Additionally, I asked for and was given some of the original data to explore more explicitly the differences by race and household status reported here.

3. The magnitude of race and marital status differences varied on different issues, but it was particularly high on the question about the war in Iraq. Wilcox, Hewitt, and Allsop (1996) examined gender differences in attitudes toward the 1990–1991 Gulf War by interviewing people in eleven cities—five in Europe and one each in Russia, Japan, Turkey, Mexico, and Israel. Such cross-national research, designed to explore the extent and source of a gender gap in foreign policy and militarization, is one among a series of promising research directions that will enable scholars to move beyond a U.S.-centric approach to questions about militarization.

REFERENCES

Carroll, Susan. N.d. "Women Voters and the Gender Gap." http://www.apsanet.org/content_5270.cfm (accessed May 9, 2007).

Cockburn, Cynthia, and Lynette Hunter. 1999. "Transversal Politics and Translating Practices." *Soundings: A Special Issue on Transversal Politics* 12 (Summer). http://www.lwbooks.co.uk/journals/soundings/archive/introduction12.html (accessed September 25, 2007).

King, Martin Luther Jr. 1963. "Letter from the Birmingham Jail." April 16. http://www.stanford.edu/group/King/frequentdocs/birmingham.pdf (accessed May 9, 2007).

Martinez, Elizabeth Betita. 2003. "Looking for Color in the Anti-War Movement." *Z Magazine*, November. http://zmagsite.zmag.org/Nov2003/martinez1103.html (accessed May 4, 2007).

Mohanty, Chandra Talpade. 2004. *Feminism without Borders: Decolonizing Theory, Practicing Solidarity.* Durham, NC: Duke University Press.

National Council for Research on Women. 2006. "Women's Priorities 2006: Executive Summary." http://www.ncrw.org/researchforaction/PollExecSummary.htm (accessed May 9, 2007).

Simonson, Karen. 2003. "The Anti-War Movements—Waging Peace on the Brink of War." Geneva, Switzerland: Centre for Applied Studies in International Negotiation. http://www.casin.ch/web/pdf/The%20Anti-War%20Movement.pdf (accessed May 8, 2007).

NOTES ON THE CONTRIBUTORS

ROKSANA BAHRAMITASH obtained her Ph.D. in sociology from McGill University. She is the author of *Liberation from Liberalization: Gender and Globalization in Southeast Asia* (Zed Books, 2005). She has recently received a three-year research grant from the Social Science and Humanities Research Council of Canada for research on globalization, Islamism, and women.

THE ESPERANZA PEACE AND JUSTICE CENTER is a community organization based in San Antonio, Texas, that works to advance social and economic justice. The center fosters dialogue and interactions among diverse groups of people as a way to address oppressions based on race, class, sexual orientation, gender, age, health, and physical and cultural boundaries. Its Web site is www.esperanzacenter.org.

LEONARD C. FELDMAN is an associate professor of political science at the University of Oregon. He is author of *Citizens without Shelter: Homelessness, Democracy and Political Exclusion* (Cornell University Press, 2004). In 2007–2008, as a member of the Institute for Advanced Study, Princeton, he is working on a book titled *Governed by Necessity*.

THE GENDER AND HUMAN SECURITY NETWORK was an informal network of activist women from around the world whose goal was to attend the Hague Appeal for Peace Conference, a large international gathering held in May 1999 in the Netherlands, and to bring a gender perspective to it.

JANELL HOBSON is an associate professor of women's studies at the University at Albany, SUNY. She is the author of *Venus in the Dark: Blackness and Beauty in Popular Culture* (Routledge, 2005) and is currently working on an oral history project about a ferryboat disaster in 1970 between the Caribbean islands of Saint Kitts and Nevis.

KAREN HOUPPERT is a freelance reporter whose work has appeared in the *New York Times*, the *Washington Post*, the *Nation*, the *Village Voice*, and *Mother Jones*. She is the author of *Home Fires Burning: Married to the Military—For Better or Worse* (Ballantine, 2005) and *The Curse: Confronting the Last Unmentionable Taboo, Menstruation* (Farrar Straus, 1999).

THE INTERNATIONAL CONGRESS OF WOMEN at The Hague was a large international gathering of women from North America and Europe who assembled in the Netherlands in 1915 to discuss and advance an agenda for peace.

GWYN KIRK is a scholar-activist who has written widely on ecofeminism, militarism, and women's peace organizing. She cowrote and co-edited *Women's Lives: Multicultural Perspectives* with Margo Okazawa-Rey, which is now in its fourth edition (McGraw-Hill, 2007). She is a founding member of an international women's network against militarism.

BARBARA LEE is a U.S. congresswoman who serves on the House Appropriations Committee; the Labor, Health and Human Services, and Education Subcommittee; the Foreign Operations Subcommittee; and the Legislative Branch Subcommittee. She is the cochair of the Congressional Progressive Caucus, the first vice-chair of the Congressional Black Caucus, and a senior Democratic whip.

CATHERINE LUTZ is a professor in the Department of Anthropology and the Watson Institute for International Studies at Brown University. Her recent books include *Homefront: A Military City and the American Twentieth Century* (Beacon, 2001) and the edited volume *The Bases of Empire: The Struggle against U.S. Military Outposts* (Pluto Press, 2008).

BONNIE MANN is an assistant professor of philosophy at the University of Oregon in Eugene. Her many years as a feminist activist inform her philosophical work. She is a founder of the Society for Interdisciplinary Feminist Phenomenology and the author of *Women's Liberation and the Sublime* (Oxford University Press, 2006).

KATHERINE T. McCAFFREY is an assistant professor of anthropology at Montclair State University. Her primary research has focused on the conflict between the U.S. Navy and residents of Vieques, Puerto Rico. She is the author of *Military Power and Popular Protest: The U.S. Navy in Vieques, Puerto Rico* (Rutgers University Press, 2002).

PATRICIA McFADDEN, Ph.D., works and writes as a radical feminist in the African and global women's movements. She resides mainly in Zimbabwe, although she is Swazi, and her scholarly interests are in the areas of sexuality, citizenship, and the African women's movement. She recently held the Endowed Cosby Chair in the Social Sciences (2005–2007) at Spelman College in Atlanta, Georgia.

SANDRA MORGEN is associate dean of the Graduate School and professor of anthropology at the University of Oregon. Her main research interests are women and public policy, the economy, and women's health. Her recent books include *Into Our Own Hands: The Women's Health Movement in the United States, 1969–1990* (Rutgers University Press, 2002) and *Taxes Are a Woman's Issue* (with Mimi Abramovitz, Feminist Press, 2006).

JULIE NOVKOV is an associate professor of political science and women's studies at the University at Albany, SUNY. She is the author of *Racial Union: Law, Intimacy, and the White State in Alabama, 1865–1964* (2008) and *Constituting Workers, Protecting Women: Gender, Law, and Labor in the Progressive Era and New Deal Years* (2001) (both published by the University of Michigan Press), and the co-editor with Joseph Lowndes and Dorian Warren of *Race and American Political Development* (Routledge, 2008).

SIMONA SHARONI is an associate professor of women's studies at the State University of New York at Plattsburgh. She is the author of *Gender and the Israeli-Palestinian Conflict: The Politics of Women's Resistance* (Syracuse University Press, 1995) and numerous other publications on gender, militarization, and demilitarization.

RON SMITH holds a master's degree in International Studies from the University of Oregon and is working toward a Ph.D. from the Department of Geography at the University of Washington. His research examines contemporary manifestations of imperialism and colonialism as well as the unique impacts of occupation on local communities and their responses to these threats.

CINDY SOUSA holds an M.S.W. from Portland State University with a focus on community-based practice and is working toward a master's in public health from the University of Washington. Her research interests include antiracist community organizing, the trauma of occupation, and personal and collective resiliency. She is on the board of directors of the Seattle Draft and Military Counseling Center.

LYNN STEPHEN is Distinguished Professor of Anthropology at the University of Oregon. Her most recent books are *Transborder Lives: Indigenous Oaxacans in Mexico, California, and Oregon* (Duke University Press, 2007) and *Dissident Women: Gender and Cultural Politics in Chiapas*, co-edited with Shannon Speed and Aida Hernandez-Castillo (University of Texas Press, 2006).

BARBARA SUTTON is an assistant professor of women's studies at the University at Albany, SUNY. She holds a Ph.D. in sociology from the University of Oregon and a law degree from the National University of Buenos Aires, Argentina, where she was born and raised. Her scholarly interests include globalization, women's activism, body politics, state violence and human rights, and intersections of inequalities based on race, class, gender, sexuality, and nation.

TERESIA K. TEAIWA is senior lecturer and program director of Pacific studies at Victoria University of Wellington, New Zealand. Her research interests include the gendered dynamics of militarism in the Pacific. She is currently working on a project to collect oral histories of Fiji women serving in the Fiji Military Forces and the British Army.

INDEX